REGENDERING THE SCHOOL STORY

CHILDREN'S LITERATURE AND CULTURE

JACK ZIPES, SERIES EDITOR

REGENDERING THE SCHOOL STORY

SASSY SISSIES AND TATTLING TOMBOYS

BEVERLY LYON CLARK

ROUTLEDGE
NEW YORK AND LONDON

First paperback edition published in 2001 by
Routledge
29 West 35th Street
New York, NY 10001

Published in Great Britain by
Routledge
11 New Fetter Lane
London EC4P 4EE

Routledge is an imprint of the Taylor & Francis Group.

10 9 8 7 6 5 4 3 2 1

Library of Congress Cataloging-in-Publication Data

Clark, Beverly Lyon.
            Regendering the school story : sassy sissies and tattling tomboys
    / Donnarae MacCann.
            p.   cm.
        Includes bibliographic references and index.
            ISBN 0-8153-2116-3 (alk. paper)
            ISBN 0-415-92891-5 (pbk.)
            1. Children's stories, English–History and criticism.
    2. Children's stories, American–History and Criticism. 3. Education
    in literature. 4. School children in literature. 5. Gender identity in
    literature. 6. Children–Books and reading. 7. Feminism and literature.
    8. Sex role in literature. 9. Children in literature. 10. Schools in
    literature. I. Title. II.Series: Garland reference library of social science ;
    v.1060. III. Series: Garland reference library of social science. Children's
    literature and culture series ; v.3.
    PR830.E38C53   1996
    813'.54–dc20   96-19804
                                                               CIP

Printed on acid-free, 250-year-life paper
Manufactured in the United States of America

CONTENTS

Preface

I suppose I could blame it all on Alice. For if I hadn't had a chapter on Lewis Carroll in my dissertation I wouldn't have gotten to teach Children's Literature. And then I wouldn't have gotten a grant to write a book on the themes of reading and writing in children's literature. Which book of course never got written. For in the process of investigating this overly ambitious topic I became intrigued by a genre that hadn't even figured as a chapter in the proposed book, though it should have: the genre of school stories.

What I liked about the first school stories I read, canonical stories in the tradition of *Tom Brown's Schooldays,* was how much they adopted the perspectives of the students as opposed to those of the teachers. How they endorsed peer codes like that prohibiting talebearing and even portrayed plagiarism with surprising forbearance. Leading me to reflect more on my own teaching.

But then I started wondering where the girls were. And as I read on, I found that the stories that most piqued my interest, the stories that seemed to be doing the most complex new work, stories like E. J. May's *Louis' School Days* and Richard Johnson's *Little Female Orators,* had something in common: they were all crossgendered. What was it about crossgendering— women writing about boys and men writing about girls—that gave play to the contradictions of the genre, contradictions otherwise buried? And why had these school stories been paid so little attention, or when paid attention, their context in a tradition of school stories ignored?

I am grateful to the NEH for a Fellowship for College Teachers, which helped to make early research for this book possible; to the Yale Collection of American Literature, Beinecke Rare Book and Manuscript Library, Yale University, for permission to quote from a volume in the Gertrude Stein collection, Adela Quebec's *The Girls of Radcliff Hall;* to the John Hay Library, Brown University, for permission to quote from Edward Everett Hale's *Mrs.*

Merriam's Scholars; to the de Grummond Children's Literature Research Collection, University of Southern Mississippi, for permission to reproduce an illustration from Elizabeth Eiloart's *Ernie at School;* and to the American Antiquarian Society, the British Library, and the Osborne Collection of Early Children's Books, Toronto Public Library, for making their collections so generously available. I am also grateful to Sherry O'Brien, Marcia Grimes, and Martha Mitchell of the Madeleine Clark Wallace Library of Wheaton College, for expert assistance with research; likewise Laura Wasowicz of the American Antiquarian Society and Maurice N. Lyon of the Silvio O. Conte Records Center and Regional National Archive; to Patrick Scott for sharing his collection of school stories; to Dee Jones, curator of the de Grummond Children's Literature Research Collection of the University of Southern Mississippi; and to Roger Clark, Travis Crosby, Susan Dearing, Elizabeth Keyser, Paula Krebs, Toni Oliviero, Dick Pearce, Steven Strang, Claudia Strauss, Jan Susina, and Cynthia Wells for reading drafts of chapters.

I am grateful as well for permission to reprint versions of essays that have appeared elsewhere. Parts of Chapters 1 and 4 appeared as "Cracking the Code of the School Story: Telling Tales About Telling Tales" in *Culture and Education in Victorian England, Bucknell Review* 34.2 (1990), edited by Patrick Scott and Pauline Fletcher. A somewhat different version of Chapter 9 has appeared as "Domesticating the School Story, Regendering a Genre: Alcott's *Little Men,*" in *New Literary History* 26 (1995): 325–344.

Introduction

Redressing the School Story, Crossgendering a Genre

Critics can no longer assume that important narratives deal with war or whales and that, as Virginia Woolf critiqued their consensus in 1929, "This is an insignificant book because it deals with the feelings of women in a drawing room." The schoolroom remains another matter.

—Mitzi Myers, "The Dilemmas of Gender"

The Awakening and the *Narrative of the Life of Frederick Douglass* are now commonly taught in U.S. literature courses, thanks to the current ferment over reconstructing the canon.[1] But rare is the adults' literature course—or anthology—that includes even such acknowledged children's classics as *Little Women* or *The Secret Garden*. Rarer still is any acknowledgment of genres marginalized by the children's literature establishment—such as the school story. Rarest of all is attention to works marginalized by such a genre—such as boys' school stories by women and girls' school stories by men. Yet such marginalized, crossgendered work can give voice to the cultural contradictions that inhabit a genre—and a culture. Such marginal cases "always constitute the most certain and most decisive indices wherever essential conditions are to be grasped" (Derrida, "Limited" 209): one must turn to marginal cases to gain insight into essences, even as one deconstructs those essences. Such transgressive work can reshape and reclaim a genre.

Those critics who theorize marginality often address race, gender, class. But not age, not children (and certainly not children's literature).[2] Cora Kaplan, for instance, has brilliantly argued that in the nineteenth century

> Female subjectivity, or its synecdochic reference, female sexuality, became the displaced and condensed site for the general anxiety about individual behaviour that republican and liberal political philosophy stirred up. It is not too surprising that the morality of the class as a

whole was better represented by those who exercised the least power within it . . . (166–167)

Namely, women, according to Kaplan. But also children, for whom the synecdochic reference becomes education, the site where adults play out competing philosophies. Kaplan points further to the elisions among "all three subordinated categories: Blacks, women and the working class," such that "whole cultures became 'feminized,' 'blackened' and 'impoverished'—each denigrating construction implying and invoking the others" (168). One might add that whole cultures are also deemed immature, "infantilized," in a construction that likewise invokes and implies the other vectors of marginality.

By examining the crossgendering of school stories, then, one can explore the intersections of gender and age, how the particularities of the one influence projections onto the other, how the other in turn resituates the particularities. Crossgendering is especially suitable for examining how a literary work can mediate conflicting codes and ideologies—in particular, the ideologies associated with adulthood and childhood, and with male and female. For when men try to imagine the subjectivities of girls, or women those of boys, they are doubly removed from that whereof they write—removed by age as well as gender. The result is that women may adopt what they recognize as an accepted code—such as the schoolboy code against talebearing—but perhaps not having fully internalized it, certainly having greater distance from it, they at times contradict the code (as E. J. May does), or they are at pains to justify it, contextualize it (as Harriet Martineau does), or they transform it (as Ellen Wood—Mrs. Henry Wood to her contemporaries—and Louisa May Alcott do). These activities are much less likely—indeed I have found very little evidence of them—in writers for whom the code seems second nature, men who once lived the code.

Of course my concern for the gender of a story's signature essentializes the author, reinscribes the gender polarities that the project of crossgendering itself transgresses—when in fact no female is simply and purely feminine, no male purely masculine. Yet this is one of those occasions that calls for what Gayatri Chakravorty Spivak has described as strategic essentializing (176). Only then is it possible to begin disentangling the myriad knottings of gender and age with language, as well as with class and race.

Or rather this is an occasion for seeking perhaps a new essentialism, one informed by the insights of poststructuralism—a provisional recognition that the concrete realities of, say, biology and economics cannot just be deconstructed but do in fact affect who we are.[3] In theorizing positionality, for instance, Linda Alcoff navigates between the pitfalls of essentializing women and of deconstructing all gender difference by examining the shifting contexts in which gender is employed, keeping sight of the need to problematize key concepts while yet being able to state what it means to be a woman—or a man—here, now, in these particular circumstances. The project of crossgendering is supremely one of positionality. When men and women crossgender, they are both "other" from that of which they write, at the same time that their views and modes are shaped by their genders and histories, by their immersions in social, political, and economic realities, and by existing literary traditions.

Later chapters address in detail how crossgendering can shape the school story. It is important first, though, to provide some background on the genre and its history.

The key distinguishing feature of the school story is that it be a story set at school, generally at the secondary level (in contrast with what have been called university novels).[4] It is often—though not always—addressed to children, and it is often written from the perspective of a child. Given the general inaccessibility of secondary school to the working classes before this century, the school story tends to be written from a middle-class perspective and addressed to a middle-class readership (though the readership of later school stories often included other classes). And given the genre ambiguities of stories set at day schools—when a story focuses on the out-of-classroom activities of a child attending a day school, we are not apt to consider it a school story—I am primarily concerned with stories set at boarding school.

Yet there are ambiguous cases, stories in which the genre has not yet congealed, stories that reveal traces, what Fredric Jameson calls the sedimentation, of competing genres (see *Political Unconscious* 140–141). Take stories that are only partly set at school, whether because the child doesn't leave for school till halfway through, or he or she leaves school early on. Or stories about children at a day school, whose activities outside the classroom are given much more attention than those inside, as indeed is also the case in boarding-school stories. What of girls' stories in which girls are educated at home with a governess? Or by their mothers? Then there are early stories that address education allegorically, with perhaps a figure called Instruction who is, for all intents and purposes, a schoolmaster (see Pickering, "Allegory" 48–49). For the most part I will be focusing on stories that can, in the narrowest sense, be considered school stories, that is, boarding-school stories. Yet I will also be making forays into contiguous realms, since it is on the boundaries that the most revealing questions are raised.

I am not primarily concerned with the mainstream, canonical school story, that is, stories following in the wake of Thomas Hughes's *Tom Brown's Schooldays* (1857), what too often is considered "the" school story. Yet I must address these stories, if only to begin to differentiate the other kind. I must delineate the features of such a genre "not in order to drop specimens into the box bearing those labels, but rather to map our coordinates on the basis of those fixed stars and to triangulate this specific given textual movement" of individual texts (Jameson, "Towards" 322).

The plots of the canonical stories, set at British boys' public schools, soon became formulaic: They feature an ordinary good-natured boy, not particularly intellectual, but keen on sports. We would see his arrival and the larks and scrapes of his early years. We would see his awe of the older boys, as well as his willingness to do the small services expected of him as a fag (a term whose meaning was not yet explicitly sexual), such as toasting bread on a fork and making tea over a fire in an older boy's study. We would see our hero rise through the ranks to the sixth form and become a creature of awe himself, perhaps a prefect and captain of the cricket team. Occasionally we might glimpse a classroom, for a paragraph or two, but we could count on spending pages and pages on the playing fields, with at least one match described in thrilling detail. There would also be other physical adventures, probably a fight with the school bully, our hero valiantly holding his own even if he does not defeat the oaf, and perhaps also the hero's rescue of his worst enemy from drowning. There might be a moral adventure too, our hero wrongly accused of, say, stealing an examination paper and staunchly bearing the blame, suffering a caning or the threat of expulsion, but refusing to tattle on the wrongdoer—and, of course, eventually being exonerated anyway. Competition (sports, the fight with the bully) is thus balanced against peer solidarity (sports, not telling tales). The story would conclude with our hero nostalgically reflecting on the joys and triumphs of his school days as he is about to leave, and perhaps with the narrator telling us the future fates of the boy and his friends: which one is to become a Queen's Counsel, which one a lord of the Admiralty, which one Bishop of Zanzibar—thereby underscoring the connection of such stories with the British imperial project. Overall, as Margery Fisher has wryly noted, "You get the odd impression that school life consists of a series of cricket and football matches and school speech days, enlivened by petty larceny, cribbing and gang warfare" (*Intent* 171).

These late-nineteenth-, early-twentieth-century stories were written mostly by men. One of the three recent books on the genre, Isabel Quigly's *The Heirs of Tom Brown*, devotes only one short chapter to girls' books and mentions few women authors of boys' school stories. P. W. Musgrave gives even shorter shrift to girls' school stories and similarly scants women authors in *From Brown to Bunter,* as does Jeffrey Richards in *Happiest Days.* Yet women writing about boys, likewise men writing about girls, have seemed especially able to illuminate the dialectics of the genre, redressing, regendering it.

Commentators such as Quigly have underscored the connection of school stories with the imperial project (3ff.) but not the gender connection. For school can curiously feminize boys as it subjects them to discipline and authority. As Quigly has noted, a young boy who fagged for an older one undertook "wholly domestic chores, considered totally 'feminine' in a period when no male would ever, in other circumstances, make toast and tea or lay and light a fire" (7). Or as George Eliot has noted of the fictional private school attended by Tom Tulliver, "Mr. Stelling was not the man to enfeeble and emasculate his pupil's mind by simplifying and explaining, or to reduce the tonic effect of etymology by mixing it with smattering, extraneous information such as is given to girls" (149). Yet the result of this regime is that "Tom became more like a girl than he had ever been in his life before"; the effect on his pride "quite nullified his boyish self-satisfaction, and gave him something of the girl's susceptibility" (149).

At the same time—and partly causing this feminization—the canonical school story is premised on the exclusion of females. The canonical school story emerges when society separates "public" from "private," "public" schooling from "private" family: the school story symbolically carves out a realm where a boy could move from a private to a more public arena.[5] And it does so by eliminating females. Excluding mothers and girls—boys were even chary of admitting that they had sisters—lent the boys authority. A move that is replicated by twentieth-century critics, who have generally failed to notice that what they call the school story developed from a tradition dominated by women.[6]

Not that men writing of boys' schools were unable to capture the contradictions of the genre, or of the schools themselves. But not until George Orwell wrote, in 1952, of his early-twentieth-century schooling did they effectively confront the contradictions "between the tradition of nineteenth-century asceticism and the actually existing luxury and snobbery of the pre-1914 age," between "low-church Bible Christianity, sex puritanism, insistence on hard work, respect for academic distinction, disapproval of self-indulgence" and

> contempt for "braininess" and worship of games, contempt for foreigners and the working class, an almost neurotic dread of poverty,

and, above all, the assumption not only that money and privilege are the things that matter, but that it is better to inherit them than to have to work for them. Broadly, you were bidden at once to be a Christian and a social success, which is impossible. ("Such" 45)

In school stories as in real schools, a boy was supposed to be both Christian and popular. Yet in most of the canonical stories, the authors pay mere lip service to Christian piety: what engages their energy is the boys' loyalty to one another rather than to adult authorities or to religious truth. Still, the underlying tension, the contradiction—even if expressed only as a momentary hesitation over loyalties—nonetheless gives life to these stories.

In the spirit of these contradictions, I want in this chapter both to exalt and to debunk the book generally considered the first school story, to pave the way for reading other, noncanonical school stories. I want to crack its codes—simultaneously decipher its meaning and shatter its assumptions. I want, in effect, to express my ambivalence about Hughes's work, an ambivalence reflected in the undertaking of my book as a whole, in which I embody my crossgendered resistance to what has usually been treated as a male genre by attending to the crossgendering of the genre. I want, in short, to call the school story into question, put it under erasure, transgress its genre and gender—place and displace it simultaneously. A simultaneity whose disruptiveness may, paradoxically, best be rendered as a series of moments.

First Moment: Debunking

Tom Brown was not the first school story. In the realm of adults' literature—or at least literature not explicitly or exclusively addressed to children—there were what Margaret M. Maison has called scholastic novels, in the 1840s and 1850s: both stories primarily about school and stories like Edward John Trelawny's *Adventures of a Younger Son* (1831), in which we gain a quick glimpse of a Squeers-like school before our hero moves on to sea fights and tiger hunts. Not to mention—speaking of Squeers—the cameos of school appearing in mainstream Victorian novels ranging from *Nicholas Nickleby* (1838–1839) to *Vanity Fair* (1847–1848) to *The Mill on the Floss* (1860).

In the realm of children's literature, school stories have an even longer history: the highlights include Sarah Fielding's *The Governess* (1749), Mme (Marie) LePrince de Beaumont's *The Young Misses Magazine* (1757), Richard Johnson's *The Little Female Orators* (1770), Dorothy Kilner's *The Village School* (c. 1783), Charles and Mary Lamb's *Mrs Leicester's School* (1809), Harriet Martineau's *The Crofton Boys* (1841), Elizabeth Sewell's *Laneton Parsonage* (1846–1848)—almost half of them crossgendered. Most of the best-known eighteenth-century writers for children—including Fielding, Kilner, Ellenor Fenn, and Maria Edgeworth—wrote at least one story set at school. These early school stories focus on the child's accession to virtue: he or she might get into a scrape or two, perhaps quarrel over some apples, but the central children behave largely in accordance with—and fully subscribe to—the moral exhortations of parents and other instructors.

School stories were particularly suited to children's literature of the eighteenth century, for in a world of middle-class secularism, "education, not right religion, now restored harmony to life" (Pickering, "Allegory" 56). These stories often lent themselves to authorship by women, who could view such writing as an extension of their traditional nurturing and maternal teaching; most of these early school stories are in fact by women.[7] More generally, the school story readily lent itself to the prevailing interest in didacticism—a didacticism we have often been too ready to look down on[8]—with the fictional instructor a mouthpiece for the author.

School stories lend themselves to didacticism because they are about schooling. They thematize their own textuality—or rather their own moral purpose. Schooling is, in part, a metaphor for the effect that the book is supposed to have, whether it endorses traditional schooling or tries to school us in subversion. A school story may contain a figure that mirrors the larger whole,[9] but, an object to be deciphered, it also replicates itself: it is not just a product but a process to be undergone. Like other genres, the school story includes a "trait that marks membership" and "inevitably divides," so that "the boundary of the set comes to form, by invagination, an internal pocket larger than the whole" (Derrida, "Law" 206)—but with a vengeance. The school story self-divides, invaginates itself, is larger than itself. A story about school is a school.

The school story thus is and is about a peculiarly marginal institution, a boundary institution between family and world, between private and public spheres. Schooling is, furthermore, addressed to marginal individuals, to those between childhood and adulthood, and adults always marginalize children and adolescents. For even now, however much we may think that we are child-centered, we still apply, unthinkingly, adult norms. When we use metaphors of juvenility, we use them to disparage: it is hardly a compliment to call someone immature or infantile.[10] School is also curiously marginalized by its being a temporary site from the perspective of the individual. It situates the student in the position of always becoming; even its ending is called a commencement. Yet schooling can be centered if every child goes to school—or it can be centered hegemonically when access to schooling is limited or segregated. Or rather it is implicated in class and other hierarchies, shaped by them, reinforcing them, though it also allows some possibility for subversion, some possiblity for giving one perspective on the marginal, on class, gender, race, ethnicity, sexuality. School is, in short, multiply a border case, a site for working out contrary impulses. Located at the fracture between adult and child, it plays out "the impossible relation between adult and child" (Rose 1), and between adults and children's literature.

As for the earliest school stories—in Fielding's *The Governess; or, Little Female Academy,* the first book-length story for children, each schoolgirl reflects on her life, admitting to her faults and how she will improve. Dolly Friendly would do anything for a friend, allow herself to be swayed against her better judgment, but now will be more moderate; Lucy Sly used to be deceitful; Nanny Spruce, too concerned about dress. Each of these stories within the story, each figure mirroring the larger whole, adumbrates the schooling that is the book's point, or rather, given that the book is largely composed of these interpolated tales, the tales do not just adumbrate but become the book's point. Yet *The Governess* also contains more fanciful stories. The governess in charge of the small girls' school tries carefully to defuse the dangerous potential of the fanciful. She explains at great length that giants do not really exist, that

> Giants, Magic, Fairies, and all Sorts of supernatural Assistances in a Story, are only introduced to amuse and divert: For a Giant is called so only to express a Man of great Power; and the magic Fillet round the Statue was intended only to shew you, that by Patience you will overcome all Difficulties. Therefore, by no means let the Notion of Giants or Magic dwell upon your Minds. (34)

Yet the mere inclusion of such stories admits their attractiveness to children, the power of the imaginative. The insistence on reading them allegorically— giants are simply large men—only underscores how they cannot be fully contained by allegory. Readers persist in imagining giants. And advice not to let something "dwell upon your Minds" is a recipe for the opposite. Fielding's story embodies conflicting impulses, to instruct and to amuse; the need for the fictional instructor's cautions underscores how fiction inevitably escapes the merely cautionary.[11]

The early school story, like other early children's literature, is thus a site for mediating conflicting ideologies regarding children and their education. It's not coincidental that the first children's literature is said to emerge— in 1744 perhaps, with John Newbery's *Little Pretty Pocketbook*—in the same decade that the novel is said to. And in the same century as the emergence of the middle class, the same century that class overtakes status, as Michael McKeon has argued, as the prime sorter of people. McKeon points to the crucial ability of the novel, at its origin, "to mediate—to represent as well as contain—the revolutionary clash between status and class orientations and the attendant crisis of status inconsistency" by organizing "the fluidity of crisis . . . into a conflict of competing interpretations" (173–174). Something similar happens in children's literature, as school stories play out the clashes and connections among the Calvinist view of the ineradicability of sin; the Lockean view of the educability of children, making it desirable to join amusement and instruction; and the Rousseauian view of the superiority of childhood to educational and other institutions, a view that spirals back to a denial of the desirability of education.[12] Children's literature emerges in this time of ferment. School stories attempt, as Jameson has said in another context, "to resolve, in the imaginary, what is socially irreconcilable" (*Marxism* 383).

Early school stories, crossgendered and otherwise, are thus worthy of study for their own sakes, for how they embody the crises and values of their age. To apply here what Spivak has argued with respect to *Frankenstein* and imperialism, such stories may contain incidental tropes and sentiments like those in later school stories, but "the discursive field of imperialism does not produce unquestioned ideological correlatives for the narrative structuring of the book" (188). These early school stories raise questions that are later buried in canonical plots; these early stories do not deserve the twilight that descended on them after Hughes.[13]

SECOND MOMENT: EXALTING

Tom Brown's Schooldays has nonetheless been unduly ignored and devalued, especially by literary critics.

Such devaluation has happened first because school stories—and with them *Tom Brown*—are generally classified as children's literature, and despite the attention granted, say, Lewis Carroll, children's literature is not accorded as much critical scrutiny or respect as adults' literature. Not all school stories have been addressed to children—not all would be considered children's literature—though all seem to have been marginalized, as if contaminated by associations with childhood.

Second, school stories have remained a marginal genre even for critics who address children's literature. Perhaps the school story is especially marginal in North America, where we tend to think of our juvenile tradition as similar to that of England—the field has not fully bifurcated into

9

"British" and "American"—so we're likely not to notice a genre that has had greater definition and visibility there than here. Witness the "canon" of children's literature drawn up in the early 1980s by Mary Ake and other members of the "canon" committee of the Children's Literature Association: the list comprises some sixty-odd books and series, including fantasy, family stories, adventure stories, but *Tom Brown* is omitted, as are all other school stories.[14] And maybe another reason why school stories have remained marginal is that, as my colleague Jan Susina reminds me, those of us who teach may feel uncomfortable about reminders of how we wield power (often unthinkingly) and how our power can be subverted. Yet for academics who care about teaching and learning—cultural critics, say, who examine not just culture, and not just its traces in texts, but also our own teaching as reproducing and subverting culture[15]—school stories comprise an ideal locus for study. Examining school stories enables one to probe the intersections of literature and pedagogy and the politics of schooling, including the conflicts in authority between and the complicities of teacher and student.

Furthermore, school stories give access to the central enterprise of children's literature. As Jacqueline Rose acknowledges, "There is no language for children which can be described independently of divisions in the institution of schooling, the institution out of which modern childhood has more or less been produced" (7). Adults construct childhood through both children's literature and schooling. Didacticism did not disappear during the Golden Age of children's literature in the late nineteenth century; its function was in part transferred to, in part epitomized by, the emergent genre of "the" school story, where the story about school became a school by pretending to disavow schooling.

In any case, although its role is now often overlooked, *Tom Brown's Schooldays* (1857) helped to mark the transition from what has been called the Age of Didacticism to the Golden Age of children's literature in English. Sometimes the watershed is taken to be 1865, when Carroll published *Alice's Adventures in Wonderland*. Yet there were earlier milestones, as F. J. Harvey Darton notes: the publication of Catherine Sinclair's *Holiday House* in 1839; of Felix Summerly's *Home Treasury* of fairy tales and other traditional stories, beginning in 1843; of a translation of Hans Christian Andersen's tales in 1846; of Edward Lear's *Book of Nonsense* in 1846; of a translation of Heinrich Hoffmann's *Struwwelpeter* about 1848 (see Darton, *Children's Books* 220–243). *Tom Brown* is at least as much of a milestone as any of these, sparking a realistic tradition of writing for children. But to the extent that the essence of children's literature is seen as fantasy or fairy tale, to the extent that the school story is excluded from the children's canon, let alone any other—to that extent *Tom Brown's Schooldays* has been denied its place as milestone, let alone watershed.

Yet *Tom Brown* had enormous impact: it is an understatement to say that it influenced the hundreds of subsequent school stories, whether the authors tacitly agreed with Hughes or set themselves in opposition (or, more precisely, agreed with some of Hughes's stances and disagreed with others). Standard histories of the genre always make Hughes central, as origin—followed by Farrar, Reed, Kipling, Wodehouse, Walpole, among many other writers.[16] *Tom Brown* also influenced stories that are not usually classified as school stories, such as the U.S. bad-boy story by Mark Twain and others. And Hughes's book has even, it has been argued, influenced the life of the public schools themselves.[17]

It has likewise influenced popular culture and also mainstream literature for adults. At the beginning of the twentieth century, the tradition of the canonical school story split into nonelite and elite strands.[18] The former comprised pop-culture magazine stories, read variously by working-class boys and by young boys of the middle to upper classes, and featuring such figures as the fat Billy Bunter, still a British pop-culture antihero. On the other hand, it also became possible to write "serious" school stories, for adults presumably, stories that questioned some earlier assumptions, stories that were less celebratory of the public school, stories that were often more willing to broach—for good or, usually, ill—the possibilities of homosexuality at single-sex boarding schools. Both twentieth-century strands, in any case, still respond to the tradition inaugurated by Hughes.

Tom Brown was, in short, a watershed. More than earlier writers, Hughes laid bare the opposition between student and teacher, undermining—and thereby underlining—the conservatism of the earlier school story. Or rather, if the disciplinary foundations of schooling in the eighteenth century succeeded in hierarchizing students even while homogenizing them, individualizing them by subjecting them to the adult gaze, as Foucault would have it, Hughes succeeded in disengaging these individuals, a little, from visibility. He empowered children. What he provided is not so much a simple opposition to what had gone before but a departure sufficiently radical to clarify the terms of the dialectic, countering the school story as it had existed previously, freezing the fluidity of the genre.

Yet even so cautious a statement needs to be further qualified. For of course the genre developed dialectically, with a sedimentary layering of old and new. In the second half of Hughes's book, for instance, Tom increasingly adopts the headmaster's views, as the book reverts to the older, pious model of school story.[19]

The statement also glosses over the way the older school stories did offer some glimmers of the subversiveness that Alison Lurie finds characteristic of children's literature; likewise the way later school stories allowed for a resistance that was nonetheless safely contained (see Inglis 177). The later stories provide a place where, away from the "the subtle mesh of the parent–child relationship" and other complexities at home, "there is a natural and accepted opposition between what pupils are supposed to do and what they will do if they get the chance" (Townsend 112). Such a story marks—and aids—a boy's passage from the family to the world beyond, as it inculcates traits (initiative, teamwork, ethnocentrism) that would make for effective colonial functionaries. It displaces adult moral authority from parents to masters, from adults whom it would be sacrilege to disobey to ones whom it would be merely inappropriate to.[20]

Hughes may not stress the opposition of child and adult, or the priority of child over adult. He may even allow the adult narrator to preach at the child reader. Yet he accommodates the child's perspective by attributing to the headmaster some of Tom's ideas of what a Rugby education is for: especially sports.[21] As an admirable sixth-form boy states in the book, "I'd sooner win two School-house matches running than get the Balliol scholarship anyday" (104). And because of the centrality of Tom's perspective, loyalty to other boys generally takes precedence over loyalty to adult authorities. For one way in which school empowers children is by distancing them from the only authority they have hitherto known—that of the family.[22] Such duplication of authority enables them to triangulate to their own.[23]

In empowering children, *Tom Brown* thus marks a change from an earlier literature written to the child to a literature for the child, portraying "children as children like to see themselves" (Avery and Bull 66); from a literature relatively undifferentiated by class and age to one that could separately address the working or middle classes, young children, or young adults; from a literature largely for both boys and girls to a sex-segregated one that allowed boys to be less submissive, if they were middle and upper class; from a literature predominantly by women, schooled so well in submission, to one where men could let boys be boys—and eventually, especially by the twentieth century, women could let girls be girls or even tomboys. From the Age of Didacticism in children's literature to what has been called the Golden Age.

THIRD MOMENT: DEBUNKING

Yet the presumed centrality of *Tom Brown,* its canonization as the origin of the school story, has warped not just the earlier but also the later history of the genre. For not all school stories written after *Tom Brown* assume the supremacy of peer loyalty, the independence from family and other adult authorities, and the ethic of not tattling that Hughes endorses. These other stories include U.S. stories for boys and girls, British stories for boys during the first two decades after Hughes, and British girls' stories.

One reason for the relative invisibility of U.S. school stories is that the United States had fewer boarding schools, in and out of literature—and these schools generated less mystique than the British public school did. Thus it is tempting to assume, when a Tom Sawyer or an Amy March attends a day school yet the vast majority of the book takes place outside the classroom, that the book is not a school story. Instead two other genres have been seen as central in U.S. literature about children.

One is what has been called the boy book, or bad-boy book, including works by Mark Twain, Thomas Bailey Aldrich, William Dean Howells. The bad-boy books, like the British school story, depict "a child's world that is antagonistic to the world of adults" (Crowley 385).[24] On some level this U.S. version is even more antagonistic than the British one, since one of the adult impositions that the boys may reject is school itself. Paradoxically, a sign of the antagonism is the ambiguous status of these books as children's or adults' literature: Is *The Adventures of Tom Sawyer* a children's story? Is *The Adventures of Huckleberry Finn?* The more adult such stories are, it seems, the more antiadult they can be. Or perhaps the more antiadult they are the more imperative it has been to remove them from the domain of children's literature.

The other genre that has been seen as central in the United States is the family story, including works by Louisa May Alcott and Susan Coolidge. Later volumes in a family-based series may become school stories—for instance, *Little Men* (1871), *What Katy Did at School* (1873)—but the best-known volumes remain focused on the family. Here too perhaps is an implicit rejection of school, this time in favor of the family—a rejection sometimes made explicit, as when Alcott's Marmee withdraws Amy from school.

In any case, what much nineteenth-century U.S. literature about children seems to have in common is a tendency to reject school—putting U.S. school stories, where they exist, in an anomalous position. On the one hand, the existence of the bad-boy book and the family story, both embodying resistance to school, enables bona fide school stories to stay closer to an older tradition endorsing adult authority. Yet the existence of the bad-boy book and the family story also scouts that tradition, undermining the authority of adults associated with school. Add to that the fact that adults now grant recognition to authors like Twain and Alcott—who nowadays has even heard of conservative school-story authors like Helen C. Knight or Adaliza Parry?—and we again confront the paradox that adults endorse what least endorses them.

Another way in which the United States diverged from Britain, in addition to having fewer boarding schools in and out of fiction, is that U.S. classrooms were more commonly coeducational.[25] And the greater heterogeneity—with respect to gender and also class and often age—may simultaneously have dimmed some of the mystique of school, its unattainability, and have vitiated the power of peer loyalty, both in literature and in the culture at large.

Whatever the reasons, the U.S. school story followed a different trajectory from that of the recognized British tradition. Consider U.S. school stories about boys. In the latter half of the nineteenth century, these stories tended to stay closer to the older, pre-Hughesian stories in tone, even when acknowledging Hughes's influence and importance. The authors of U.S. boys' stories often frown on fighting (countering what they misread as Hughes's endorsement of it)[26] and give mixed messages about talebearing, or even endorse it. And that is true whether the author was a man or a woman. In later chapters I'll be addressing some women writers of boys' stories, so here let me cite some men: In Oliver Optic's *In School and Out* (1864), the hero readily overcomes any initial reluctance to tell his principal about a secret schoolboy society—thereby firmly placing himself "on the side of law and order" (250). Edward Eggleston, in *The Hoosier School-Boy* (1883), is more ambiguous: the hero does submit to a whipping by a tyrannical master rather than tell who put gunpowder in the school stove, yet the narrator equivocates by saying that the boy "ought, perhaps, to have told, for the offence was criminal; but it is hard for a high-spirited lad to yield to a brutal threat" (68–69). It's not until the twentieth century that prep-school stories like Claude Moore Fuess's *The Andover Way* (1928) or sports stories like Elmer A. Dawson's *Garry Grayson at Lenox High* (1927) enact and enforce the ethic prohibiting talebearing.[27]

As for British boys' stories, Musgrave has rightly pointed out that the true definer of the genre was Talbot Baines Reed, in such works as *The Fifth Form at St. Dominic's,* which appeared in the *Boy's Own Paper* in 1881–1882 (112). The flood of school stories that followed in the 1880s, 1890s, and beyond essentially reworked the tropes that Reed assembled, echoing the low profile he accorded religion and the high profile accorded games. Between Hughes and Reed there had been a few writers like H. C. Adams and T. S. Millington writing school stories, but largely in the pre-Hughesian evangelical tradition.[28] So on some level the real progenitor of the canonical school story, the author of the true prototype, is not Hughes but Reed.

And as for British girls' school stories, there were, as with U.S. stories, relatively few of them, and again at least partly because of social context. Nineteenth-century middle-class girls were often educated at home by a mother or governess, and we are unlikely to consider the story of such a girl's education a school story. A middle-class British girl was also more likely than a boy to attend a day school, so that a story of her activities, if it does not focus on her classroom experiences, will again not seem like a school story. Even when a girl did go away to school, it was likely to reproduce the family context. Nineteenth-century British girls who attended school generally went to small private schools, modeled on the family, run by ladies of modest means. Such a school, with its pupils of diverse ages and its high ratio of adults to pupils, encouraged dependency and discouraged peer solidarity—unlike the more public girls' school, the larger endowed or proprietary school run by academic professionals, that started emerging after 1850 and especially after 1870.[29]

In any case, when a story did send a girl to school, it thereby suggested the desirability of authorities other than parents, and it became potentially dangerous. Occasionally, as in works by Evelyn Sharp, who was to become a suffragist and journalist, a girls' school story does indeed probe the disjunction between school and family, illuminating the subversive potential of school. More often girls' stories by writers like Mrs. (Mary) Molesworth, L. T. Meade, and Christabel R. Coleridge stress the congruence between family and school, certainly more than that between school and the world outside: If school marks a transition between family and world, girls' school stories are likely to focus on the first phase of the transition, boys' school stories on the latter.[30] In part the emphasis on family counters the possibility that a girl might find some independence at school. Yet also girls were never supposed to enter that world outside but to cycle back to the family—or a family—after school. As Nina Auerbach has said in a discussion of *The Prime of Miss Jean Brodie* (1961), "No girl can experience the effortless transition whereby the holy wars of school become those of adult reality, as they do in Tom Brown's tribute to his friend East . . ." (172).

Furthermore, if girls tend to be seen more in relation to others, as less independent than boys, as more caring and connected (to use the terminology of latter-day feminists like Nancy Chodorow and Carol Gilligan), a girl would be expected to continue to interact with her family a good deal. Families were less apt to relinquish connections with a girl who went to school, and a girl might be less apt to sever connections with her family than a boy would (certainly she was not likely to hide the fact of having brothers, as a boy might hide having sisters, almost as carefully as he would hide having a first name). And if girls tend to connect and to identify with authorities, then their conflicts are likely to be different from those of boys. Girls' school stories are less likely to set up a "clash between authority and the individual," between adult and child—what John Rowe Townsend sees at the heart of the (canonical) school story (112). Instead, girls' stories are more likely to be framed as a clash between adult authorities—between family and school authorities. Even in the boys' story in the *Tom Brown* tradition that most implicates family, F. Anstey's *Vice Versa* (1882)—significantly, a work of fantasy—the conflict between family and school is framed as a conflict between the (wrong) individual and (school) authority. Father and son have exchanged bodies, and the father is sent to school: the key conflict continues to be between child and adult, as in other boys' school stories, the father here becoming educated in the boy's perspective. In a girls' story, on the other hand, what conflict there may be is between family and school authorities (or between girls adhering variously to one or the other), thereby minimizing direct conflict between child and adult—yet the existence of a gap in authority does create space for subversion.

Mostly, though, family and school authorities reinforce each other. Such mutual reinforcement, in girls' school stories, allows less play for peer loyalty, at least in its oppositional forms. Before the twentieth century and the appearance of popular stories by Angela Brazil and the like—with such titles as *For the School Colours* (1918) and *A Popular Schoolgirl* (1920)— British girls' authors were reluctant to endorse peer solidarity and school-child codes, including that against talebearing, or else they tacitly assumed the codes without confronting any resulting dissonance, emphasizing connections with adults rather than conflict. Perhaps the authors did not want to emphasize the subversive dangers of school. Or perhaps they did not need to confront such issues in order to tap subversive energies. For going to school could itself be an act of subversion, still a privilege for middle-class girls, far from the more boring necessity that it was for their brothers.

The subversive potential of girls' school is best expressed by Sharp in *The Making of a Schoolgirl* (1897). When Becky goes to school, she encounters standards other than those of her older brother Jack. She can then move beyond Jack's contradictory dismissals of girls' schools as variously no fun or no work, dismantling the pronouncements while still liking the boy. She learns, for instance, that other girls can be real people too, honorable people, "that, in spite of the general inferiority of the sex, there actually seemed to be a sense of honour among girls as well as boys" (37). She has overheard girls talking in the dormitory at night about talking in the dormitory at night—which they are on their honor not to do. By showing that girls have a sense of honor, she undercuts Jack and his proclamations. But she also undercuts the girls and their protestations, for defending their honor seems to entail violating it. The gaps and contradictions among authorities enable Becky to start triangulating to her own authority, to become a person in her own right, sensitive to others' needs but not subservient to them. As Toril Moi might say, Sharp's deconstruction of patriarchy reveals "the paradoxically productive aspects of patriarchal ideology (the moments in which the ideology backfires on itself, as it were)," which enable Becky—and enabled Sharp too—"to counter patriarchal strategies despite the odds stacked against them" (64).

More typical in late-nineteenth-century British girls' school stories is a less conscious dismantling, a profusion or confusion of norms. Such disarray is of course appropriate in a time of transition, a time when girls' schools increasingly adopted the modes of boys' public schools yet also attempted to amalgamate values from both the boys' school and the Victorian family.[31]

We can find such disarray, such potential dismantling, expressed as ambivalence toward the code against talebearing and toward the replacement of parental with school authority, in Annie Buckland's *Lily and Nannie at School* (1868). We are told that Lily depends too much on the "commendation of others" (177), especially the commendation of her peers; she is therefore tempted to subscribe to the code against talebearing. When she comes across older girls reading *The Heir of Redclyffe*, a book forbidden because it is a novel, the others want her to promise not to tell Mrs. Stafford, their governess (as the head of a small private girls' school was often called—yet another reproduction of the family context).[32] Lily hesitates yet is eventually lured into the secret readings. One girl responds to Lily's reluctance by expostulating that "if people make ridiculous rules, we enter into the absurdity by keeping them"; she goes on to accuse Mrs. Stafford of tyranny and adds, "Why, did she not say herself the other day, that the reason the Italians were so uncivilised and debased, was because the Pope would not let them read what they liked?" (89). Although this firebrand is elsewhere shown to be less than admirable—she throws blame for a misdeed on another, an action despicable according to both adult and schoolchild codes—Buckland gives the girl surprisingly persuasive Thoreauvian arguments.

Lily's reading of the forbidden novel and succumbing to peer solidarity are not, however, endorsed. The episode is introduced by the narrator's saying, "Whatever you do, my young readers, be careful never to engage in the concealment of a secret" (81)—a secret from adult authority, that is. Lily herself loses sleep over her lapse. And when she reveals her misdemeanor at home during the holidays, her mother is grieved by the deception and disobedience; the mother goes on at length to indict such "a secret arrangement," to tell her child to "beware of the first step in a crooked course" (124)—to endorse, in short, telling tales to adult authorities.

Later, most of the sixteen girls in the school plan a midnight feast—they are not going to steal fruit from the pantry, or from the head's orchard, as boys in a boys' story might, but simply break into the closet where their own fruit baskets are kept. They decide not to tell the virtuous Lily and her twin Nannie. Nevertheless the plans go awry and the miscreants assume that the twins have somehow found out and told Mrs. Stafford. Yet no: Lily did not know about the plans—and thus has not been forced to choose between tattling and disobedience, between loyalty to adults and loyalty to peers. She is merely suspected of tattling by some not-so-admirable schoolfellows—and the moral valence of dubious suspicions by dubious girls remains conveniently ambiguous.

The book's ending too is ambiguous. Nannie gratuitously falls ill and dies, and no attempt is made to draw a lesson like the good dying young or the virtuous being closer to God. It's as if the point of Nannie's death is to prevent Lily from returning to school—returning would have been, we are told, "almost too great a trial" (221). But why protect Lily from the discipline of returning to school? Does danger lurk in the examples of the other pupils? Does the moral ambiguity of their actions infect the school? Or is the death simply a convenience for ending the book? Might there be in fact some dangers in reading this book—some necessity for cutting it short—for all that it seems to endorse school and other adult authority? Do we and Lily need to be protected from the temptation of relying on the "commendation of others," of subscribing to the schoolgirl ethic, protected from the subversive potential of school for girls?

By heightening disjunctions and the conflict of loyalties—rather than resolving contradictions—a book such as Buckland's starts unraveling the fabric of the canonical school story, and perhaps for that very reason such books have been ignored. The canonization of *Tom Brown* has pushed this and other versions of school stories—especially stories that do not focus on boys or are not about public schools or are not British—into the penumbra of literary history. Yet such stories often confront issues that the more canonical story glosses over.[33]

To find issues such as peer loyalty treated with due complexity, to find the fullest manifestations of their tensions and contradictions, and of the tensions and contradictions between child and adult and between home and family—to deconstruct the genre, as it is typically constructed—we need to seek outside the mainstream, outside the accepted canon of the school story. Acknowledging the interdependence of canonical and noncanonical, we can redress the genre by redressing, regendering it.

Or perhaps by crossdressing it. Since school stories are so gender marked, it becomes easy—not just easy, vital—to address questions of gender, to examine both the instability of gender and its potency. And critics who address the portrayal of crossdressing in fiction can offer insights applicable to writers who effectively crossdressed as they wrote. Sandra M. Gilbert and Susan Gubar suggest that twentieth-century men and women writers have had different attitudes toward the fictional portrayal of crossdressing, with "modernist literary men seeking to reinscribe traditional gender hierarchies and modernist women seeking to overturn those hierarchies" ("Sexchanges" 773).[34] Gubar suggests elsewhere that for female modernists crossdressing could variously be an attempt to attain the power of men (thereby devaluing women), a recognition of brooding self-division, or a complex shifting awareness of androgynous possibility. With respect to school stories, women who crossdress in their writing variously write with greater assurance and with less: greater if they believe in a fluid sense of self, if they feel that characters lack true essences but simply wear different guises in different situations and genders; less if they feel intimidated by writing about a gender accorded more public status.

More profoundly, as Marjorie Garber has urged, crossdressing can provide *"a space of possibility structuring and confounding culture:* the disruptive element that intervenes, not just a category crisis of male and female, but the crisis of category itself" (17, Garber's italics). The texts I go on to explore may not be traversed by the explicit figure of the transvestite, yet there is some play with clothing and disarray—a sow dressed as an usher, a boy garbed in a blanket, various others playing pranks with substituted clothing, or dunking an effete boy. This play functions as unmarked transvestism, creating a "transvestite effect" (Garber 356)—marking the traces of the literary transvestism of the authors.[35] Other school stories, ones that are not crossgendered, may display the transvestite—witness the "Slaves of the Lamp" in *Stalky & Co.* or the travesty of "Enoch Arden" in *The Making of a Schoolgirl.* Yet perhaps in crossgendered stories we find "the submergence of something that is more powerful when masked or veiled—that is, when it remains unconscious" (356). For crossgendered stories embody a profound category crisis, destabilizing both genre and gender.

Yet another way to describe the possibilities of crossgendering is through Hélène Cixous's notion of bisexuality: not the kind that is "a fantasy of unity" but "the *other bisexuality*"—"that is to say the location within oneself of the presence of both sexes, evident and insistent in different ways according to the individual, the nonexclusion of difference or of a sex" (104, Cixous's italics). Crossgendering can allow a woman to express the masculine in herself—"the other that I am and am not, that I don't know how to be, but that I feel passing, that makes me live—that tears me apart, disturbs me, changes me, who?" (105)—at the same time that it heightens her sense of femininity; correspondingly for a man, his femininity, heightening his masculinity. In part such work may reinscribe the same, reinforcing the status quo, but it harbors the seeds of subversion as well.

Crossgendering may be especially revelatory with respect to the school story. For the book that continues to be seen as both epitome and origin, *Tom Brown's Schooldays*, is situated at a time of transition with respect to gender. Victorian thinking seems, at midcentury, to have undergone an important shift in orientation: if at the beginning of the century the opposite of "man," that which defined the term's limits, was likely to be "child," by the end of the century it was likely to be "woman." Or to put it differently, if early in the century the ideal of manhood included traits that could be considered androgynous, then by the end of the century the ideal was more likely to include traits that could be considered adolescent or even boyish.[36] Hughes would then seem to register some of the complexities of the transition, as a man writing through the child and attempting to accommodate both "androgynous" and "masculine" versions of manliness, ostensibly portraying the former as more childish than the latter while yet showing Tom as progressing, in effect, toward the former. Even more revelatory are explicit crossgenderings, men writing of girls, women of boys.

Sometimes—as I detail in subsequent chapters—a woman writer of boys' stories tries to write like a man, as Mrs. G. (Annie) Forsyth Grant does in books like *The Boys at Penrohn* (1893) and *The Beresford Boys* (1906)—thereby endorsing the masculine, attempting to stifle the feminine, implicitly devaluing women though she may also be indulging in some Irigarayan mimicry, parodying male voices. Sometimes, like E. (Emily) J. May, she is self-divided, bringing contradictions to the fore with great urgency, at the same time that she devalues characters who, like herself, are women. Sometimes, like Louisa May Alcott, she is bisexual, in Cixous's sense, allowing an interplay between masculine and feminine, an interplay that allows Alcott to express the otherness in herself while yet remaining the same. It is fitting, then, that Alcott chooses not to hide behind a husband's name, as Forsyth Grant does, nor behind initials, as May does, but names herself with both her father's Alcott and her mother's maiden name May. In all three cases, though, and more generally, crossgendering women emphasize the interface of family and school more than male writers of boys' school stories do.

On the other hand, when the occasional man writes about girls' schools, he sometimes seems able to empower his girl characters in a way that women have found difficult—he seems to grant them some of the freedoms that he himself experienced at school. Yet he cannot write of girls without some anxiety, an anxiety that often plays out in his portrayal of a fictional male proxy, whether it is George Mogridge's genial Old Humphrey or H. G. Wells's earnest guardian Oswald. And men, especially British men, seemed unable to write of girls at all during the heyday of the canonical school story in the last half of the nineteenth century.

Women writers too found ways of projecting their discomforts, often by traversing a class, racial, or ethnic boundary. In the mid-nineteenth century Mrs. (Mary Martha) Sherwood and C. (Charlotte) Adams might find a spokesperson in, curiously, a laboring-class woman—as if they had to dramatize their sense of estrangement from their subject by elevating someone who was excluded from boys' schools not just by gender and age, as they themselves were, but by class. Later in the century authors of crossgendered school stories, women such as Mrs. (Elizabeth) Eiloart and men such as Edward Everett Hale, would project some of their own otherness and their ambivalence about their estrangement from that of which they wrote onto racial or ethnic others.

Or in terms of the literary system, the marginalized school-story writers that I engage with here often wrote stories that were in dialogue with other genres. Kilner and Alcott, for instance, wrote school stories that intersected with domestic fiction, though to rather different effect: Kilner as if reluctant to disengage from the family context, before the school story had fully emerged as a genre; Alcott more overtly challenging what had by then become the canonical story by reconceiving it. Or Wood wrote a school story that was also a sensation story; Hale, one that was also a sermon; Wells, one that was also a treatise.

The remaining chapters explore such issues in discussions periodized—before *Tom Brown,* during the height of his influence, afterwards—in a way that reinscribes the centrality of Hughes even while calling it into question. Some of the earliest and latest stories, discussed in Chapters 2 and 11, are by men writing about girls, men such as Lamb and Wells.

Most of the crossgendered school stories, from the eighteenth to twentieth centuries, are by women writing about boys, women such as Kilner, May, Sherwood, Wood, Alcott, Julia A. Mathews, and D. Wynne Willson. Sometimes the stories are explicitly addressed to children; sometimes not.[37] In all cases, writing against the grain brings the grain into bold relief. Writing at cross purposes lays bare the contradictory welter of purposes circulating in the culture. Less committed perhaps to both the literal and literary systems of and in which they were writing—their works marginalized with respect to gender, genre, and generations—these writers felt less need to present a perfect front.

NOTES

1. For elaboration of ideas in this paragraph, see my "Not for Children Only."

2. For further discussion see my "Fairy Godmothers."

3. Feminist theorists who work this vein include Alcoff, who theorizes positionality; Spivak, who speaks in passing of strategic essentializing; Ferguson, who interweaves the essentializing of interpretation with the subversion of genealogy; Friedman, who calls for a politics of negotiation; Haraway, who writes of situated knowledges; J. Scott, who historicizes the concept of experience. Kristeva's discussion of a "third generation" of feminists, in "Women's Time," can be read as congruent too. Still other feminists, such as Christian, in "Race," have resisted the impulse to deconstruct all along.

4. Note the implications of the nouns associated with the two genres: the first are generally called stories, the second novels—another sign of the lower status and marginalization of school stories. Yet "story" remains more flexible and accommodating than "novel," less implicated in a particular historical and social context, even at the same time that it is more commonly associated with children (an association that I want both to question and to celebrate), so at the risk of reinscribing the hierarchy I will continue to use "story."

5. My use of the terms here is provisional, in quotation marks—in accordance with Kerber's review of the rhetorical uses and limitations of the concept of separate spheres.

6. In his essay discussing the history of the school story, for instance, Wright mentions none about girls or by women—not recognizing that one of the two traditions he traces, that following Farrar's *Eric* (1858), derives from an earlier tradition of stories predominantly by women.

7. As Myers notes, eighteenth-century women authors often portrayed women as valuable teachers, rational educators, thereby countering demeaning stereotypes of female passivity and sentimentality ("Impeccable Governesses" 34–35; see also her "Dilemmas," "Socializing Rosamond," "Taste"). In "Romancing" she points to "an alternative discourse that privileges affiliation over achievement, human interrelatedness over scientific reason" (101; see also her "Reading"). And in "Erotics" she notes how teaching enables a woman to bridge "private and public spheres of human endeavor" and hence, in Edgeworth's case, participate "in the reconstitution of British cultural identity occasioned by Revolutionary conflict" (4).

8. We too easily ignore the extent to which works that we consider free of didacticism nonetheless purvey moral values. See P. Scott, "John Bull" 4–5, for an illuminating discussion of how the nineteenth-century shift in children's literature from the didactic to the normative did not eliminate the transmission of values but simply displaced it. See also Tompkins, 17ff., for discussion of how in mid-nineteenth-cen-

tury sentimental novels the aesthetic and the didactic were not in opposition but rather overlapping: what we are now tempted to castigate as didactic is often directly engaging itself with the world—and with the language that shapes that world. Richardson deconstructs the dualistic model that underlies most histories of children's literature, which pit didacticism against the imagination ("Wordsworth"); as does Rose, who suggests that what the trend toward a less conspicuous narrator "denies precisely is language—the fact that language does not simply reflect the world but is active in its constitution of the world" (60); see also Lesnik-Oberstein 38ff. But see Jackson, writing of eighteenth- and early-nineteenth-century children's literature: "School tales seem to have brought out the worst in many writers, given the number of sinister and dictatorial governesses and teachers they spawned" (147–148).

9. That is, "the myriad letters, books, tombstones, wills, inscriptions, road signs, maps, birthmarks, tracks, footprints, textiles, tapestries, veils, sheets, brown stockings, and self-abolishing laces that serve in one way or another as figures for the text to be deciphered or unraveled or embroidered upon" (B. Johnson 18). In a school story the figure might be a student composition.

10. Or at least, I would argue, primarily so. If there are hints of the positive in ascribing juvenility, these hints are usually suppressed, siphoned off into the occasional positive term ("childlike") so as to preserve the power of the more common negative ones ("childish," "immature," "puerile"). For further discussion of these issues see my "Thirteen Ways."

11. For another gloss of this passage, see Briggs, "Women Writers" 226–227.

12. For discussions of the philosophical underpinnings of eighteenth-century children's literature see, e.g., Jackson; Kowaleski-Wallace; Lesnik-Oberstein 37–99; Pickering, especially *Locke;* Richardson, especially "Wordsworth"; and Summerfield.

13. See Downs-Miers for a parallel argument with respect to *The Governess.*

14. The list is annotated and memorialized in Nodelman's three collections.

15. See Poovey, "Cultural Criticism" 620.

16. For the fullest histories see Reed, *Old School Ties;* Quigly; Musgrave; and J. Richards, *Happiest Days.* But also see Bristow 53–92; James; Mack, *Since 1860;* Nelson, *Boys* 56–86; Orwell, "Boys' Weeklies"; Osborne; Petzold; Protherough; Reed, "Public Schools"; J. Richards, "School Story"; P. Scott, "School Novels"; Wright.

17. See Quigly 49 and Honey 1ff. On the other hand, it seems likely that the rise of the public school, endorsing the values that it did, did much to enshrine *Tom Brown* and other public-school stories as the canonical school stories.

18. See, e.g., Musgrave 10ff. The timing is coordinated with a more general shift in critical consciousness with respect to children's literature: F. Hughes argues that shortly after the turn of the century, about 1910, "The 'serious novel' would have to earn its laurels, or win its spurs, at the cost of being unsuitable for women and children" (544)—that the (adults') novel received critical recognition by estranging itself from a family readership, establishing barriers based on age, sex, and class, and allying itself with "realism" rather than fantasy. See also Jameson, who notes that a breakdown of "older realisms" gave rise not just to modernism but to the "culture industry," that is, mass culture (*Political Unconscious* 207).

19. See P. Scott, "School and Novel" 52–55. In reacting against those who focus on the first half of the book, Nelson (in "Sex," an essay later revised and incorporated in *Boys*) identifies *Tom Brown* with earlier views that stress pious submission. I am more inclined to view Hughes as ambivalent, transitional, poised between an androgynous, spiritual ideal of manliness and one that celebrates physical toughness— more inclined to agree with J. Richards that the book "is a mirror of the changing nature and structure of Victorian values, a vital point of intersection between ideas that had been dominant and ideas that were to become so" (*Happiest Days* 24).

20. But see Jan, who says that "what these stories illustrate is really no more than youthful high spirits and the art of letting off steam without any serious consequences, but *school as such is never criticized:* the teaching function or the content of

lessons are never mocked" (108, Jan's italics). Certainly the school story is largely conservative, supportive of society's institutions. Only relatively late did the educational misfits, the Hucks and Kims who escaped from school, become "the voice of truth or nature, which, in fact, were often the same" (Pickering, "Allegory" 63). Yet the potential for subversion was always present.

21. The priorities of his real-life headmaster at Rugby, Thomas Arnold, were religious principles, gentlemanly conduct, and intellectual pursuits (in ascending order, according to J. Richards, *Happiest Days* 31, 44, though most commentators have assumed the reverse); he encouraged exercise simply as a means to stay healthy. Still, Arnold was sensitive to the child's point of view, even if he gave priority to an adult moral perspective. He can be seen as trying to channel the boys' interests: he converted the boys' makeshift self-governance outside the classroom to a system of prefects that reported to the headmaster (see Mack, *1780 to 1860* 40; Newsome 39–40). Subsequent attitudes toward sports, later in the century, reflect an even more complex interplay between boys and masters. Masters and headmasters may have initiated the emphasis on games in the 1850s as a way of disciplining the boys' unruliness (see Mangan 16ff.), yet they were building on the boys' preferences. The late-nineteenth-century mania for games in British public schools was both a pandering to boys' interests and a way of disciplining their energy—and also an admission that complete control was impossible. The resulting eclipse of academic achievement both denied what schools and masters, on some level, stood for and enabled them to exert even greater control over the boys, creating "compliant, uncomplicated, not-too-well-read boys who would challenge neither the intellectual nor the moral authority of older men—at least not openly" (Mangan 106).

22. Honey stresses how utterly the middle-class Victorian family transferred authority to the public school: "the completeness of the transfer to an alternative community—a distinctive emotional milieu capable of generating its own set of values—as the common practice of an influential section of society, probably has no parallel among advanced societies" (147).

23. As B. Johnson points out in another context, students are empowered when they "must respond to the contradiction between *two* teachers. And what the student learns in the process is both the power of ambiguity and the non-innocence of ignorance" (83, Johnson's italics). For an account of recent school stories in which children are implicitly empowered, directly or indirectly, by the alternative authority of teachers, see Smedman; see also Trousdale. But see Hildebrand for the argument that portrayals of school in recent award-winning books are largely negative.

24. Or a "retreat from adult experience" (Trensky, "Bad Boy" 516). See also Avery, *Behold* 197–206; Fiedler, *No!* 263–267; Geller 245–250; Hunter; and Jordan.

25. Beginning in the first half of the nineteenth century, U.S. schools were predominantly coeducational and thus congruent with institutions that children had experienced before school—namely, family and church—even if not with the workplace or with the gender differentiation of adult roles in the family (see, e.g., Hansot and Tyack).

26. See, e.g., Geller 247 and J. Richards, *Happiest Days* 33–34, for discussion of Hughes's attitude.

27. The best discussion of twentieth-century U.S. school stories is Saul's. For additional discussion of U.S. prep-school stories, see Saul and Kelly; of U.S. sports stories, see Erisman and Evans; yet another strand that emerged about the turn of the century in the United States was the girls' college story. Meanwhile, in Britain, the boys' school story was moving in the opposite direction: late-nineteenth-century stories generally endorse peer loyalty unquestioningly, and only in the twentieth century do we find statements comparable to that in *The Hoosier School-Boy*, in which an admirable adult criticizes the code. In Hugh Walpole's *Jeremy at Crale* (1927), for instance, a respected housemaster may honor a boy's unwillingness to tell about the actions of others but he nonetheless makes clear his disagreement with this "ridiculous code of honour" (201).

28. There was also Bracebridge Hemyng, whose more antic and adventurous *Jack Harkaway's Schooldays* (1871+) harked back to the likes of Trelawny's *Adventures of a Younger Son* (1831), stripping the school story of piety and probability, making it the prolegomenon to a series of adventures, resumed in *Jack Harkaway after Schooldays, Jack Harkaway in America,* and the like, by various authors.

29. See Pedersen, "Women's" 68–71, 83, and Pedersen, *Girls'* 36ff.; see also Burstyn, Fletcher, and Vicinus (*Independent Women* 163–210) on British girls' education in the nineteenth century. For discussion of how nineteenth-century stories reflect the historical background, see Rowbotham 113–140. Girls' school stories, though generally only twentieth-century ones, are starting to receive recognition too: see Cadogan and Craig 111–124, 178–205, 227–262; Drotner, "Schoolgirls"; Frith; Vicinus, "Distance"; also Grey 64–77.

30. Or more precisely, in Molesworth's case, as Reimer has argued, even school is something to be retreated from, and when a character runs away from it she "is not lighting out for the world so much as coming in from the cold" (9). For elaboration of the ideas presented here and in subsequent paragraphs see Clark, Introduction.

31. See, e.g., Vicinus, *Independent Women* 164. In discussing inconsistencies in the works of a writer of girls' stories, Mitchell suggests that L. T. Meade grafts the emotional content of women's concern for friendships, feelings, and family onto organizational structures derived from boys' stories ("Children's Reading" 58).

32. Or rather a blurring of school and family. As Pedersen has noted, before about 1860 the word *governess* could refer to any lady who taught, whether in a home or in a school—what differentiated her from a schoolmistress was her class standing rather than her institutional context (*Girls'* 102–103).

33. It is also worth noting that the hegemony of the canonical stories (coupled with the marginality of the school story in the grander scheme of literature) has rendered invisible several veritable masterpieces—works that can be considered masterpieces, as I argue in "Heading," even in terms of New Critical criteria, "serious," high-culture criteria such as psychological depth and verbal wit: notably, A. H. Gilkes's *Boys and Masters* (1887), Sharp's *The Making of a Schoolgirl* (1897), D. Wynne Willson's *Early Closing* (1931), and, least forgotten though still insufficiently recognized, Antonia White's *Frost in May* (1933).

34. See also Gilbert's "Costumes." For a subtle reading of modernist female crossdressing, more specific to crossdressing and less applicable to crossgendering, see Benstock 181.

35. A literary transvestism that sometimes achieves the destabilizing effects that Kahn describes as "narrative transvestism," which she ascribes to males utilizing female voices in the eighteenth century; and the ideological dislocations that Wolfson finds in Byron.

36. I am oversimplifying, yet as Newsome suggests, "Whereas Coleridge had regarded manliness as something essentially adult, Kingsley and Hughes stressed the masculine and muscular connotations of the word and found its converse in effeminacy" (197). Or as Poovey would put it, "the characteristic feature of the mid-Victorian symbolic economy" is "the articulation of difference upon sex" (*Uneven Developments* 6). See also Nelson's discussion of the shift from an androgynous spiritual ideal of manliness to one focusing on physical toughness ("Sex," *Boys;* similarly Green, "Robinson Crusoe" 46; K. Reynolds, esp. 50–62).

The American case is perhaps more complicated; certainly cultural and literary historians have sometimes seen the early nineteenth century as marked by anxiety over femininity. Fiedler, for instance, expresses his dismay with the feminine "bourgeois sentimental novel" in *Love and Death* (75ff.), though he often sees "important" nineteenth-century U.S. authors as evading gender in favor of an "innocent homosexuality" (348ff.). Yet I am inclined to see this account as a projection of twentieth-century values: now that the divide between masculine and feminine is so important to us, we are inclined to see those who are not so concerned as feminine. Demos does in fact note a shift in the United States that parallels the one in Britain (103–104); Rotundo too charts an increasing willingness among American men to embrace boyishness and an increasing fear of being womanly (*American Manhood* 255–279).

37. The works by Hale, Wood, and Wells, among others, were addressed to adults. One additional way in which I work the margins is, then, by working in the margins between children's and adults' literature.

PART I
BEFORE *TOM BROWN*

ANXIOUS PROXIES AND INDEPENDENT GIRLS

CHARLES LAMB AND OTHER EARLY MEN

After *Tom Brown's Schooldays* it was rare that a man would write a school story for girls. Perhaps men felt less qualified as gender segregation in children's literature increased. Perhaps they found less to interest them in stories of girls, as boys' stories increasingly allowed scope for scrapes and adventures. Perhaps a growing cult of manliness forbade much interest in anything associated with girls—or if not so much a growing cult then a redefining of the boundaries of manliness, where the crucial boundary was no longer between man and child but between male and female, inhibiting male crossgendering.[1]

Even before 1857, when the desire to educate was salient in most children's literature and girls may have seemed more quintessentially educable, more malleable than boys, it was not all that common for men to write of girls. But Richard Johnson, Charles Lamb, George Mogridge, and, in the United States, Jacob Abbott did so. And doing so allowed them to push beyond the established, to play with difference. As Cixous states, "Rare are the men able to venture onto the brink where writing, freed from law, unencumbered by moderation, exceeds phallic authority, and where the subjectivity inscribing its effects becomes feminine" (106). None of these four men was entirely freed or unencumbered or excessive: three of them included adult male proxies to allay some of their anxiety over crossgendering. But focusing on a girl still enabled each to address some of the feminine in himself, to speak from a position of marginality, to start dismantling the patriarchal.

The earliest crossgendered school story would seem to be Richard Johnson's *The Little Female Orators; or, Nine Evenings Entertainment* (1770), which follows the mode of Sarah Fielding's *The Governess* (1749).[2] The young ladies of a boarding school take turns telling stories every week.

What is prized in their stories is not originality: they're allowed, almost en-couraged, "to repeat, from their Memory only, whatever useful had occurred to them, as worthy of Notice, in the Course of their Reading" (3). More important than originality is the moral lesson to be drawn from each story—as their governess demonstrates when each pupil completes her tale. And as Johnson himself enacts, when he appends moral lessons to tales borrowed from other writers. More important still is the fact that the young ladies are telling borrowed stories, not narrating the kind of confession that enabled Fielding "both to construct and to reform character" (Burdan 11).

Most of the girls derive their stories from their reading, whether they relate what they call an Oriental tale, a satire of London society, or a tale about "the savage and wild Americans" (R. Johnson 46). And Johnson does too—the slippage in authority and authorship continues beyond the bound-aries of the text. For he has borrowed rather heavily—indeed, by current standards, plagiarized—from Richard Steele and others.[3] And thus he fur-ther complicates the gender valence, complicates what it means when a man writes about a girls' school—though most of Johnson's borrowings (other than the book's framework, modeled on *The Governess*) are from men.

Johnson's choices of stories are relatively liberating to British middle-class children, offering new perspectives, sometimes alternative values. Most are at least partly set in an exotic locale—either North America or the Middle East—in keeping with a Rousseauian strain in early children's literature, exalting noble savages (see Jackson 154–157). Many of the stories also in-clude some fantastical element, such as a mystical vision or a ring that con-fers invisibility. We can gauge some of the subversive potential of such sto-ries by the need the governess feels to offer caveats. She reprimands the first storyteller for telling a story from a book that the girl had read during her father's absence: "It might have been a Book of bad Morals and Principles, in which, it is not at all unlikely, she might have met with something new, which might have equally dwelt on her Mind, much to her Prejudice" (14). The governess likewise adjures us not to believe an American Indian account of the hereafter, not to consider such stories "Realities."

Yet these caveats cannot erase the imaginative force of the stories themselves: their distancing through exoticism and fantasy grants freedom to the imagination—if nothing else freeing the imagination to draw less pre-dictable morals than would be possible with more prosaic narratives. And the governess's quickness to correct an error or misjudgment also implies endorsement of views that she does not correct: the story centering on the ring of invisibility, for instance, seems to endorse the spying enabled by in-visibility, as long as it is applied to worthy ends.[4] On the other hand, many of the stories place an instructor figure within the tale (if not a prosaic educator then a genie) or else adjacent to it, one young lady prefacing her remarks by adverting to the teachings of her Pappa (the same young lady who read in Pappa's absence, thereby creating a tension between Pappa's physical absence and moral presence). So even without the moralizing section entitled "Observations" that follows each tale—the sectioning out making the observations simultaneously prominent and skippable—the instructiveness of the tales is overdetermined. Yet the meanings of such instruction are nonetheless unstable.

The attitudes toward women promulgated in *The Little Female Orators,* for instance, are sometimes stereotypical. We learn of the commonplace that women are prey to the lures of vanity, "the Love of Praise" having been "implanted in the female Bosom" (44). Yet Johnson is also capable of adjurations that, however slightly or ambiguously, enlarge the roles available to his girl readers: "Pursue, my dear Children, the Paths to Knowledge and Science: These will afford you solid Employments, of which nothing but Death can rob you. You will then live respected, for a sensible Woman will always command Respect . . ." (35). The young ladies are to pursue science— or is it sense? What are we to make of the slippage between learning science and being sensible? Elsewhere Johnson seems to employ a modern usage when he includes under the purview of science the lifelong study of a single mineral. So is he retracting his largesse when he reverts to the sensible, limiting his encouragement to traditional spheres of women's knowledge, making a science of domesticity? Or is he using sense as a cover for science, subversively hinting at an enlarged sphere for women while yet providing a sop for traditionalists?

The most intriguing playing out of gender issues occurs in the eighth and penultimate tale, in which the English traveler Inkle, stranded in the Americas, surviving an attack by Indians, is befriended and loved by the Indian maid Yarico, whom he eventually betrays into slavery. The text of Johnson's tale is almost identical to that in *The Spectator* (1711)—the gist of which Richard Steele himself borrowed, as he acknowledges (Bond 1: 49), from Richard Ligon's *True and Exact History of the Island of Barbados* (1657).[5] And it's a tale that permeated eighteenth-century thinking: as late as 1819 Charles Lamb was writing enthusiastically of a theatrical rendition (Lucas 1: 184–186). For the most part, Johnson simply reparagraphs Steele and omits an occasional quasi-erotic or erotic reference—he omits "Gallantry," "amorous," "Love," "Naked."[6]

Johnson also modifies the import of the story by the context he provides. This is after all an exemplary story told at a school. Furthermore, in introducing the narrative, Sally Readwell states her desire to counter stories in which "instances are given of the ill Conduct of young Ladies" (84). Her statement is mirrored within the tale she tells (that is, within the frame narrative provided by Steele, which she reproduces): the virtuous Arietta responds to stories of the inconstancy of women by saying, "You Men are Writers, and can represent us Women as unbecoming as you please in your Works, while we are unable to return the Injury" (87). She then tells her countertale of Inkle and Yarico (thereby belying the inability she has just proclaimed,[7] though not the justice of her accusation).

In Steele's version of the story—and in Johnson's crossgendering too—gender is salient, yet racial difference is also significant. Other eighteenth-century versions of the tale stress the racial difference, "the contrast between the faithless Christian and the faithful Indian" (Price 9), to the extent that Yarico's precise race is less important than the fact of difference: Inkle encounters her, in various versions, in America, in India, in Africa; in a 1738 rendition she is described as both "A *Negro* Virgin" and an "*Indian* Maid" (The Countess of **** 6, 9, reprinted in Price, author's italics).

As for Johnson's Inkle, he is someone whose father "had taken particular Care to instil into his Mind an early Love of Gain" (89), and hence he repays Yarico's devotion when they arrive at Barbados—"notwithstanding that the poor Girl, to incline him to commiserate her, pleaded her Condition" (93)—by selling her into slavery and fetching a higher price because of her "condition." At the intersection of two spheres of difference, the intersection heightened by her pregnancy—by that which both underscores her femaleness and will body forth the mingling of the two races—Yarico becomes a metaphor for the plight of both nonwhites and nonmales. Though of course, as Peter Hulme points out, the sentimentalizing of her story, its various displacements, tend "to obviate all mention of English settlement of Carib lands," tend to screen the imperialism being enacted during the Carib Wars of the 1770s and 1790s—and earlier (259).

Upon completion of Sally's recital, her schoolmates discuss how they will use this story to counter their brothers' stories—family connections are never distant in Johnson's book. But the governess soon "give[s] them to understand, that they were to make a quite different Use of what they had heard" (R. Johnson 94). She provides an allegorical gloss that ignores gender and race, though it does implicitly address mercantilism, another nexus of the tale: Inkle embodies "the fatal Effects of early Prejudices"—not the prejudice of, say, calling Indians savages or, worse, of enslaving them but rather "the Love of Gold" (94). The governess is hinting perhaps at Martin Wechselblatt's critique, that the merging of "sensibility" and "primitivism" in the Yarico tales bolsters the views of the rising commercial classes. Yet in criticizing love of gold, she criticizes the extremity of greed, not trade itself; by making excessive greed a lightning rod, her comments help to naturalize the expansion of trade. In any case, the governess continues, temporarily losing sight of her original gloss, by noting that the lovers will henceforth epitomize faithfulness and faithlessness: "The Name of *Yarico* will be pitied and revered by future Posterity; the Name of *Inkle* will never be repeated, but when Mankind are at a Loss for an Epithet to call something by, that is too horrible to be told by its own name" (95, Johnson's italics). Though of course, as Lawrence Marsden Price notes, "After a century of praise the name of Yarico was rarely heard again" (138). Still, Johnson attempts to name the unnameable, to capture, however ambiguously, what has been excluded from his world.

Now perhaps we shouldn't make too much of what Johnson might be attempting here. He may be "the best known" of late-eighteenth-century hack writers for children (Jackson 103) but he was nevertheless a hack writer, author of some ninety-one books in twenty-four years, most of the books "borrowed" to varying degrees from other writers, most of them published anonymously or pseudonymously, most of them for children since that was what paid best. A reviewer of another of his volumes, published in 1769, castigates Johnson's "catch-penny method of vamping up old publications under new titles" (quoted in Weedon 38), and the same criticism could be made of *The Little Female Orators*. Yet he chose to include the Inkle and Yarico tale, reinforcing its protofeminist framing, in a book for children— while none of the forty-seven versions of the tale found by Price seems to have been addressed specifically to children.

What finally do we make of this tale addressed to a reading audience of (perhaps) young ladies, a tale purporting to recount a story told by a woman and retold by a young lady, further glossed by that young lady's governess, a tale borrowed by a male author from another male, who in turn had it from yet another? Richard Steele's attribution of the story to Arietta— a gender change from his source, Ligon—lends authenticity (it is a tale about a woman and by a woman) and channels more sympathy toward the hapless woman of the tale, but perhaps also the teller's insistence on her gender underscores how, from Steele's perspective, this tale offers only a partial view, that of a woman. The need for some supplementation may be further underscored by its physical supplementation, in *The Little Female Orators,* by eight other tales.

The subversive impact of the story is also undercut somewhat by the governess's appended glosses: the young ladies' protofeminist reflections may be "innocent," according to the narrator, but young ladies should in fact make quite a different use of the story. Perhaps too the subversive effect is muted by the position of the tale in the volume, as the penultimate story: no tale of the perfidy of woman follows, it is true, but instead a preachy disquisition on the pursuit of pleasure, closer to the discursive tone of the governess's pronouncements, thus effectively reiterating the governess's perspective. And the tragic outcome of Arietta's tale may imply the impossibility of gender and racial equality. But still, neither Arietta's feminism nor her anti-imperialism is directly refuted.

And in allowing his young ladies to give voice to a story presumably from a woman's perspective, and potentially protofeminist, Johnson allows his girl characters somewhat more independence than most contemporary women authors did. Like other men writing about girls' schools, he seems to show some willingness to attribute to girls more independence from adults than women writers did. Perhaps a man's portrayal of childhood is inevitably colored by his own boyhood memories. Perhaps his sense of decorum differed from that of women writers, and he felt less need to protect the status of females by showing them behaving with great propriety. Or perhaps he felt that adult females would feel the need to hamper girls.[8] For Johnson attributes repression to the adult female—the governess—while subtly, even if ambiguously, empowering the young ladies.

Charles Lamb more strongly castigates adult women on behalf of children in a famous 1802 letter to Coleridge:

> Mrs. Barbauld['s] stuff has banished all the old classics of the nursery; & the Shopman at Newbery's hardly deign'd to reach them off an old exploded corner of a shelf, when Mary ask'd for them. Mrs. B's & Mrs. Trimmer's nonsense lay in piles about. . . . Think what you would have been now, if instead of being fed with Tales and old wives fables in childhood, you had been crammed with Geography & Natural History.? **Damn them.** I mean the cursed Barbauld Crew, those **Blights & Blasts** of all that is **Human** in man & child.— (Marrs 2: 81–82, Lamb's emphasis)

Yet despite castigating the didacticism of contemporary women writers— writers neither "man" nor "child"—Lamb goes on to produce relatively didactic stories for children himself.[9] For *Mrs Leicester's School* (1809)[10] is another book in the mode of *The Governess,* with girls at school telling stories, stories here variously by Charles and Mary Lamb. Charles's letter to

Coleridge reveals his ambivalence toward women authors, castigating Barbauld and Trimmer while yet praising tales told by "old wives"—and getting Mary to serve as his surrogate at the bookstore, even as he proceeds to coauthor books with her. If women writers of school stories are more likely than men to emphasize connections with family, then Charles would seem to enact some degree of womanliness by writing with his sister.

Furthermore, by following the mode of *The Governess,* the Lambs could be said to write in a women's tradition, a tradition inaugurated by a woman. Yet although they eliminate most of the moral glossing by a preceptress, they still mute the voices of the young ladies of whom they write. As in Johnson's book, we do not get the girls' own stories in *Mrs Leicester's School,* or not exactly. The girls do not seem to have borrowed their stories from other sources, yet the tales are redacted by an instructor, since "what is very proper and becoming when spoken, requires to be arranged with some little difference before it can be set down in writing," paring away "little inaccuracies," and providing "a more formal and correct appearance"; the narrator adds, "My own way of thinking, I am sensible, will too often intrude itself, but I have endeavoured to preserve, as exactly as I could, your own words, and your own peculiarities of style and manner . . ." (283). Such a disclaimer simultaneously reveals a concern for verbal verisimilitude and negates it, denying the girls their own voices at the same time that the undertaking as a whole endorses their stories.

And on the whole, the Lambs' project merits more attention than it has hitherto received. Brother and sister are ripe for rediscovery, revaluation, given the way they deconstruct such binaries as male and female, adult and child—as Jane Aaron has recently argued. Marginalized as the children of servants, as borderline insane (Mary especially was in and out of institutions after committing matricide), they offer a critique of the increasing paternalism of British society, including that of high Romantics such as Wordsworth and Coleridge—"a protest against this new demarcation and separation of child, male, and female roles" (Aaron 54). Aaron concludes that through writing Mary "seeks to mediate between warring elements," while Charles "perpetually encodes the possibility of a balanced and playful interchange between the various contradictory parts of the individual psyche" (207). Not that Charles altogether evades the paternalistic in his approach to women and children, but he does give more play to alternative perspectives than his male contemporaries do.

Mrs Leicester's School, in any case, provides a rare opportunity to examine parallel school stories by a man and a woman. Charles and Mary seem to have worked at muting differences, tempering their tales because of their coauthoring, certainly addressing each other as a salient portion of their audience.[11] Yet some differences remain.

Consider their two tales about the frightful effects of reading. In both a girl begins with certain weaknesses: in Mary's story, weak eyes that make it desirable to limit reading; in Charles's, a tendency to be fearful and depressed. Both girls lack or forgo proper guidance and read material that they should not. Neither girl reads what she comes across word for word, as it was "meant" to be read: the book that Mary's girl reads has had key pages torn out; Charles's girl was young enough that she did not understand all the words, a circumstance that "probably made [the stories] appear more strange and out of the way to me" (319). In both the effects of reading are deleterious. In both the girl is cured by removal to a more wholesome setting, where there are more people to interact with.

It is significant, however, that Mary's girl reads about Mahomet, while Charles's reads about witches. The frightful is associated, in each case, with the other gender. It may also be significant that each girl is rescued by someone of the same gender as the bugbear, Mary's by a male doctor, Charles's by a female relative. Mary defuses the potential gravity of what she is dealing with—infidels—through humor: after the girl states that she has read "that those who believed all the wonderful stories which were related of Mahomet were called Mahometans" and that she "concluded that I must be a Mahometan, for I believed every word I read," the doctor notes that "it was a new case to him, he never having attended a little Mahometan before" (309, 310). Charles, on the other hand, is quick to let us know that women are not as powerful as poor little Maria Howe has come to believe: "I was not old enough to understand the difference there was between these silly improbable tales which imputed such powers to poor old women, who are the most helpless things in the creation, and the narrative in the Bible . . ." (319).

The two stories also convey subtly different attitudes toward reading. Mary's tale reveals "the dire effects of locking little girls away from books" (Marsden, "Shakespeare" 49), and she flirts with the efficacy of reading in effecting religious conversion while yet parodying the notion that merely reading a holy book will convert one—for we are not to take seriously Margaret Green's conversion to Mahometism. But we are to take seriously, in Charles's story, "that I had read myself into a fever" (310). We are to admit that too much solitary reading can overheat the imagination: to admit, in short, the efficacy of reading. Not for Charles the fear of not being allowed to read.

As for the collection of stories as a whole, Charles is slightly more willing than Mary to interrupt his presumed child narrators. In her seven tales Mary provides adult interpolations only twice, and only at the ends of tales. One such interpolation appears at the end of the first tale, when the adult narrator explains that in the future she will avoid mentioning interruptions *"unless materially connected with the stories"* (289, Lamb's italics).

In his three tales Charles interrupts twice, both times in the midst of the same tale. And the nature of one of Charles's interruptions is quite different from any of Mary's. In her account of reading about witches, Maria Howe has also been telling of gazing at a picture of the Ark and deciding, if there were another flood, which pretty creatures to save and which ugly ones not to. She goes on to call herself foolish for considering any creature ugly— "Doubtless a frog or a toad is not uglier in itself than a squirrel or a pretty green lizard; but we want understanding to see it" (318). Charles's adult narrator then feels called upon to note,

> *Here I must remind you, my dear miss Howe, that one of the young ladies smiled, and two or three were seen to titter, at this part of your narration, and you seemed, I thought, a little too angry for a girl of your sense and reading; but you will remember, my dear, that young heads are not always able to bear strange and unusual assertions; and if some elder person possibly, or some book which you have found, had not put it into your head, you would hardly have discovered by your own reflection, that a frog or a toad was equal in real loveliness to a frisking squirrel, or a pretty green lizard, as you called it; not remembering that at this very time you gave the lizard the name of pretty, and left it out to the frog—so liable we all are to prejudices. But you went on with your story.* (318, Lamb's italics)

Charles may be interrupting the written text here out of his own anxiety with such autobiographical material,[12] in this story about feverish overreaction to one's reading, yet the comment functions as a put-down. A put-down only underscored by his attribution of the original impetus to the other young ladies, to their tittering, and further underscored by Charles's allusion to an "elder person" or book as the source of an idea that the girl is hardly likely to have come up with herself.

The last story in the volume, though, is the one in which Charles's anxiety over crossgendering comes through most clearly and most brilliantly; it is also the one story that allows a girl some independence—at least in outward circumstances—for it strips her, temporarily, of the family context emphasized in other stories.[13] Five-year-old Arabella Hardy finds herself on board a ship without any female companion. Charles is at some pains to explain the circumstances: the girls' parents have died in the East Indies;[14] her relatives want her to return to England; the young woman who was to have accompanied her has suddenly taken ill; this is the last ship to sail this season; a decision has to be made quickly since the ship is about to sail; and, as Arabella says, "At last the captain, who was known to my friends, prevailed upon my relation who had come with us to see us embark, to leave the young woman on shore, and to let me embark separately" (327). Thus this five-year-old girl gets what fictional boys have to wait a few more years for in Captain Marryat's thrilling pages: a trip to sea. Though without adventures—for the ship is quite tamed and domesticated, her preceptor a gentle, womanly man, someone who instructs her about dolphins and porpoises, someone who calls the potentially frightening clamors of the wind music.

And this Charles Atkinson—this Betsy, as the other sailors have nicknamed him—serves as Charles Lamb's proxy. Like other men writing for girls, Charles shows anxiety not so much about whether he is qualified to undertake the task (as women tended to when writing about boys) as what it means to do so. Lamb is at some pains to show that although Atkinson has some feminine traits, he is still manly. He may possess "a gentleness of manners, and a pale feminine cast of face, from ill health and a weakly constitution," but he also "had a great character for bravery, and all sailor-like accomplishments" (327).[15] Atkinson may not particularly like the nickname Betsy, "but he submitted to it the better, as he knew that those who gave him a woman's name, well knew that he had a man's heart, and that in the face of danger he would go as far as any man" (327). He may act the role of the heroine in a play got up for Arabella's amusement, but his relationship to her is like that of a father—he blesses her "as a father would bless his child" (329). Lamb's gender anxiety seems particularly acute at the end, when Atkinson dies, and the character's femininity and masculinity are both strongly asserted: in Aaron's words, Lamb has here "compressed much of his ambivalence concerning the question of gender roles and authority" (33). For the final illness stems from a wound "which he got in the desperate attempt, when he was quite a boy, to defend his captain against a superior force of the enemy which had boarded him, and which, by his premature valour inspiriting the men, they finally succeeded in repulsing" (Lamb 330). In the next breath Arabella adds, "This was that Atkinson, who, from his pale and feminine appearance, was called Betsy. This was he whose womanly care of me got him the name of a woman, who, with more than female attention, condescended to play the hand-maid to a little unaccompanied orphan, that fortune had cast upon the care of a rough sea captain, and his rougher crew" (330).

Curiously, given the focus on Atkinson's actions throughout the tale, Arabella suggests that it is Atkinson's death, more than anything else, that made an impression on her: "His death, which happened just before we got to England, affected me so much, that he alone of all the ship's crew has engrossed my mind ever since" (329). Stressing the impact of his death perhaps hides the impact of his womanliness, masking Lamb's uneasiness with the latter (whose situation, we might wonder, is what Arabella has described as "uneasy and unnatural"?). Perhaps androgyny is dangerous: such a womanly man isn't viable. Or perhaps someone capable of "more than female attention" must go beyond the passivity ascribed to women by achieving the ultimate passivity of death.

Thus in the tale with the external trappings of what would shortly become the boys' adventure story—potentially the most "masculine" story in the collection—Lamb indulges in a peculiarly heightened crossgendering. Certainly he sets the tale on board ship not so much to make it possible for the girl to be independent (though it does do that, a little) as to emphasize her dependence. He didn't have to make her so very young, only five. He didn't have to stress how the sailors waited on her, stress her dependence on their attentions. He didn't have to emphasize Arabella's effect on men— "I believe the homage which I have read that men universally pay to women, was in this case directed to me, in the absence of all other woman-kind" (329)—thereby empowering her girl readers even as it frames them as objects of male regard. And in writing of a girl's incursion into a world of men, Lamb regularizes his undertaking in the tale—his own incursion, inversely metaphorized by Arabella, into the world of females.

By the middle of the nineteenth century, men writing for girls seem to have felt more need to justify themselves. In prefacing *Lessons Worth Learning for Girls* (1851), George Mogridge (here going by the name of Old Humphrey, a pseudonym he had used for a number of popular moralizing works, when he wasn't pretending to be Peter Parley) explains his decision to write for girls by suggesting that they too should "have books to amuse and instruct them as well as boys" (vii). He goes on to defend himself against the charge that he may know too little about girls by saying, "What do I know? You shall hear. I know that the head of a little girl is like the head of a little boy; for it very often has but little wisdom in it, and requires to be furnished with information. And the heart of a little girl is like the heart of a little boy, often being the seat of bad passions, which stand in need of correction" (vii–viii). Mogridge may not be directly addressing the notion that it would be demeaning to write for girls—he seems concerned simply to defend his ability to write for them. Yet perhaps some anxiety about demeaning himself is fueling the anxiety of his defense.

It is significant, in any case, that he says that a little girl's head is like a little boy's, a little girl's heart like a little boy's. For he shows some willingness to make his little girls more like little boys than contemporary women writers did, granting them somewhat more independence and spunk. He seems in fact to be drawing upon his own experiences in school. The Rev. Charles Williams, his biographer, recounts an elaborate practical joke from Mogridge's school days: one evening when the master was out, when the boys boasted of how bravely they'd fend off robbers, they found the building—apparently—besieged. The boys succeeded in chasing an intruder out of the house. But when the usher asked for a volunteer to accompany him in inspecting the grounds, the boys cowered in bed; only George eventually agreed to go. Then after a fearful tour of the premises, "the usher having raised [the boy's] terror to the utmost pitch, burst into a loud laugh, declared that the robber was only the servant girl, dressed in her master's clothes, and told him that the whole affair was contrived—principally by the schoolmistress—to punish the boys for their boastful expressions of courage" (Williams 73). Williams then proceeds to protest such practical joking because of the potential for disastrous consequences—in contrast with an earlier description of how schoolmates had perpetrated an elaborate joke centering on a presumably haunted house, and the affair, far from being disastrous, is potentially efficacious in curing a belief in ghosts. Williams (and perhaps Mogridge, as Williams' informant) projects the pleasure of practical joking onto fellow boys and the onus onto a woman. In children's literature, however, females are never allowed such rude practical joking.

Certainly the girls in Mogridge's "The Best Scholar in the School," a story in Lessons Worth Learning, never engage in anything so disruptive. In fact, the point of the story is to show the right religious way to behave. The older girls in Mother Barnes's village school have been set tasks to be performed within a week—working a sampler, hemming a handkerchief, learning a hymn, finding illustrative Scripture passages—and a prize will go to the girl "who is the most regular in coming to school, who behaves best when here, and who does best the tasks which have been set" (28). Most of the girls assume that the prize will go to clever Caroline Hawker, the girl who is quickest at her studies, knows the most games, skips rope the best, runs fastest. But of course—typical of the moral tale—it goes to the slow but steady Susan Price, "the most diligent and obedient" (33).

Still, an early incident suggests some of the rewards of misbehavior. For one girl manages to get behind Mother Barnes and mimic the schoolmistress's actions. The girl may be quickly squelched: Mother Barnes knows perfectly well what is going on behind her, because she has been watching the girl's shadow. The overt point of this episode is to show how observant Mother Barnes is—and perhaps to hint that she will not be misled by substanceless foolery. But the episode does give some play to play, does allow girls to revel, a little, in mischief.[16] And thereby "The Best Scholar in the School" suggests the power of peers more strongly than contemporary women writers of girls' stories do. Women writers may suggest that girls may be misled against their better judgment, yet Mogridge suggests a more general, seemingly more entrenched clash of values between children and adults: "If young people valued the good opinion of their teachers as highly as they do the applause of their companions, many an hour that is now passed in folly would be spent in the attainment of wisdom" (30).

Two other stories in Mogridge's volume allude to school. In "The Beginnings of Sin," two sisters, both schoolgirls, discuss the desirability of mending a rent in a frock before it gets large and read a story about two men who have been schoolfellows together. One man has been frequenting a public house, and he quickly degenerates, eventually finding himself "plunged into the dreary prison for theft" and then "transported for life beyond the sea" (73). Thus should the young girls learn to take a stitch in time. The story as a whole functions as an emblem of how girls should read stories and apply morals, translated across gender, to themselves. On another level, it reveals how Mogridge is himself reading girls through males, translating male actions into those of girls.

In "The Bamboo," on the other hand, an old gentleman is visiting a school for young ladies and, when asked to tell a story, tells about the bamboo and its many uses; he concludes that if the lowly bamboo can provide "food, clothes, dwelling, fire, bedding, furniture, medicine, shields, walking-sticks, paper, baskets, ropes, umbrellas, and water-pipes," then "what ought you to be, who have qualities so much higher and better than it possesses?" (106). The old gentleman is of course Mogridge himself—is in fact revealed as Old Humphrey on the last page.[17] Thus does Mogridge dramatize his relationship with his audience, perhaps assuaging some of his ambivalence about writing for girls by portraying himself as both different from yet close to them. On the one hand, the differences between the old gentleman and the young ladies are overtly described only in terms of age: "There they were, youth and age. He of the grey hair, and they of the rosy cheek. He of the thoughtful mind, and they of the light heart" (99). Yet the masculine pronoun remains—even if Mogridge masks the gender difference by adding a difference in number—and the contrasting ascriptions of mind and heart are congruent with the gender valence. By setting up oppositions and then collapsing them in a way that masks gender, Mogridge may mute some of the opposition, convey some approach to closeness, at the same time enacting slippage among categories. Like Charles Lamb in "Arabella Hardy" and unlike most women when they write boys' school stories, Mogridge includes a proxy, an emblem of his own rhetorical situation.

The United States tended not to have a clearly demarcated school-story genre, in part because there were fewer boarding schools here. And the myths of democracy do not seem to have fostered as marked an interest in the doings of the elite, in the fictional doings of children who might go to boarding school—at least not before the twentieth century. Or rather the middling classes, generally whites of northern European extraction, were assumed to be the norm—and by failing to acknowledge the existence of recent immigrants, never mind blacks, and by ignoring urbanization and industrialization, early U.S. children's literature reinforced the power of this hidden elite.[18] By fostering assumptions that everyone was middle class, when of course not everyone was, the elite hid its exclusivity.

Perhaps too the myth of family togetherness was stronger in the United States,[19] so that a large percentage of the stories about boarding schools, like Optic's *In School and Out* (1864), tend to be about military schools—schools that can discipline boys who are otherwise incorrigible. Nineteenth-century children, even elite boys, simply did not expect to go away to school. Certainly U.S. stories tend to be apologetic about sending a child off to boarding school, tend to have elaborate explanations for why the child is there (not unlike Lamb's elaborate explanations for why Arabella boarded that ship to England).

The prolific Jacob Abbott—one of the best known of early-nineteenth-century U.S. writers for children, the only one with "the rare gift of making goodness seem both credible and attractive" (Avery, *Behold* 89)—briefly addresses girls' schooling in his Lucy books. He does not grant Lucy much independence—in part perhaps because she is very young (though that did not prevent Lamb from granting Arabella greater independence), in part perhaps because she doesn't leave home to go to school. She remains very much in a family context.

Like Mogridge, Abbott feels obliged to include some explanation of why he is writing about and for girls. He hopes, after his successful series of Rollo books, "that the history of [Lucy's] life and adventures may be entertaining and useful to the sisters of the boys who have honored the Rollo Books with their approval" (*Stories* 5). In part Abbott may have wanted to expand his audience, though that need not be entirely the case, for girls, then as later, were accustomed to reading stories featuring boys. In part Abbott was expressing genuine commitment to the education of girls: he helped to found two girls' schools, at one of which he taught for several years following the publication of his Lucy books, a seminary committed to teaching moral values but also to more academic training than was usual for girls (see Gay).

In *Cousin Lucy's Stories* (1841) we briefly see five-year-old Lucy going to a family school, which is to say "a school for the children of one family, though several other children went to it" (49), a school funded by a family since there was no other school nearby. In his *Rollo at School* (1839), Lucy's cousin Rollo is able to attend a more established school, Miss Mary's coeducational farmhouse school. Yet when Abbott decided to address the education of a girl, he tells something less like a school story, in books that do not include the word *school* in their titles, and provides a more domestic context.

As in *Rollo at School,* much of the teaching in *Cousin Lucy's Stories* is done through interpolated stories, such as one about a man getting caught in a quagmire because he was so indecisive. Many of the remaining scenes are expressly didactic too, as when Lucy's mother adjudicates responsibility in the loss of Lucy's bubble pipe down the heating register—the actual dropping was perhaps merely an accident, but the opening of the register without leave was a misdemeanor, and the refusal of Lucy's brother Royal to give back the pipe when his sister wanted it was, even worse, morally wrong. More than other crossgendering men—certainly more than Lamb— Abbott's stories are governed by didacticism. And that may partly reflect their differing sources of inspiration. Lamb drew on his own experiences, perhaps refracting them through his sister. Abbott, however, spent much of his adult life teaching. That was a strength in that it kept him in touch with children; as he has said of another work, whatever success it had "arises from the fact that I was surrounded, while writing it, by one hundred children, with whose wants and difficulties and dangers I was fully familiar" (quoted in E. Abbott 56). But it was also a weakness, for he is ever the didact.

In the subsequent *Cousin Lucy at Study* (1842) Lucy, now a year or two older, continues primarily in one-on-one instruction—with her older brother Royal, with her father, with an older girl named Mary Jay—and the emphasis is almost as much on teaching the teacher as it is on teaching Lucy. When ten-year-old Royal tries to teach Lucy simple sums, we see his mistakes, how he starts with the difficult rather than the easy, until seventeen-year-old Miss Anne explains to him "that teaching is a kind of ladder-making" (20). And he learns to start where Lucy is, getting her to draw 1's and

2's and 3's. Or rather, 1's and 3's and 2's. For Lucy wants to move on to 3's after working on 1's, even though Royal does not want her to. And we learn that they are both wrong, Lucy because "he was her teacher, and therefore she ought to have obeyed him," and Royal for reasoning "that, because two comes before three in numeration, therefore it ought to be made first" (41). We learn further how Royal should discipline Lucy—as Miss Anne would, by giving "some slighter punishment, just enough not to make her cry" (so as not to be "the cause of making disturbance in the family"), such as telling only a pretty long story rather than a long one (43). Thus Miss Anne teaches Royal, who teaches Lucy, a crossgendered chain appropriate in a crossgendered book, though the existence of such a chain and the consequent undermining of the middle term, of Royal as a teacher, may sow a whiff of subversion with respect to the authority of one's elders.

The final arbiter in all this teaching, the last link in the chain, is Lucy's father. We witness his lesson on why windows open as they do; we learn about the account book he gives Lucy for her allowance. We also witness him giving advice to Mary Jay. Mary Jay has asked what Lucy's mother wants taught, so the family invites the young girl over and the father pontificates. One should teach children what they can be taught, as opposed to making them learn by rote. One should teach not history (what can a young child understand of a rebellion?), not geography (what does a child understand of distances? Lucy doesn't understand that a mountain can be higher than a steeple)—or not unless one gets a suitable book on such subjects to make a beginning with them, perhaps one by Jacob Abbott—but rather reading, writing, spelling, arithmetic. The final arbiter is thus not Lucy's mother but her father. Abbott too needs an adult male proxy. Like Mogridge and Lamb, he seems to have felt the need to dramatize his rhetorical situation, though his proxy remains in many ways more distant from the child, as the teacher of her teacher even if also her father—much as Abbott distanced himself from the contours of what I have loosely considered the school story, encapsulating it in what is essentially a family story and thereby offering his young scholar less independence than Johnson, Mogridge, or Lamb do, as he underscores the patriarchal context of a midcentury girl's education.

Notes

1. See, e.g., Nelson, "Sex"; Newsome 197; Poovey, *Uneven Developments* 6; K. Reynolds 50–62.

2. Which Johnson had more directly plagiarized the previous year, transcribing sections of it in *Letters between Master Tommy and Miss Nancy Goodwill* (see Weedon 31).

3. As was common in eighteenth-century publications for children: many tales first appearing in the *Tatler* or *Spectator* or *Rambler* reappeared in publications by

John Newbery and others (see, e.g., Barry 51–52).

4. In other eighteenth- and nineteenth-century British children's literature, such eavesdropping would not be considered honorable.

5. For a history of the story, an accounting of more than forty-five different versions in English, French, and German between 1657 and 1830, see Price.

6. He likewise makes a reference to pregnancy more oblique, and possibly more criminal, by changing "to incline him to commiserate her Condition, told him she was with Child by him" (Bond 1: 51) to "to incline him to commiserate her, pleaded her Condition" (R. Johnson 93). And he adds a didactic paragraph with overtones of Rousseau: "Let not the vain, tho' polished European imagine, that the tender Passion of Love is known only to his Clime: It is peculiar to every Region of the Earth; and, perhaps, among even Savage Nations, it is more *pure* and *sincere* than among us" (90, Johnson's italics).

7. But see Wechselblatt, who would point out that her tale, like that of other heroic epistles, "articulating the contradictions in women's lives, while circumscribing what one is to do about them" (206), is ultimately limiting and ineffectual, dissolving "the act of male betrayal in the rhetoric of female self-betrayal" (203), dissipating urgency through pathos.

8. For a contrasting view, see Myers: she argues that through emphasizing pedagogic intent a contemporary woman writer like Edgeworth may not so much constrain her females as "rewrite . . . cultural stereotypes of females as passive victims at the mercy of external circumstances and their own undisciplined emotions by granting girlhood the potentiality for rational agency and self-command," affirming "that girls can achieve control of their wits and hence in some measure their lives" ("Socializing Rosamond" 55).

9. Riehl suggests, in *Charles Lamb's Children's Literature* (8ff.), that Lamb was forced to do so out of financial expediency: he turned to children's literature because of financial difficulties, and in order to sell it, he needed to moralize, though his literature for children often shows signs of ambivalence. The Lambs, in fact, minimized moralistic intrusions, not mechanically tacking on a moral at the end of each story. For an illuminating discussion of the Romantic engagement with fairy tales, deconstructing the dichotomizing of fantasy and reason, of fairy and moral tales—and for discussion of how Lamb's statements betray his fundamental conservatism (40)—see Richardson, "Wordsworth."

10. The editor of the edition I used indicates that the book was first published in 1809, as do Carpenter and Prichard, but Riehl dates it to 1808 (*Children's Literature* 101), and Marrs dates it variously 1809 and 1808 (1: xxvii, xliv).

11. Courtney (167) posits a good deal of mutual influence in the writing of these stories. See also Riehl, *Children's Literature* 104.

12. See Riehl for a discussion of how Lamb continues reworking the content of the tale in a later Elia essay—where Lamb reaches the resolution "that night-fears were a more or less normal phase in the development of the imagination" (*"Mrs Leicester's School"* 140; see also Summerfield 261–262).

13. It was also apparently Wordsworth's favorite (see Marrs 3: 15, n. 4). As for the general prominence of family, of domesticity, in these stories, Riehl finds Charles uncomfortable with it, and is quick to blame Mary: "He seems not to have chosen his own ground in *Mrs. Leicester* but to be confined within the limits which Mary set" (*Children's Literature* 104). Marsden, in "Letters," rightly argues that Mary's stories focus on maternal absence—yet what makes the absence so acute are the familial contexts.

14. Not until Juliana Ewing's *Six to Sixteen* (1875) and Frances Hodgson Burnett's *The Secret Garden* (1911) do women authors use the same premise—an orphan returning to England from India—to create relatively independent girl characters.

15. Courtney praises Lamb for thereby creating a modern tone in this tale (168). In the mid-twentieth century, though, Anthony is uneasy about the crossing of

genders: this tale "shows a marked struggle with the limitations of the theme imposed upon him [presumably by Mary]. Arabella Hardy threatened at any moment to assume the trousers of an India House clerk" (97)—to assume, in short, Lamb's extraliterary profession.

16. A similar reveling—and a similar undermining of adult authority—appears in Williams' recounting of Mogridge's own days at a dame school: "'The first rudiments of education were received by me at a dame-school. In the shadowy school-house of those days I can still discern the dim outlines of a certain young gentleman standing on a form behind the door, with a pointed cap on his head; but as to his express identity, the considerate reader will not trouble himself to inquire.' George doubtless had his failings; but these did not detract from the general character which truth requires to be given" (21). Mogridge did not always submit to higher authorities. Nor do his schoolgirls, at least not when the authority is a woman.

17. And is revealed as Mogridge in Williams' biography—for though Williams never mentions *Lessons Worth Learning for Girls,* he nonetheless describes Mogridge as often visiting a school for young ladies and alludes to the content of the story when describing an elucidation of the uses of bamboo (315).

18. Yet see Quinlivan for a discussion of Jacob Abbott's children's books focusing on black children. On the ignoring of urbanization and industrialization see, e.g., Boles 514ff.

19. Remember Honey's comments on the completeness with which the middle-class Victorian family transferred authority to the public school. MacLeod says of the United States at this time, explaining the family focus in children's literature, "In a society constantly jostled by change, the family was the most stable social institution in view, and the only one that seemed to offer any guarantee for social stability in the future" (*Moral Tale* 29). Avery attributes the fact that the family story is "a genre at which American writers have always excelled" to an early Puritan emphasis on the family (*Behold* 2).

DOROTHY KILNER AND OTHER EARLY WOMEN

The Tom Brown of M. Pelham's (Dorothy Kilner's) *First Going to School; or, The Story of Tom Brown, and his Sisters* (1804),[1] one of the first crossgendered school stories by a woman, is not like the later, better-known Tom Brown. For Kilner's little boy does not fight a bully. He does not glory in football and cricket. And, above all, he respects learning. Kilner's book might thus seem to be all that Thomas Hughes's was rebelling against—a pious manual of behavior more than a story to delight children. Yet Kilner's book is in its own way as effective at challenging received opinion as Hughes's, at challenging the codes associated with schools and with school stories—but more through manifesting contradictions than through coherent argument and more through thematic texturing than through narrative plotting. The book undermines its own pious endorsement of learning, depicts tensions between what it means to be civilized and what it means to be bestial, and creates a central generic disjunction—is the book a school story or a family story? And in these respects it is representative of other boys' school stories by women writing in the eighteenth century and the first decades of the nineteenth: it crystallizes key themes and questions.

Nevertheless, on the surface, *First Going to School* may seem pious and reactionary. Before he leaves for school, Tom is wildly enthusiastic about going because, as he tells a visitor, "I shall learn to read, and write, and cypher, and learn French, and Latin, and Greek, and I cannot tell what beside, but I shall learn to be very wise" (10). Once he goes, Tom does well at his lessons: his master commends him to the other boys as an example of diligence, and he does so well on a weekly examination that he "took the places of two boys much older than himself" (89).

Yet there is an undercurrent in the book that runs counter to the boy's professions—and it is, in fact, the one early children's book addressing education that Samuel F. Pickering, Jr., singles out as also celebrating high spirits (*Moral Instruction* 155).[2] Even at the beginning, Tom's ecstasy of enthusiasm for school is cut short when he falls and hurts himself, as if quite literally to undermine his enthusiasm. And later, on the morning that Tom leaves for school, he reasons,

> My Papa tells me that he was [comfortable and happy], when he went to school; and he says he is sure I shall, if I am a good boy. And as for the people being all strangers to me, what does that signify? They will not be strange long.
>
> And then I shall have such nice games of play, which it is impossible I can have at home.
>
> I shall play at cricket, and trap-ball, and prisoners'-base, and fives, and basting the bear, and I do not know what besides.
>
> And then when I come home at the holidays, I will teach them all to my sisters, and that will be good fun. (52)

When musing to himself, instead of for an adult audience, it's not academic learning that Tom is most looking forward to. He may briefly admonish himself to be "a good boy," but he is simply parroting what an adult authority has said. And he soon launches into what clearly interests him most, what he describes most vividly and at greatest length here—games—much as the book overall subtly undermines the value of academic learning through the greater vividness of its extracurricular episodes. This early Tom may not be so utterly unlike that later Tom Brown after all. At the same time, though, despite his enthusiasm in the quoted passage for trap-ball and basting the bear, and despite his assertion that it is impossible to "have such nice games of play" at home, this early Tom quickly returns in his imagination to his family circle and to the feminine—half the fun, it would seem, will be teaching the games to his sisters.

Kilner's Tom is, in effect, suspended between family and school, between home and peer influences, much as the author is suspended between the family story and the school story. The resulting work can therefore seem, to a twentieth-century reader, inconsistent and disjointed. Sometimes we may be able to rationalize the inconsistency—as we can when gauging whether Tom reveres learning—as a disparity between what a character professes and what he "really" feels. Sometimes what strikes the twentieth-century reader as inconsistent was common in children's books of the time.

The book does not always seem, for instance, to be addressed to children—at least not to children as we now understand them. But then again that was often true of eighteenth and early nineteenth-century children's literature. Partly that may reflect what Michael McKeon describes as the categorial instabilities of genres, the welter of contradictions they may exhibit as they emerge (37ff.). Partly it may reflect some categorial instability in the construction of childhood, for the concept of childhood was in flux, many people still inclined to treat children as miniature adults. Partly it may reflect a tendency for exponents of didacticism to become caught up in their pontificating and to lose track of their audience. In any case, like other early authors Kilner may, through showing the inadequacies of certain adult authorities, be able to criticize practices she does not approve of, but she also reveals cracks in the facade of adult authority, subtly empowering the child.

Consider another crossgendered school story: Ellenor Fenn's *School Dialogues for Boys: Being an Attempt to Convey Instruction Insensibly to Their Tender Minds, and Instill the Love of Virtue* (1783). At times it seems to be addressing boys about to embark on schooling, at times their mothers. Fenn admits as much in her preface, and sometimes the anecdotes recounted in her story tell of faulty mothers and nursery maids who improperly indulge or threaten a young boy—it is hardly boy readers that such examples are meant to instruct. Later too, in books with a didactic import, there remains some slippage of audience. In E. J. May's *Dashwood Priory; or, Mortimer's College Life* (1855), for instance, the narrator may state that "our volume is intended for those who have not yet commenced their own life at Oxford" (240). Yet her discussion of what happens when one allows boys to overwork is hardly addressed to schoolboys but rather to parents and masters.

Like other early children's authors, then, Kilner addresses adults not so much through her address to the child (the mode that we now validate) as side by side with her address to the child. In glossing a story about a boy who didn't learn at school and whose parents didn't like to see him punished, for instance, Tom's mother says that the parents "deserved to have labels stuck upon their backs, for neglecting to let a cane be laid across his, when he was such an idle little boy as not to mind his book" (30). While such a comment may explain to a child reader that parents who seem cruel may nonetheless have the child's interests in mind, it still seems more addressed to parents than to children. And, furthermore, in castigating remiss parents, Kilner approaches treacherous ground: she may displace the inadequate parents onto a family other than that of Tom Brown and into a story within the story, but she is opening the door to criticism of parents. And children are not supposed to criticize their parents, even implicitly, as Tom's father later makes quite clear: "After I have told you my determination on a subject, I do not, you know, approve of farther importunities . . ." (84–85).

Another node in the network of disjunctions is attitudes toward education. Mrs. Brown acknowledges the practical uses of education but emphasizes the moral ones: "I would wish you, whilst you diligently apply to your learning, to be careful to cultivate your temper; otherwise, however wise and learned you may be, you will never be much loved by any body" (28–29). Tom himself, however, stresses the practical: "When I get to school, I shall learn so much you will be quite surprised; and then, when I am a man, I shall either be fit to keep a shop, or to be a merchant, or a banker, or a miller, or a farmer, or a captain, or a clergyman, or a gentleman, or a king, which ever trade I like best, Papa says" (11). Ah, yes, gentleman or king. Some of his other pronouncements likewise reveal the "immaturity" of Tom's understanding. When his mother describes how a would-be apothecary is "such a dunce as to mistake the name of one drug for another, and so ignorant as not to know to whom they are to be administered," Tom reduces the explanation to something within his ken, namely spelling: "Aye, to be sure, . . . if a man were such a *great* blockhead as not to be able to tell what r,h u,-b,a,r,b, [*sic*] or what g,u,m spells, I think he might perhaps make a mistake" (20, Kilner's italics).[3] Yet for all that Tom's views on the practicalities of education may be implicitly undermined, they are never directly challenged. Does Kilner have a sense that children would be able to grasp subtleties of tone—to recognize the humor of Tom's misunderstandings? Is she—anachronistically, it would seem—catering to adult norms of "cuteness" in children? Is she providing a double narrative that entertains adults even as it informs children?[4] Certainly the slippage here, between the moral and practical uses of education, echoes a slippage in the culture at the time between the religious and the secular.

Or let's look at matters of genre. Even the form of the book suggests a straining away from consistency, for not till halfway through does Tom set out for school. And once he gets there we don't get a close view of school. Instead there is an interchange of letters, so we hear as much about events at home.

One might argue that Kilner lacked precedents and was simply mixing what we now see as separate genres, the school story and the family story. In fact, all early school stories—and all girls' school stories, before and after Hughes—have tended to mix family and school, even when a child went away to school. Yet Kilner did not lack models for stories set entirely at school (even if children at school might keep thinking of home). There was Fielding's *The Governess* (1749) and the many books that followed in its wake, including those by Johnson and the Lambs, books that focused on the stories told by girls at school. Then there was Kilner's own *The Village School: A Collection of Entertaining Histories, for the Instruction and Amusement of All Good Children* (c. 1783) and also her *Anecdotes of a Boarding-School; or, An Antidote to the Vices of Those Useful Seminaries* (1790), both preceding *First Going to School*. The former is about a day school attended by boys and girls of the laboring classes; the latter, about a girls' finishing school.

True, in both of these earlier books, Kilner may be writing from direct experience in a way that she wouldn't be in writing of a boys' school. *Anecdotes* is set at a middle- to upper-class girls' school of a sort that Kilner might have attended. *The Village School* depicts a coeducational school for the laboring poor, the kind of school that Kilner might have come in contact with as a teacher or benefactor. And her emphasis on the family in *First Going to School* may simply reflect her interest in writing about that with which she was most familiar.

And thus perhaps the emphasis on family is also a sign of her gender. For, early and late, women writers of school stories, whether boys' or girls' school stories, have incorporated attention to family—have found, in short, a way of including females in the story. As Elaine Showalter has noted, in women's novels men generally achieve manliness with the help of instruction by the various women in their lives, not "through separation from women" (137).

Fenn, for instance, prefaces *School Dialogues for Boys* with excuses for writing the book, for rushing it into print, stressing her motherly concern for a particular boy about to go to school and her interest in helping other mothers. And in the story itself the family is often invoked. Parents visit. An ancient letter is treated with special reverence because it was written by a boy's ancestor. Boys frequently reflect on what their parents would think. And family is often invoked metaphorically: an older schoolmate is likened to an elder brother, the masters to parents.

In some school stories by women, family members may even take precedence over school authorities. In "The Cautious Mother," in *Juvenile Anecdotes, Founded on Facts, Collected for the Amusement of Children* (1798), Priscilla Wakefield tells of a mother careful to excise unsuitable passages. The virtuous Theodosius, sent to school and asked to read from a drama by Mme de Genlis, requests a pencil since "there is the awful name which I dare not repeat; and my mamma used always to draw a line through those words which she did not choose we should say" (402). The master is so struck by the practice that he then proceeds to engage in it himself. Thus does a mother gain sway over a master, through her son, when he reads the work of another woman, whose words are put under erasure.

Harriet Martineau likewise validates family in *The Crofton Boys: A Tale* (1841). The school becomes a metaphoric family: the housekeeper's conversation reminds Hugh of his mother's; the master is compared to a father. And even if other boys belittle "home doings"—such as the thorough personal washing that Hugh's mother recommends—Hugh constantly turns to his mother as his spiritual guide, "the best friend he had in this world" (179), whether she is physically present, or they exchange letters, or he simply reminds himself what she would have him do in a given situation.

Other members of Hugh's family figure too. His older brother Phil is at Crofton too, and through hearing Phil tell of the school, Hugh has learned something of schoolboy codes. At school Hugh constantly wishes Phil would help him more—would regularly listen to him repeat his lessons, given that Hugh has so much difficulty. But Phil is chary of his time because he doesn't want to lose his own place in class; he is also perhaps a little ashamed of Hugh, wanting to dissociate himself from "a little brother that was scarcely any better than a girl:—and consider how you talked on the coach, and what ridiculous hair you had,—and what a fuss you made about your money and your pocket,—and how you kept popping out things about Miss Harold, and the girls, and Susan" (125). Martineau thus acknowledges some of the gender anxiety boys at school seem to have felt, yet she displaces much of it onto the not-completely-admirable Phil.

Furthermore—and radically unlike canonical school stories—Hugh is openly fond of his sister Agnes. When he undergoes a lengthy recuperation from a serious accident, she is the "person in all the world [he] would like best for a companion" (134). So she stays with him at his aunt and uncle's, not far from Crofton. Once he is lamed, Hugh tyrannizes over Phil yet eventually acknowledges his tyranny; with respect to Agnes, however, he not only tyrannizes over her but, "If any one had told him that he was tyrannical, he would have been as much surprised as he had been at Phil's tyranny over him" (151). Hugh may not have realized that in asking her to leave the room when a Crofton boy visits he has confined her to her own fireless room, dark and cold, but he should at least have realized "that he had used her with a roughness which is more painful to a loving heart than cold and darkness are to the body" (151). And thereby Martineau comments on how boys fail to respect their sisters. Hugh may eventually prefer not to be waited on by his sisters, something he had once liked and expected, but it's not so much out of respect for them as an urge to compensate for a crippling disability, to try "to be more independent in his habits than any one else" (186).

As in these other pre-Hughesian school stories, Kilner's *First Going to School* allows for the presence of the family—only even more so. For the book is only precariously a school story, a precarious melding of school and family stories. An emblem of the countervailing strains between family and school is the contrary implications of the title and subtitle: *First Going to School* and *The Story of Tom Brown, and his Sisters*. The strains are further compounded by the fact that, on the 1804 title page, the key words of the subtitle are set in larger and bolder type than the words of the main title. Is the book about "first going to school" or about "Tom Brown, and his sisters"? The latter subject would vitiate the former, given that middle- and upper-class girls did not go to school with their brothers, if indeed they went to school.

Given all these inconsistencies, given all this slippage, perhaps one could say of the book something like what Jane Moore has said of Wollstonecraft's *Vindication of the Rights of Woman*: that "the text radically subverts the extant binarism of genre and gender difference of the 1790s" (167). Certainly Kilner enacts slippage, deferral, subversion of the binary, not just in the plot but in the texture of her text. The second half of the book, in particular, comprises an exchange of letters, a slippage among authorities, a slippage only underscored when correspondents defer writing to others. At one point Tom writes for his cousin Peter, who has hurt his hand,[5] in response to a letter from Tom's sister Mary, who was writing for their father, who was preoccupied with business matters.

The key thematic site of slippage in the book is the interface between animal and human: there is a continual questioning of what it means to be animal and what it means to be human, whether a father is telling animal fables or some schoolboys dress a pig in an usher's clothes. This questioning is appropriate in a story that addresses the education, the civilizing, of children, both at home and at school, but it also keeps undermining the premises of education, as we are constantly reminded how bestial we are, despite our educations.

Of course, another function of the concern for animal rights prominent in much eighteenth-century children's literature[6]—however it may have been initiated by Locke in an attempt to lead children away from cruelty and generally toward benevolence[7]—is to serve as a metaphor, however unconscious, for other groups that were treated as inferior to men but should be granted rights: especially women and children. The women who wrote for children about animals and advocated attention to neglected rights may have been acting on the womanly virtue of empathy, but they were also in some sense writing about themselves and about their audience. And perhaps the less conscious they were of such linkages, the more passionate they could allow themselves to become, and the more objective they could seem to remain. Though of course the issue is even more complex—for often these authors want children not to become too concerned about animals but rather to recognize the need to keep animals in their place, even be willing to kill them if doing so will benefit humans. The animal metaphor thus becomes a trope for keeping inferiors inferior even as it grants them rights that verge on equality—and thus it is suited for the contradictory feelings that women (and other marginalized groups) are apt to have had about their own and others' places. Associating children with animals both allows for the possibility of taming the wildness of children and also distances them from full humanity.

Early on Tom is likened, variously, to a "stuck pig," a "little lamb," a horse. Soon the metaphoric references give way to real animals. Tom tries to hit an intruding dog that has snatched a hen from the family's yard, and he and his mother discuss whether one can "punish" a "brute," whether punishment is predicated on the ability to reason. At school he wants a pony to replace the boys whom he and his cousin had drafted to draw a makeshift carriage. Tom's father indicates that he won't crop the ears of the family's pony Hob, even though Hob would look better with smaller ears, since doing so would cause unnecessary pain, and such cruelty to dumb creatures would be wicked.

Tom's father also composes animal fables, duly moralized, based on the family's rabbits, calf, and sow. When writing to Tom of the birth of nine rabbits, he states, "Five of them are exactly like their mamma (though I believe I ought to say *mother,* lest if they were to know I talked of their *mamma,* they might laugh at it as much as the boys at your school) . . ." (66, Kilner's italics). Mr. Brown pokes gentle fun at Tom—and implicitly equates Tom with animals.

Mr. Brown goes on to discuss whether human moral attributes can be applied to animals, whether the cow is at fault, whether the cow deserves blame—as would be the case "if she had understanding to direct her conduct"—when she followed

the dictates of her appetite, and clamber[ed] over the bank into the next field, for the sake of regaling her palate with some of the nice clover grass: nor was she contented, when there, to eat with moderation; but, like all sinners who have once broken through the bounds of duty, she proceeded to add one crime to another, and to indulge in gluttony and excess, till she was so ill she could not stir, and would certainly have died in a very short time, had not the Doctor came, and given her relief by pouring some proper medicine down her throat. (67–68)

Then, in keeping with the genre of the animal fable, Mr. Brown educes a moral: while pitying the cow, "I cannot say I feel much compassion for those persons, who, regardless both of the suggestions of reason and the laws of God, indulge themselves in the excesses of eating and drinking, till they destroy their constitutions, and bring upon themselves many painful disorders" (68). Or in going on to discuss the cutting off of a sow's ear, after it has been torn by a dog, Mr. Brown pontificates over "the pains and disagreeable circumstances of our lives," which will shortly "pass away and be forgotten, like the sow's ear"—only, unlike the sow and her pains and consequences, "the *effects* of our conduct respecting our sufferings or joys, will last *for ever* (69, Kilner's italics) Mr. Brown uses the animals as exempla to illustrate his advice, carefully drawing distinctions between human and beast—much as education was supposed to lead to sharper distinctions, humans differentiating themselves more sharply from animals. At the same time, though, by applying human attributes to beasts, even if playfully, Mr. Brown subtly humanizes the animals and vice versa, thus erasing some of his careful differentiation.

The climax of the book—if such an episodic work can be said to have a climax—likewise harries the boundaries between human and beast, through a cross-species crossdressing: cousin Peter describes a prank in which several schoolboys get a sow and her pigs into a dormitory, dress the sow in the clothing of an usher (master) and tie it to the usher's chair, and dress the pigs in nightcaps and gowns and put them in boys' beds. In the maelstrom that ensues, as Peter concludes, "Such a racket as hogs, boys, masters, maids and mistresses all made, grunting, squeaking, laughing, hallowing, scolding and chattering, altogether—sure never was heard since the foundation of the first school was laid" (98). Thus are the usher and boys exposed as bestial, especially the perpetrators. So bestial, in fact, that their leader, refusing to apologize to the usher, is expelled from the school—is thus proclaimed ineducable, like a beast. This confounding of human and beast occurs not just in the plot but in Kilner's sentences, semantically and syntactically. In the passage just cited, all the humans—masters and maids as well as boys—are syntactically confounded with the hogs, the hogs in fact acquiring precedence. They are semantically confounded as well, the various verbs, from *grunting* to *chattering,* difficult to sort out and assign.[8]

In the context of all this concern about bestiality, we may start wondering whether it is significant that Tom's most willful sister, the one most likely to dispute with him, is named Kitty. Or we might wonder about Tom's wish, when home again at the end of the book, that his sisters could wear trousers to play games with him: "When you run, your nasty frocks are as much in your way as the night shirts were in the pigs. When you hop, when you skip, when you ride on the poney, when you get over stiles or clamber any where, they are always in the way, and are sure either to get torn, or dirtied, or to throw you down (118). Are girls, explicitly compared to pigs, more piglike than boys? Or is their awkward clothing, hampering their ability to clamber over stiles, a sign of a lack of bestiality?[9]

The closing pages of the book confound humanity and bestiality in other ways as well. We learn that the poor pony Hob has been lamed by stepping on some broken glass someone had carelessly thrown in the road. A few pages later we learn that Peter is "lame in his hand" because, while cutting a pole for a cart, another boy hit the hand with a hatchet. Peter and Hob would seem to be akin. Furthermore, we learn that the sleeve of Peter's coat has had to be cut so that he can wear his arm in a sling; the cutting of this coat echoes the cutting of the usher's coat, when the naughty schoolboys dressed the sow and tied it to a chair. Is Peter then, despite receiving an education, despite seeming more mature—more educated—than Tom, ultimately a beast who simply tries to dress like a human? Having segregated humans and beasts to project an ideal of education in which one progresses away from beasts toward some civilized ideal, Kilner nonetheless seems to recognize an affinity between beasts and humans and thus undercuts the ideal of progress.[10]

Of course, to some degree, I am imposing too neat a picture on the book. I am reading it through the filter of hindsight, despite seeing a subsequent history of—to oversimplify—a struggle toward consistency, toward neatly segregated opposites (one pole of which is the tradition inaugurated by the later Tom Brown). Yet the ingredients I focus on are there in Kilner's book—there is a striving for an ideal of education that separates one from the beasts as well as a sense that one is always already implicated in bestiality after all.

Kilner thus raises key questions, an ability that may be due in part to her own metaphoric crossdressing, to her being a female writing about a boys' school. Other women authors seem to have been similarly insightful, similarly empowered to raise questions, when writing about boys' schools. It's as if in writing about boys' schools they didn't have to be as constrained as they would have been in writing about a girl's education. At the same time, since they were generally less familiar with boys' education, they could be more inventive, could give greater play to their imaginations—and they could project their desires for freedom onto boys. Certainly the episode about dressing the pigs is more exuberant—and grants children more independence, even if it is branded as naughty—than anything in Kilner's girls' school story.

Kilner's other school stories are in fact worth examining in a little detail. They too lend themselves to deconstructive readings, whether they are about boys' schools or not.[11] *Anecdotes of a Boarding-School* conveys some ambivalence about the treatment of superstition, more about whether girls should tell tales, and a good deal about whether it is desirable to send a girl to boarding school in the first place. Or take *The Village School*. This book seems at first a fairly straightforward—if heterogeneous—account of how children ought to obey and will be rewarded. The aptly named Mr. Right tells the schoolchildren a story about a good dog and a bad one, Syphax and Cato, and later explicates it. But first he asks Roger Riot how the boy liked the story. Roger responds, "I like it very well; but I do not see what I can learn from it, except that cross dogs will not be liked so well, nor live so comfortably, as good natured ones" (71). He has of course missed the point that the adult wants to make, so Mr. Right goes on, at great length, to stress that "neither will cross boys; and though the story I have been telling you has been about dogs, yet you may be assured, that it would be just the same with children"; in fact, "those children who are good, though they should be even as ugly as Syphax, will, like him, when once people know their sweetness of temper, be loved and encouraged as he was" (71).

Yet maybe Roger is not so wrong. For even though he has not made the equation between dogs and people, he has seen to the economic heart of Mr. Right's message. When Roger says that cross dogs will not live as comfortably as good-natured ones, he states rather starkly the materialistic argument for goodness that the book promulgates: the good village children get Christmas boxes containing dolls and bats and peaches, while the bad children are threatened with rods and confined in cellars. We may be meant to dismiss Roger's comments, both because we know he is a naughty boy (his teasing has even led to the death of another) and because he misses part of the allegory. Yet perhaps he sees the Emperor's New Clothes more truly than the adult authorities do. And thereby, in sketching a child's perspective, the book starts dismantling adult preachments.

As also happens at the end. For there Kilner's didacticism becomes self-immolating. The kindly and virtuous schoolteacher Mrs. Bell has taken a poor sick woman into her house and stays up nursing her and also making a shirt for a neighbor. How is Mrs. Bell's virtue rewarded in this book that so meticulously rewards the virtuous and punishes the naughty? Her house catches fire and she dies in the conflagration, her flesh "so entirely consumed as to make it impossible to distinguish Mrs. Bell from the poor woman she had charitably assisted" (88). Thus does Kilner provide "a convenient conclusion to the otherwise endless tale" (Carpenter and Prichard) —or perhaps the "one real excitement which not even the moral that Kilner draws (to be careful with candles) can dampen" (Jackson 147).

The narrative text too does violence to Mrs. Bell. The paragraph following that on the conflagration starts to provide closure, adjusting the narrative to incorporate the shock of Mrs. Bell's end into the moral frame of the book as a whole: "Thus concluded the life of that most valuable member of society; much lamented, and much beloved, by all the inhabitants of Rose Green; and an irreparable loss to all the rising generation of that place"(88). But the book does not end there. The narrator tacks on yet another one-sentence paragraph: "From this fatal accident it is to be hoped, that every body will learn to be extremely cautious not to leave candles burning near linen, nor, indeed, any where, without constantly watching, that they may not do mischief" (88). In insisting on pointing an unrelated little lesson, the narrator partly plasters over the obvious moral of the fatal event, but she also reminds us to seek morals and hence to recognize the obvious one. For surely the fire shows us that—contrary to the message of the rest of the book—virtue can go unrewarded in this world. Thus does the book undermine its own premises, as it undermines Mrs. Bell's.

Finally, the tension created by two modes of characterization in *The Village School* is subversive as well. Most of the children are given names that typify them: Eliza Giddy, Hannah Right, Anne Dawdle, Jacob Stedfast. And the characters are true to type; by and large they don't change. Roger Riot cannot seem to stop being riotous—running against Anne Trundle and bruising her, cutting Peter Limp's leg by throwing a hatchet at him (again Kilner lames a boy named Peter with a hatchet), spoiling Samuel Strut's clothes with rotten eggs. The characterization that governs most of the book implies that change isn't possible. Yet the presumed purpose of the book is not just to maintain good children in their goodness but to reform naughty ones. Kilner's concern for education and change creates grounds for questioning the allegorical mode of naming she has adopted, though she does not pursue the questioning.

In the later *Anecdotes* Kilner uses both allegorical and more neutral names. Most of the good girls have neutral names: Martha Beauchamp, Kitty Long, Miss Lloyd. The bad girls, on the other hand, are likely to have names like Miss Grumpton, Miss Sneak, Miss Fangly, Miss Creedless. Later still, by the time she writes *First Going to School*, Kilner has abandoned such allegorical naming, relying instead on "ordinary" names—the John Doe of Tom Brown.[12] Part of the difference may be due to the fact that in the third book, compared to the first, she is dealing with a different class of children— middle-class children whom she may feel closer to, less inclined to distance herself from through allegorical naming (though the typicality of Tom's name engenders its own distance). And compared to the second book, Kilner feels less ambivalence about the desirability of sending children—in this case, boys—away to boarding school: it's as if she expresses some of her mixture of feelings in the second book through her mixture of modes of naming. Or perhaps her increasing abandonment of allegorical naming is a sign that she recognized its limitations.

As for where all that leaves *Tom Brown's Schooldays,* Hughes may or may not have been familiar with Kilner's work. But he was familiar with the kind of literature that it purported to be, the kind that exalted piety and virtuous behavior and gave little overt scope to fun and games. And it is in part in reaction to such literature that he wrote his school story a half century later. Yet the trend toward homogenization that he fathered tends to obscure the value of the kinds of inconsistency that Kilner's work embodies.

Not to mention the ways she is perhaps consistent, the ways she suggests alternate modes of reading. A book like *First Going to School* may perhaps be read more profitably as a poetic text than a narrative one, more for its thematic texturing than for its plot. Once we see the centrality of the issue of bestiality, the book seems much more unified. The plotting may remain episodic, and there are still events that seem thematically extraneous. But we no longer need to raise such overarching, implicitly condemnatory questions as whether the book is indeed a school story. Or rather, we can decide that our preconceived notions of unity do not apply—that they need perhaps to be deconstructed. We need to read against the grain of established codes, both the codes of the school story and those associated with education at the time. For Kilner's is a story that questions schooling in the broadest sense, questions its civilizing functions.

NOTES

1. M. Pelham was a pseudonym used by Kilner and also presumably Sir Richard Phillips (though in neither the *National Union Catalog* nor the *British Museum*

General Catalogue can I find titles specifically attributed to him under that pseudonym). In fact, Nelson (*Boys* 56)—and before her Maison—briefly refers to *First Going to School* as being by Phillips. Yet the copy she refers to was published five years later, and the copy I consulted states that it is by the author of *The Village School* and *Perambulation of a Mouse*, both recognized Kilner titles. Furthermore, bibliographer St. John attributes *First Going to School* to Kilner (272), as do such critics as Darton (*Children's Books* 162) and Pickering (*Moral Instruction* 205). Once again I am working in the margins here, at the boundaries of gender attribution—as I examine a work that is a boundary case for school stories, even if it might turn out not to have been crossgendered.

2. Jackson claims that the ability of Kilner and her sister-in-law, in their school stories, "to give a touch of reality to homely childish activities and to restrain somewhat the moralizing impulse distinguished their efforts above those of many others" (146).

3. And perhaps Mrs. Brown's understanding is undermined here as well—since she does not address his level of understanding and, once misunderstood, does not explain her meaning further. Perhaps, too, Kilner herself is implicitly undermined, since her project in the book subsumes Mrs. Brown's.

4. For a discussion of the often contradictory pulls of the double audience for children's literature—an audience comprising both children and adults—see Shavit 63ff. and Knoepflmacher.

5. Lameness and disability are here more a plot device, to get a different character writing, or perhaps a thematic device, than a means of taming through pain—and feminizing—as they would be in subsequent women's stories about boys' schools (see Chapter 9). Though there is a recurring trope of disability, the book opening with Tom's fall, and various animals are later crushed or otherwise disabled.

6. See, e.g., Jackson 166–168.

7. See Pickering, *Locke* 12.

8. The confounding also appears on the previous page when Peter refers to "the young gentlemen pigs" (97)—referring ostensibly to the pigs but the metaphoric equation that makes the pigs gentlemen also makes the gentlemen pigs. Earlier confoundings—not associated with this incident—include Mr. Brown's humorous closing of a letter by sending "all the kind loves of your mamma, (I beg your pardon, your *mother*), your sisters, your rabbits, pigs, &c. &c. with which I am commissioned . . ." and Tom's more earnest statement, soon afterwards, "I am very glad to hear that my mamma (O dear, I never can remember to say *mother*) and all my sisters, and beasts are well" (70, 71, Kilner's italics).

9. Similar questions are raised—their salience reinforced—when Peter likens the dressed pigs to himself: "I think they must have tumbled and stumbled as much as I did one day, when I dressed myself in my mamma's gown" (108). The boundary between human and animal is like that between male and female—there, but nebulous.

10. Kilner may have been especially drawn to recognizing the affinity between beasts and humans because of her earlier experience in writing *The Life and Perambulation of a Mouse* (1783–1784), in which she writes a first-person narrative from the perspective of—and is entirely sympathetic to—a mouse. In discussing eighteenth-century theories of the fable, Noel observes that, particularly later in the century, critics were inclined to see the animal fable—fables like Mr. Brown's—as expressing man's unity with nature (12ff.).

11. The fiction by Kilner that least lends itself to deconstructive reading is perhaps her best-known work, the one that has been reprinted in a volume of *Masterworks of Children's Literature*: namely, *The Life and Perambulation of a Mouse*. The story is episodic, as we follow the mouse through a number of households and overhear a variety of conversations—and thus any inconsistency in what is preached from one household to the next is not particularly troublesome to a twentieth-century reader.

This episodic, even picaresque, form naturalizes inconsistency. For extended discussion of Kilner's *Anecdotes of a Boarding-School*, see my "Reconstructing."

12. As Hughes explains in the preface to *Tom Brown at Oxford* (1861),

> I chose the name "Brown," because it stood first in the trio of "Brown, Jones, and Robinson," which has become a sort of synonym for the middle classes of Great Britain. . . . As to the Christian name of "Tom," having chosen Brown, I could hardly help taking it as the prefix. The two names have gone together in England for two hundred years, and the joint name has not enjoyed much of a reputation for respectability. This suited me exactly. I wanted the *commonest* name I could get, and did not want any name which had the least heroic, or aristocratic, or even respectable savour about it. Therefore, I had a natural leaning to the combination which I found ready to my hand. Moreover, I believed "Tom" to be a more specially English name than John, the only other as to which I felt the least doubt. Whether it be that Thomas à Becket was for so long the favourite English saint, or from whatever other cause, it certainly seems to be the fact, that the name "Thomas" is much commoner in England than in any other country. The words "tom-fool," "tom-boy," etc., though, perhaps, not complimentary to the "Toms" of England, certainly show how large a family they must have been. (ii, Hughes's italics)

4   TELLING TALES ABOUT TELLING TALES

E. J. MAY AND OTHER TALEBEARERS

In the course of the nineteenth century, school stories, especially boys' school stories, increasingly registered a questioning of authority, increasingly addressed the potential for conflict between child and adult—through the tropes of insurrection, fagging, and talebearing. Of the three, the trope that most directly confronts the conflict between child and adult authority is that of the schoolboy insurrection; but it has such subversive potential that it rarely appears in school stories, not even by way of allusion. As for the trope of fagging, of younger boys serving older ones, it embodies a caricature of adult–child cooperation that serves to consolidate peer authority; at the same time it can show the abuses of an unequal power relationship even more clearly than adult–child interactions do, because of a sense that it might be inappropriate for a boy to exercise power over another, whereas adult power often seems natural. Although common in post-Hughesian boys' school stories by men, this trope appears very rarely in boys' stories by women, perhaps because of gender differences in Victorian psychosexual economies: women could perhaps imagine the girls' equivalent, the rave, the worship of a senior girl or mistress from afar, more readily than the institutionalizing of the relationship that was endemic in boys' public schools and the abuses to which such institutionalizing could give rise, the license it could give for the exercise of cruelty.[1] Instead, the trope that best provides a locus for examining the effects of crossgendering is the third of the trio: that of talebearing.

Yet before going on to tell tales about telling tales, I'd like to examine one of the few direct presentations of a schoolboy insurrection in a school story: in Maria Edgeworth's "The Barring Out; or, Party Spirit" (1796).

Schoolboy insurrections—barring out the masters—occurred in real schools. In the sixteenth and seventeenth centuries such revolts were even ritualized: shortly before Christmas, the boys would bar out the masters and demand the granting or extension of holidays (Cathcart 50; Thomas 66–67). But by the eighteenth century the barring out had become rare, more a protest "against what were regarded as singular acts of tyranny or infringements of ancient privileges" (Cathcart 52) than a regular means of negotiating authority. And when it did occur, it could more readily go out of control: in the late eighteenth and early nineteenth centuries, public schools like Rugby, Harrow, Eton, and Winchester experienced serious disorders; one at the last required the intervention of the militia (see Honey 6). Yet almost all school-story writers seem to have found the trope too dangerous to broach, as if fearing that readers would sympathize with the rebels (as is the case when such an insurrection occurs in novels that provide a glimpse of school before moving on to the real adventures, in adventure stories like Frederick Marryat's *Rattlin, the Reefer* [1836]). In "The Barring Out," then—what P. W. Musgrave calls "probably the first recognisable English school story" (26)—Edgeworth effectively redresses the avoidance of such writers as Ellenor Fenn, who in 1783 simply alludes to schoolboy rebellions at Eton and Harrow and dismisses them by having a boy say, "The master always is conqueror; the boys get nothing but chastisement, contempt, disgrace;—they shew their evil dispositions, or want of judgment; and are either flogged, or expelled, according to the degree of their guilt" (*School Dialogues* 2: 112). And Edgeworth by and large succeeds in the aim she states in her preface: to avoid "the common fault of making the most mischievous characters appear the most *active* and the most ingenious" (vi, Edgeworth's italics)—though some ambiguity remains, some vestige of glory still adheres to the schoolboys' strike for freedom. As Mitzi Myers notes of Edgeworth's stories for children, not only do "educators invent children" but "children turned educators invent juvenile selves that simultaneously support and subvert parental premises" ("Dilemmas" 83).

Edgeworth succeeds in large measure because of her characterization of Archer, the leader of the insurrection. He is intelligent; he has a sense of honor and nobility, willingly going without food himself to feed his confederates; he is simply misguided about power, about the instability of mob allegiance, about what is reasonable. He disparages blind obedience to Dr. Middleton, only to find that his companions won't blindly—or even with reason—obey him. He assumes that what a majority wants must be right, until "He saw that the majority, his own convincing argument, was against him" (103).

The boys under his command start splintering off—and it's the leader of a subgroup who serves as the lightning rod for the schoolmaster's retribution and also enacts the rebellious boys' concern with material supplies. Earlier this despicable Fisher had switched allegiance from De Grey, the virtuous student leader, to Archer because De Grey refused to do a translation for him. When Archer and De Grey compete for a premium, a prize, Fisher fans the rivalry by taking bets. He incites boys to tear down De Grey's playhouse. He rarely thinks of anything loftier than his stomach: during the barring out he misappropriates funds and hoards buns. He is stupidly credulous of a gypsy woman, and he has poor control of language: he can't even understand puns.[2]

Also contributing to Edgeworth's success is that her adult authorities behave with restraint. Instead of attacking the rebellious boys—and thereby fostering sympathy for the underdog—they leave the boys largely to their own devices, wait till the latter tire of being, in effect, barred in. And the punishments afterwards are mild. There is no flogging, popular though that was at the time in boys' schools, though Fisher is eventually expelled.

Edgeworth likewise adds resonance to her story through redefining terms: to convert Archer to true goodness, she needs to redefine his understanding of such concepts as honor and reason. Yet these terms often reveal slippage rather than neat redefinition, thereby eroding some of the neatness of the solutions she proposes. Take the matter of reason. Early on Dr. Middleton has prohibited the boys from going to a certain building, for reasons that he prefers not to name. (Later he reveals that a gypsy with a contagious fever had slept there, and the doctor had not wanted to alarm the boys by telling them.) Archer's response to the prohibition is to proclaim, "I won't be governed by any man's reasons that he won't tell me" (84). Later the boy learns not to confuse an insistence on reasons with true reason, not to—in Dr. Middleton's words—rebel "against the just authority which is necessary to conduct and govern you whilst you have not sufficient reason to govern and conduct yourselves" (112). And Archer and his crew are encouraged to rely on their reason: when De Grey comes to parley he brings breakfast, so that if the rebels agree to surrender they will do so for the sake of reason, not for the sake of their stomachs. De Grey states, "When we yield, I hope it will not be merely to get our dinner, gentlemen" (107)—and he strategically includes himself among those who would yield. The boys, however, belie their reliance on reason, admitting that fasting Archers would have been easy to persuade, "but Archers feasting are quite other animals" (106). Animals indeed. Later, after the boys surrender, Archer is again invited to exercise his reason. Dr. Middleton invites him to name his own punishment, to "show me that you now understand the nature of punishment" (113). Then, "proud to be treated like a reasonable creature, and sorry that he had behaved like a foolish schoolboy" (113), Archer declines the opportunity, deferring to the doctor. Thus, paradoxically, a boy shows that he is reasonable by abdicating his reason.

Such redefinition occurs not just in the story's themes but in its images: Edgeworth redefines, revalues, the tenor of a prison trope, when the boys' attempts at a barring out effectively become a barring in. Early on the school is associated with prison, from the boys' perspective: "The moment the hours destined for instruction, or, as they are termed by school-boys, school-hours, were over, each prisoner started up with a shout of joy" (83). The interpolation of the phrase "as they are termed by school-boys," to excuse or explain the term "school-hours"—a term that hardly needs explanation—provides a context for the remainder of the sentence: it situates the perspective from which schoolboys are seen as prisoners, namely, that of the boys. Later, after the insurrection has gone its course, the rebels tear down their fortifications, glimpse the playground outside, and "the countenances of these voluntary prisoners" brighten (111). The schoolhouse is again a prison, yet now not when the masters rule but when the boys do; the boys have presumably learned that it was not the rule by just adult authorities that made school a prison but the attempt to overcome such rule. Still, some vestiges of the earlier valence remain. Dr. Middleton decides that for two months the insurgents will return from the playground a quarter hour earlier than the rest of the boys. Once again the schoolroom is the site of punishment, reinforcing the boys' earlier views of it.

Still, despite the slippage of terms—or rather because of such slippage, a slippage that enables her to plumb the complexity of the issues she broaches—Edgeworth has the skill to present an account of a schoolboy rebellion that is surprisingly (to a post-Romantic reader) sympathetic to the nonrebels.

Few authors were as brave. Most instead addressed the nexus of authority through the trope of talebearing—that "major schoolboy sin" (Musgrave 28). The conflict posed by the trope is this: What should a child do when another breaks an adult-sanctioned rule? Should she tell tales—becoming, as it were, a tattling tomboy? Or should she remain loyal to peers by remaining silent, upholding the schoolchild code against talebearing? As George Orwell has written of the contradictory pulls he experienced at school in the early twentieth century, "You were bidden at once to be a Christian and a social success, which is impossible" ("Such" 45). You were bidden to tell and not to tell.

Certainly some kind of schoolchild code against tattling must have existed at least since 1546, when the *Oxford English Dictionary* first notes the appearance of "tell tales out of school." Yet most pre-Hughesian stories allowed it little play. If in the eighteenth century the disciplinary power of school established for its subjects a "compulsory visibility" (Foucault 187)—visibility to adults—then it was not until the next century that fictional schoolchildren were able to establish their countercode, one that conferred a measure of invisibility.

Or more precisely, the parameters for applying the code against talebearing were limited, before Hughes.[3] The code is never absolutely present or absent but rather negotiates a shifting terrain. Even in a real school in the early twentieth century, the code was not absolute: Orwell notes that sneaking "was the unforgivable sin," yet qualifies his statement by adding, "except in a few rigidly defined circumstances," such as sodomy ("Such" 36).

Many early writers simply assumed that telling tales was both acceptable and desirable; they valued moral goodness over peer loyalty, fidelity to God over fidelity to friends. In the anonymous *Tales of the Academy* (c. 1820), for instance, the virtuous Osric thinks nothing of telling his master of the romantic Paul's fancies about becoming a hermit to re-enact *Robinson Crusoe*—and there is no hint that Osric is anything but right to tell on Paul.

Even as late as George Lawrence's *Guy Livingstone* (1857), an adventure story in which the brief description of Guy's sojourn at public school serves as a sauce to whet our appetites for the later Byronic exploits of our hero, there is some evasiveness about talebearing. After a classic fight with a bully, "Guy walked out without a glance at his prostrate enemy; and going straight to the head of the house, told him what had happened" (19). Even if Guy told only of his own part in the affair, and the head inferred the rest, most late-nineteenth-century schoolboys would accuse Guy of sneaking. He should have waited till the head had discovered the fight—maybe let the bully do the sneaking—or at least have waited till assembled schoolboys are asked who was responsible and then manfully owned up. But Guy is not accused of sneaking. Instead he is acclaimed by his schoolmates, some fifty of whom are eager to write the lines imposed on him as punishment.

Thomas Hughes, however, is not so evasive. Or rather in *Tom Brown's Schooldays* he displaces the literary tradition of the past onto Tom's past: a weakness of the preparatory school that Tom attended before Rugby is the extent to which the ushers encouraged "tale-bearing, which had become a frightfully common vice in the school in consequence, and had sapped all the foundations of school morality" (61). At Rugby, on the other hand, an admirable sixth-form leader won't pry even when he knows there is bullying going on: "That only makes it more underhand, and encourages the small boys to come to us with their fingers in their eyes telling tales, and so we should be worse off than ever" (104). Later the sixth form proclaims that reporting incidents to masters is "against public morality and School tradition," and "any boy, in whatever form, who should thenceforth appeal to a master, without having first gone to some praepostor, and laid the case before him, should be thrashed publicly, and sent to Coventry" (139).[4] The need for such a proclamation suggests that the code is not yet second nature. At least not for the older boys, though, curiously, it seems to be for younger ones. For Tom and his friends believe in the code implicitly, even doubting the propriety of telling older boys of Flashman's bullying. Instead they resolve as a group to defy the bully—acting on the advice of an older boy who has conveniently overheard their deliberations (such coincidences frequently allow the heroes of canonical school stories to avoid the taint of talebearing while yet averting the direst consequences).

Thereafter the boys in British school stories need no such proclamations. Imagine Kipling's Beetle tattling on Stalky, or Wodehouse's Psmith on Mike. Stories that follow in the wake of *Tom Brown* may at times pay lip service to Christian piety, but they really celebrate boys as boys, their loyalty to one another rather than to adult authorities or to the higher truths of religion.

With one important exception: Frederic Farrar's *Eric; or, Little by Little* (1858), though it follows *Tom Brown* by a year, is still in the tradition that gives religion precedence over peer loyalty.[5] Like many other books that overtly endorse adult authority—especially earlier stories and later girls' school stories—*Eric* offers a complex portrayal of peer loyalty and the code against talebearing. As he wends his downward way, Eric is too attached to peer loyalty: it may seem admirable that he refuses to tell which boys have been using a crib even though that means he himself seems guilty. But his loyalty derives from too intense a hunger for popularity—too great an eagerness to win the "favour of man," resulting in "forgetfulness of God" (103). We are in fact told with approval of two boys who tell or threaten to tell tales. Yet while stressing the boys' courage in braving their peers' contempt, the narrator nevertheless undermines their example. In one case, he explicitly disavows it: "I do not recommend any boy to imitate Owen in this matter" (23). He also distances us from the incident by making it occur before Eric arrives at school and by never allowing Eric to become very close to Owen, for all that Owen is always on the side of truth and justice, the side that Eric's better nature keeps urging upon him. In the other case, the narrator simply shows a boy threatening to tell a master about widespread cribbing, a boy concerned that a friend is being deprived of his rightful standing in the form, but we then get caught up in Eric's drunken debauchery and never learn the aftermath. Furthermore, though the boy had been encouraged to take a stand against cribbing by an admirable older boy, the narrator refers to the advice as "well-meant, though rather mistaken" (142).

Before Hughes, too, several early writers, especially women writing of boys' schools, women ranging from Ellenor Fenn in 1783 to E. J. May in 1850—and May more than anyone else—explore the issue of talebearing and elicit the contradictory interplay between adult authority and peer loyalty. These women may then leave their fictional incidents unresolved and the implications unexplored, but they do raise key questions: Under what circumstances should a child tattle on others? Should his fundamental allegiance be to peers or to adults? Will tattling cause him to forfeit any chance of influencing his schoolmates? For whose good does he tattle—and how does the valence shift if he will benefit materially from the tattling? Margaret Atwood, adopting the persona of a nineteenth-century writer who wrote one of these probing, problematic school stories, might almost be addressing such fictional incidents when she writes, "There was something they almost taught me / I came away not having learned" (27).[6]

Probably the earliest boys' school story by a woman is Fenn's *School Dialogues for Boys: Being an Attempt to Convey Instruction Insensibly to Their Tender Minds, and Instill the Love of Virtue* (1783). Like other early writers of school stories, Fenn portrays respect for adult authority. Perhaps she is remembering her own experience at a girls' school, which would have allowed less independence than a boys' school generally did. Or it may be that a woman's way into a school story—and often her justification for writing one—is as a mother, and hence as an adult authority herself. Fenn's preface supports such a notion, for she apologetically excuses any stylistic infelicities on the grounds of motherly urgency—she has written the book hastily so that a particular boy about to enter school will be fortified "against the contagion of bad example," and rather than sacrifice "the conduct of her darling Child to her own vanity," she is willing to brave "censure on her style" (1: x, xi). She makes it clear, furthermore, that she includes mothers in her audience: she wants to assist a fellow mother by writing pages "sprightly enough to engage the attention of her darling son to those maxims which it is her constant aim to instill" (1: xiv).

Yet the role of mother helping other mothers is not the only role she enacts in the preface—for in a flight of fancy, something that she never allows in the fiction itself, she likens herself to a kite flyer, a masked old woman "personating youth," a spider who has "long spun in a corner, and now venture[s] to fix my web in a more conspicuous situation," and a schoolboy who has now "placed my exercise upon the desk" (1: xx–xxi). If Fielding could allow some fantasy to intrude in interpolated tales in *The Governess* (1749), Fenn could allow it only in her preface—the site, usually, of greater grounding in our world outside the fiction. Fenn's imaginative flights are, furthermore, confined to her conceptualization of her role. It's as if she not only feels the need to disinfect the fiction itself of mere fantasy but also finds it so inconceivable that she write such a book (even though she published it anonymously), that she has recourse to fantasy to imagine doing so. At the same time, the metaphors suggest her need to locate herself androgynously, writing across gender, even across species.

In any case, given Fenn's general endorsement of adult authority, we might expect her not to endorse the schoolchild code against talebearing. But as with other perceptive writers of early school stories, that is not entirely the case. Not even in Fenn's girls' school story—for in *School Occurrences: Supposed to Have Arisen among a Set of Young Ladies, under the Tuition of Mrs. Teachwell; and to be Recorded by One of Them* (1782), she acknowledges the tensions precipitated by the schoolchild ethic. The admirable Miss Sprightly has lent the key that enabled her schoolmates to help themselves to Miss Greedy's cake: she uneasily decides not to tell Mrs. Teachwell, given her own technical innocence and her fear of being "reproached as an informer," but she also resolves "never to be prevailed upon to be an accessary [*sic*] to what she knew was wrong" (39). Later Miss Sprightly hesitates to tell Mrs. Teachwell that another young lady has abstracted a letter from the mistress's table; fortunately Mrs. Teachwell determines what has happened without being told. Yet this evasion of a difficult moral decision—whether Miss Sprightly should tell or not—attests to the force of the prohibition against tattling. Not only does the admirable Miss Sprightly subscribe to the ethic, not only does Mrs. Teachwell not challenge the prohibition, but the author dextrously extricates herself, as the guilty young lady has extricated the letter, while yet guiltily, like Miss Sprightly, providing a key.

Fenn is similarly evasive in *School Dialogues for Boys,* where she pays even more attention to talebearing. At one point several boys are planning to go out of bounds. Frankling, a frank boy if nevertheless mischievous, declines to go, and when asked if he will tell on the others says he will not unless asked. The more completely admirable Sprightly (clearly akin to Miss Sprightly) is even more implicated in the cabal—for when Subtle pretends to call for help, just out of bounds, Sprightly goes to his aid. Subtle urges that now that Sprightly has broken one rule he might as well join the party, but Sprightly refuses. Sprightly later muses that "if the boys be discovered, they will think that I told of them, and will reproach me" (1: 145)—he is, in short, attuned to the code against talebearing. And if he too is accused, he could tell the truth, "but it will appear like an invention; the boy who so ungenerously drew me into the scrape, will never own the cheat which he put upon me" (1: 145). Sprightly's friend Gentle agrees—"Your excuse will seem like an artful tale" (1: 146)—yet proposes consulting the older Sensible, urging that Sprightly need not name names. Sprightly concurs, realizing that Sensible would then be able to vouch for his story. Sensible in turn tells the two that they "have judged very properly": "You would have been sorry to be suspected of seeking to disclose the faults of your schoolfellows; unhappy to be supposed guilty; and miserable to have appeared so base as to excuse yourself by any falsity or evasion.—Now you are perfectly safe" (1: 147, 148). Thus Sprightly has indulged in some mild talebearing—to another boy rather than a master, but to an older boy who functions as something of an assistant master. And content with having preached her lesson— that a boy in such a predicament should at least consult an older boy—Fenn proceeds to forget the incident: we never learn if Subtle and the rest are caught, never see Sprightly squirm out of the difficulty.

Still, this dialogue is immediately followed by another in which talebearing and Subtle again figure, as if to resolve the previous crisis by displacement. Frankling freely admits to the prank of having placed rotten apples in the bed that he shares with Goodwill. When the usher Mr. Wiseman states, "I command you to tell me all who knew it," Frankling responds, "Sir, if I Must.—Young gentlemen, will you not rather confess yourselves?" (1: 156). So Thoughtless, Careless, and several others come forward. But not Subtle. Chatter then chatters on, alluding to Subtle, and Easy implicates Subtle as well. Neither Easy nor Chatter incurs sanctions, from boys or masters, but Frankling's refusal to name names—"I named nobody, Sir" (1: 157)—provides the preferred model of behavior. Frankling goes on to insist that he himself was the perpetrator and is the only one meriting punishment, offering to write all the punishment lines allotted to various boys, but Mr. Wiseman pardons the boy for his "noble disposition" and excuses the misdeed as "merely the offence of vivacity and mirth" (1: 158). As for the serpentlike Subtle, Mr. Wiseman exclaims, "How ungenerous! to tempt a companion to play a trick; then leave him to take all the punishment" (1: 159)—and Subtle's punishment is that each of the others will lash him five times. Fenn thus acknowledges the code against talebearing and allows Frankling, its leading exponent, to be worthy, to have his behavior endorsed by the master (even if it's not explicitly adherence to the code that is endorsed). But Fenn seems reluctant to endorse the code fully—certainly she hasn't allowed even worthier boys like Sprightly and Gentle to enact it unambiguously. And by having the boys lash Subtle, she makes them the instruments of adult authority, punishing the greatest offender, namely, the boy unwilling to tell tales about himself. Yet this displacement of the punishers also subtly empowers the boys, paving the way for the emergence of peer solidarity.

Maria Edgeworth's "Tarlton," a story in *The Parent's Assistant; or, Stories for Children* (1796), likewise endorses parental and other adult authority. As the title of the volume suggests, Edgeworth, like Fenn, envisions her role as a parent's auxiliary[7]—as was the case in her own life, for her children's stories originated as tales told to her many stepbrothers and stepsisters, and on some level she served as her father's assistant, writing tales congruent with his ideas on education.[8] Certainly she relied on him for information and background for her boys' school stories (see Butler 159, n. 2). Crossgendering stories was thus feasible, in part, because of her close relationship with her father.

In "Tarlton," as in her other stories, Edgeworth succeeds in not making the naughty too attractive—Edgeworth's "bad children are never attractive, and her good ones hardly ever impossible" (Barry 179). "Tarlton" focuses on Hardy, a courageous, good boy, wrongly accused of stealing apples and of attempting to poison a dog guarding a neighbor's apple tree. Far from having been involved in the attempt, Hardy was trying to rescue the dog.

The story might more aptly be named after Hardy; certainly it begins and ends with him. The eponymous Tarlton is simply not given much scope. Nor is the latter's insurrectionary energy seductively attractive—he is not a Byronic hero. Rather, he's the kind of villain who always plays safe, sending his schoolmate Loveit after the shuttlecock in the lane forbidden to the boys, sending the servant Tom out to poison the dog (the displacement of the crime onto a servant is a measure both of how heinous such treatment of animals is and of how villainous Tarlton is). Yet Edgeworth chooses to name the story after Tarlton, and thereby she subtly subverts the moral import, naming the story after that which must be expelled. Though Hardy too is metaphorically expelled, even if only momentarily: he was locked into a closet called the Black Hole for having gone out of bounds (when rescuing the dog). So Hardy anticipates Tarlton, in a sense, or possibly Tarlton expresses what is latent in Hardy, the potential for even a good boy to be governed by peer values—or rather by what Edgeworth defines as selfishness.

Here too, as in Fenn's story, communal values are in ascendance and again they serve not the interests of the boys in opposition to the masters (as they would in later canonical stories) but those of the adult moral authorities. Tarlton may harp on a kind of group loyalty to get boys to participate in unworthy escapades, getting them to swear, "Stand by me, and I'll stand by you" (5). But ultimately he espouses isolated individualism: "Every one for himself in this world!" (10), he proclaims, after refusing to help free Loveit from an entangling hedge as they flee the fierce dog. Contrast that with Hardy, who, on the next page, quietly rules a sheet of paper for Loveit (the ruling of a page itself expresses the kind of constraint and restraint that is desirable, that enables creativity and community).

And it is Hardy who, even when caught with the poisoned meat—he had snatched it from the dog—refuses to implicate others: "I have no pardon to ask, I have nothing to confess; I am innocent; but if I were not, I would never try to get off myself by betraying my companions" (15). Though of course Hardy had promised not to betray Loveit; like other early authors, Edgeworth justifies adherence to peer loyalty by superadding the sanctity of keeping a promise. And even later, when the handkerchief that had wrapped the meat is found, Hardy simply denies that it is his. Fortunately it sports the initials "J. T."—and as soon as his trace is discovered, Tarlton feels no compunction about telling tales: "Upon my word and honour, sir, I'll tell you all; I should never have thought of stealing the apples if Loveit had not first told me of them; and it was Tom who first put the poisoning the dog into my head. It was he that carried the meat . . ." (19).

The master Mr. Trueman provides further—even if tacit—endorsement of the code against talebearing. He refuses to press Hardy to reveal his supposed confederates, as urged by the usher, given that "truth and honour are not to be expected amongst thieves" (18). Mr. Trueman may here be disparaging Hardy's sense of honor. But his implication that honor would require not revealing one's confederates paradoxically endorses the code.

Overall, Edgeworth succeeds in co-opting the code against talebearing—that mainstay of solidarity among boys against the masters—for the purposes of adult moral authority. For she associates the worst violations of the code with the mischief-makers, boys who would, in later stories, be staunch adherents.

A number of subsequent crossgendered works touch on talebearing. Priscilla Wakefield's *Juvenile Anecdotes* (1798) includes several brief stories that take place at school. In "The Grateful School-Fellow" a boy named Danvers repays the generosity of the Milton family when he tells a master of seeing an older boy beating the youngest Milton boy. Danvers is in turn beaten by older boys for being a telltale, but he does not tell tales about this latter incident: "I scorn to tell tales for my own sake, however ill-used I may be; but *now* I suffer in defence of my friend, and for the gratitude I owe to my benefactors, Mr. and Mrs. Milton" (398, Wakefield's italics). That is, he expresses loyalty to adults, even if they are not the adult authorities of the school. Wakefield has prefaced the tale with some hairsplitting about the telling of tales: she admits that talebearing "is an odious fault" and that perpetrators are disliked, even despised, but one should distinguish "between the tattler, who repeats every inadvertent action, with a malicious design to make mischief, and the boy of true courage, who dares appeal in an open manner to his master, at the risk of being scoffed at by his companions for a tale-tale [*sic*], when he sees the weak oppressed by the strong, and is unable to redress the injury" (396). Wakefield draws the line between tattling and true courage differently from the way it would be drawn in a later canonical story: even though helping the weak would still be admired, Danvers would nonetheless be considered a sneak and should have attempted to fight the bully himself, despite the physical odds. And the need to begin the anecdote with a disclaimer implies—at least to a latterday audience—a narratorial urge to protest too much.

In Susannah Strickland's *Hugh Latimer; or, The School-Boys' Friendship* (1828), the code is strong yet under pressure. Hugh is tempted to tell the headmaster Mr. Vernon why he and his friend Montrose left school bounds without permission—they were helping a black peddler, and a full explanation would require telling tales about how the other pupils mistreated the peddler. Yet the strongest adherent of the code is Montrose, who later proves to be too vulnerable to social prejudice—he temporarily deserts Hugh because the boy's widowed mother is in trade. So can we fully respect Montrose's upholding of a code endorsed by peers if he later shows himself unduly influenced by peer pressure? As for Hugh, the central character, a boy with no failings except a tendency to feel a little downhearted when his schoolmates snub him, he is willing to break the code to save a friend, to save Montrose from the brunt of Mr. Vernon's wrath—which could simply indicate the strength of his friendship, if it weren't that he is also saving himself. The plot crisis is finally averted by one of those timely coincidences that mask ideological crisis: the arrival, in this case, of an uncle ex machina, willing to tell the full story.

More subtle is *The Crofton Boys* (1841), in which Harriet Martineau acknowledges the code against talebearing while carefully hedging her portrayal of it. A new boy named Holt unwittingly violates it, telling the usher that other boys are teasing him and the hero Hugh and thereby preventing the two from studying. The other boys of course become angry. As Martineau explains, Hugh "believed it was settled among schoolboys . . . that it was a braver thing for boys to bear any teasing from one another than to call in the power of the master to help. A boy who did that was supposed not to be able to take care of himself; and for this he was despised, besides being disliked, for having brought punishment upon his companions" (75–76). Martineau is unusual in providing a rationalization for the code, a rationalization whose emphasis on bravely bearing teasing, rather than on opposing adults, could sit reasonably well with adult authorities. At the same time, though, she makes it clear that she is simply reporting Hugh's belief and, furthermore, that she is reporting what Hugh believes that schoolboys believe—doubly distancing herself from the code.

Still, when Hugh later declines to tell who was responsible for pulling him off a wall and thus laming him, his mother encourages him in his stance. In part, perhaps, Mrs. Proctor is co-opted into accepting the child's perspective, yet also her endorsement of Hugh's stance defuses the extent to which talebearing enforces opposition between adults and children.

More strikingly—and more effectively defusing it—the code is implicitly invoked against an usher, for telling boys of the prattling he overheard when Hugh was on his way to school for the first time. An admirable older boy muses "that though it was not wise in Hugh to prate about Crofton on the top of the coach, it was worse to sit by and listen without warning, unless the listener meant to hold his own tongue" (63). In later canonical stories masters would respect the boys' code but would not be expected to practice it themselves. By making the code apply to masters as well as boys, as a matter of good manners, Martineau further diffuses opposition between boys and masters. Overall, she skillfully positions the code in her own economy of piety and manners, yet the complexity of her treatment is also testimony to shifting norms. As midcentury approached, the code and its contradictions became increasingly salient.

Witness *Reuben Kent at School; or, Influence as It Should Be* (1844), in which the evangelical American Helen C. Knight unquestioningly supports adult authority, though even she hesitates to let her virtuous schoolboy violate the code. A sign of her religious emphasis is her choice of hero. Three boys are rooming together—a temporary measure, the narrator assures us, for the rooms usually accommodate only two. One of the three is naughty, verging on wicked, someone who says he hates all teachers; one is pious; one is drawn in both directions. In a later story we would expect the hero to be the boy in the middle, someone with whom the middling range of readers could identify. But in Knight's book the hero is the pious Reuben and, true to his subtitle, he draws others in his godly wake.

Some disobedient boys, including one named Harris, have taken—stolen—food from Mr. Ashby's cellar. Since Reuben has noticed some suspicious behavior, Harris decides to implicate the boy by giving him some of the food—hoping to seal Reuben's lips by making him an accessory.

Does the strategy work? Of course not—sort of. It hadn't occurred to Reuben to tell, but now that they mention it, he is reminded of the behavior of another boy in connection with a prank involving a powder-train (an anticipation of the gunpowder prank that recurs in other U.S. school stories, such as Edward Eggleston's).[9] This other boy had denied knowledge of that prank, and Reuben decries the way the boy lied to screen others who deserved punishment; he adds, "I would not lie to save myself, and I would not lie for others" (50). And as for then being called a telltale, "That would be bad, . . . but not half so bad as to have my conscience keep telling me, I was a liar" (50).

Still, Reuben temporizes regarding the stolen food. He asserts that he would tell all if asked, but he will not apparently volunteer the information (nor does he seem to have volunteered information to adults in connection with the gunpowder incident). Furthermore, despite his avowals, despite his confidence that he would "never flinch from speaking the truth," he does feel "a slight shrinking to disclose what he knew of the affair" (52). And despite the narrator's reference to the near-"perfect peace that grew up within his bosom," Reuben's awareness of the "suspicious eye" of the boys (52) sullies the perfection of that peace.

Knight temporizes in the plotting as well. For matters never reach a crisis that requires Reuben to tell tales to an adult. Instead, his comments touch the heart of one of the culprits, who then confesses his guilt to Mr. Ashby. Yet we never learn how much this boy has confessed—did he implicate other boys as well?—nor do we witness his punishment nor that of the other culprits. Knight has, in short, evaded the problem.

She also evades it—like Fenn in the previous century—by displacing some of its echoes onto the next incident in the story. Reuben and his classmates are supposed to be copying their themes, but someone has taken the boy's quills and penknife. Reuben makes no accusations. He stoically bears the imputation of laziness—of being "unfaithful to yourself" and of "set[ting] a bad example" (65). And thus Knight gives Reuben the chance to show some of the moral courage shown by later heroes when they take the blame for a misdeed but refuse to tell tales. Yet Reuben does so without having to renege on his principles: he doesn't know, after all, what has become of his writing implements. But he must have a pretty shrewd idea, given his previous difficulties with Harris. Knight thus garners some of the positive associations of stoicism that the talebearing topos would later elicit while avoiding the onus of making her hero tell tales.[10]

The climactic treatment of talebearing appears exactly at midcentury, seven years before *Tom Brown's Schooldays*. E. (Emily) J. May's *Louis' School Days: A Story for Boys* gives full play to the contradictions associated with talebearing, even if not so much intentionally as unintentionally—not so much through the turmoil of a character's reflections as through what might seem to be confusion in the narrative. *Louis' School Days* would not perhaps be considered better than *Tom Brown's Schooldays,* but it is more revealing: it shows the schoolboy code under pressure, leading to uncertain, even contradictory, results. Published in 1850, May's book was in its fourth edition by 1855[11]—its popularity shows its resonance for readers in this decade of transition from adult to schoolboy codes in children's literature, from loyalty to Truth to loyalty to peers. May is pathbreaking in the way she problematizes talebearing.

She writes what is arguably the most conflicted boys' school story by a woman, and her stances toward talebearing are emblematic. On the one hand, deciding whether to report other boys' misdeeds to adult authorities is a litmus test of peer solidarity: boys expect other boys not to tell tales. Yet closing one's eyes to another's misdeeds is not right in the eyes of God. And like other early school stories, *Louis' School Days* is a profoundly religious book: it's clear that school authorities are to be obeyed; only bad boys disobey.[12] Certainly Louis Mortimer is committed to obedience, yet his popularity soars and plummets. Wrongly accused of using an illicit translation to help him with exercises, Louis at first names names but then is revered for taking the blame due another boy and for forgiving the boy for not speaking up. Louis then preens himself on his virtue, divulges confidential information to an adult, fears to confess to a practical joke and thus implicate another, is accused of stealing apples but refuses to tell tales to clear himself, and finally is restored to good favor. May seems a little uncertain at times in charting Louis' popularity—it's hard to see how, at his most priggish, he remains popular. And her treatment of talebearing reflects a similar uncertainty: sometimes Louis seems aware of the code against talebearing, sometimes not; sometimes boys punish those who violate the code, sometimes not. It's worth examining these incidents in detail.

When Louis is accused early in his first term at Ashfield Academy of using the illicit translation, he thinks nothing of implicating others. He feels no compunction about saying who had put the book in question near his books; he denies having taken it out of a classroom and attempts to incriminate a boy named Ferrers. But others believe that Louis, the newer boy, is guilty—and he is "looked upon as an unworthy member of the little society to which he belonged" (70), not just by Dr. Wilkinson but by his schoolmates in the upper classes. Still, there is no indication that Louis' unpopularity is due to tattling. Instead, it seems due to his being presumed guilty of cheating, to having been caught, to denying the charge instead of confessing—and hence presumably, given all the evidence, lying.[13]

Yet soon afterwards we are assured that there is indeed a schoolboy prohibition against telling tales. A younger boy admits to having seen Ferrers fetch the illicit book but prefaces his admission by saying, "It won't be telling tales out of school to tell you, Louis" (95–96). Young Alfred has a sufficiently keen sense of schoolboy honor to know that he should not tell a master what he has seen, though it may be acceptable to tell another boy. And Louis knows enough by now to admonish Alfred not to tell others about Ferrers' action—not to tell tales to clear Louis of suspicion. Yet the endorsement of the code here underscores how, earlier, Louis was violating it. Furthermore, it's curious that, as in *Tom Brown,* younger boys seem to have a surer grasp of the code than some of their elders do. Are older boys, as they approach adulthood, increasingly co-opted by adult authority? But then why would an older boy like Louis (more or less) increasingly adhere to the schoolboy code?

Later, after Ferrers has confessed to his dire deed and Louis has been basking in moral approbation, the latter is charmed by an imprudent and flattering family friend, a Mrs. Paget, into prattling on about school life, particularly about Ferrers. The prattle then becomes known at the school, thanks to a boy who has overheard Louis' conversation and subsequently enrolled. Thus the virtuous Louis, who had prevented Alfred from tattling even to save Louis' reputation, has in effect been tattling to an outsider: one boy angrily calls him a telltale and hypocrite.

His consciousness heightened with respect to telling tales, Louis then encounters several boys and a servant with what must be illicit apples. Louis doesn't want to bear tales, as he tells his virtuous friend Charles, but he feels uneasy about not doing so. He states that the servant Sally "is always doing forbidden things for the boys" (262). Charles urges him to tell Dr. Wilkinson, but Louis doesn't want to "get the boys into such a scrape" (262), nor does he want to be called a sneak. And despite Charles's admonitions that "If they are bad boys they deserve it," and that "if we conceal evil, when we may remove it by mentioning it, we make ourselves partners in it" (262),

Louis doesn't tell. He doesn't question whether the boys have indeed committed evil, as a twentieth-century reader might (when a child raids the cookie jar, do we consider her evil or simply naughty?). Instead he tries to dodge the incompatibility of schoolboy and Christian codes through uneasy evasions about fearing to be called a sneak and also through class and gender prejudice, latching onto the maidservant as the most guilty party.

Later still, Louis is reluctant to admit to a practical joke, to having taken what turns out to be the only copy of an essay that his older friend Hamilton wants to submit for a prize. Louis is even more reluctant, once found out, to divulge who had put the idea into his head: "I do not mean to say who was with me. He was not to blame for what I did" (295). Through the adroit questioning of Hamilton, who has strong suspicions about which boy it was anyway, Louis nonetheless lets the name slip. In the give-and-take that follows, another boy remembers Louis' indiscretion with Mrs. Paget and accuses him of being "a tell-tale—a traitor—in the camp" (296). Yet Louis is astute enough to counter the charge: "If there hadn't been another as great . . . you would never have known of me; but you bear with him because you can't turn him out" (296). That is, the indiscretion with Mrs. Paget would never have been discovered if a new boy had not told on Louis. And Louis' phrasing here suggests May's uncertainty: Louis does not stop at the semicolon but goes on to vitiate his argument—why shouldn't the boys have to bear with Louis too because he can't be turned out? Furthermore, it's not the new boy who is distrusted here, as when Louis accused Ferrers of using an illicit translation and brought opprobrium on himself. And while it is true that this dialogue may catch some of the slips and uncertainties of actual conversation, May does not elsewhere seem to be aiming at this kind of verisimilitude: she might almost be trying to make Louis self-deconstruct.

Well schooled by now in the niceties of schoolboy honor, Louis subsequently refuses to tell Hamilton whom he suspects of a later theft of apples. Louis is wrongly accused but refuses to state his suspicions; Hamilton expostulates against Louis' "mistaken notion of honor," which leads to "doing an injury to others as well as yourself. You must remember, that these evil-disposed boys are still mixing with others, to whom their example and principles may do much harm, independently of the evil done to themselves by being allowed to sin with impunity" (308). Louis responds,

> I am called a tell-tale, and I know I deserve it; but the worst is, they call me a hypocrite, and say that religious people are no better than others. I could bear it if it were only myself, but it is more, and I have

given reasons for them to say all kinds of things. . . . But do not make me tell any more tales. I have promised, Hamilton—I dare not—I *will* not break my promise! (309, May's italics)

The overabundance of excuses shows how strongly Louis is drawn to the schoolboy code, despite its conflict with his understanding of Christian principle. He admits that he does not like being called a telltale. We may or may not fully believe him when he claims that it is worse still to be called a hypocrite and therefore bring opprobrium on religious people. And in case all that is not enough—and presumably it isn't, for what follows is the most telling reason with Hamilton—Louis has promised not to tell.

And Louis doesn't. But he is cleared—the wrongly accused schoolchild inevitably is in school stories, as if the author too doesn't dare trust only in heavenly rewards. The virtuous minor character Charles steps forward to make an accusation to Dr. Wilkinson—thus becoming a telltale, though he is not so called. As Hamilton tells Louis (thereby becoming, in a dizzying regress, a kind of telltale himself), Charles told Dr. Wilkinson that the culprit was surely not Louis but probably one of the boys to whom Charles had earlier seen the maid Sally give apples. Sure enough, when accused, Sally confesses—or rather blames one of these other boys—thereby herself becoming a telltale and deflecting some of the opprobrium we might otherwise be tempted to assign to Charles. In fact, Hamilton goes on to admire what he calls Charles's "truthful independence" (318).

But what are we to make of Charles's talebearing—and of Charles himself? Why, with all his "truthful independence," didn't he tattle about the earlier apple incident when it happened, especially given his willingness at the time to berate Louis for not tattling? Will Charles tattle only to save a friend? But surely that is not sufficiently principled. Will he tattle only when he is certain of his accusations? But he wasn't certain here. And what should we make of his relative unpopularity, the fact that "never once, from the first day he came to school, had he on any occasion incurred the displeasure of his masters; and yet no one cared for him, for he had lived only for himself" (265). Much as some opprobrium is deflected from Charles to the dubious Sally, some that might earlier have adhered to Louis is now deflected to the paragon Charles.

Nevertheless, Louis likes Charles, and Hamilton admires the boy. Further endorsement is that Charles wins the medal for good conduct at the end of the term. Of the various prizes, this one is, Dr. Wilkinson has told us, "the greatest of all" (129). There had, in fact, been considerable fanfare when Louis had won it the previous term, after having silently borne scorn and blame: Louis had not only been chosen by Dr. Wilkinson—thus being rewarded by an adult authority for not tattling—but had received the acclaim of his schoolmates. So Charles is merely following in the footsteps of Louis, the character with whom the reader presumably sympathizes. Yet the luster of Charles's meritorious conduct is slightly dimmed when we learn that Hamilton, the most likely other candidate, has privately withdrawn from the competition. Why he should withdraw is never made clear—as if the purpose of telling us is only to tarnish Charles's achievement. Furthermore, May buries the announcement of the medal in a paragraph detailing many prizes, unlike the many paragraphs that had heralded the award to Louis.

Still, Charles wins the medal. And, overall, his virtue is endorsed. Even his talebearing is not for the sake of personal aggrandizement but to clear the name of another (though we might be forgiven for wondering if the prospect of winning the medal had been entirely absent from his mind).

Yet despite this endorsement of the talebearing Charles, May lacks the courage of her convictions. The progress of her story shows Louis more or less increasingly accepting the schoolboy prohibition against bearing tales, despite its conflict with the dictates of religion—with the necessity of expunging evil. We are led to believe that Louis is nonetheless religious and will eventually enter the ministry. Still, toward the end of her story only Charles, a relatively peripheral character, and with all the ambiguity accorded by lack of popularity, violates the schoolboy code in the name of religion.

Now maybe we shouldn't make too much of May's inconsistencies. It's important to keep in mind, as Gill Frith has noted with respect to girls' stories, that schoolchild codes are often just narrative devices, "subject to adaptation according to the demands of the narrative. . . . What matters, in fact, is not *what is done,* but *who does it.* Whether the character concerned has the reader's sympathy, or the reverse" (118–119, Frith's italics). And that's true in part. But the inconsistencies also illuminate the fault lines of conflicting loyalties and ideologies. Other writers are rarely guilty of lapses as resonant as May's—either their technique is equal to their story or they choose a plot that evades the contradictions associated with talebearing.

As is true of May in her sequel: *Dashwood Priory; or, Mortimer's College Life* (1855), set partly at Oxford, evades the contradictions, giving little play to talebearing. It's as if Louis—or Mortimer, as he is here called—is now too virtuous and steady to allow much interesting incident to happen to him, something that May tries to make up for through a flurry of physical displacements in the book, skimming from one locale to another.[14] In only two incidents is anything like talebearing broached. The first is merely a brief mention. Still at Ashfield Academy, Louis learns of the straitened circumstances of Ferrers, who has been obliged, upon the death of his father, to become apprenticed to a stationer. We might not make much of the fact that the boy who tells Louis of Ferrers' plight is referred to offhand as an informer—"'It is a just punishment for him,' said the informer" (50)—even though Ferrers had been involved in a talebearing incident in the first volume. Yet later when Louis does visit Ferrers—and visits him out of interest and concern, unlike others who come merely to gape—Ferrers says, "I don't believe you come to carry the tale of what the apprentice is doing, and how he looks. I know *you* are above that . . ." (62, May's italics). Thus May displaces the code against talebearing to a realm more acceptable to adult moral authorities: in part the code encompasses loyalty to a (former) schoolmate, but it is also redefined as a matter of Christian kindness, of not rubbing in a change in fortune, not allowing oneself to be governed by the superficial niceties of social standing.

In the other incident, at Oxford, something like talebearing does occur, though it is carefully hedged and qualified, as if May now has control of this trope (or Louis now so fully subscribes to religious authority that talebearing is less fraught with anxiety). Through the machinations of his cousin Frank—whom May has allowed to regress to some of the careless practical joking that had characterized him early in the previous volume—Louis has agreed to host a musical gathering in his rooms, subject to certain conditions, including an early hour of adjournment. Yet Frank and his friends become boisterous and rowdy; they deceive Louis as to the hour and lock the door so that he cannot get out. When a don or two come to object, Frank goes so far as to fire a pistol he has found lying around (he says he thought it wasn't loaded), though fortunately no one is hurt. Visiting with faithful old Hamilton the next day, Louis tells the whole story, for Louis is still bound to the young man by ties of friendship. Yet Hamilton has now received his degree and is serving as Louis' private tutor—is, in effect, a college authority. Hamilton gets the revelers to sign a statement exculpating Louis and presents it to the Head of the college. The onus of talebearing is thereby displaced onto Hamilton, a peer who is no longer a peer, and dissipated even further by his ability to persuade the guilty parties to incriminate themselves: Louis seems little to blame for either the rowdiness or the talebearing. Nor does May get at all exercised about the issue. She seems to know better how to control the contradictions, how to tidy the traces of disruption associated with talebearing.[15]

Yet in *Louis' School Days* the trope does cause disruption. Poised on the cusp of change, May documents the fissures between (and within) a religious view of authority and a newer child-centered one. She registers the tensions between new expectations and old conventions, or between the conventions of school and the outmoded conventions of the pre-Hughesian school story, or between the precanonical and the canonical school story, or perhaps between instructing and delighting the reader, or rather between overt and normative indoctrination. She marks the stresses that arose in the transition to a children's literature increasingly segregated by gender and class, a literature that could allow middle- and upper-class boys increased authority. The transition, in the history of school stories, from views espoused primarily by women writers to those espoused primarily by men.

For the gaps in the book, the inconsistencies, can be explained in part by May's crossdressing. She is a woman who provides only the initial of her first name on the title page, hiding the "Emily" behind the "E."[16] She has not herself attended the kind of boys' school of which she writes: at one point she admits that she will not "particularize the subjects for examination" since "my classical and mathematical ignorance might cause mistakes more amusing to the erudite reader than pleasant to the author" (114)—an unnecessary admission, for rare was the school story, before or after Hughes, that particularized such subjects. And May includes no comparable disclaimer in the sequel; she even sprinkles her dialogue there with a few shopworn Latin and Greek phrases, a *multum in parvo* here, an *argumentum ad hominem* there, an alternate manifestation, perhaps, of her uneasiness.

May tentatively takes on the trappings of male authority, yet she is anxious and apologetic. It may be that in *Louis' School Days* she is writing about her experience in a girls' school, dressing it in trousers, in effect anticipating the stresses of the transition from private to public girls' schools, from an emphasis on dependency to one on peer loyalty, a transition that started in the midst of the century whose midpoint she straddles (see, e.g., Pedersen, "Women's" 68ff.). Or she may be bringing her experience of girls' schools to bear on what she has heard of boys' schools. Or even if she is simply rehearsing what she has read in earlier school stories, she does not acknowledge that, as an outsider, as a woman writing of a boys' school, she can bring insights and interrogations that most men seemed unable to.

May's uneasiness is reflected in the roles she allots the most prominent women in the book, marginal though they remain. Neither the servant Sally nor the family friend Mrs. Paget is altogether trustworthy, one abetting a kind of stealing, whose perpetrators would oppose talebearing, the other abetting a kind of talebearing. Women are thus associated both with those who might oppose talebearing, not wanting their evil deeds to come to light, even if they indulge in it themselves, and those who elicit it, however imprudently.[17] It is significant that neither of the males who tries to elicit talebearing—Charles, Hamilton—is seen as imprudent. May displaces onto Mrs. Paget, the imprudent elicitor, some of the negative associations readers might have with talebearing (though also, perhaps, showing the undesirability of talebearing by associating it with a woman, and thereby undermining some of May's own authority and import). Similarly, Sally's association with some evil boys (or are they naughty?) serves as a lightning rod for their evil (she led them astray) and as a marker of their evil (their actions must be dubious if their confederate is both a woman and a servant): she may simultaneously be a sign of their evil and also, if she led them astray, if she is somehow responsible, imply that they are merely naughty. By intensifying the sense in which the boys are both, the presence of Sally intensifies the hesitation between—and consequent foregrounding of—the evil and the merely naughty, much as, overall, May foregrounds and intensifies contradictory attitudes toward talebearing.

And much as these women are ambiguously associated with both opposing and eliciting talebearing—and with negative sanctions either way—so perhaps is May: she has trouble locating herself, locating a narrative stance. Yet despite—or perhaps because of—her uncertainties, May broaches fundamental issues: she hints at the deviousness of all authors who tell tales about telling tales (as I am doing now). Is telling tales in the sense of telling on someone ever far from telling tales in the sense of lying? Can we ever trust what we are told? Is there inevitably something dubious about the teller? May foregrounds and problematizes authority, including her own. And by calling into question the cosmetic unities of subsequent male authors, who gloss over the ways in which peer authority undermines adult authority, including that of the author, May sheds light on the fissures between (and within) the predominantly female tradition of the school story before Hughes and the male tradition, the public tradition, afterwards.

Notes

1. In girls' school stories, fagging is never an issue, unlike schoolgirl raves, which were prominent in late-nineteenth- and twentieth-century girls' school stories (and schools—see Benson 39–41; Vicinus, "Distance"). And even men writing of boys didn't express much of the trope's sexual potential before the twentieth century and the elite school stories.

2. Not that such wit is worth emulating—as Archer notes, one boy "has puns in plenty; but, when there's work to be done, he's the worst fellow to be near one in the world—he can do nothing but laugh at his own puns" (97).

3. Here I disagree, in emphasis at least, with Pickering, who states that most early children's books warned children against becoming telltales, a statement that he qualifies by noting, "Exceptions to this kind of advice appeared for the most part in books for very young children for the lower classes . . . or in books written primarily for girls" (*Moral Instruction* 169). For accounts that chart some of the code's shifting

terrain—specifically toleration of talebearing in some twentieth-century British schools—see Auden and Raven.

4. Sending to Coventry—the shunning of a schoolchild by the other children—inverts the code against talebearing in that it shows the fracturing of schoolboy solidarity. Yet it also reinforces such solidarity by providing sanctions. As inversion, it may be a suitably symmetrical punishment for talebearing. As reinforcement, it perhaps allows for rehabilitation.

5. It's significant, as P. Scott notes, that it is a story about a private school rather than a public one, a school where small-group moral responsibility prevails ("School Novels" 163, 177). Among later canonical stories, the most one can hope for is that a boy will experience some inner turmoil, as in George Manville Fenn's *Burr Junior: His Struggles and Studies at Old Browne's School* (1891). When Burr takes the blame for something he thinks his friend Mercer has done, for instance, we see him silently curse his friend, assure himself his mother would believe his innocence, be overcome by the thought of what his uncle would think, almost capitulate. But Burr holds out, and is cleared, and so is Mercer. Fenn gives some play to the complexities of the code but evades a full working out of its implications by rescuing the boy anyway.

6. Atwood is writing as the later Susannah Strickland (see the discussion of *Hugh Latimer* below), after the latter has married and emigrated to Canada. The "they" who "almost taught me," in "Departure from the Bush," are animals, representatives of the wilderness. The poem would thus seem to be addressing the opposite of what *Hugh Latimer* addresses, if the civilizing effects of school are opposed to the effects of the Canadian bush, though maybe what is almost learned is not so very different.

7. She had originally called it *The Parent's Friend* but the publisher changed the title to *The Parent's Assistant* (see Pollard 349).

8. A favorite crux in Edgeworth criticism has been the extent to which Richard Lovell Edgeworth was responsible for inspiring and shaping Edgeworth's work, whether for good or (more often) for ill—see Butler 6ff.; Davie 68; Harden 17ff.; Murray, *Edgeworth* 25ff.; Murray, "Edgeworth"; Newby 10ff.; Omasreiter 195. As Myers has noted, "paternal influence has usurped even more space in studies of her work than in her life" ("Dilemmas" 77). Though indeed, as Myers points out, Edgeworth "needed a relational motive to write, whether her father or another of her family"; with respect to her father, "he was the sole determinant of neither her literary nor her private identity, but a commanding presence within a larger relational field that changed over time . . ." (77).

9. A prank notably absent from British school stories (except for Sherwood and Kelly's *Boys Will Be Boys,* 1854)—as if gunpowder plots might savor too much of Guy Fawkes, of what the authors would consider sedition against just authority. Mack cites one contemporary headmaster as especially fearing rebellions—barrings out—on Guy Fawkes Day (*1780–1860* 82).

10. Contrast the treatment here with that in Knight's more heavy-handed school story about girls. When the teacher leaves the room, in *Annie Sherwood; or, Scenes at School* (1843), the girls engage in some illicit talking. Even the eponymous Annie momentarily forgets herself and responds to a question. When Miss Wallace returns, having overheard some of the noise, she asks those who have been speaking to stand up, but "no one moved. Annie, who had expected to see them all comply with this command, as they had all broken the rule, looked up and down the class in astonishment" (29). Then she herself rises—not immediately, mind you, though the narrator doesn't make anything of that. When individually asked if they have disobeyed, some of the girls confess, others lie, and Miss Wallace reproves the class for disobedience. Annie is later scolded by her schoolmates: "If you had only kept your seat . . . we should all have escaped one severe lecture" (35). Annie responds that "I only told the truth respecting my own conduct" (35). But one girl retorts that Annie's wondering look around the class was as good as telling, and accuses Annie of think-

ing herself a saint. And there the incident is left, in a narratorial impasse.

11. Though of course it didn't compare in popularity to *Tom Brown's Schooldays,* which went into a fifth edition within seven months (see P. Scott, "School" 35).

12. With the possible exception of Louis' cousin Frank, who is a carefree practical joker during the first half of the book but then settles down and even wins prizes at the end of the second term (though May allows him to revert to his earlier ways in the sequel, *Dashwood Priory,* to provide some vivid incidents at Oxford that would not otherwise have attended the sedate Louis). Through Frank, May can make the point that hard work counts more than natural ability, for Dr. Wilkinson decides not to give the idle and mischievous Frank a prize at the end of the first term, despite Frank's strong examination results. Dr. Wilkinson even overrides the recommendation of an outside examiner. Then, as if feeling a little guilty about depriving Frank of his award, May makes him work hard the second term and win several prizes. Still, rather like the private girls' schools that Pedersen describes ("Women's" 69), this private boys' school tends to reward boys more for their behavior, for working hard, than for achieving academic excellence—or rather, May and Dr. Wilkinson are drawn both ways, acknowledge both kinds of merit, even if they try to reward one more than the other.

13. That greatest of childhood offenses in nineteenth-century Britain: "It was so obviously a mortal sin that there was no point in constructing a moral tale round it; one did not moralise to children about murder. The very word 'lie' became an obscenity; 'untruth,' 'story,' 'fib,' 'whopper,' 'crammer' were substituted for it" (Avery, *Childhood's Pattern* 141).

14. A flurry of displacement hinted at by the clash between the main title and the subtitle—is the book set at a priory or a college?—and displaced even further by the elevation, in the U.S. edition, of the subtitle to the title.

15. Not so for other contradictions, such as whether it is appropriate to strive for earthly glory at college—which Louis both does and does not do, rather like his relationship with talebearing in the earlier volume.

16. Her name is so well hidden that at least one early reviewer, quoted in the advertising supplement in the U.S. edition of *Dashwood Priory,* assumes she is a male—"someone who can recall his own youth." And although her gender is correct in Allibone's *Critical Dictionary* (1870), her first name is given as Edith (she is described as being "favourably known as the author of a number of juvenile works which have obtained considerable celebrity both in England and in the United States"); it's not until Kirk's supplement, two decades later, that her name appears as Emily, though even then the compiler lists only a late work of hers, apparently not connecting her with the Edith in the earlier volume. The confusion continues into this century: U.S. libraries, according to the *National Union Catalog,* tend to call her Edith; British libraries, according to the *British Museum General Catalogue,* are more likely to call her Emily, differentiating her from a contemporary called Edith May, who published poetry in the United States.

17. Sally may be so outside the system—beyond the pale—that she can be associated with both ends of the talebearing spectrum, both those who oppose it and those who endorse it. She may, in effect, be someone for whom the codes do not apply. Perhaps that's true for Mrs. Paget too? And what of Charles? Does his exemplary virtue somehow place him beyond the pale, somehow feminize him, as if ordinary schoolboy rules cannot register his virtue? Is May, in short, broaching the incompatibility of schoolboy codes and Christianity?

5 AT MIDCENTURY

MARY MARTHA SHERWOOD AND OTHER TRANSITIONAL WOMEN

Like E. J. May, other midcentury women who wrote of boys played out increasing tensions and contradictions in the school story—before, in 1857, *Tom Brown's Schooldays* consolidated a new stance, a stance that vested authority in the boys themselves. These women not only invoked Christian and moral virtue, reiterating earlier themes, but also anticipated later ones, tentatively questioning adult authority and broaching the possibility of increased peer influence. Three works in particular, all British, all overlapping in theme and approach, serve as compendia of the intersections between early and late school stories: Mrs. (Mary Martha) Sherwood's *Robert and Frederick: A Book for Boys* (1842), her and Mrs. (Sophia) Kelly's *Boys Will Be Boys; or, The Difficulties of a Schoolboy's Life: A Schoolboy's Mission* (1854), and C. (Charlotte) Adams's *Edgar Clifton; or, Right and Wrong: A Story of School Life* (1852).

All three books create a gap between school and family, one that allows for some disjuncture between adult authorities. Families are crucial here, in part because of the way they are structured: as in much early children's literature, the moral is driven home through a contrast between good child and bad child—in this case it is good and bad cousins, sometimes contrasted at length, sometimes in passing. In addition, the central characters are fatherless—and that is partly why the boys need to go off to school. In part such familial structuring enables some bridging between family and school, some merging of the two; the schools are in fact small private schools that function like families. Yet the fact that the boys are fatherless hints as well that the authors are not convinced that other boys need to be sent away to school. A gap remains between school and family, allowing room for some questioning of adult authority and for the emergence in each novel—perhaps necessitating the emergence, to bolster adult authority—of a figure from yet another realm, a preindustrial realm: a laboring-class woman.

The most coherently crafted exemplars of the early school story—the least conflicted, at least on the surface—are those by Sherwood.[1] Born in 1775, she was one of the best-known authors of children's books in the early nineteenth century. She has also been described as "the most fiercely didactic of all writers of the moral tale"—though in later life she "reached the belief that 'salvation was wholly unconditional, a free gift of Divine love, that every creature was safe in the hands of his Creator and his Redeemer'" (Carpenter and Prichard). In the first volume of *The Fairchild Family* (1818), though, she created one of the most infamous scenes in children's literature: when siblings quarrel, their father takes them to a gallows to see the remains of a man who had been hanged, a man whose quarrels with his brother had culminated in murder.[2] A couple of years later she prepared an expurgated version of the first school story, Fielding's *The Governess* (1749, 1820), leaving out imaginative tales and infusing the whole with evangelicalism.[3] Sherwood had mellowed somewhat by the time she wrote her two boys' school stories, though Christian teaching is still central.[4]

Her moral purpose, for instance, is imparted through the deployment of polarities. The good-boy–bad-boy polarity had been a staple of eighteenth-century children's literature, though the boys were then apt to have allegorical names like Tommy Playlove and Jacky Lovebook. In *Robert and Frederick*, Robert is good and Frederick bad. Robert is the kind of boy who volunteers to tutor the youngest boy at school and unshirkingly accepts blame for a theft he has not committed.

Frederick, on the other hand, shows his mettle as soon as we are introduced to him: he pelts a laboring-class woman with a pellet of paper. Later Frederick deceives his little cousin Willy into straying from the yard, then helps to scare him, so that Willy runs away and almost plunges into the millstream—to be saved by the Jenny Groves whom Frederick had previously pelted. Not one to mince words, the narrator tells us, "How often has that ill-will, which has begun in as little a thing as poor Willy's offence against Frederick, ended in murder!" (54). But the narrator is one to mince incidents, allowing Willy to be rescued.

At school the opposition between good boy and bad translates into an opposition between two parties, as in Edgeworth's "The Barring Out" (1796)—and Frederick, of course, joins the wrong party. Yet Sherwood goes some way toward deconstructing the polarity, in keeping with Christian principle, for the virtuous party, that of Edward Somerville, both is and is not a party. As Robert explains, Somerville "will not have a party; but there are some of us who call him our king because we love him so much, and there is nothing we would not do for him" (157). Robert adds, "I think there always will be parties in schools" (157). Though there aren't any—at least they are not clearly defined—in the subsequent *Boys Will Be Boys,* by Sherwood and her daughter.

The polarities in *Robert and Frederick* are further compromised by Sherwood's desire to make the leader of the less virtuous party, Frank Faulkner, relatively admirable, in fact quite admirable by the end. It's not finally the revered Somerville but Faulkner who first senses, of the assembled schoolboys, that Robert is innocent of a suspected theft.

And the polarities are compromised by conflicts in characterization: one of Sherwood's impulses is to portray characters as static types, either good or bad, to convey moral judgment, yet she also wants to allow characters to reform. Early on, when Robert is fretting over what he can do to keep Frederick from bad influences, Somerville suggests letting matters take their course, letting the Creator work in His mysterious ways. So far so good. Somerville assumes that humans cannot effect changes of character: characters are static types; only God can wreak sudden conversions. But soon afterwards Somerville urges his counterpart Faulkner to rescue Frederick from the clutches of the wicked schoolboy John Greaves. At issue here is whether sudden conversions from one type to another are plausible, or whether change is more gradual and conflicted. Sherwood decries books that show sudden conversions, for even when the Holy Spirit descends it is "always carrying on a warfare with the old cor[r]upt nature; and though always conquering, yet never approaching to any thing like an agreement" (319). Yet if the Holy Spirit "always conquers," why exert oneself to change? The paradoxes of her Christian beliefs—that individuals can and cannot change—reinforce the paradoxes of her characterization—that characters are unchanging types and that they can nonetheless change.

Implicated in both theories of character is Sherwood's treatment of Frederick's illness. On the one hand, his moral invalidism is of a piece with his physical invalidism, the latter a bodily manifestation of his ill deeds. Yet the physical illness also becomes an agent of moral regeneration, an instrument of divine goodness, making the boy daily "more and more sensible of the utter meanness and selfishness of all his past conduct" (344). His body is not just a moral marker of a static character but an instrument that enables him to undergo moral change.

Much as his physical and moral functioning are impaired, so is Frederick's cognitive functioning. Or rather the cognitive is deficient if not allied with the moral—and here Sherwood is countering advocates of natural reason, like Edgeworth. Frederick relies too much on mere reason. So do the followers of Frank Faulkner, who call themselves Frankensteins—as if to hint at reason gone amok. One of Mrs. Moss's great weaknesses is her feeling that her son Frederick can find his way to religion when he is ready (a view uncomfortably close to Somerville's); hence she will wait until his reason matures; meanwhile she relies on reason to guide her children "by letting them discover from experience what are the natural results of every mode of acting; as, for example, that sickness and pain are the consequences of greediness . . ." (23). Yet Mrs. Moss's reasoning is contradictory: she argues that reason is already Frederick's guide, though his reason is not yet sufficiently mature to lead him to religion. In fact, Frederick uses his reason to violate the dictates of right religion: he consistently uses such powers as he has "not to find out what was good and right, but what would bring him to his object in the way least disagreeable to himself" (42).

So Frederick falls prey to the senses, especially that of taste: his "head was too full of toasted muffins and other eatables to leave room for the operations of his boasted reasoning faculties" (168). His desire for such delicacies as tea and cake leads him into bad company—he agrees to "go chum" with Greaves, the worst boy in the school. And it is appropriate that a schoolboy jest that Frederick falls for, early on, pivots on eating—on eating candle ends. In general, as the narrator says, a person should not "expect his senses to assist him in escaping a temptation" (269). It is the sense of sight, in fact, that finally betrays Frederick into the sin that leads to the book's climax, for once he has caught sight of Faulkner's money box, he cannot resist the temptation to steal.

And in succumbing, suffering the consequences, and eventually learning the error of his ways, Frederick paradoxically shows the truth of his unwise mother's assertions—that he will find his way to religion when he is ready, that he will be taught virtue by experiencing the consequences of his sins.

Sherwood and Kelly's *Boys Will Be Boys* is similarly religious, at least in intent. There's a good boy and a naughty boy—now, more than a decade later, Brewster is not as bad as Frederick, just (as the title implies) high spirited.

Yet countering the Christian thematics is the book's financial, materialistic plotting, a focus on the things of this world—for all that the virtuous Reginald's financial plotting is for the sake not of himself but of his brother James. Little James keeps pining for his older brother, and Reginald tries to figure out how to get James to Mr. Masefield's school. He knows how much his mother is able to pay and what James's school expenses would be: a child younger than eight is charged 25 pounds, though if he has an elder brother and the two sleep together the charge is only 21.

One way that Reginald gains funds is through an arrangement made by his grandfather. Dr. Prichard, financing the educations of Reginald and his cousin Brewster, will supply the same funds to each: if one has more expenses than the other, the other will be granted a like sum, to spend as he sees fit.[5] Fortunately, the naughty Brewster has been racking up charges. One prank eventuates in a broken tumbler and salt cellar (worth 5 shillings); another results in a smashed window, among other damage (9 shillings 7 pence).

Then there are details about Reginald's slow accumulation of other funds: 5 shillings here, 3 there, amounting to a total of 20 pounds 14 shillings 7 pence, or some 5 shillings 5 pence shy of the necessary 21 pounds. Now if it weren't for Reginald's pride and independence it would not be difficult to come up with the remaining money. He could ask his grandfather. Mr. Masefield and his wife would be happy to accommodate him by charging James somewhat less. Even a repentant naughty boy, who has tempted Reginald to do wrong and has offered a bribe of 5 shillings, gives that 5 shillings to the Masefields to be set aside for James—since of course Reginald would be too proud to accept the money directly. If only, as Brewster laments, he could have been guilty of "another piece of mischief" (289) to increase the amount his grandfather will give Reginald—and thus do Sherwood and Kelly find value in mischief, especially given the way, as the title avers, boys will be boys. And given the way the authors endorse materialism. As a reviewer of Sherwood's autobiography (which was edited by Kelly) has said, addressing the whole of Sherwood's work, "After ever so careful and conscientious a perusal, reading all the didactic parts, and skipping nothing that was dull, what remained longest, and left the most real impressions from her books, was their strong appreciation and exaltation of beauty, wealth, rank, elegance, and all worldly advantages whatever" (Review of *Life* 362).

In Adams' *Edgar Clifton,* too, religious education is paramount, though instead of spotlighting the contrast between good and bad (or good and not-so-good) boys, Adams focuses on the improvement of a not-so-good boy. She relies on a theory of character that might lend itself to a linear plot of progression, whereas Sherwood gives more credence to a static conception that might lend itself to a plot of community.

Yet, in fact, Adams' book is less linearly plotted than Sherwood's.[6] Like much early children's literature, *Edgar Clifton* is repetitive and cyclical, veering toward what Sandra A. Zagarell has called narratives of community, episodic narratives that focus on "the continuous small-scale negotiations and daily procedures through which communities sustain themselves" (503). Such works may be particularly congenial to women, for whom "it is really a question of another economy which diverts the linearity of a project, undermines the target-object of a desire, explodes the polarization of desire on only one pleasure, and disconcerts fidelity to only one discourse" (Irigaray 104). Although Clifton does progress toward goodness, the rhythm of the story depends on repeated encounters with small temptations, "great ones being but rare; and as we conduct ourselves under these petty trials so are our habits formed for bearing patiently or otherwise the real ills of life" (C. Adams 141). Each cycle starts with Clifton making a decision—whether he decides not to sacrifice pocket money to help the worthy poor or in his eagerness to pick some grasses falls into a river—and in each case he acquits himself poorly, muses on what he has done, and, especially later in the book, attempts to redress his wrongs. Adams may thereby capture some of the instability and nonlinearity of gradual change, but the effect is more reiterative than cumulative. In short, while Sherwood creates static characters who presumably change through linear plotting, Adams creates a developing character who essentially stays the same.

Adams also tends to be more egalitarian than Sherwood. True, in all three novels Christianity is to some degree egalitarian, making all to some degree peers before God. Pupils may, for instance, teach other pupils, becoming authorities for one another. Yet the emphasis on egalitarianism is strongest in *Edgar Clifton,* where Adams seems little concerned whether boys will inappropriately help one another, whether they might band together against adults.[7]

In the social sphere as well Clifton learns some measure of egalitarianism: he learns to look beyond a boy's family background, learns that he should not look down on little Bennet because the boy's father is in trade. His virtuous friend Harwood reminds Clifton of "the common origin of all men" and of "the constant rise and fall in station of persons in our commercial country," not to mention the fact that "many of our first families . . . had their origin far below that of John Bennet"; finally Harwood hints "that it was beneath him thus to tease the little boy" (106). Again, though, Adams seems to belie her intentions. For her plotting implies that she does look down on Bennet. For one thing, she compounds his class marginality by making him the youngest boy, and although the youth of the youngest schoolboy in *Robert and Frederick* gives him, as we shall see, greater access to truth, Bennet's seems simply to contribute to Clifton's desire to persecute: juvenility effectively reinforces lower-class status. Furthermore, Adams punishes Bennet's father with financial reverses for the purpose, it seems, of calling forth Clifton's benevolence: Clifton makes a small sacrifice so that he can then pay for Bennet's education. What is important is the effect not on Bennet but on Clifton; reduced to the instrumental, Bennet is effectively punished so that Clifton can be educated. Bennet is finally so marginalized that he fails, at the end, to make it to Clifton's coming-of-age celebration, unlike every other character, major or minor; instead Bennet writes a letter from India, that convenient repository for the fictionally excessive.

Nor is Bennet the only character who suffers reverses for the benefit, it seems, of Clifton. Clifton's cousin Laura, whose presence he finds galling, is rewarded with smallpox[8]—though happily without significant scarring, and Clifton's eventual settlement of an estate on her enables her to marry a man of small means. The worthy laboring-class Robert Lee, in whose presence Clifton has felt uncomfortable because of his own lack of charity, is also struck down—giving Clifton another chance to act charitably, this time providing employment. The adversities that strike those whom he early considered his enemies subtly reinforce Clifton's early views, as if to show that all will work out as he secretly desires if only he seems to comply with adjurations to respect other people. All meet with adversity, it would seem, to justify Clifton's paternalistic benevolence.

Whatever egalitarianism Adams is advocating has clear limits with respect to class. Clifton helps the worthy poor in a manner that keeps them firmly in their place: there is no question of helping Robert Lee attend school, as Clifton helps Bennet. Nor—except for the final roll call enumerating the fates of both major and minor characters—do we hear of Robert and his mother again, once they are shepherded to Clifton's family estate.

In all three novels issues of authority assume some prominence and even urgency. Most of the adults in these works are worthy of respect. Yet Adams' relative egalitarianism starts fraying some of that authority. In the other two works, adult authority is frayed through the treatment of jests and talebearing.

In *Robert and Frederick,* for instance, we are told that the truly religious do not perform jests, or practical jokes: only a boy like Greaves, "a thorough young quizzer" with "much genuine ill-nature" (205), so indulges. So what do we make of the fact that an admirable graduate of the school plays a prank on Greaves, replacing the latter's clothes with some disreputable ones? True, it's in return for a similar prank perpetrated by Greaves, enabling him "to feel for a little while, in your own person, something of what it is too much your delight to make others feel," to realize further "that one who, like yourself, is ever forward in practical jests, is liable—and deservedly so—to be the jest of other persons, and of persons perchance of more wit, or, if not, of more ill-nature" (244). Yet what of the perpetrator of the prank on Greaves? Does he possess more wit or more ill nature? Can one indulge in a jest without tarnishing the Christian and gentlemanly principles that the young man then goes on to extol?

Even harder to assimilate is Sherwood's provision of a recipe for how to prepare pieces of yellowish apple with slips of burnt almond so that they look like candle ends. The purpose of such preparations? To "deceive children who are not in the secret" (187), children such as Frederick, who has been deceived into trying to eat a candle end. This jest, we are told, is inappropriate. Yet is the jest inappropriate only because, as Robert later argues, Frederick "is not up to these sort of things" (195)? Then why does the narrator elsewhere argue that the truly religious don't indulge in jests—and why provide a recipe?

Further testing the limits of adult authority is the issue of talebearing, a trope prominent in both of Sherwood's works. In *Robert and Frederick,* Robert largely adheres to the code, though his adherence is aided by a promise not to tell who did in fact steal the money from Faulkner's money box (namely, Frederick). And one of the ways in which Frederick is shown to be less than admirable is through his readiness to tell tales with respect to the candle-end jest. The code is tarnished a bit, though, when its strongest adherent is Tim, a disreputable village boy who abets erring schoolboys. The bad boy Greaves too dims its luster, translating it into bribery, with the help of the colloquial language of lower-class thieves: he promises not to "peach" on a servant whom he has seen near the money box—in order to get her to say whom she had just passed leaving the vicinity (namely, Robert). Conversely, the inimitable Jenny Groves, with all her "simple" virtue, is not averse to telling a few tales—contributing to the revelation of the true culprit.

In the subsequent *Boys Will Be Boys,* in which the code seems to have even greater force, it also generates some complex maneuvers. Here it is the naughty but basically upright Brewster who is reluctant to tell on others, while the virtuous Reginald always gives precedence to duty. In the end, duty bids that he tell tales about a prank involving some gunpowder—tell tales at least to his cousin Brewster—though not before honorably revealing his intent to the guilty parties. Brewster readily agrees to confess his own part in the gunpowder plot, "perceiving the folly and worse than folly of which he had been guilty" (144),[9] but he has been confined to the schoolroom. So Reginald goes to Mr. Masefield to get permission for his cousin to come to the master's study, providing some intimation of what Brewster has to say.

Thus is the responsibility for talebearing shared between the two cousins, diffusing the blame and thereby hinting that, for all its virtue, talebearing is nonetheless blameworthy.

Yet if Sherwood, Kelly, and Adams are beginning to question adult authority and hence anticipate subsequent writers of canonical school stories, these three midcentury women nonetheless base their questioning on very different premises from those that would shortly dominate. For adult authority is here questioned in part because the school is less hermetic, much more permeable, than it would soon become in canonical school stories: the school is less clearly separated from the family (and hence females are less clearly excluded from the story), and the school is also less clearly separated from the surrounding community (and hence neighboring members of the laboring class are less clearly excluded).

As in other school stories by women, school is like a family, whether it is explicitly compared to one, the assembled boys called an "assembly of the family" (Sherwood, *Robert* 359), or the master's wife plays a role in the life of the school (as in *Boys Will Be Boys*). In *Boys Will Be Boys* Sherwood and Kelly are also unusually successful at making us care about the good boy—even though the not-so-good one gets the best scenes—in large measure because the story begins with Reginald and places him in a family context. We see him with a younger brother who looks up to him as a father, with sisters and a mother, with the grandfather who pays for his education. That is, Sherwood and Kelly put to good use one of the favored tropes of women writers, the sense of relationship with the family—a feeling perhaps especially acute in this book by mother and daughter—to give meaning and credibility to a standard didactic trope, the good-child–bad-child contrast.

Furthermore, since the fathers of the central characters in each book have died, the emphasis is on female family connections—enhancing the presence and valuation of women. For the most part these three authors, like others writing at midcentury before the cult of physical toughness and stiff upper lips, see manliness as comprising a "blend of compassion and courage, gentleness and strength, self-control and native purity" (Nelson, *Boys* 37), an ideal that parallels contemporary ideals of femininity. So perhaps it is not too surprising that in *Robert and Frederick* the most admirable adult, the only adult who is truly religious and wholly unflawed, is a woman, Robert's mother. True, the sadly flawed Mrs. Moss is female. Yet it is striking that the headmaster—he who is usually devoutly worshiped in school stories, both canonical and noncanonical, whether in *Tom Brown* and *Stalky & Co.* or in "The Barring Out" and *Little Men*—is portrayed in

Sherwood's volume with less than full approbation. He works his students hard and is an admirable classicist, yet too much a classicist: "All his ideas of what is valuable, or otherwise, in a human character, were imbued with the spirit of these heathen books, so that, as Christians, we must feel that we are truly sorry it was so" (146).

Or in *Boys Will Be Boys,* in which mothers are more peripheral, there may be the despicable village woman Betty Lea, an accessory to the gunpowder plot, but she is offset by the admirable Mrs. Masefield, the master's wife, even if the latter remains more in the background. Or in *Edgar Clifton,* Clifton's inadequacy is often measured against the virtues of a cousin who is a girl. This Laura is Clifton's closest competitor in an archery contest (the other schoolboys are handicapped by having spent their disposable incomes not on bows and arrows but on donations to the worthy poor). Adams is eager to show the measures Clifton will take to win, using his influence over Laura to distract her, getting her to lower her bow at his command. Yet she remains gracious, acknowledging that "Edgar cared a great deal more about winning the prize than I did, so it is better as it is" (51); she seems to realize that although her cousin is the physical victor, she wins the moral victory. Adams' choice of this game to portray in thrilling detail and also the point she wants to make are significant. A few years later canonical authors of school stories would provide detailed accounts of cricket or rugby matches so that the reader could enjoy the thrill of competition, the authors thus endorsing competition. But Adams wants to show the deleterious effects. When, on the same day, Clifton proposes a game of cricket, his fellow pupils decline to play, his behavior at archery—so clearly not cricket—having given rise to "a feeling nearly amounting to shame . . . , and they wished for the present to keep themselves as much as they could away from him" (59). Thus Adams succeeds in foiling male sports,[10] in part by focusing on a sport in which females could compete with males, a sport that not infrequently, in nineteenth-century fiction ranging from Alcott's *Under the Lilacs* (1878) to Eliot's *Daniel Deronda* (1876), becomes the site of a contest between male and female that likewise tests masculine and feminine roles.

Beyond the family, though, there are community connections—and here is where these three midcentury school stories differ most from others. Earlier boys' school stories by women generally include more interaction with the neighboring community than would later be allowed in canonical stories: in *School Dialogues for Boys* (1783) Fenn's schoolboys talk with miscellaneous adults who are passing through; in "Tarlton" (1796) Edgeworth provides a compassionate neighbor who mediates, to some degree, between boys' and masters' perspectives, while in her "Eton Montem" (1800) the townspeople help to reveal the villainies of the bad boy; in *The Crofton Boys* (1841) Martineau situates Hugh's aunt and uncle in the neighborhood of the school, giving him a place to visit and, once lamed, to convalesce. Later canonical stories, on the other hand, generally de-emphasize interactions with the local community and stress the ways in which school prepares boys for the world of empire—witness Kipling's Stalky, who extends his stalking to India.

Sherwood, Kelly, and Adams, however, allow the immediate community to impinge directly on school affairs and in a manner quite unlike earlier or later school stories, for the community impinges in the person of a laboring-class woman. And this figure plays an important role in the book, whether she resolves the complications of the plot or provides a moral touchstone or even speaks as an authorial mouthpiece. The closest parallel to these midcentury works is perhaps Edgeworth's turn-of-the-century tales, for she sometimes allows neighbors to intervene usefully in school affairs, yet she does not give this role to women of lower social status. This reliance on someone doubly outside the school—as a woman and as a member of the laboring classes—to resolve a key conflict is unique. In fact, it counters prevailing trends: Orwell later wrote of the public-school "contempt for foreigners and the working class" ("Such" 45); such contempt for the working class, likewise the lower middle class, is true of public-school fiction too. Nor is it altogether missing here: witness the laboring-class reprobates Tim and Betty Lea; witness further Clifton's initial disdain for Bennet, whose father is in trade. Yet the affirmative role played by some laboring-class women is telling. It's as if the stresses of relying on Christian virtue and high-minded moralizing are causing increasing discomfort, and not having worked out internal resolutions, these midcentury women turn to something outside the usual province of the school story.

Who are these pivotal laboring-class women? In *Robert and Frederick* Jenny Groves is a crucial truth-teller, someone who is instrumental in setting the plot to rights: Robert is rescued from the wrongful accusation of theft in large measure because of her intervention; she is likewise not averse to telling the naughty Frederick's mother about the boy's dangerous exploits—such as teasing a small cousin so much that the frightened child nearly plunges into the millstream, whence he is fortunately saved by the ubiquitous Jenny. Whether it is acceptable for Jenny to tell tales because she is religious or because she is lower class, she is crucially unconstrained by secular upper-class codes.

Jenny is in fact the clearest spokesperson against Mrs. Moss's mistaken views, Jenny's lower social class somehow enabling her to speak the truth. Countering Mrs. Moss's rather incoherent ramblings on laissez-faire childrearing and natural reason, Jenny explains that "reason is oftener busy on the wrong side than the right" (88). Later, impressed that little Marley was the one schoolboy to stick by Robert when the latter was accused of theft, she declares that such "a firm, fixed persuasion of anything . . . is most times built upon the truth. No one can force his belief; but truth has often forced belief contrary to many suspicious appearances" (355). Though why Marley's certitude is better than anyone else's is not clear—unless we believe that age, like class, is a medium for distilling virtue. The truth-tellers in this book are generally marginal, like little Marley, like laboring-class Jenny, thereby enacting the Christian belief that the last shall be first, the untutored wise, contrary though that is to the presumed import of the book—namely, to educate children.

Twelve years later in *Boys Will Be Boys,* a laboring-class woman is likewise instrumental in bringing the plot to a happy conclusion—even though she is somewhat more incidental, less of an authorial mouthpiece. Remember how Reginald plots to find the funds to bring his younger brother to school, as his cousin Brewster racks up expenses. Brewster happens to mention Reginald's financial woe to a neighbor, someone whom Brewster has fortunately injured in one of his escapades so that he pays her frequent visits to make amends. She in turn tells a farmer's wife of the boys' predicament—whereupon the farmer's wife rushes to the school, as Dr. Prichard is picking up his grandsons, and blurts out how she would be happy to supply the school with free butter to make up the difference in James's school fees. Thus does the boys' grandfather learn of the boys' problem, which he quickly resolves, only too happy to make up the small sum.

Two years earlier, in *Edgar Clifton,* interactions with the nearby village are similarly important. The archery contest, for instance, takes place at the home of a neighbor. More important still is interaction with the widowed Mrs. Lee and her son Robert. Mrs. Lee serves as a touchstone, underscoring, early on, how much Clifton needs improvement when he fails to contribute to her relief (it's at her expense that Clifton purchases a bow and arrows and is enabled to go on and best Laura). Clifton feels, for instance, that Mrs. Lee is accusatory when she comes to thank the other boys for their contributions (though of course, as an obliging member of the worthy poor, she wouldn't dream of accusing her betters). Later Clifton helps her son Robert when the latter is disabled. And finally Clifton provides a niche for mother and son at his family estate, for Robert as carpenter and Mrs. Lee as washerwoman.

The neighboring communities, in short, become metaphors for the world beyond the school, allowing this world to impinge upon school—even to set schooling to rights—and also perhaps preparing the boys for the outside world, not the world of empire but the hierarchies of the British class system. Yet the way that they show communities impinging on their fictional schools sets Sherwood, Kelly, and Adams apart from their predecessors and hints at the authors' anxiety about changes in their world—as if they want to deny the changes arriving with industrialization. For it is not a midcentury industrializing world that the boys and schools are embedded in but rather one that harks back to rural, preindustrial traditions. Now much children's literature has harked back to a time shortly before its time of writing, as if the authors can do no better for children than to invoke the times of their own childhoods. Other children's literature, eager to dissociate itself from the past, superimposes a version of a group's past onto an individual's; in *Tom Brown,* for instance, the preparatory school that Tom attended before Rugby is guilty of lapses—such as encouraging talebearing—that no subsequent public-school boy would tolerate. Sherwood, Kelly, and Adams, on the other hand, do not encapsulate and discard the past but integrate and even celebrate it. The stresses of industrialization are starting to tell, and by harking back nostalgically to an idealized notion of village life, one that emphasizes beneficial interconnections within the village, between high and low, the authors can try to negate the ills of industrialization.

On one level, it is true, these three midcentury authors may be dramatizing their estrangement from their subject by elevating someone who was excluded from boys' schools not just by gender, as the authors themselves had been, but by class. Yet turning to the community, specifically a preindustrial community, likewise hints at an increasing sense of normlessness: the traditional authorities are no longer fully adequate—not the family, not the masters, not even God. Nor are the authors prepared to vest full authority in the boys. Instead they shore up what authority they can patch together by turning to outsiders, specifically to laboring-class women.

NOTES

1. Or in which she had a hand. In what follows I will often refer to both single- and coauthored books as hers.

2. For a defense of Sherwood's scene in its original context, see Keith.

3. Though as Richardson points out, Sherwood then inserts "a surprisingly energetic tale which is, if anything, more imaginative than the one it replaces" ("Wordsworth" 38).

4. Cutt suggests that after the early 1830s "entertainment takes precedence over religion" in Sherwood's works (87; but see Demers 145). In the twentieth cen-

tury, commentators often look at Sherwood's later writings, especially her autobiography, with some surprise and delight, especially in contrast with her better-known, earlier works—better known in the nineteenth century in part because of their conformity to prevailing norms of didacticism and, eventually, because of their defining a norm that later practitioners moved away from (see Darton's edition of Sherwood's autobiography, which differs from that of her daughter, S. Kelly, by including more of the pranks and adventures, less of the preaching; see also N. Smith xviff. and M. Wilson 127ff.).

5. The narrator is a little nervous about any implications that there should be "a regular distribution of all property" (28)—God obviously ordains inequality—and so stresses that the arrangement teaches "a lesson on unnecessary expenses" (29). Though she is indeed implying some of the egalitarianism that she fears.

6. Demers similarly finds some of Sherwood's work "linear and thesis bound" (135). *Robert and Frederick* is in fact as carefully plotted as latter-day detective fiction—is in fact an early avatar of the detective story, as Frederick's guilt is carefully hidden from general knowledge, then, at a climactic gathering, suddenly revealed.

7. Further tending toward egalitarianism is that adults may be shown as subject to the same temptations as children, and may in turn be influenced by children. For discussion of how evangelical doctrine and stories counterpose to "the earthly hierarchies of age, sex, and rank a spiritual antihierarchy in which only humility brings power," see Nelson (*Boys* 8).

8. A reward as well for her unwomanliness in helping to rescue Clifton from a river accident.

9. Sherwood and Kelly's is the British school story least heavy with moral disapproval of a gunpowder plot—the escapade is portrayed as a prank, not as an exemplar of treasonous evil, even if it is referred to in passing as a "gunpowder-treason plot" (68).

10. As Sherwood does, temporarily, in *Robert and Frederick*: the money taken from Faulkner's box was to be used to purchase gymnastics equipment.

PART II
DURING THE HEYDAY
OF THE CANONICAL STORY

After 1857 the school story became preeminently one in which boys will be boys (in a way that Sherwood and Kelly could hardly dream of) at a boys' public school. Or rather *Tom Brown's Schooldays* crystallized gender segregation. By decreasing the importance of domestic and religious influence (though that is not exactly what Hughes himself did, that is the effect of his influence), Hughes made it more difficult for women to write about boys' schools and also, curiously, for men to write about girls' schools. And that despite the fact that contemporary men in other contexts—Lewis Carroll, George MacDonald, L. Frank Baum, Henry James—were quite happily writing about girls falling down rabbit holes or encountering goblins or getting caught up in tornadoes, or young women trying to find their niche in society.

Yet during the heyday of the canonical school story, no Englishman would be caught dead writing a school story for girls. I have found no girls' school story written by a British male, not even a girls' story set partly at school, from 1857 to the turn of the century. However feasible it may have been for a writer of fantasy, such as Carroll or MacDonald or Baum, to use the persona of a girl, or for a writer for adults, such as James, it seems not to have been feasible in a more realistic work addressed to children—or at least in a work with a more realistic setting.[1] In part, that may be because the boys' school story had become a recognized genre; men inclined to write a story about school had a ready outlet. But it also seems likely that men were disinclined to cross the gender barrier because of increasing gender segregation—because their masculinity would somehow be impugned if they did so. If a British male were inclined to transgress boundaries during this time, he would not write of a girls' school but instead, like F. Anstey in *Vice Versa* (1882), write a fantasy about a boys' school—young Dick exchanges bodies with his pompous father, to considerable satirical effect, thus anticipating the satiric emphasis that emerged when men once again crossgendered school stories in the twentieth century.

Certainly everyone who did write a crossgendered story between *Tom Brown* and the end of the century was either nonmale or non-British or both, nor did these mavericks particularly ape *Tom Brown*. Crossgendering became the province of those who lacked privilege in a literary system that exalted the male and the British. Perhaps not being fully privileged by the school-story genre, which is to say the public-school-story genre, enabled one to sample the forbidden.

That was especially so for those who were doubly unprivileged—for U.S. women. U.S. women not only crossgendered stories in some quantity in the second half of the nineteenth century, but often to remarkable effect. Their work so poorly fits the prevailing definition of the school story that it could be ignored, not even particularly recognized as school stories—and thereby the women were freed to do some pathbreaking work. I will be discussing two such pathbreaking works in later chapters on Louisa May Alcott and Julia A. Mathews, the one informing a boys' school with values considered feminine, the other constantly testing issues of gender as she portrays a "feminine" boy. Another author who invites extended attention, Ellen Wood (Mrs. Henry Wood), happens to be British; but her identification with the popular genre of sensation fiction also gave her a promising vantage point, as she sensationalized the school story. In effect, Alcott and Wood enacted the wrenching of crossgendering by wrenching the genre, crossing it with other genres—domestic and sensation fiction.

There were as well other works that, if less daring, also broached some questioning of rigid gender boundaries. And most have another element in common, besides being crossgendered school stories, whether they were written by British women, U.S. women, or U.S. men. That element is an unusual degree of attention and also, in a way, respect paid to one or more characters representing a traditionally denigrated other: in the United States, usually blacks; in England, usually someone from France or Germany (if not yet someone from the colonies).[2] As Cora Kaplan has pointed out, in nineteenth-century fiction, class, race, and gender reciprocally constitute one another, denigrations of each implying and invoking the others; thus a story about a governess like Jane Eyre distills the instabilities of both class and gender. Similarly, in the United States, the racial other can embody the instabilities of both gender and racial identity, gender and race invoking each other in associative chains of meaning, imbricated in each other's cultural meanings. If, in other words, as Spivak has argued, "the active ideology of imperialism . . . provides the discursive field," fueling "the narrative energy" of the likes of *Jane Eyre* (180), then race is the discursive field in U.S. fiction. Race itself of course is imbricated in the imperialist project, often in the form of paternalistic benevolence toward and re-education of blacks—what Spivak calls "the terrorism of the categorical imperative" (181).

Crossgendering authors of school stories can thus play out their own marginality, if they are marginalized by being women and/or Americans, by valuing characters who are marginal because of race, and in a way that embodies shared myths of nationhood. During and after the Civil War, cultural myths in the United States focused on uniting a divided people and on rethinking the position of African Americans—myths that could be distilled as the story of the relationship between two individuals, a black and a white, Jim and Huck. A significance that is only heightened if the story is set during the Civil War. In England, the sun was never setting on the empire, and a story of the relationship between an English child and someone of a different nationality or ethnicity could do the cultural work of rationalizing empire.

And to the extent that the racial or ethnic other is granted individuality in such a relationship, he or she is accorded some measure of respect. This respect for the other, this breaching if not yet demolishing of traditional hierarchies, is particularly striking given that the canonical school story, set at a British boys' public school, is decidedly ethnocentric, endorsing the aims and attitudes of empire as it prepares boys to become colonial functionaries.[3] Respect for those who are not just ethnically but racially different from the crossgendering author—respect that enables them to become preceptors for both characters and readers—then serves in part as a metaphor for the wrenching of hierarchy enacted by the author's crossgendering, becomes yet another playing out of the transgression.

Not that school stories had never before paid respect to the racially other. One strand of eighteenth-century children's literature in English, influenced by Rousseau's ideas on the noble savage, portrays the plights of "the black boy from Jamaica," "the Asiatic princess," or of "Congo in search of his master"—to cite the titles of representative works (see Jackson 157). Writing about blacks or Asians seems, for whites, to have served as a metaphor for expressing that—or a displacement of the fact that—one is writing for a generational other, for children. Yet given that British and U.S. schools were usually wholly white, such exoticism is difficult to incorporate in a "realistic" work about school—unless one incorporates a tale within a tale, as Johnson did in *The Little Female Orators* (1770), when he told of Inkle and Yarico. Still, writers of school stories did find ways of alluding to such parallel otherness. Strickland, for instance, lets us know in *Hugh*

Latimer (1828) that it is inappropriate for boys at Hugh's school to tease a black peddler, the black thus becoming a moral touchstone. But the racial other is not directly portrayed (and Strickland is guilty of a more negative portrayal of otherness when she makes poor Pedro's master a cruel Jew). Even more fleeting are Martineau's hints, in *The Crofton Boys* (1841), at the debilitating effect of India on Europeans, how it has spoiled a boy who ends up at Crofton—hardly a positive portrayal of the impact of racial otherness. In short, never before had respect for the racial or ethnic other been so central to the story.

The various U.S. women who crossgendered school stories in the last half of the nineteenth century include Anna Bartlett Warner, sister of the best-selling author Susan Warner and creator of "I Would See Jesus" and "Jesus Loves Me" (see Foster 73). *The Prince in Disguise* (1862), a brief evangelical story, is a particularly adept synthesis of the sentimental novel and the school story. Austin May[4] is the newest of the six (white) boys at Dr. Carn's school. Austin is religious, his one ally in the household the black servant Chloe. The other boys persecute him: they tease him about kneeling to say prayers; they intrude when he seeks solitude for religious contemplation. They even get Dr. Carn, none too religious himself, to contribute to Austin's misery—by curtailing the Sunday trips to church from two to one. But Chloe reports this state of affairs to the nearby minister, and he invites the school to his home. There he regales them with food and an inviting illustrated talk—first with respect to three powerful men of the world, a king, an emperor, and a sultan; then, having duly built suspense with respect to three "princes in disguise," a cobbler, a man in prison, and a martyr burned at the stake. Thanks to the patient example of Austin, himself a prince in disguise, and helped by the minister, one or two boys are brought closer to godliness by the end of the novel. The messianic zeal of the novel is directed, in short, toward the boys: the crucial boundary categories, delimiting what the narrator hopes to act upon, are those of age and gender. Or rather religion becomes a third source of cleavage, the narrator reaching across the first two to effect a change with respect to the third.

And the crosscutting interplay of the three can be subversive. The story opens with a discussion of where the new boy Austin could have gone after church. Surely he didn't stay behind to take communion. When one boy asks, "What if he *did* stay for that?," another explains that "why, then, he's better than the doctor: and *that*'s an act of insubordination" (6, Warner's italics)—rather clearly setting out how religion can subvert secular authority derived from age. Sure enough, the relatively carnal Dr. Carn is dismayed by young May. "Very improper!" he expostulates, for communion "is altogether too sacred a solemnity to be made a spectacle,—and without leave, too!" (7). In general, from Dr. Carn's perspective, Austin is "not enough of a boy" (57)—not sufficiently resistant, that is, to religious authority, too resistant instead to school authority.

Warner includes among her most admirable characters two women who are black servants, and thus simultaneously breaches hierarchies with respect to class, race, and gender. She portrays Chloe and Dinah without great condescension, given the time when she was writing. Yet such leveling or reversal is always under the aegis of religion; the women may be sanctified by religion but they are also subordinated by it. As "one of the Lord's people" (28), Chloe helps Austin to be a "standard bearer" for the Lord, comforts him, and knows when to turn—through the mediation of the mulatto Dinah—to the minister, the Rev. Mr. Beryl.

Chloe is also the medium through whom Warner introduces military discourse. Such discourse is a staple of the canonical school story: in *Tom Brown's Schooldays* the headmaster invokes the church militant to engage the boys in the endeavors of the school (and Edward Everett Hale would too, as if to assuage his anxiety over writing about women), even as he implicitly underscores the connection between the public school and the militarism of the British Empire. In *The Prince in Disguise* such discourse appears in connection with the evangelizing of the schoolboys. Chloe says to Mr. Beryl, "But now, Massa Beryl, you be de captain o' dis yere little Sweet Springs company—and dere's one of 'em hard set upon. 'Most had de sword knocked out of his hand, he has, like Christian" (54). Mr. Beryl allows such talk, though he does not initiate it and only reluctantly, as if it's in quotation marks, uses it himself: "It is kind of you, Chloe, to help the captain—as you call me—all you can" (54). Warner thus allows readers to have the analogy, allows such talk to attract her boy readers, without fully endorsing this laboring-class view of the church militant—a view further distanced by its being expressed in dialect (much as the schoolboys' use of colloquialisms is supposed to entice the reader but also indicate that what is voiced is not fully endorsed by a narrator who uses standard edited English) and perhaps also by its speaker being a black woman (who attempts to bolster her views by alluding to the work of a white man, John Bunyan, specifically his Pilgrim named Christian). Still, the military metaphors are apt given the Civil War provenance of the novel. It is appropriate, furthermore, that the character whose language hints at the wartime context—at a time when some people, at least, were fighting a holy war to end slavery—is herself black.

Warner also uses another trope traditional in school stories, though more to the fore in girls' stories than in boys': that of feasting. A version of the trope appears as early as Fielding's *The Governess* (1749), in which young ladies quarrel over a treat of apples. Yet most early children's literature—such as Sherwood's *Robert and Frederick* (1842)—focuses more on controlling one's appetite than on indulging it. Warner is one of the first fully to indulge this trope that gains prominence in the late nineteenth century and continues to be voiced in twentieth-century pop-culture stories by Enid Blyton and others—which wouldn't be complete without a clandestine midnight feast. Warner is able to shift the nineteenth-century valence of this trope—instead of being a sign of a boy's badness, physical hunger is both an avenue to and a reflection of spiritual hunger—in part because of a parallel between this secular feast and the early communion incident, making the feast an earthly embodiment of communion. And in part because she approaches from the angle of a sentimental novelist, someone who celebrates domesticity, including the preparation of food.

For Dinah's preparations for the minister's feast, her cutting and rolling, her wiping and paring, are described in loving detail. Then we are treated to a lavish description of the groaning board: the table under the trees, the white cloth, the pink and white crockery, the golden apples, the dish of cut-up peaches, the plum cake, the baskets of little cakes (some twisted, some heart-shaped), the plates of tarts and turnovers and bread, the milk and ham and beef, not to mention the carpet of grass and the dancing sunbeams. Perhaps the emphasis on preparation and visual appearance, together with minimal attention to the actual eating, mitigates the carnality of appealing to physical appetites. Still, as with the military metaphors, Warner both eats her cake and has it. She sacralizes the feast, making it a fitting complement to the concern over partaking of wine and wafer that opened the book—it too an absent feast, the eating not directly described.

Warner's sacralizing of the domestic and quotidian is akin to that in her sister's *The Wide, Wide World*. And much as the women in such sentimental novels are able, "By ceding themselves to the source of all power, [to] bypass worldly (male) authority and, as it were, cancel it out" (Tompkins 163), so is the boy in *The Prince in Disguise* able to bypass worldly (adult white male) authority as he submits to God. At the same time, though, in Spivak's terms, the book can be read as "an allegory of the general epistemic violence of imperialism, the construction of a self-immolating colonial subject for the glorification of the social mission of the coloniser" (185)—or if not fully self-immolating then self-effacing, as Chloe and Dinah serve not just God but also Austin. In this school story that is also a domestic story, it is hard, as Kathleen Diffley has said of contemporary works, to find "alternative roles for black characters to play" (645).

There were likewise some U.S. men who could be said to crossgender the school story, though only if one is flexible about what constitutes one. Take Oliver Optic's *Poor and Proud; or, The Fortunes of Katy Redburn* (1858). Eleven-year-old Katy is an entrepreneur who makes molasses candy and gets other girls to sell it—until, as so often happens in these rags-to-riches stories, she is helped by rich connections, in this case long-lost relatives. School is a luxury that the girl cannot afford until her business is well established and her mother well enough to lend a hand—or until, at the end, Katy comes into an inheritance as the granddaughter of a Liverpool merchant.

And even then school is mentioned only in passing, Optic's work thereby being emblematic: school is absent from his plot, as men absented themselves from girls' school stories. School provides an alibi, proving Katy's innocence of a misdeed; she has to wait till a half-holiday to follow one of her employees and catch the girl in dishonesty. Still, Optic manages to incorporate the canonical trope of the fight with the bully—even if it's not exactly at school. Katy's champion defends her from a boy who would intimidate her into giving him some candy. Thus does Optic transpose a staple of boys' school stories to a story for girls, as if he didn't know what else to do when portraying a girls' school, or as if to mask his uneasiness over writing for girls.

For Optic is apologetic about having written a girls' story. In the preface he apologizes not exactly for having written for girls but for having written a story that may seem a little improbable—"for Baron Munchausen and Sinbad the Sailor were standard works on my shelf in boyhood, and I may possibly have imbibed some of their peculiar spirit" (5). As if Katy's adventures are improbable for girls but not for the boys that Optic usually writes of. And as if he, like Carroll or later Baum, could somehow be excused for writing about girls if the story is somehow a fantasy.

Or take Glance Gaylord's *Miss Howard's School* (1866). Gaylord focuses on the teacher, Mary Howard, who, like Katy, has a mother to support: as in many other nineteenth-century works, a woman can be allowed to work only out of family necessity. He shows the process by which Mary tames the village children—what few of them need taming—and earns the gratitude of the villagers to the extent that they will, after this first term, provide permanent rooms for her and her mother, instead of making her board around from family to family.

Mary's main problem at school is Squire Wilson's son Johnny. He hides the school bell, destroys the school flower bed, and is generally disrespectful. Mary tames him through kindness, playing upon his inherent goodness so that he starts feeling guilty about the honor of having been chosen to buy confectionery and nuts for the school picnic (yet another feast). Finally she does what a canonical schoolboy hero would do: she rescues Johnny from drowning. And like the difficult schoolboy in many school stories by women, Johnny is tamed through temporary laming. In the course of his extended recovery from a broken leg, he finally overcomes his pride and asks Mary to forgive his pranks.

More noteworthy than either of these two works—and better fitting the rubric of the crossgendered school story[5]—is *Mrs. Merriam's Scholars: A Story of the "Original Ten"* (1878), by Edward Everett Hale. A minister, Hale enacts what Ann Douglas has seen as the nineteenth-century alliance between the clergyman and the lady—as does Warner's portrayal of Mr. Beryl. Douglas has suggested that the prevailing sentimentalism of the era enabled clergyman and lady "to cross the cruel lines laid down by sexual stereotyping": "She could become aggressive, even angry, in the name of various holy causes; he could become gentle, even nurturing, for the sake of moral overseeing" (*Feminization* 10). And perhaps they could be even more so when they crossgendered stories. Warner could be militant, writing of/through boys; Hale, nurturing, writing of/through women.[6] Hale's novel too combines elements of the sentimental novel and the school story—not to mention the Civil War story and the liberal story sermon.[7] In fact, writing some sixteen years after Warner, after the sentimental novel had lost much of its ascendancy in middle-class culture, Hale experienced the advantages and disadvantages of belatedness—not the least of the advantages, perhaps, was that he felt that he, a male, could attempt a story about a middle-class woman.

Hale was, in any case, someone spoken by contrary discourses, someone whom William Dean Howells could describe as "an artist in his ethics and a moralist in his art" (quoted in Billman 203): Hale was, for instance, the author of the parable "The Man without a Country," intended to rouse the somnolent during the Civil War. Hale writes at the intersection of preaching and teaching—on education, but only marginally about school, as befits someone who has claimed "that school was always a bore to me" (*New England Boyhood* 16).[8]

At the same time he writes a rather secular novel, compared to the sentimental novels celebrated by Jane Tompkins, novels in which the domestic becomes ritualized sacrament. Hale's mission is more this-worldly than other-worldly, adhering more to the word of one Harry Wadsworth than to that of God, and more concerned to create Paradise on earth than to attain one in heaven. And the site for playing out difference is less the boundary between heaven and earth, or even that between youth and age, than that between blacks and whites.

Mrs. Merriam's Scholars is a sequel to *Ten Times One Is Ten* (1870)— and perhaps Hale is emboldened to address girls' schooling by the male-oriented framework provided by his earlier book. For there he propagates the meliorist gospel of Harry Wadsworth, a "most manly and most womanly fellow" (3), someone who had set a shining example in helping others. The four planks of his movement entail looking "up and not down," "forward and not back," "out and not in," and lending a hand (96). Which all means to think positively and to help others, whether through giving alms to the worthy poor, planting trees in the center of town, teaching newly freed slaves, stamping out the demon drink, or rescuing someone from desperadoes. Here, in short, is the genteel ideal of public service as conceived by the arbiters of culture during the Gilded Age (see R. G. Kelly 64ff.). Wadsworth's gospel spreads tenfold every three years, like a chain letter, each convert influencing ten more. After twenty-one years Congress needs to meet no longer than three weeks annually, newspapers are so short of shocking news that they have to publish fiction to fill out their pages, and "Coal was at half price, because they mined by machinery, and the workmen had forgotten the mystery of striking" (93). Here is a social philosophy that assumes the efficacy of charitable benevolence (ignoring structural contradictions), that ignores the perspectives of workers (replacing them with machines, depriving them of unions, and even within the sentence replacing them with a referent-less "they"), and that values cultural activity, including the writing of fiction like Hale's.

In its way *Ten Times One* is as imperialistic as the canonical school story, but with a somewhat different gospel. Like the authors of British public-school stories, Hale had an effect on the world outside the book: within a year of its publication he had heard from "some fifty persons, in different parts of the world, who called themselves, more or less definitely, 'Harry Wadsworth people'" (vii).[9] Thus does Hale preach while he writes, his writing an extension of his other calling. In fact this novel—what Hale calls a parable—has the texture more of a tract than of fiction, the exempla of benevolent acts and exciting rescues trailing off into tallies of converts.

In general, *Ten Times One* and some of its sequels enact a heightened sense of the interconnections of fiction and "reality." Hale affects reality in these fictionalized tracts and is affected by it. Yet not without anxiety. As he insists in the preface to *Mrs. Merriam's Scholars,* set during the Civil War, the exploits of Rachel Fredet are probable, or at least possible, for he "narrat[es] nothing of importance in her life, which has not been done under similar circumstances by ladies well known to me" and, in fact, in some respects, he has been "obliged to tone down the true picture" (v). Hale may be too much a literalist in calculating fictional probability, yet relying on true narratives nonetheless enabled him to counter some of the norms of the time, to depict women active beyond their accepted sphere—and that despite his being someone "to whom public activities of women became increasingly distasteful" (Holloway 99). If during the course of the nineteenth century it became increasingly difficult for writers in the genteel tradition—and Hale was a writer and editor firmly in that tradition—to portray plausible men, men who were both genteel and manly,[10] then Hale solved the problem by killing off his androgynous Wadsworth and replacing him with a woman.

The Mrs. Merriam of the sequel is mentioned in *Ten Times One*, though she is sufficiently marginal that Hale proceeds to confuse her and another woman of the Original Ten disciples, as to which one lives in Brooklyn, which in Florida, which one runs a girls' school, which a club for newsboys. By retrieving what was forgettable in the original story, Hale revalues the marginal. And the interchangeability of the girls' school and the newsboys' club itself underscores his concern to address the marginal—and the slippage that always occurs among the marginal, whether marginalized by gender or class in addition to age. Yet by making the story a sequel, and by situating it in what he calls, on the title page, the Ten Times One Series, he also subordinates it to the earlier masculine frame, just as the Original Ten, and all the subsequent tens, are but disciples of a founding male.

In *Mrs. Merriam's Scholars* itself, Hale further marginalizes the girls' school even as he addresses it, for he doesn't focus on Mrs. Merriam's school but rather follows four (white) girls as they leave and go on to perform suitable tasks—including teaching. Still, we do get a quick recounting of how Mrs. Merriam, or Aunt Mary, has run her model school:

> If a girl must be sent away to school, and sometimes she must, it is to Aunt Mary's that I should send her. Twelve scholars, and only twelve; there was no capturing a poor girl by Aunt Mary's reputation, and then turning her off among forty thousand others to assistants, so that Aunt Mary never saw her face. They saw her face,— and she saw theirs. She saw through and through them, and loved them heart and soul with genuine motherly love. A simple home life they had there, but they could go over to New York when Aunt Mary said the word,—or, as Rachel said, they could pull the string of the

shower-bath and let the whole rush of water come. Best of all, nice girls came together and studied together and walked together and talked together. (14)

Note, first, the ambivalence still about whether girls should even go to school—"If a girl must be sent away to school."[11] Though after this token acknowledgment of misgivings, Hale expresses very little ambivalence—what the girls learn from Aunt Mary is well worth learning in this surrogate family bathed in "motherly love." The passage also indicates the possibility of interacting with the outside world, here specifically New York. This last, the engagement with the world outside, beyond the realm of the family, may hint at a masculine imprint, given how rarely women writers for girls allude to such a world in school stories; in any case, it prepares for the focus of the rest of the book, and, in fact, the girl invoked here, Rachel, is the one who will most fully engage with the outside world.

Still, Hale seems uneasy with his feminine focus, an uneasiness underscored by the instability of his narratorial perspective early on. The closer he comes to the girls' perspective, it seems, the more he has to emphasize his own. As the girls ready themselves for the performance that is to cap their school careers, he retreats to the audience, emphasizing his and our distance from the girls—"you and I," as he says, "hob-nobbing with Madam L'Estrange and with Dr. Farley" in the audience (15). Yet the next paragraph takes him backstage with the girls:

> You see it is "our school," not merely Aunt Mary's school. Indeed, this is "our play," not Mrs. Merriam's play. It is "we" who are responsible for the name and fame of this school, not Aunt Mary alone. Indeed, to say truth, "we girls" have a notion of the name and fame of the school far wider and grander than Mrs. Merriam has. "We girls" think it is the central establishment in the education of the world, and that such little, one-horse go-carts as the University of Oxford, or Yale or Antioch College, or the Polytechnic, or the College of the Propaganda, may as well hide their inferior heads in the comparison with "our school."
>
> That is what "we girls" think, and Mrs. Merriam, alias Aunt Mary, does not think so. (15–16)

The narrator's use of the first-person plural links him with "we girls," even as he calls the linking into question with quotation marks, whether he means thereby to show that he is quoting the girls or to emphasize the provisionality of his linkage with them.[12] He gains further distance from "we girls" when he hints at the absurdity of their thinking themselves the center of the educational universe—though he also hints that it is no less absurd to consider Oxford and other male bastions central, especially by the time his list of the founts of wisdom gets to "the College of the Propaganda." His statement that Mrs. Merriam disagrees distances the girls' perspective too. Though the disjunction is mitigated by his use of *and* in the last sentence rather than *but,* even if the *and* may also, defying logical opposition, diminish the seriousness of what the girls and Mrs. Merriam believe. The net effect, in any case, is to deconstruct both what "we girls" think and what they do not.

The first chapter ends as the curtains go up on the drama, setting the stage for what would soon become a staple of girls' school stories: the amateur play or charade. Yet the next chapter begins both with an avowal that the reader will not see the girls' end-of-term performance after all and with the abrupt intrusion of the author as hypothetical character:

> "My dear Mr. Hale, life is not made up of little stage-plays in the back parlor.
> "Is this the entertainment to which you invite us?"
> Thus Mrs. Grundy addresses me severely.
> "Dear Madam," I say in reply, "your words are words of truth and soberness. Of this little stage-play and the applauses which greeted it you shall hear never a word more. Let it be forgotten, dear Mrs. Grundy, as is your own mother's appearance as Marcia in Addison's Cato at the Leicester Academy in the spring of 1805, when George Grundy won her maiden heart by his irreproachable Marcus."
> For us, we have far graver cares before us. (18)

It is as if a male writing a book for girls has need of all the trickiness and indirection of women authors of the time, writing works that Sandra M. Gilbert and Susan Gubar describe as palimpsestic (*Madwoman* 73). For Hale here asserts his masculinity, extricating himself from his association with "we girls" as he puts down the stereotypical Mrs. Grundy. He even invokes his own name, as if to verify that he is separate from the characters of which he writes—to verify that he is not, like them, fictive. Yet bringing his name into this fictional context also backfires: if "Mr. Hale" is here a fiction created by Hale, can we be sure that Hale is not in some sense a fiction too? And hasn't Hale hoped through his work to affect the world outside the fiction, as the first volume in the series has? Isn't he trying, in effect, to make his fiction into nonfiction? Furthermore, at the same time that Hale puts down Mrs. Grundy, pointing out her inconsistency, he also accedes to her request—he does not portray for us "this little stage-play" prepared by Mrs. Merriam's scholars. Yet he does not give her what she wants—she presumably is castigating anything so frivolous as a stage-play in favor of "truth and soberness." Instead he provides a story of adventure, high moral adventure perhaps, but without the pious sermonizing Mrs. Grundy would presumably prefer: as the narrator later insists, "No, Lily; no, Emma! never fear me. I should like to stop and moralize, but you would not like to. And I have taken you into my keeping these five-and-twenty chapters, and they shall all be story and no moralization" (20).

On another level Hale does portray a drama after all, the drama comprised by his novel, as is underscored by the title of the closing chapter, "The Curtain Falls," a phrase that likewise closes the book. In part he is being dismissive of his story, heightening its unreality by reminding us of its fictitiousness. Yet the last chapter also functions as his final dismissal of Mrs. Grundy—he has provided one of those "little stage-plays in the back parlor" after all. If in the nineteenth century the parlor served as a site between the public world of strangers and the private world of family, and if, after midcentury, private theatricals became a way to act out the daily negotiations of social masks and disguises,[13] then this stage play, both proffered and withheld, is a rehearsal for the girls' subsequent actions: Rachel plays a "masculine" role in both dramas, or rather "masculinity" is, in both theaters, both proffered and withheld. The border sites of school and private theatricals prepare her for the deceptions and dangers of a more public role.

Furthermore—to return to the cited passage—the narrator puts down Mrs. Grundy through invoking earlier authorities, mostly male, thereby further underscoring his difference from her and from "we girls"—Addison, Cato, George Grundy, but also, and significantly, Charles and Mary Lamb. For "Leicester Academy" alludes to the then-well-known *Mrs Leicester's School* (albeit published in 1808 or 1809 rather than the 1805 that Hale invokes),[14] and thereby to a male predecessor who had written girls' school stories, a male role model who can assuage some of Hale's anxiety over authoring a girls' story.

Nevertheless *Mrs. Merriam's Scholars* is only marginally a story about Mrs. Merriam's school: after the first chapter "we girls" have left it behind. Yet two of the four young women graduates do go on to teach. One, Thekla, teaches Sunday School, getting a class of young men interested in self-improvement. Her class is populated by "'hobble-de-hoys,' boy-men or man-boys, who had strayed into the school" (110). She attempts messianic work across a gender and class boundary, a boundary reinforced by metaphors of juvenility—the boundary itself reified in the hyphen ("boy-men," "man-boys") bridging the adult and the juvenile.

But for all that Thekla teaches young men—or rather inspires them to appoint themselves her knights and then to set about improving themselves—her sphere is circumscribed. For she concentrates on fulfilling "her duty in her mother's family," though the narrator tries to laud her importance: she may think little of what she does because it seems so ordinary, while "the work of hospitals and of freedmen's schools seemed a little outside the common run. It was something more like what people generally write books about. And Thekla did not yet know, that the extraordinary things in life are, from the nature of the case, the least important" (109–110). Hale throws out a sop, insists that a young woman can play an important role within the family, but he protests too much: the tenor of the rest of the book, its focus on the more active Rachel, someone "a little outside the common run," and on actions "more like what people generally write books about" belies his claims. Not to mention his failure to sacralize these household tasks or indeed to describe them with any specificity. At the same time, though, the narrator is reminding us in this passage how fictive the rest of the book nonetheless is, how it's "more like what people generally write books about": he both heightens the unreality of the book and erodes the boundaries between fact and fiction.

The rest of the book addresses the more public activities of Rachel, who heads south at this time of Civil War to teach freedmen, "contrabands," first in Washington and then in Virginia. Hale thus makes his scope national, embroiling his female teacher in the public issues of the day, again perhaps mitigating his choice of female subject.

As does his choice of metaphor: Hale gives preference to discourse associated with masculine realms. When Rachel first plunges into her duties at school, she is sanctified by the discourse of Hale's own high calling. She reads from the Bible, leads her students in the Lord's Prayer and in a hymn. And the chapter ends: "There had been no laying on of hands, but none the less her ordination was divine" (59).[15]

More frequent still, in this work of secular evangelism, is military discourse. I won't enumerate all the instances when Rachel's work is described in terms of battles and requisitions and campaigns. Suffice it to say that her maps and globes are "'weapons of precision'" and that she enters her version of "'the service'"—as if with orders to act "with courage verging upon boldness, with boldness verging on audacity, and with audacity just touching on the edge of rashness" (54, 60). A metaphor that slides into realization when Rachel actually does march her students about, "by way of showing them what it was to obey, and what it was to command" (62). So when, a little later, Rachel tries to restore order after a disruption by ringing a bell and achieves "a certain 'parade rest'" (66), Hale has destabilized the metaphor—"parade rest" is simultaneously the narrator's self-conscious military metaphor (he has signaled this and other military metaphors by setting them off in quotation marks) and also Rachel's imitation of a procedure that seems to appeal to her students.

Hale is careful, though, never to desex Rachel. She always remains feminine in appearance and demeanor. Never does Hale speak of her as "more of a man" than her persecutors or protectors—though such was indeed said of some courageous women teaching in freedmen's schools at the time (see Jones, "Women" 55–56).

Hale is also careful to situate her with respect to family connections, thereby drawing on discourse more common in girls' school stories—though he uses family primarily as an ideological matrix to move beyond.[16] Mrs. Merriam's school may have been like a family, small, but Rachel's classes contain fifty to eighty pupils.[17] Nor do the children board with her. And she and they are transient: not only is she moved to a second school but she has to cope with high absenteeism and, at least in the first school, the fact that the children themselves are in transit. Nor is she concerned just with teaching but also with the environs of the school, coping with sabotage to the schoolhouse, with smallpox in the neighborhood, with threats to her own safety (a Union general in Virginia gives her pistols and teaches her to shoot). So it is difficult for her school to be familial.

Rachel has been personally deprived of the familial as well, for she is free to undertake this work because, unlike Thekla, she doesn't have a family whose needs take precedence: eighteen years old, she is "an orphan, and her only brother and sister were so placed that she had not, and could not claim, any share in their training" (40).[18] She is not enmeshed in the family connections that both protect and stifle the other three graduates. Nor does her family situation require her to work to support others, unlike Optic's and Gaylord's heroines. Instead she works for the sake of her country, of humanity, of principle. Hale may implicitly invoke a family context for "we girls" at the beginning when he calls their teacher Aunt Mary, but he is at pains to divest Rachel of any such actual encumbrances.[19]

Nor does Hale hamper Rachel with a husband. None of the four young women becomes engaged during the story; instead Hale undercuts the possibilities for romance. Early on he notes that Rachel helps a surgeon attend to an injured railway brakeman and coyly adds, "We must even skip that splendid surgeon of the Ninth New Jersey . . ." (20), though of course

Hale doesn't, not altogether. What he does skip is the potential for romance: "No, Florence, he did not offer her marriage. He never saw her again, and she never saw him, and they never heard of each other. And that is the last I ever heard of him. The accident detained them two hours. And I will not tell another word about it" (21). For Hale wants to tell a story of work rather than of romance, of ambition rather than the erotic.[20] And here, once again, when he wants to differentiate his tale from stories written by women, or stories that he thinks a woman might want him to have written, he condescends to an imaginary female auditor: he displaces his discomfort with his invention of himself and his book by inventing an audience he can feel superior to, the very personalizing of the audience—addressing someone named Florence—making it possible to be all the more condescending. Those of us who are not named Florence need not feel directly addressed; even those who are can assume he is referring to some other Florence: Hale allows readers to join him in feeling superior to readers who insist on romance—to, on some level, themselves.

Hale even frees Rachel of some of the bureaucratic constraints that most teachers of freedmen faced—thereby granting her greater independence than the norm. True, she is summarily moved from one post to another, from Washington to Virginia, but then she is the one who decides to stay on in the Virginia community where she has started a school, even when the Union army moves on. Nor do we ever see her report to a male supervisor, as women teachers of freedmen always did, never mind live under his thumb in a mission home.[21]

Hale writes, in short, of something like what Alcott lived—when she went to Washington during the Civil War to nurse the wounded—yet Alcott had trouble embodying her public experience in her novels, except, fleetingly, in Work (1873). Hale writes of a woman active in the public realm by divorcing her from the familial matrix in a way that Alcott could not. When a man attempts to embody the subjectivity of a woman, he destabilizes her traditional sources of identity even as he destabilizes the genre.

Yet a kind of connectedness, verging on the familial, comes from Rachel's devoted Tirah, her woman Friday, also an avatar of Harriet Beecher Stowe's Topsy, someone for whom there is never a question of having any other family. An escaped slave, Tirah arrives in Washington just after Rachel does, and "this redeemed Friday . . . like her godfather gave twofold the duty of a slave, with all the love and loyalty of a freeman" (77). Thereby "much of the friction of life was unexpectedly lifted from Rachel's shoulders" (77). And the narrator launches into more praise of household drudgery: "To do errands well—this alone is a great duty. It gives to angels their name, and that name has, on the whole, become the noblest name of all. For Rachel, from the moment of Tirah's reporting for duty, there was no physical drudgery in life. Never did she carry a book from her lodging to the school" (77). We see little in the book of what Hale refers to as drudgery, his praise of ordinary duties again belied by the attention paid to Rachel's out-of-the-ordinary work, also by his feeling it necessary to relieve her of the "great duty" of "physical drudgery"—not to mention his implication that physical drudgery is merely a matter of carrying a book to school. Rachel is in short freed for public work—just as Thekla's domestic work frees others in her family—by the devotion of someone who is a slave in all but name.[22] Barbara Christian has pointed out how the image of the Southern white lady is reciprocally implicated in images of black women: how the white lady's delicacy required the construction of the black mammy to do one kind of dirty work; how her chastity required the construction of the loose black woman to do another kind; how her Christian piety required the counterbalance of the conjure woman ("Shadows"). Hale may not be extolling the virtues of a Southern white lady, but he too can exalt a white woman, ennobling her, enlarging her sphere, only at the expense of a black one. He can, in effect, devote his attention to a white woman—giving her public scope despite his own distaste for feminism—only because he depicts, within the book, people with even less status.

And Hale does so by stereotyping the black woman, and blacks more generally. He may simply have been acceding to the thinking of the time, but the thinking of the time conveniently enabled him to give scope to a white woman by allowing a black woman to become what Zora Neale Hurston (29) and others have called the "mule of the world." Emblematic of his blindness is his portrayal of Tirah's arrival. We first become aware of her existence when we overhear her singing a verse of a hymn telling Jesus "I am coming home!" and then, to the same tune, a verse about stealing "missus' setting hen" (63). The juxtaposition comprises, we are told, "Flat blasphemy!" (63), in its equation of worship with stealing. Hale fails to acknowledge how the two verses are in fact related, one portraying escape, the other rebellion—both of which Tirah has just enacted by stealing herself away to Washington.

Elsewhere too Tirah represents extremes for Hale. She is not only docile, devoting herself slavelike to Rachel, but also more rambunctious than other African Americans. At school "this wild-cat from the plantations" (66) is apt to pop out of her seat without permission to talk to passersby, unlike other blacks, an activity that those in authority learn to accept "probably as the antics of a lunatic are received in the East as tokens of a certain inspiration. In Tirah's case they were so well meant, and frequently so shrewd in execution and successful in result, that it was impossible to chide them seriously" (76). Thus does Hale project Tirah's attributes onto other kinds of otherness: across mental, geographical, and cultural boundaries.

Tirah becomes, in short, a distillation of a Northern white liberal's views of Southern blacks. For, oblivious of cultural differences in values, Northern white teachers often did find blacks "hard to manage" in school: blacks had not, after all, practiced the discipline of sitting still in white Protestant churches from an early age, nor was the notion of punctuality according to clock time familiar, even when clocks were available, nor was regularity of attendance always feasible, given the difficulties of subsistence living.[23] Yet Hale encapsulated all these challenges in a single person, a singular person, otherwise docile, thereby making Rachel's classes more controllable—and individualizing difficulties as quirks, ignoring the larger social context, homogenizing differences.

Hale likewise homogenizes differences in his portrayal of Southern whites. By the end of the book we are led to believe that Southern whites of a certain class standing fundamentally respect and appreciate a Northern interloper like Rachel, yet historians such as Sandra E. Small and Jacqueline Jones suggest that Southern whites would have little to do with the Yankee schoolmarms of freedmen's schools. Poor whites would at the least be envious of black schooling—Georgia, for instance, did not offer universal public schooling until 1873. And planters would be unlikely to appreciate having former slaves inculcated with such values as independence.[24] Hale would thus seem to be seeking to heal national divisions by uniting white elites from the North and South, admixing a token black. He translates key differences from race and region to class by making elite whites supportive and protective of Rachel and poor whites responsible for arson and threats of personal violence—scapegoating in particular a couple of drifters, already geographically displaced, who are eventually expelled. In fact, the resistance to the freedmen's schools and their teachers was much more widespread among Southern whites, and the immigrants who were effectively expelled were apt to be the Northern teachers, fearful of violence (see Small 387). Hale's melioristic philosophy assumes, however, a norm of good will; it cannot function in a more divided society.

But back to the complexities of Tirah. On the one hand, she is treated with moral seriousness: she is allowed to figure in the final tableau of ten who will go on to propagate Wadsworth's word. But only just barely—she is the last person called, for all that another character, already on the platform, tells her sweetly, "If anybody belongs here, . . . it is you" (268). On the other hand, she provides comic relief: her idea of how to use a bed, when first introduced to one, is to creep in head first, placing her feet on the pillow—as we see when we follow the gaze of amused whites;[25] and after incendiaries attempting to destroy the school have been foiled, Tirah, confused, still runs off to the woods with the school's precious globes, trying to protect them.

At the heart of Hale's treatment of Tirah is his desexing of her. When she first arrives, a philanthropic senator's wife wonders "how she knew that this was a girl" (65). Pea-jacketed and hardly demure, Tirah lacks the trappings of white femininity—until, perhaps, she is reclothed in items culled from boxes sent by benevolent societies. Yet subsequently too Tirah performs not just duties in line "with the culinary instinct of her race" (124), race here already effacing gender, but ones that would be gender typed, from the perspective of whites at least, as masculine[26]—in keeping with the narrator's masculine nickname for her, Friday. Both Rachel and Tirah learn to shoot, for instance, but "the pistol practice wasn't wholly in Rachel's line" (143), and Tirah becomes the better shot—and keeps some incendiaries at bay by shooting their jack-o-lanterns square in the forehead. In fact, for Tirah, being able to handle firearms "was the crowning evidence that she was indeed free" (142). The reductionist thinking here,[27] together with the somewhat ludicrous shooting of jack-o-lanterns, undermines the value of her skill.

Tirah is also more likely than Rachel to behave in a military way, more likely to keep watch or patrol the grounds. On one occasion she extinguishes some attempts at arson and then, to make it appear that the schoolhouse is being guarded by the Union army, she "put on a soldier's overcoat, which one of the privates had left to be mended, and twisted up for herself an imitation of a foraging cap. In this costume she passed the window on the inside occasionally, and so kept up her patrol till morning" (136). Rachel has earlier crossdressed in play, in a stage-play, and looked, if anything, dashing—in a "long blue soldier's coat, and with Colonel Sleeman's sash," even if she has drawn a "ferocious moustache" on her lip with burnt cork (16). Tirah's crossdressing is in earnest, more hastily improvised, more functional than dashing. On the whole, for the white Rachel military discourse—both clothing and language—tends to affirm the high seriousness of her purpose, for Warner's Chloe it verges on the faintly ridiculous, and for Tirah it is indeed ridiculous, especially at first, another inversion of the bedclothes. It may, to some degree, broaden the potential scope of Tirah's activities, open up some masculine realms to her, create space perhaps for what Cixous calls the "other bisexuality." Yet it also reinforces her subordination, as a black—the racial subordination taking precedence over white-defined gender identity.

In portraying the most respected African American in the book, a preacher, Hale tries to move beyond stereotype, but he is not entirely successful. Take the man's name—"The Rev. John Bottle, whose name always seemed ridiculous to Rachel, though she came to esteem the man thoroughly . . ." (138). In part perhaps a white reader is educated to see beyond the ridiculous here, like Rachel, though a whiff of the ridiculous remains, "always." Similarly with his preacherly exhortations: he is "sublime even in his blundering pronunciation and wayward accent" (189). More telling is Hale's description of Rachel's boarding, at one point, with the Elder Bottle and his wife. That Rachel and her colleague do so is taken as "a display of confidence in the race" (205).[28] Where Rachel and Jane Stevens had before been "monarchs" of their own home, they now in effect recognize that "there is no question in history so difficult as that question, how the Roman republic got on so well for centuries with two consuls" (207). This republican imagery recurs soon afterwards in connection with their disposition of the schoolhouse: "They were habitually the monarchs—or, if you please to be accurate, the consuls—there" (215). Yet what has disappeared in this second iteration is the doubleness of the consuls, the existence of difference. We never see any difference between Rachel and Jane, though they have had to adjust to living together and to running the school together, a school that Rachel started though Jane has more seniority as a teacher. Instead the crucial difference is race, to the extent that the "two consuls" in the first iteration are, in effect, not two individuals but two races subsuming four individuals.[29]

At the same time there is surprisingly little friction between the white teachers and the black preacher—or between the teachers and the black community generally. Historians have found that Yankee teachers reserved their harshest judgments for "native black religious leaders, whom they condemned as drunken, adulterous, profane, and power-hungry men" (Jones, *Soldiers* 154). The Yankees simply could not fathom a religion based more on hope and joy than on self-denial and guilt.[30] Nor were blacks particularly attuned to a Northern-style work ethic or other capitalist values, nor were they necessarily eager to trust any whites. Hale evades the issue in part by making the Rev. Bottle not a native religious leader but an army chaplain who has, like Rachel, decided to stay on in the community. Once again, Hale glosses over difference.

To gain some perspective on Hale's portrayal of Tirah and the Elder Bottle, it's worth looking at contemporary portrayals of blacks. Too typical is Margaret M. Brewster's *Charlie Hubert; or, Consecrated Gifts* (1857), another crossgendered story partly about school. A benefactor sends the impoverished Charlie from Pennsylvania to an academy in South Carolina, where he lives with the pious Mrs. Lincoln, whose name history would soon invest with irony. He encounters the slovenly Aunt Amy, a free black who has chosen to live on Mrs. Lincoln's plantation and to place her money in Mrs. Lincoln's hands—and who is meant to provide comic relief, though not for voluntarily giving her money to a slaveholder. She may technically be free, but she is granted even less agency than Tirah, allowed less bubbling up of irrepressibility. On the estate Charlie becomes a kind of missionary to the "black servants," and, like Rousseau's noble savages, the blacks in turn educate him:

> Sometimes remarks from devout, but ignorant old negro servants would strike him with great force, and set him to thinking afterwards upon the subject of that spiritual illumination which was claimed by some of them, and which did seem to be possessed in such a degree, as to level the human understanding with regard to the *great essential truths* of the Gospel. (139, Brewster's italics)

Yet Brewster so hedges their power to educate that she all but denies it: it's not what blacks say that is important but how they "set him to thinking"; they do not necessarily have access to "spiritual illumination" but rather claim it (some of them) and merely seem to possess it (in passive constructions that make them less consciously active); and finally it's only with respect to the Gospel that "human understanding" is thereby leveled (or perhaps the Gospel is so powerful that it alone can overcome rigid social barriers). Still, this white author does show the racially other as an instrument of Christianity, both here and, more violently, when another character is converted only after his evangelizing friend is killed by Commanches.

Very different is Harriet E. Wilson's character Frado, of *Our Nig; or, Sketches from the Life of a Free Black, in a Two-Story White House, North, Showing that Slavery's Shadows Fall Even There* (1859), who is as irrepressible at school as she is repressed in the white household where she lives. Her (white) schoolmates so enjoy her antics—such as filling a master's desk drawer with cigar smoke so that he will shout "Fire!"—that, even when they get the blame, they "would suffer wrongfully to keep open the avenues of mirth" (38). Yet Frado is granted narrative subjectivity. We feel how she is tortured by the Bellmonts and see how her antics at school are the bursting forth of "pent up fires" (38). At the same time, she is less passive than white sentimental heroines as she "acts out her dreams of independence and superiority, however unguardedly and humorously. She is not shorn of all aggression or self-esteem as is generally the case in the sentimental novel"

(Gates 143). Unlike the African-American Wilson, the white Hale grants subjectivity not to Tirah but to whites like Rachel, so Tirah's antics are framed as quaint, for all that they have subversive potential.

Their potential is like that of characters created by Hale's aunt by marriage, in *Uncle Tom's Cabin* (1851–1852), especially black characters other than Uncle Tom. Christina Zwarg argues that a character like Sam, in both caricaturing and enforcing Emersonian rhetoric, is not just acting out capitalist patriarchy in blackface but subverting it: Sam "manages a textual escape from the entrapments of patriarchy," an escape that "becomes Stowe's model for the escape of each 'sambo' in the text, each portrait done in blackface, each projection using this ironic doubling in a feminist way, moving beyond and back to value all at once" (287).

Hale, in any case, moves beyond some of the stereotyping that Brewster portrays, creating space for its subversion, but he also reproduces it. Poor whites may be "surly, sulky, crafty, ill-natured," but blacks are stereotyped as "willing, stupid, affectionate, good-natured . . . , lazy of habit but quick for gratitude" (132).[31] Or look at Hale's use of dialect for presumably humorous effect, for color, as it were: "Ah! you nose it was me. But I was frightened dat time, Miss Janestevens, w'en dey all come in so solum" (258). Hale is not just finding orthographic means for representing sounds, such as the rapid-fire joining of *Jane* and *Stevens,* but he condescendingly writes *knows* as "nose," presumably adding humor with such "eye" dialect. And it's significant that Tirah's speech here, like that of most blacks in this novel, is more inflected with dialect markings—more divergent from the norm of the narrator's language—than that of any other nonnormative group, such as poor Southern whites and working-class Yankees.

Look further at Hale's proffering of the Black English conjugation of the verb "I dun": the present of the first person singular is "I dun it"; the imperfect, "I dun dun it"; the perfect, "I gone dun dun it"; the pluperfect, "I dun gone dun it"; the first future, "I gwine dun it"; the second future, "I dun gwine dun it" (97–99). Rachel shares the list, copied in Tirah's handwriting (though Rachel has apparently been the one to codify it), with a fellow teacher. The ventriloquism enables condescension, as Jane acclaims Rachel: "This is too funny. You are as bright as you are good" (99). The recording of the grammar is, on the one hand, an act of respect. This language is worth recording. But the act is also patronizing, like the "respect" accorded black students when visitors to Rachel's school ask to hear students sing spirituals rather than recite lessons: the conjugation is recorded more for its quaintness ("too funny") than for its truth, a condescension reflected in the decision to spell *done* "dun." And more respect goes to the white who presumably codified it than to the blacks who spoke it, or the black who wrote it out. The ventriloquism becomes even more complex when Hale appends the following footnote: "I owe this charming piece of philology to Miss Lucy Chase of Worcester. If only she would write the history of the Contraband teaching, 'much of which she saw, much of which she was!'— E. E. H." (97). The footnote comprises a whiff of "reality" that simultaneously increases the reality of the story (this really happened) and reminds us of its fictionality (the marginalization of the note within the story, its typographical distinctness, underscores the difference between fictive and real). And it is notable that Hale is standing on the shoulders of a white woman, repeating the words she has recorded, the words of blacks. The white woman serves as a mediator, between white man and black men and women.[32] The way to blacks, for a white man, is through a white woman; the way to write about a white woman, without being too demeaned oneself, is to place her in authority over blacks.

Still, Hale is groping toward a mode that can free African Americans from the shackling conventions of domestic fiction—given that, in near-contemporary domestic stories, "black characters who threw off their bonds generally risked appearing disloyal to those they served or inessential to the domestic principles that readers had learned to expect" (Diffley 645). If, in a story called "The Brothers" (1863; later entitled "My Contraband"), Alcott starts pushing beyond such boundaries by setting her work in a hospital, a setting "both domestic and national" (Diffley 652), Hale succeeds through his use of a school setting—through his merging of domestic fiction and the school story, making Tirah not just a servant but also a student, and an assistant in the school setting as well. In his attempt to provide an education for Tirah, Hale starts to educate the nation.

And Hale is also, despite his preference for keeping women out of the public arena, groping toward a mode that can free a white woman from the conventions of domesticity. We might assume that Rachel's stay in the South will be temporary: the average Yankee teacher stayed about four years.[33] Yet we do not, in the novel, see her leave. And for a while at least she has considerable scope for activity, even adventure.

All together, Hale's is a story more of work than of romance, more of adventure than of domesticity. It is a story that alludes more to *Robinson Crusoe* (1719), for good or ill, than to other literature, certainly than to other school stories. A story whose discourse is more military than romantic, Rachel metaphorically fighting battles like the men she works near. A story that ends with a tableau yet, unlike that epitome of domestic stories, Alcott's *Little Women* (1868), the final tableau portrays not a scene of family togetherness but ten stalwart individuals who will go on to educate ten others, a human chain letter, to heal perhaps divisions within the nation and certainly to make a difference in the world. It is a story that enforces racial difference while pretending to ameliorate it, that enforces racial difference to enable greater gender equality among whites, a story that transgresses gender and racial boundaries in part to reinforce them.

Still, Hale does succeed in destabilizing established relationships in his school story. Warner essentially reproduced the prevailing relationships between black and white: for all that Chloe and Dinah provide paths to the truth, they remain, in religious terms, handmaidens; and in social terms there is never any hint that they should be anything but servants—though of course Warner was writing during the Civil War, before the national imagination had had as much opportunity to dwell on the implications of freeing blacks. During this time of political instability, she may have been fearful of disturbing the social structure, not to mention her narrative. Hale, on the other hand, creates an inherently unstable situation in his portrayal of Tirah: she is both servant and student. Both are positions that can be conceptualized as inferior, but the latter role hints that she may have a different future. Much as her irrepressibility does, for it enables the irruption of what established institutions cannot contain. Furthermore, Hale makes his narrative less tidy than Warner's: instead of being a synthesis of two genres, domestic fiction and the school story, it is a more cumbersome amalgam of several, including such nonfictional genres as the sermon. This untidiness too allows for the irruption of what cannot be contained in traditional modes. Hale thus "reflects some events not caught so clearly by others," as a recent critic has noted (J. Adams 115), even if he does not ultimately know what to do with them. Hale thinks he has written a parable about the difference that a benevolent individual can make in the world. Yet he has actually written a parable about nineteenth-century white liberalism—and about twentieth-century liberal feminism. He underscores the extent to which access to the public realm, for white women, depends on subjugating others. His attempts at teaching continue to reverberate, to sound warnings, for those of us who teach.

NOTES

1. Even if the characters in a school story are not necessarily realistic, the canonical stories "comfort us with idealised projections of ourselves" (Tucker 147).

2. The colonies figure in Anstey's *Vice Versa,* but only as trigger or catalyst, and by way of a material object rather than a person: the Garuda stone from India inconveniently—or conveniently—grants wishes.

3. See, e.g., Briggs, "Reading" 7. In late-nineteenth- and early-twentieth-century British popular school stories, the French master or mistress is always a figure of

fun (see Dhingra 50–55): as novelist Belinda Blinders (Desmond Coke) notes, underscoring the norm through parodic exaggeration, "At most Public Schools crimes among the members of the Staff are, in fact, confined to the French Master . . ." (39). See also Musgrave on xenophobia in school stories (101, 152).

4. A surname that, in another context, Douglas finds particularly girlish (*Feminization* 21), Austin thus perhaps representing an androgynous ideal.

5. Though since the white male author, while starting with a girls' school, is particularly concerned with a white woman graduate who goes on to teach at a co-educational freedmen's school, he could be said to cross race as much as he crosses gender.

6. And perhaps he was writing through women in another sense as well. For in the preface to a volume in his collected works he describes some real co-workers, a group who called themselves the original ten, after Wadsworth's Original Ten in *Ten Times One Is Ten*. Hale goes on to acknowledge that all were "mixed up with the evolution of the story" (vii). And with respect to the five women, "If we had the original manuscript of the book I suppose we should find the handwriting of each of these ladies" (vi).

7. For discussion of the shift, in the nineteenth century especially, from the doctrinal to the story sermon, see D. Reynolds.

8. And whose one boys' school story, "The Good-Natured Pendulum" (1869), tells of boys applying their scientific knowledge of pendulums to make school hours fly by twice as fast.

9. For an account of the clubs and journals spawned by the book and its sequels, see Hale, Jr., 2: 128–132.

10. See R. G. Kelly 72, 78.

11. In 1892, in an article entitled "Where Shall Polly Go to School?", Hale is still ambivalent about sending Polly outside the home to school.

12. His use of similar locutions in *A New England Boyhood*—"we four," "we boys"—suggests more connection than provisionality, though the use of quotation marks likewise hints at distance, here between boyhood and adulthood.

13. See Halttunen 188.

14. As I note in chapter 2, there is some instability in scholarly opinion: some date it 1808 (Riehl, *Children's Literature* 101; Marrs 1: xliv), some 1809 (Bator 281; Marrs 1: xxvii).

15. Similarly, drawing on the language of political discourse, she achieves in this chapter an "inauguration" and the winning of an "empire." Elsewhere in the book are invocations of "apostles" and "prophetess" and "martyr," not to mention "queen" and "monarch" and "consul."

16. If the metaphoric nexus of actual freedmen's teaching entailed a tension between military and agricultural metaphors (see Jones, *Soldiers* 24, 86), then the tension in Hale's work is primarily between military and familial metaphors.

17. In this and other physical details, Hale's account is generally consistent with the historical record regarding freedmen's schools—see, e.g., Botume; Jones, *Soldiers* and "Women"; Pearson; Small; and Thorpe. Though Hale does make some omissions. He does not stress, for instance, how wide the age range in such a school could be, from six to sixty (Small 393)—possibly he is trying to avoid what he might consider infantilizing the race as a whole.

18. In this she is like actual women teachers of freedmen in Georgia between 1865 and 1874, for about a third were orphaned; another third had only one surviving parent (see Jones, *Soldiers* 31).

19. What, furthermore, does it mean when her black landlady in Washington is likewise called aunt, Aunt Dolly? Is Hale creating a family? Is he travestying it? Is he feeding into the stereotypes that contribute to the image of Aunt Jemima? Or is Aunt Dolly akin to Aunt Mary, to Mrs. Merriam? And if so, what are the reverberations for Aunt Mary? Does it defamiliarize the familial?

20. For discussion of how the two desires have been perceived as incompatible for women, and of how women writers have played out possibilities, diverging from standard plots, see Miller. Hale may offer a woman a plot of ambition, but he sees such a plot as incompatible with the erotic.

21. Jones reports, in "Women," the tensions between the mostly female and experienced freedmen teachers sent out by the American Missionary Association and their always male and often inexperienced supervisors—though teachers sent to rural outposts managed to evade some degree of male control. Still, even in Washington we never see Rachel reporting to a male authority. Possibly the women who reported their experiences to Hale chose not to emphasize their conflicts with white male authorities. Certainly the published correspondence of one such informant—Lucy Chase, whom Hale cites in a footnote—does not discuss such conflict, but then again her and her sister's correspondence has been edited by a white male who does not even mention their names on the title page (see Swint).

22. The attitude displayed here is conistent with the historical record: as Small notes of freedmen's schools, "Dedicated teachers saw no inconsistency in expecting the Negroes . . . to serve as domestics" (391).

23. See Jones, *Soldiers* 111–118; Botume 43–45, 68ff.

24. See Jones, *Soldiers* 80–81; see also Swint 68ff. Botume betrays an attitude similar to Hale's when she shows herself willing to castigate the behavior of whites of the lower classes yet reluctantly admits that those whom she would call ladies were reserved with her (231–232).

25. Contrast that with Booker T. Washington's account of himself—also newly arrived at school—learning to cope with bed linen: "The sheets were quite a puzzle to me. The first night I slept under both of them, and the second night I slept on top of both of them; but by watching the other boys I learned my lesson in this, and have been trying to follow it ever since and to teach it to others" (866). Here we have Washington's own account, from his own perspective, without an amused sense of the ridiculous.

26. Given that most black women slaves were expected to do "masculine" work, working in the fields—and often, like Zora Neale Hurston's Janie, they preferred working in the fields to domestic work (see Jones, *Labor* 22, 27; Fox-Genovese 172)—the gendering of Tirah's duties is less clear from an African-American perspective. For an early discussion of "one of the supreme ironies of slavery"—that to extract the greatest labor from the slaves "the black woman had to be released from the chains of the myth of femininity"—see Davis 7ff.

27. In a description that is contrary to the historical record. For most blacks found different ways of symbolically enacting their freedom: especially by going to school. Even Hale himself, reporting on freedmen's schools some thirteen years earlier, stresses "the enthusiastic readiness of the freedmen to learn. . . . [M]en, women, and children knew that there was power in letters" ("Education" 533). And for black women in particular "freedom had meaning primarily in a family context": it enabled the reunion of family members and greater stability of family relationships (Jones, *Labor* 58; see also Tate 103). Tirah, however, is shown as resistant to school learning (as willing to learn only because her much-worshiped Rachel decrees it) and as devoid of family (not carefully extricated from it, as Rachel is).

28. Perhaps especially since Hale leaves it ambiguous whether the two women are more guests or tenants—they would seem to be on a fairly equal footing with their hosts, though again we do not see exactly how domestic affairs are managed, who, for instance, dines with whom. Such a living arrangement was unusual among the teachers of freed blacks: in her examination of twelve Northern white women's accounts of teaching in freedmen's schools, Small finds only two mentions of white teachers entertaining blacks in their homes and one mention of subletting a house from blacks who then provided meals (391). Jones notes that the American Missionary Association "insisted that white teachers exhaust all other possibilities before decid-

ing to live with black families," and white teachers "rarely considered contact with blacks as 'company' or 'society'" (*Soldiers* 186, 188).

29. This culmination of political discourse in a republican image could, on the other hand, be taken as Hale's response to an emphasis that Crandall has found in nineteenth-century fictional portrayals of U.S. schools: an emphasis on images of empire, the schoolmaster a stern and physically abusive autocrat. Hale effectively displaces this chain of associations onto the British, for at the end we encounter an English visitor "who hated schools, and always had, since he was flogged at one almost daily" (263). We never witness any corporal punishment within Rachel's various schools, just the threat of violence from without—yet another displacement of the violence of schooling.

30. See Jones, *Soldiers* 67. Nor is the difference simply a matter of race, for an elite Northern black teacher like Charlotte Forten Grimké could also find it "amusing" to watch the "gymnastic performances" of a black singer, "quite in the Ethiopian Methodists' style" (98).

31. Elsewhere Hale attempts to translate the pivotal difference from race to social status, contrasting "the laziness and theft and lying of slaves" with "the industry and honesty and truth of freemen" (183)—though in the context of whether anyone can succeed in teaching the newly freed to change from their old ways. His views are consistent with those of Northerners teaching in freedmen's schools—who "saw the Negroes as culturally backward but not inherently deficient" (Small 391).

32. And perhaps I, a white woman, am tempted to focus more on the racial errors of a white man than on those of a white woman because of my own need for a buffer between me and racism, because of my difficulty in extricating myself from the racism that pervades U.S. society. If Hale used blacks as a way of attempting to convey a more egalitarian mode for women, I am using Hale as a way of attempting a more egalitarian acknowledgment of blacks.

33. Which is longer than the average tenure of a schoolteacher in New England at the time, namely, two years (Jones, *Soldiers* 45). Teaching was almost always a temporary occupation—in fact, although fewer than 2 percent of Massachusetts women were teaching at any one time before the Civil War, some 20 percent of white women had been teachers at some point in their lives (Schwager 346).

CROSSING GENDER WITH ETHNICITY

ELIZABETH EILOART AND OTHER BRITISH WRITERS

In England between 1857 and the end of the century, when no man crossgendered a school story, British women did. They did not particularly ape Hughes. They continued to play out many of the concerns of pre-Hughesian school-story writers. They continued, furthermore, to set their boys' school stories not at public but at private schools. Perhaps they were more familiar with private schools, probably having attended such schools themselves. Or perhaps, like the parents in one of these crossgendered stories, they chose schools that enabled them—and enabled fictional families—to continue to have more impact: our hero's parents choose a small private school "as more homelike than a public school, and yet as one where he would get accustomed to a new and a more extended world than he had at home" (Goddard, *New Boy* 18).

Like other feminine practices of writing, practices that "will never be able to be *theorised*, enclosed, coded," as Cixous has argued, such stories "will always exceed the discourse governing the phallocentric system; [they] take place somewhere other than in the territories subordinated to philosophical–theoretical domination" (109, Cixous's italics). And as with contemporary U.S. stories, British women expended, embodied, some of the excess in an other, displacing their own sense of otherness, though usually through an ethnic rather than a racial other, an other that they treated with unusual respect, given the "contempt for foreigners" (Orwell, "Such" 45) endemic in contemporary boys' schools, in and out of literature. It's as if women like M. Betham-Edwards and Julia Goddard were domesticating world relations, miniaturizing them, though they focused on the European community rather than the British empire. In effect, they redressed some of the belligerence in the earliest boys' adventure stories by the likes of Frederick Marryat, where the enemy was most likely to be French,[1] by promoting harmony with the French and other Europeans, domesticating warlike impulses.

Elizabeth Eiloart, whose school story ranges as far afield as New Zealand, domesticates the warlike as well.

M. (Matilda) Betham-Edwards' *Charlie and Ernest or Play and Work: A Story of Hazlehurst School* (1859), published two years after *Tom Brown's Schooldays,* is little affected by Hughes's work. Like other midcentury women, Betham-Edwards creates a curious amalgam of earlier and later trends; in particular, she grafts eighteenth-century-style interpolated tales and attendant sermons onto a late-nineteenth-century attitude of amused indulgence of the naughtiness of children. Yet like the other works discussed in this chapter, other works not caught up in the Hughes frenzy, it revalues the ethnically other.

The revaluation of the ethnically other is what one might expect from someone who went on to interpret French life and character in numerous books—earning herself the honor of being named by the French government, in 1891, an *Officier de l'Instruction Publique de France,* probably the first Briton so named (*Mid-Victorian Memories* l-li). Betham-Edwards was also more egalitarian than many other Victorians, her friends including feminists and Marxists, even if she did not always share their beliefs.[2] And she was someone who chose not to write stories of her own school experience. As a governess-pupil, for instance, she witnessed the taunting of a tradesman's daughter, pupils accusing the girl of filthiness while, naked, the girl stood in a tub. Yet in her fiction, "instead of describing school life, as depressing from the moral point of view as that portrayed by the great Brontë," Betham-Edwards describes herself as taking "refuge in idyllic scenes and ideal portraiture" (*Reminiscences* 84). Or, rather, in transmuting the experience into that of boys at a boys' school, she transformed a potential scapegoat into an exemplum.

The exemplum in *Charlie and Ernest* is Ernest. But it's not until well into Part II that we meet this blind German musician, who is taken in by Mr. Grey so that the English boys can practice their German and Ernest can practice English. Part I is dominated by little Charlie, "dearly fond of fun and mischief" (2).[3] Deprived of a holiday treat, he decides to play truant, runs away, becomes lost, spends the night in a shepherd's hut, breaks his arm, and the next day returns to school repentant.

What is striking about Charlie is that he is a likable, naughty child, not a bad exemplum but what would soon be called a pickle or madcap, thus heralding a trend in late-nineteenth-century children's literature. Similarly prescient is the narrator's tone, self-consciously indulgent of a child's "quaint" reasoning, when Charlie sets out on an escapade with—"Let me see—a map for guide, a knife to defend myself, a book for quiet minutes, apples for delicacies, and the immense sum of six shillings and sixpence by way of funds. I only hope that no poor person will want to borrow it of me, in order to set up a shop. I should get interest certainly, but I like to be my own banker" (14). Like the canonical school story, this one gives some play to the child's perspective, yet lurking in the background is an adult who finds such reasoning quaint. And in the guise of frivolity Betham-Edwards gives voice to the capitalist underpinnings of British society: we are meant to read Charlie's notion of lending and banking as a charming indictment of his understanding, yet it also allows some of the hidden underpinnings of a schoolboy's class privilege to emerge.

It's true that in breaking his arm Charlie enacts the traditional equation of invalidism and accession to virtue, an equation prominent in children's literature of the first half of the nineteenth century—and even appearing in *Tom Brown,* where associating with the sickly but virtuous Arthur is improving for Tom. Yet for all that Charlie claims that "this broken arm has given me a world of experience" (128), his accession to virtue is not foregrounded; his moral education is, furthermore, displaced in the second half of the book when Ernest appears. For Charlie's transient invalidism is transmuted into Ernest's permanent handicap: as one of the masters says, Ernest "has the misfortune to be blind, if indeed any thing can be called a misfortune which God sees fit to give us,—but though he cannot see, he can feel all the beauty of nature, and when you hear him play you will envy him. For God never takes one thing from us but he gives us another; and we are all rich if we did but know it" (131).

Ernest, in fact, harks back to the portrayal of children in earlier children's literature—as does the language describing him. He is triply unlike the British schoolboy enshrined in the Hughesian school story, for Ernest is not only German but physically handicapped, and since he is a musician who must expect to work for his money—unlike Charlie and the other schoolboys—his class background and expectations are different as well. Yet there is no question of anyone treating Ernest with anything but respect. No boys snub him so that they can then stand corrected (as might happen in a canonical story—or indeed in Adams' *Edgar Clifton* [1852]—if one of the boys were to have a father who has made his millions in trade instead of inheriting wealth and status). Instead, Ernest becomes "a great favourite" because "he was so gentle and obliging, so patient and affectionate, that no one could help loving him, and whatever quarrels took place among them, he was always the peace-maker" (142). Ernest is, in short, to be taken as a model, as Mr. Grey emphasizes to Charlie at the end of the book, noting what "good use" Ernest has made of his "few advantages," industriously earning a living despite his blindness and youth, patient and happy despite being "deprived of all the beautiful sights around us," and overall—"think of his courage, his gentleness, his sweet disposition, his brave independent spirit, and lastly, of his thankfulness to God" (163–164). Ernest's function as model is overdetermined by his triple otherness, an otherness that sets him so apart from the "ordinary" boys like Charlie that his virtues may seem unattainable, or unnecessary, for an ethnocentric Briton. It may be all right for Ernest to work, because he has to—but what about Charlie? What real incentive does he have to work at school? Perhaps too Ernest's foreignness excuses his lowly class status—there is little danger of the boys treating him as anything other than an exotic, little danger of being infected with a desire to cross class boundaries.

Also harking back to earlier children's literature is Betham-Edwards' constant iteration of a class-based apothegm, whether it is voiced by a fisherman casually encountered at the seashore or enunciated as the moral of an interpolated tale or directly articulated by Ernest: one should be content with one's lot—that perennial Victorian pablum for those who would strive to rise out of their God-given place.[4] Not that characters in canonical school stories would disagree; they simply wouldn't find much occasion to mention it in their hermetic worlds of class and gender homogeneity, nor would the narrator feel compelled to be so overt about driving home a moral. Perhaps the iteration of the apothegm in the interpolated story of an enchanted top (a poor boy should be content with his lot since he would be uncomfortable at school) also serves to keep Ernest in his place as a mere visitor at Hazlehurst school, defusing potential subversion. Yet, still, Betham-Edwards' favorable portrayal of Ernest also opens the door to some questioning of British class hierarchy—the one hierarchy so sacrosanct in nineteenth-century British children's literature, certainly in the school story, that virtually no one ever thinks to question it.

Betham-Edwards also opens the door to some questioning of British xenophobia. For, unlike the Hughesian story, *Charlie and Ernest* is set at a private school where more attention seems to be paid to learning German than to learning Latin, a curriculum that sounds more like that of a nineteenth-century school for girls than that of one for boys. Yet Betham-Edwards can thereby overcome some of the ethnocentrism characteristic of the more canonical school story, encouraging as she does learning not just about the ancients but about one's European contemporaries.

Certainly Betham-Edwards provides positive portrayals of the French and German masters. The British headmaster Mr. Grey is as usual ideal, but these other two are too—these masters who in more canonical stories would be accorded little respect (partly because their subjects would be so marginal) and who would eventually, certainly by the twentieth century, be treated as figures of fun (or, in more lowbrow stories, as sinister). An early glimpse of the French master does suggest some of these less respected qualities, an anticipation of Enid Blyton's Mam'zelle, that constant butt of practical jokes who yet defuses open hostility by laughing at herself: "Mr. Emile the French master put salt by mistake on to his gooseberry tart, instead of sugar, which occasioned great laughter, and which he joined in very good-naturedly" (35). Yet Mr. Emile's character is otherwise unimpeachable.

Even more respect accrues to Mr. Müller, Ernest's fellow countryman and he who introduces the boys to Ernest. The German master is frequently allowed to preach at us, like Mr. Grey. The man further provides a site for playing out earlier and later modes of children's literature. He is someone the boys never keep secrets from, like an eighteenth-century preceptor, yet they are open with him not so much because it is the proper thing for an obedient child to do but because it is fun: "for he was so good-natured and fond of fun, that unless anything was against the rules, he always joined in it as heartily as any of the boys themselves" (143). As in earlier school stories, like Strickland's *Hugh Latimer* (1828), Betham-Edwards is in effect urging kindness toward outsiders—toward Germans like Ernest and Mr. Müller. But she makes the outsiders central, preceptors—with a cosmopolitanism absent from any other school story I have come across.

Mr. Müller likewise garners status through his storytelling. His interpolated tales are reminiscent of interpolations in the earliest school stories, such as Fielding's and Fenn's and Johnson's: he tells, for instance, an eighteenth-century-style allegory of the battle of the books. The potential subversiveness of the interpolated tales—their ability to break free of constraining reality—is held in check by the constant straining after moral applications, a straining only emphasized when the purport of one tale is to explain what a moral is. Sometimes the strain of deriving a moral is revealed through contradiction: after Mr. Müller tells his story of the enchanted top, about a poor boy who is granted his wish to be rich but is then so unhappy that he gladly returns to his former condition, Charlie wishes he had such a top. Mr. Müller expostulates, "You shock me! Here I have been telling you a story to show you the folly of wishing, and now you begin by wishing the first thing. No, no, Charlie, depend on it, we are best off as we are, without fairies, or genii, or enchantments of any kind, for we never know what is good for us, and should be getting into all sorts of scrapes" (124). Yet as Betham-Edwards acknowledges through Charlie's response (reminiscent of that of Kilner's Roger Riot), telling such a story may not so much curb a desire for fairy tales and their accouterments as foster it.

And perhaps it's only in a fairy tale like "The Enchanted Top" that a boy can be altogether converted from laziness to industriousness. We are told that Charlie learns moral lessons, but we never see him fully act on them— even near the end he still cares more for play than for books. Only in an interpolated tale can goodness reign supreme.

Or in Ernest. The story of his background, his exemplary struggle to survive, functions like the interpolated tales. It even echoes the tale of the enchanted top: like the boy in the story, Ernest finds himself in an alien school environment. But he knows enough to know his place, to know that he doesn't belong. Ernest too is an interpolation, a bit foreign to the text. Not part of the family.

I won't here detail the many ways in which *Charlie and Ernest* does in fact provide a family context, but I will note that, like later writers of girls' school stories, and also like Anna Warner, Betham-Edwards devotes some attention to food—though at the same time she masks its importance. Mr. Müller rewards the boys with a supper for contributing regularly from their pocket money to a fund enabling Ernest's friend Otto to come to England— instead of wasting the money "on knick-knacks and cricket-bats" (147). He fails to mention what such boys, in and out of school stories, are most likely to have spent their money on—namely food, like the sausage rolls and jam tarts with which the master eventually rewards them. He gives the boys what they presumably weren't all that interested in, simultaneously denying their interest in food and acknowledging it.

By the time E. (Edith) C. Kenyon[5] and Julia Goddard turned to writing boys' school stories, several decades later, the canonical story had crystallized. So it is not surprising that they include some canonical tropes. Yet both continue to be very much influenced by the earlier evangelical tradition. Kenyon's Jack, in *Jack's Heroism: A Tale of Schoolboy Life* (1883), may ride in a balloon and on a bicycle, may burn a letter and rescue someone from a fire, yet the advice of his missionary father is to fight the small battles of life and not worry about grand heroic actions, to discover, on his knees if necessary, true humility and forgiveness. Which Jack does, sort of. He finally dies after his daring rescue of the headmaster's daughter from a fire— as if such heroic excess is too much for a mere mortal, or for the story's purported moral, and Jack has to be quickly translated to a more spiritual realm.

More interesting for my present purposes is Goddard's *Philip Danford: A Story of School Life* (1890), in which there is a school bully and a wrongful accusation, accompanied by even more concerted efforts at spiritual regeneration. And like Betham-Edwards, Goddard reveres people from the Continent, this time from France: the French master and the eponymous Philip, a boy whose great-great-grandfather was a royalist killed during the French Revolution.

Someone has been guilty of disturbing the new French master's clothes, which had been laid out in preparation for his going out. Clothing, like eating, is a favorite trope for women writers (remember how the schoolboys in Kilner's *First Going to School* [1804] dress the sow in a master's clothes). If crossdressing adumbrates crossgendering, then clothing is an important nexus in crossgendered stories, disarray in dress adumbrating disarray in narrative expectations. The wrongful accusation may, furthermore, be a standard trope in the canonical, post-Hughesian school story, but by comparison with the more typical crimes of which a boy might be wrongfully accused—stealing money, stealing an examination paper—this one, disturbing the arrangement of a master's clothes, seems minor. Its significance would seem to be symbolic—the real crime is the resonance of the disarray.

In any case, the paragon Philip knows who is guilty but doesn't tell. Seen in the vicinity, he is blamed, and caned, and mortified. Most of the four culprits would eventually come forward to exonerate him, but the bully Timmins threatens the others if they dare—even, it appears, if they dare to tell Philip how sorry they are. Nor is Timmins moved after being rescued by Philip from drowning; in fact, as one boy notes, with an acuity unusual in school stories, "I believe he'll dislike Danford more than ever for having saved him . . ." (98).

What supports Philip in his honorable stance is not so much the code against talebearing as a promise not to tell, that favorite crutch of school-story authors uncertain whether to endorse the code. Certainly talebearing is not mentioned in connection with Philip's deliberations, only in connection with another episode: whether two little boys will tell on Timmins for bullying them. Witness further Goddard's distancing herself from the code in the following passage, not clearly espousing it, even faintly condemning it:

> At school it is too much the custom for the strong to tyrannize over the weak; and complaints were worse than useless, for they brought upon themselves, even amongst those who, in a measure, were sorry for them, the odium of being tell-tales, a character no schoolboy likes to incur. Hence much that is suffered by younger boys, and no one seems inclined to lift a finger to make it otherwise. (48)

Goddard had earlier shown some discomfort with this "curious code of honour in force amongst schoolboys" (42) in *The New Boy at Merriton: A Story of School Life* (1882). A boy named Andrew has promised not to tell how he obtained a baby owl. And even though threatened with expulsion, he refuses to reveal his source because he has promised not to. He is of course saved by the confession of the boy who had given him the owl, someone who names no other names. The confession nevertheless gets other boys into trouble—a situation that canonical schoolboys would avoid at all costs—yet "the greater portion of the school, instead of blaming him for the disclosures he was making which involved themselves, felt a sudden relief from a sense of meanness and injustice . . ." (62). And they clap, later cheer.

As for *Philip Danford,* it's particularly unfortunate that the person who has been persecuted is the French master, M. Lavalle. For Philip likes the man, in part because of their shared French heritage. M. Lavalle is drawn to Philip too, even willing to abrogate some of the hierarchy between master and pupil. We find M. Lavalle wondering, early on, how Philip can continue to be courteous, seemingly bearing him no grudge, after the accusation; he even tells Philip, "I am very sorry that you got a caning through me. If I had known, I would not have said a word. You have always been my very best pupil, and—I am very sorry" (29). It seems to be important that the two develop some kind of personal relationship. Is Goddard then, in a "womanly" fashion, allowing feelings to take precedence over principle? Or is it acceptable for a master to bring himself down to a boy's level, to want a boy's approval, only if he is a foreigner and therefore suspect anyway? Or is the implicit leveling that occurs here fostered by the Christian outlook that infuses the text?

In any case, other boys have found M. Lavalle suitable prey for pranks, partly because he is new, partly because he is foreign. Dr. Brierley may state that it is "a shameful and un-English act to insult a foreigner by these petty annoyances" (21), yet his need to admonish the boys shows how natural—and how naturally "English"—their behavior is. The iteration of "un-English" and "foreigner" only emphasizes M. Lavalle's alien status. The persecutions then stop after Philip is wrongly caned—as if the punishment of someone who is in effect a fellow countryman of both victim and tormentors, both the Frenchman and the English boys, somehow exorcises the desire to persecute.

At the same time the punishment is an important teaching tool, in a throwback to earlier children's literature, the child purified through suffering, not least because the suffering is unmerited. Philip learns to go beyond his brooding reserve after the caning, pushing himself to interact with his schoolmates: "Well, I don't care much about football, but I'll go in for a game, just to show the boys I can play as well as any of them" (42–43). A far cry that from canonical attitudes toward sports.

Paralleling the wrongful accusation and the caning—and furthering their pedagogical impact—is an illness that Philip incurs after rescuing Timmins from drowning. On one level the illness is a plot convenience—it keeps Philip out of school and seems, alas, to deprive him of eligibility for academic prizes. Yet Philip's disability is also morally nurturing, like that of Martineau's Hugh (and, to a limited extent, Betham-Edwards' Charlie), as he continues to school himself in patience. For Philip eventually struggles his way to forgiveness of Timmins and the other culprits.

Family context is important here too, for Philip is a day boy, returning daily to his grandmother and sister. And his sister Gabrielle is his confidante, even his conscience. Telling her his woe and eliciting her sympathy help him to regain his self-respect. Nor is she unworthy by the standards of canonical school stories: despite socializing with the daughters of the headmaster, she never lets slip the truth that would clear her brother (a fortitude congruent with the Christian context of the book as well—she allows Philip to suffer his way to true nobility). During his convalescence she becomes Philip's agent at school, going to the prize-giving—moving, listening, seeing when he cannot, and reporting back to him. Philip even seems at times to prefer his sister, Goddard's proxy, to his schoolmates.

Not the least of the family context is Philip's ancestry: the boy is fascinated by his grandmother's grandfather, whose portrait seems to approve when he undertakes a right action. It's also through this ancestor that Goddard gets to have nobility and heroism both ways, both physically and spiritually: while reveling in the story of his noble ancestor Philippe, a man who died trying to defend his king, Philip tries to learn a less physical and more Christian heroism. The ancestor serves as inspiration, leading Philip toward Christian virtue and forgiveness.

Thirty-three years earlier, Thomas Hughes portrayed both physical and spiritual views of manliness, the latter, dominant in the second half of *Tom Brown,* superseding the former.[6] Goddard similarly portrays both, with the spiritual temporally succeeding the physical. But the physical view of heroism is more thoroughly subordinated in *Philip Danford,* textually encapsulated in the account of the ancestor, not enacted by the eponymous hero. Its mere presence may acknowledge that some ideal other than the spiritual is possible, but Goddard's book more consistently embraces the spiritual ideal.

Philip constantly struggles to be Christian, to be a Christian hero, a prince in disguise like Warner's Austin. He learns not to seek revenge but to forgive, not to seek grand heroic actions but to emulate those whose "lives have been full of grand patience and endurance, and of suffering hardships uncomplainingly, and not knowing that they were heroes of any kind" (64). Philip does indeed achieve some of this heroic stature, though it requires continuing struggle.[7] And he is avenged at the end, not suffered to forego physical prizes and to make do only with spiritual ones, for the culprit is finally unmasked, and the coveted conduct prize goes to Philip. Gabrielle later reports that Dr. Brierley "said you were a hero of the best kind; so now I am sure that I may put you down as one. And will not father and mother be pleased to hear all about it. Phil, I must write a long letter to India with nothing else in it but this" (123). Thus does Goddard get her authorial representative to inscribe Philip's virtue while using the family to invoke an international nexus, this time not the European community but the outposts of empire. With its focus on a spiritual ideal, and with its invalided central character who undergoes spiritual renewal, Goddard's book may run counter to the tide of late-Victorian thinking: the book is a throwback to earlier school stories.[8] But it also anticipates later thinking in its attempts to transcend insular nationalism.

At the end of the nineteenth century and the beginning of the twentieth, on the other hand, the Scottish Mrs. G. (Annie) Forsyth Grant wrote boys' school stories that are essentially mainstream. Not that they received much favorable recognition at the time, but their plotting and tone—jolly, not especially religious—conform to the canonical. Unlike other crossgendering women Forsyth Grant wrote stories very like the boys' school stories then being written by men, as if to demonstrate that there really wasn't much scope for women in the genre, for doing something distinctive—though it is possible that Forsyth Grant's feminine signature, the foregrounding of the "Mrs.," makes us all the more aware of the masculinity of her discourse, making the discourse parodic.

Still, her stories are relatively indistinguishable from scores of others written at the time; certainly she does not make prominent use of the racial or ethnic other. She writes, with an overexplanatory, overexclamatory style, of typical and topical incidents: rescues from bullies, rescues from drownings, wrongful accusations, cricket and races, a rescue from a train in a tunnel, the burning of a manuscript. She doesn't trouble herself much over talebearing, either ignoring the code or invoking it without fretting over its implications.

If her emphasis at times differs from that of some of her male contemporaries, it's perhaps because Forsyth Grant is writing somewhat more in the tradition of *Eric* than that of *Tom Brown,* or rather more in the tradition of *Tom Brown* than of *The Fifth Form at St. Dominic's,* the tradition of the earlier pious stories: her schoolboys can still sob out repentance for their misdeeds and put an arm around their closest friends—a mode of masculine behavior that largely went out of style in the 1860s and 1870s.[9] Certainly *The Boys at Penrohn: A Story of English School Life* (1893), her earliest and perhaps best-known work, borrows directly from Eric: a beloved younger brother dies by falling off a cliff and to no avail—though in this case it's not the hero's virtue that lapses, despite the memento mori, but his popularity, a significant shift. Forsyth Grant also allows her boys to be, at times, somewhat womanly—in, for instance, their tenderness to a younger brother—and allows a younger boy to appear "fair and rather girlish" (*Penrohn* 9). All this without reprisal by the other boys, though the author does kill off the girlish younger brother. Or, in *The Beresford Boys: A School Story* (1906), she amputates the arm of a weak, good-hearted boy, a boy neither bright nor good at games, though never actually called effeminate— yet not so that he can be morally educated by the experience but to enable the reunion of two other boys, estranged friends, one comforting the other in this time of sadness.

Forsyth Grant largely avoids physical fighting, allowing boys to face down a bully, talk him around rather than fight him. Her plots too tend to veer away from the linearity more common in the canonical story, the scenes serving more to give us samples of school life than a sense of a boy's progress: the narrator introduces a classroom scene, for instance, by stating, "Perhaps we might look in for a short while just to see how our friends conduct themselves at lesson time" (*Burke's Chum* 51). Like Adams' *Edgar Clifton* (1852), the novels veer toward the narrative of community—episodic, devoted to the dailiness that sustains communities. Forsyth Grant's sketchy plots likewise tend to place greater emphasis on vicissitudes in the friendship between two boys, boys who "adore" and "worship" each other, than on the individualistic moral and/or social development of one of them. Contemporary male authors of boys' school stories generally did not describe such passions—and certainly didn't describe them with Forsyth Grant's jolly frankness and sense of isn't-this-the-way-the-world-ought-to-be. So at times *The Beresford Boys* reads like a girls' school story with raves and crushes—with the addition of physical adventures that girls were unlikely to be allowed to encounter. In these respects Forsyth Grant may be bringing something of a woman's sensibility to the boys' school story.

Yet for the most part what eruptions there are in the text tend not to be gender coded nor, indeed, to be significantly different from those in works by males. In *The Beresford Boys,* for instance, a boy called Meredith wants to become "a famous World-traveller, a Colony-founder, an Empire-builder, a Continent-explorer, a ————" (181). He talks of the North Pole, Uganda, the Caribee Islands, the valley of the Wingicarribee in New South Wales, of "Chicago, Maracaybo—Bosnia, Polynesia—Kimberley, Tasmania—Corea, San Domingo—Dakota, Nova Zembla—Shikoku, Alabama————" (62). Thus does Forsyth Grant, like Kipling and other contemporary male writers, prepare her schoolboys for the world-hunger of British imperialism. Thus does she contain and minimize the racial and ethnic other, keeping it exotic. Thus does the world after school, and the literary world beyond school stories—namely, adventure stories—seep into the novel.

The seepage is reinforced by the quirkiness of the illustrations in this volume, illustrations presumably by Forsyth Grant's schoolboy son. He is more interested in illustrating the exotic throwaway references, such as to a tornado in Oklahoma, than in picturing the actions, such as they are, of the plot. A reference to what the would-be world traveler calls the Grand Lhama of Tibet, sitting on a cushion, calls forth an illustration that echoes Tenniel's Caterpillar in Wonderland. A boy's wishing another at "the bottom of the sea" (252) inspires a picture of the boy underwater, accompanied by fish, whale, and octopus. Similarly, when one boy tells another, "I believe that if you were going to be beheaded, you would keep on talking after your head was off!" (247), there is a picture of a beheading. If the illustrations function as schoolboy commentary on what is of interest in the tale, then they are doubly subversive: showing the schoolboy reader as reading the story at a tangent, and highlighting the eruption of imperialism and adventure stories in the text. An eruption that, in part, tames the exotic, makes it decorative whimsy more than serious object. Still, a woman writing a fairly canonical school story could be tentatively subversive, perhaps especially when in league with a schoolboy, both agents a little out of the stream fed by the main promulgators of the canonical school story. Or perhaps a mother writing for her son (as, we shall soon see, Elizabeth Eiloart did), and with her son, can have a heightened sense of the tension between school and family, and can find herself subtly subverting the former in favor of the latter.

The capstone to this discussion of British works is one of the earliest crossgendered books to follow *Tom Brown's Schooldays,* a topsy-turvy near-parody that violates more norms than the other books discussed in this chapter—including the norm of the chapter that, in the late nineteenth century,

British school-story authors crossed genders by crossing ethnicity. For in *Ernie at School* (1867) Mrs. (Elizabeth) Eiloart crosses not just ethnicity but race, like the writers of contemporary crossgendered works in the United States.[10] She thus confronts the imperial project more directly than other school-story writers do—though perhaps she can return us to some of the premises with which I started the chapter. For, in effect, Betham-Edwards' Ernest has, eight years later, become Eiloart's Ernie, less formal, less earnest. And eating is again salient. Eiloart's Ernie is an early avatar of Billy Bunter, the fat boy of twentieth-century pop-culture school stories—his name as well known in England as Superman's in the United States Ernie may not be fat— he is presumably the lightest boy in his dormitory room—but he is incorrigibly lazy (even games are too much work) and constantly preoccupied with food. And, like Billy Bunter, he serves as the catalyst for mad scrapes.

On some level Eiloart has transposed traditionally feminine qualities to Ernie, or rather works through her own feminine concerns in his person. Take his preoccupation with food, from his introduction to school fare (another boy assures him that the Yorkshire pudding, which the boys call stickjaw, is made with tallow), to a midnight feast (pork pie, raspberry jam, cake, apple puffs, sausage rolls, ginger wine), to food begged at an inn on a school outing (gooseberry pie, rice pudding, cheesecake, shrub), to a breakfast upon arriving at his uncle's in New Zealand (coffee, bread, bacon, cutlets, pickles, marmalade, black currant jam, anchovies, honey), to a climactic cannibal feast—a meal that Ernie serves to itinerant Maoris because he fears they might feast on him instead (veal pie, cake, ham, jam, marmalade, Guinness stout, Bass pale ale, then bread and butter and tea with cream). Not that boys are uninterested in food. But the emphasis on food, and specifically the topos of the midnight feast, or forbidden eating, appears more often in the girls' school story than in that about boys. Transgressions in boys' school stories are more likely to entail stealing or cheating—so that even when boys do engage in forbidden eating, as in Edgeworth's "Tarlton" (1796) or May's *Louis' School Days* (1850) or Kenyon's *Jack's Heroism* (1883), to choose crossgendered examples, the focus of the transgression is more the stealing than the eating.[11] Yet ever since the argument over who will get the best apple in *The Governess* (1749), transgressions in girls' school stories have characteristically focused on food. In Buckland's *Lily and Nannie at School* (1868), as I have noted in Chapter 1, girls considered incorrigible indulge in a midnight feast, not stealing the food, not even from the school's larder, but getting it from their own food baskets. And by the twentieth century the midnight feast had become a staple of popular girls' school stories by Angela Brazil, Enid Blyton, and others.[12] Eiloart finds her way into the boys' school story, in effect, by starting with a girls' topos, in the first adventure that Ernie stumbles into at school.

A topos that she modifies, to invest it with more of the thrills that she may associate with boys. Ned, a good-natured but mischievous boy, stashes a pot of jam in another boy's bed, and when the boys are disturbed by an approaching master, Ernie dives into the bed and upsets the jam. So, of course, Ned has to wash out the sheets and hang them out the window to dry, and when a sheet falls, Ernie is lowered to fetch it—only to be glimpsed by a visitor, the retired schoolmaster Mr. Simpkins—leading to a slapstick routine in which adults keep coming to the boys' room, see nothing amiss, and eventually decide that Mr. Simpkins has had one too many rum punches. Thereby doubly undermining adult authorities. For not only do the authorities fail to catch the boys, but the figure of absurdity in the escapade is Mr. Simpkins, someone who "lost no opportunity of inveighing against present manners and customs, especially in educational matters, as savouring too much of over-indulgence," someone who "never spared the cane and spoiled the child" (37, 41)—the archrepresentative, in short, of adult authority, even if he is only a past master and now passé.

Traditional authorities such as Mr. Simpkins and the didactic kind of children's literature that he would have favored—and that Eiloart is reacting against—are further undermined through the moral tag with which she concludes the chapter:

> MORAL.—Young people's books ought always to have a moral. I'm going to write mine now, so if you don't like to read it (I never did myself when I was young) you can skip it and go on to the next chapter. Old gentlemen shouldn't be too fond of rum punch; if they are, they can't always expect to be believed, even when they're most undeniably speaking the truth. (43)

The lesson, in short, is directed to the erstwhile schoolmaster, not to the boys. Eiloart thereby disposes of both earlier models of school authority and earlier models of school story—in a passage that captures some of the archness of her style.

She thus plays with traditional themes such as the midnight feast and with traditional authorities, undermining them through humor. She further undermines a theme such as eating through subverting its effect. For if eating—or not eating—is a way in which girls can shape themselves, their bodily contours,[13] it has no such effect on Ernie: he can make a pig of himself without ending up looking like one.

And that's despite his strong aversion to movement—another transposition of the feminine, given that middle-class women commonly lacked freedom of movement—though eventually, paradoxically, Ernie moves more than virtually any other fictional schoolboy. He is someone who would rather sit and shiver than exercise, would rather ride than walk, and certainly is not interested in games. One of the characteristic ways he gets into scrapes, in this book and in the earlier *Ernie Elton, the Lazy Boy* (1865), is by hitching unauthorized rides—riding uninvited yet unruffled in someone else's private carriage, sneaking into a wagon even though the driver has denied him permission. Such delicacy with respect to self-propulsion is gender coded as feminine, even if the impertinence with which he cadges rides is not.

Other ways in which Ernie is feminized, in effect, in both *Ernie Elton, the Lazy Boy* and *Ernie at School,* are through his association with babies and his clothing. Babies seem to like him—or at least he keeps ending up caring for them, having babies foisted on him, which he then unavailingly tries to dispose of. And his scrapes often involve a drenching, so that he has to wear clothing untypical of a European male, whether it is a gender-neutral blanket (which he has to make do with for some days in New Zealand) or an adult woman's gown. Or, more precisely, Ernie is frequently garbed in such a way that it is difficult to pin down who he is—whether another boy has drawn whiskers on his face with burnt cork while he was sleeping, or he becomes so ragged that his New Zealand uncle doesn't know who he is. Ernie remains a cipher who dons and doffs guises, some of them crossgendered—echoing Eiloart's own agility.

Nor is Eiloart averse to the depiction of tears. Ernie and Ned do avoid tears at school, but as a matter more of expediency than of manliness: "They would have been quite thrown away upon either master or boys, so, like a wise fellow, Ned reserved the display of his handkerchief for occasions when it was likely to be really useful . . ." (80)—such as when the two boys want to con pies from a cook or passage to New Zealand with a sympathetic Irishwoman. Tears are going out of fashion, among boys, though they work with women—they still work, that is, in crossgendered contexts.

In these varied respects—eating, immobility, association with babies, dress, crying—Ernie could be said to be effeminate, yet his schoolmates never call him a sissy or use any other term of gendered disparagement. Indeed, if at the end of the book Ernie's uncle is concerned to "make a man of" the boy, it is to cure Ernie not of effeminacy but of "babyish nonsense" (218, 223). Eiloart would seem here to be harking back to the polarity governing the early nineteenth century, between man and child, such that being a man entails putting away childish things, rather than the polarity that was superseding it, between man and woman. Her reliance on such early norms allows her to feminize Ernie without degrading him. Ernie may not be as favorably portrayed as earlier schoolboys who followed "feminine" ways—this lazy boy is hardly striving for spiritual perfection—but neither is he castigated for being effeminate, as he soon would be in school stories by men.

At the same time, the flippancy of Eiloart's style and her refusal to castigate Ernie's sloth and greed—her willingness to find it instead somewhat amusing—situates her squarely in late-nineteenth-century modes, even more so than Hughes's earnest *Tom Brown's Schooldays.*

Furthermore, if Ernie is frequently portrayed in feminine terms, the plot is in effect increasingly masculinized—as Ernie is pushed further and further out of the orbit of home and school, finally propelled out of England by the threat of a beating. There is, first of all, the movement from the first volume, with Ernie at home, to the second, at school. Early in the second volume there is the midnight feast, when Ernie is lowered out of the school building to fetch the sheet and then returned to the safety of bed—much as, in the book as a whole, there is a movement away from school and from the relatively domesticated school story. The first chapter of *Ernie at School,* describing Ernie's first day, gives us some insight into the school routine (mostly to show how Ernie violates it). The next two focus on clandestine nighttime activities, first the midnight feast, then another slapstick escapade that culminates in the housekeeper clobbering Mr. Simpkins, taking him for a thief. Then there is a chapter devoted to a school outing, culminating in Ernie and Ned's ride back, hiding behind umbrellas on Miss Primmins' phaeton. The remaining six chapters focus on Ernie and Ned running away from school, taking a ship to New Zealand—thereby impinging on the genre of the boy's adventure story, though Ernie's adventures on the ship are those of a nursemaid more than a cabin boy—and ending up at the home of Ernie's not-altogether-welcoming uncle. The boys stay in New Zealand upwards of seven months—their parents never, it appears, becoming unduly alarmed—and then return with some relief to the relative sanity of school. And since, at the end, Ernie's father eventually "had the good fortune to obtain a situation in a government office for him, where one of the more onerous duties is to read the *Times,* he gets on pretty well, and at any rate considers himself a very hard-working person, and sometimes wonders how public affairs would go on without him" (247–248). Our glimpse of Ernie's future does not, in short, intimate a brilliant career as a lord of the Admiralty or the Governor General of Fiji—or as a barrister practicing before the Supreme Court of the Gold Coast Colony, as Eiloart's real-life Ernie went on to do[14]—but, satirically, of the smugness of the bureaucratic functionary.

In any case, unlike other British writers of boys' school stories, even though their volumes are governed by imperial imperatives, even though they are indoctrinating readers to become the advocates and builders of empire, Eiloart more fully acknowledges imperialism by taking us to the far reaches of empire. Other writers of school stories may, like Ellen Wood or indeed Frederic Farrar, expel characters from England as a way of purifying the school; still others may send their boys off, at the end, to fight for the glory of the empire. But in almost all other cases—an exception is the popular magazine serial of the 1870s featuring Jack Harkaway—the overseas scenes happen offstage, not as direct action in the text. Even Kipling tells of Stalky's exploits in India only in the last chapter and only once Stalky is an adult, and we hear of these exploits only second or third hand. Eiloart goes further than other writers of school stories in letting her characters physically escape from school to the outposts of empire, thus undermining school and its value, an undermining heightened by having the runaways face only mild reprisals.[15] And in doing so she allows the imperialism undergirding the school story to emerge with more salience than in other school stories.

Where other crossgendering Englishwomen present a Frenchman or a German for our edification, Eiloart presents a Maori. If in the United States at this time the other, for members of the white middle class, would be a black, in Britain the lines of cleavage could be class, ethnicity, or race.[16] Or rather Eiloart presents the Maori not so much for our edification, or his. Although she avoids some of the grossest stereotypes, she fails to present him and his kinsmen with complete respect. Despite writing at the height of what the British called the Maori wars, she does not portray the Maoris as warlike. Instead she domesticates this indigenous group that, for the British, were a node of competing discourses, a people simultaneously fierce and poetic: Eiloart largely subsumes violence in the trope of sociable eating.

One night back at school, the boys had tossed Ernie with their doubled-up bolsters, pretending he was the "chief of the Cannibal Islands" (49). The boy who had instigated the game—having read about tribesmen who carry a chief on the points of their spears, then toss him up and catch him some seven times—can't remember at first which "savage people" it derived from: "I don't know whether it was the Highlanders, or the Ancient Romans, or the Cherokee Indians . . ." (47). So it is irrelevant, within the logic of the book, that the Cannibal Islands were more commonly Fiji than New Zealand. Or rather all too relevant—all too indicative of the imperialist tendency to consider all outgroups equivalent, all savage.

On the one hand, cannibalism is an extension of Ernie's preoccupation with eating. Cannibalism was also, perhaps especially to late-nineteenth-century Britons, the "nadir of savagery" (Brantlinger, *Rule* 185), "the archetype of everything monstrous and appalling in primitive cultures" (Green, *Dreams* 80)—and the game thus adumbrates the savagery of boys. Early during his stay in New Zealand, when Ernie dresses for some days in a blanket, a neighbor says, "I'll pin it round, and you'll look like one of the natives dropped in for a visit" (215)—Ernie is, in his way, "uncivilized," "going native." Later Ernie reads of an act of aboriginal cannibalism in Australia (the victim "was only one of themselves, so it don't so much matter, but I suppose if they eat blacks they will whites, if they can only get them. Like them all the better, I shouldn't wonder" [226]). So when confronted with the Maori Wangeriri on his uncle's doorstep, Ernie's thoughts fly immediately to the dangers of cannibalism. Mobilized by fear, he serves Wangeriri and cohort with the choice delicacies prepared against the return of his uncle and others from a pig-hunting expedition.

Now this pig-hunting expedition is a reprise of an earlier hunt for Ernie and Ned in England. Their headmaster had had trouble deciding which of two simultaneous calamities was worse, the disappearance of the two boys or of four suckling pigs. When the headmaster's nephew went off to fetch Ernie and Ned from a neighbor's bed, he of course found the pigs instead.[17] The New Zealand pig-hunting expedition is likewise a displacement of a kind of human head-hunting, of Europeans hunting for Maoris, or Maoris for Europeans: Ernie imagines the returning hunters "peppering [the Maoris] off as they do the pigs" (233). Thus the book invokes a chain of signifiers— European boys, pigs, Maori adults—marginalized variously by age, species, race, and nationality, and all of them hunted.

In any case, the visit of the Maoris is presumably an occasion for humor: we glimpse these indigenous people devouring the feast and "really behav[ing] very well, considering that knives and forks and the other appurtenances of a civilized table were not much in their way" (233). Then, indulging in jam and marmalade, "they didn't understand eating them on bread, but helped themselves out of the pots with their teaspoons" (233). And finally they sip tea in more or less proper British fashion, Ernie pouring it out "as well as a lady" (237)—thus is gender incorporated in the chain of signifiers as well, a British boy feminized by the encounter with the other. The "humor" of this mad tea party derives in part from the miscommunication engendered by the Maoris' broken English: when Wangeriri says, "Me want eat" (229), Ernie's imagination readily supplies the wrong direct object. Yet the "humor" derives even more from the counterpoint between Ernie's hospitable actions and inhospitable thoughts (the alacrity with which he reaches down his uncle's stock of Guinness and Bass is fueled by his imagining the Maoris being hung once they are caught) than from the presumed ineptitude of the Maoris.

For the most part—and with the exception, a big exception, of the fact that Ned calls the Maoris niggers—Eiloart's portrayal of Maoris avoids some of the worst excesses, certainly compared to earlier depictions of "savages" in children's literature. Kirsten Drotner, for instance, points to a crude woodcut appearing in the magazine *Children's Friend* in 1832, accompanying an article on New Zealand, and notes that it "is a common illustration for the periodical's missionary tales describing the alleged barbarities of foreign peoples" (*English Children* 52): both the depiction of torture in the illustration—a child is about to thrust a dagger into another, tied to a tree—and the use of the same illustration to embellish descriptions of diverse indigenous peoples, in various issues, underscore the crudeness of the imperialist imperative here. Or Claudia Marquis points to the crudeness of Jules Verne's *Among the Cannibals* (1867), a tale published the same year as Eiloart's but one that characterizes the "New Zealanders" as the most cruel and gluttonous of anthrophagi (2).

Eiloart also manages to avoid some of the virulent racism endemic in adventure fiction of the 1880s and 1890s.[18] And Eiloart's representations are a far cry from the stereotypical cartoons that—to drift somewhat afield geographically—would appear in such children's literature as Helen Bannerman's immensely popular *Little Black Sambo* (1899), a story whose text would seem to be set in India (tigers, *ghee*) but whose illustrations portray grossly caricatured Africans, or rather minstrels in blackface.[19]

Eiloart's work echoes an early strand of children's literature that made gestures in the direction of the Rousseauian noble savage, that treated blacks and other nonwhites with a measure of respect—witness the portrayal of the black peddler in Strickland's *Hugh Latimer* (1828), discussed in Chapter 4. Certainly the illustration of the tea-party scene in the nineteenth-century edition of *Ernie at School* that I used gives the Maoris "dignified" (though Europeanized) facial features and body proportions, whatever we make of their garb: one wears a Native American headdress, another a three-cornered hat and epaulettes. In neither build nor dress (nor the absence of tattooing) are the Maoris represented in their own terms, as characteristically Maori; like the illustration in the *Children's Friend* three decades earlier, this one depicts generic "natives." For like other Polynesians, Maoris tend to have solid builds rather than the somewhat slender ones that Eiloart's illustrator accords them; nor do they generally have the aquiline noses some of them are here accorded. As for dress, while we may expect indigenous peoples after European contact to assume a kind of bricolage—one comes across Ninja

Ernie makes tea for the natives. Reprinted courtesy of de Grummond Children's Literature Research Collection, University of Southern Mississippi.

Turtle and Woodstock T-shirts around the globe—the Eiloart illustration goes beyond the plausible. Even the three- or four-feather Maori headdress, the feathers radiating from the back of the head more or less at right angles, has here been translated into a full-feathered Sioux one, as if the illustrator couldn't think how else to depict a feathered headdress. Also noteworthy are the tricorne and epaulettes, sported by the figure whose facial features seem least European, the figure who, gazing out of the frame to the right, is least assimilated, compositionally, to the party, less even than the background figure that is Ernie. Their motley costuming makes the Maoris, like Ernie, simultaneously difficult to pigeonhole and figures of fun—makes them the mimic men, "not quite/not white," prevalent in colonial discourse (Bhabha 132), their similarity to Europeans traversed by a difference that shades into menace, a menace most strongly evoked by the unassimilated figure of the "native" Napoleon.

Eiloart and her illustrator thus fail to represent the Maoris on their own terms. Yet they do not portray the Maoris as particularly disgusting— only as lacking fluency in English language and manners. Ernie may silently describe the baby that takes a fancy to him as a "horrid little beast!" (235), but then his opinion is never to be trusted, and the imprecation is not much worse than what he has said of another baby when he called it "the heaviest, dirtiest, nastiest little brat that ever was" (166).[20] In fact, when Ernie threatens to abandon the burdensome Maori baby outside, on the ground, a white neighbor protests, "No, you wont [sic], young fellow. . . . I dare say its mother thinks as much of that young copper-colour as my wife does of any of hers . . ." (238).

Eiloart does, furthermore, have the grace to provide Wangeriri with a name that sounds plausibly Maori, even if the *e* would, in European transliterations, more commonly be rendered as *a* or *i*. She had probably heard of place names like Wanganui and Rangiriri because of the fighting between the British and the Maoris. In fact, the *riri* of Wangeriri provides a subversive subtext, for it means quarrel or anger (see Tregear): the Maoris called the fighting in the 1860s, what the English have called the Maori wars, *te riri pakeha,* or white man's quarrel (Sinclair 131). Not that Eiloart was aware of all that. She probably just came up with a name that sounded plausible— yet the reason it would sound plausible, in the 1860s, is because of its association with warfare. Wangeriri's name thus has an edge of fierceness, even if that is not what Eiloart emphasizes.

For the narrator says that Wangeriri "was really, like the rest of the Maories about that part of New Zealand, a peaceable quietly disposed person enough, although rather formidable in his appearance" (228); he was just passing through with some of his tribe and hoping for a little refreshment. And when Ernie's uncle returns he assures Ernie that "Wangeriri's no more of a cannibal than you are" (241). Though given the boy's gluttony, and his having been tossed as a cannibal chief, he might be justified in finding little comfort in the comment. A white neighbor's statement is a little ambiguous too: "So you've been taking old Wangeriri and his wife—the quietest couple in New Zealand—for cannibals! *They* eat you! They're too good judges!" (240, Eiloart's italics). As if—to miss the "humor" here—they might choose to eat a choicer morsel of British boyhood. In any case, quietness, peacefulness may be virtues in a native from Eiloart's point of view but not necessarily from a Maori's, especially in the context of European contact. For the "Maori wars" were very much in progress when Eiloart published *Ernie at School*. True, she sets her story on the Middle Island (now South Island), away from the main fighting. She thus evades the issue—and also signals her uneasy awareness of her evasion through her self-conscious geographical sidestepping, by attributing peaceable natures specifically to "the Maories about that part of New Zealand."

Eiloart's choice of New Zealand too, as the place to send Ernie and Ned, may have been governed by a sense that the Maoris were more admirable than other "savages," more admirable than, say, indigenous Australians (who become a lightning rod when Ernie reads of their alleged cannibalism); that is, she may have chosen to write of a group whom she could portray with some respect. For the notion of the noble savage seems to have persisted longer with respect to Maoris than with respect to other indigenous peoples. Brantlinger encapsulates common views when he notes in passing that Victorians were apt to think that "Africans were made of coarser stuff than the sensitive and poetic Maoris" (*Rule* 187).[21] Or rather, in the welter of competing discourses, ascriptions of negative qualities to Maoris are apt to be accompanied by—at times superseded by—ascriptions of positive ones: a writer in the *Cornhill Magazine* in 1865 sketches the spectrum of contemporary views when he describes "outlying colonists" as considering Maoris "half-tamed cannibals with European vices and Maori lawlessness" while "Friends of humanity" consider them "nature's noblemen and our superiors" ("Maori Sketches" 498).[22]

Even in their first contact with Europeans, Maoris were portrayed as admirable: the eighteenth-century explorer James Cook described them as "a brave warlike people, with sentiments void of treachery" (quoted in Sinclair 32). And during the "Maori wars" in the 1860s, tales abound of their sportsmanlike behavior: more than once Maoris sent food to British soldiers with whom they were fighting so that the fight could go on (Sinclair

144). The *Cornhill* writer said that "their dash, in one or two actions, has been equaled to the charge of Balaklava" ("Maori Sketches" 509–510). A recently resigned Minister of Native Affairs claimed in an 1865 letter published in *The Times*, "No campaign has ever been fought so little creditable to the British arms" (Fitzgerald): though he may have been primarily castigating the British military, he also showed respect for the Maoris. A military historian has stated that the Maoris were "on the whole the grandest native enemy that [the British soldier] had ever encountered" (quoted in Sinclair 144). Even a settler—one of those "outlying colonists," writing in self-justification to a British audience—stated that "the respectable English settler . . . likes their pluck [and] admits their intelligence . . ." ("Settled" 312). A good deal of respect seems to have devolved, in short, from the reputation for fierceness. The *Cornhill* writer suggestively yokes the two attitudes together, as if the force of the one intensifies the other, indeed provides an excuse for turning to the other: "It is not to be expected that from colonial reports we should hear much of Maori poetry. Their late armed resistance has earned for the natives a 'nigger' hatred, Yankee in its expression, nor even in England do we expect much sympathy with the Taillefers of Maori chivalry . . ." ("Maori Sketches" 509).[23] Yet in the process of constructing the Maoris as admirable the fierceness is often erased, the Maoris becoming notable for being "sensitive and poetic."

Eiloart's work is part of that process of erasure. For she wants to domesticate Wangeriri and his compatriots—domestication being, for her, a virtue—even if she has some "fun" at their expense, depicting a tea party in brownface. She controls them through humor and domesticates the potential for violence through the trope of eating. If, as Spivak has argued, Bertha Mason must immolate herself to let Jane Eyre "become the feminist individualist heroine of British fiction," enacting "an allegory of the general epistemic violence of imperialism" (185), then Eiloart, instead, domesticates the possibility of violence. She does so partly by erasing some of the historical record, erasing what was happening among Maoris on the South Island in the 1860s near Otago, near where Ernie's uncle lived—namely, a liquor craze (see A. Ward 222). Writing for children, of children, she censors the violence occurring in New Zealand as she wrote, likewise the drinking.

Or rather she translates these activities into the eating endemic in children's literature, not just in its sociable form as midnight feasting in girls' school stories but in a more aggressive form in works like the British *Alice's Adventures in Wonderland* (1865) and, a century later, the American *Where the Wild Things Are* (1963). Both Enlightenment and evangelical writers had earlier urged children to dam their appetites: in *The Governess* (1749), for instance, greediness for apples must be repressed. Eiloart, on the other hand, like Carroll, and like Anna Warner in *The Prince in Disguise* (1862), was one of the first to celebrate eating. The nurturing and agricultural metaphors of much early literature for children thus culminate in the feast that follows the harvest. Or rather, if the child is that which is cultivated, in early literature, and hence implicitly that which is to be eaten, then subsequent children's literature embodies the return of the repressed, the children becoming the eaters. Eiloart, then, gives play to the extreme embodiment of the discourse of cultivation—and to the fear of being eaten—when she invokes the trope of cannibalism. But she does so only to scout it in favor of culinary domestication.[24]

For despite the lurking hints of cannibalism, eating is a domestic activity in *Ernie at School*. Ernie's Maori feast not only domesticates the Maoris but also domesticates him: it "civilizes" him as nothing before has done. There's no danger of Ernie going native. He's no Mistah Kurtz. Even when he dresses in a blanket, ostensibly like a native, the effect is humorous; he is not internally affected. Yet it's only when he serves food to the Maoris that we ever see him doing anything for anyone else. It's only then that he is explicitly compared to the feminine, when he pours out tea "as well as a lady" (237). The encounter becomes a parable for the impact of imperialism on the mother country—what Nancy Armstrong calls Occidentalism, the way projections onto non-Europeans, segregating them from Europe, in turn changed Europeans, "the sense they had of themselves as a nation of men and women, the uses to which they put their own bodies, the form and content of their desires and fears and therefore the basis for an identification among Europeans" (4).[25] Tamed by fear, feminized without losing caste—finally socialized, in effect, to the schoolboy custom of fagging, in which a younger boy might prepare tea for an older one—Ernie becomes civil, developing an appreciation for being civilized that he has never had before, sufficiently socialized to be able to return to school.

Through strategic erasures, then, Eiloart constructs a Maori that is capable of domestication—and of domesticating the European—yet remains other. Much as she erases the tattooing that was distinctive of Maoris—she never alludes to it—to inscribe her own reading of them. In other words, it's Ernie and Eiloart who cultivate and effectively cannibalize the Maoris. If Ernie is in turn cultivated and cannibalized, it's only by the author, not, reciprocally, by the Maoris.

Yet perhaps it's also admirable that Eiloart lets the Maoris remain other—that she does not straitjacket them into a European mold. She does not, for instance, feel compelled to Christianize them—as her contemporaries

Mrs. Aylmer and W. H. G. Kingston did, in juvenile works featuring Maoris.[26] Eiloart allows Wangeriri and cohort to continue on their own way after their encounter with Ernie. Perhaps because Ernie and the story would in fact be returning to England, not staying on to colonize New Zealand, Eiloart did not need fully to assimilate the Maoris.

Yet if Eiloart allows some respect for an individual like Wangeriri, her individualizing of the story nonetheless vitiates some of its impact. Ernie may be undermined but not British institutions more generally (even if some potential for that remains). The *Cornhill* account of the Maoris states, "Our civilization and our religious teaching seem to be alike failures, which leads us to doubt if our civilization and our religious teaching, as exhibited in New Zealand, are of the best sort" ("Maori Sketches" 511). But Eiloart deflects—rechannels—such possible institutional criticism onto the individual subject.

Or consider her treatment of the trappings of canonical school stories—and of schools. Ernie may, in traveling to New Zealand, find himself so tired of tending a baby that he decides that "Latin's a great nuisance, but there are worse things than that in the world . . ." (168). Ned may, once arrived in New Zealand, find himself working harder at chores than he ever had before and hence discover "that there are harder things in life than lessons, and that if you want to get on in this world you must not be always in mischief, however great your natural talents that way may be" (217). The academic is here lauded, though, significantly, in absentia. The excitement of the boys' adventures on the way to and in New Zealand belies the enthusiasm for school.

And sometimes Eiloart undermines adult authority in a fully conscious way. When discussing one boy's willingness to tell tall tales to bewilder Ernie, the narrator notes,

> I'm not defending Paul; his notions of morality were certainly eccentric, and one never meets with anything of the kind amongst grown-up people—who always tell the truth fairly and boldly out, without any shirking or equivocation whatever—who never desire the servants to say "not at home" when they're comfortably lounging in dishabille over the fire, or say all sorts of civil things that they're as far as possible from meaning; no, *we* never do such things, young folks, so there's no excuse for such as Master Paul, with nothing but good examples amongst all the papas and mammas of his acquaintance. (107–108, Eiloart's italics)

Yet Eiloart's stance, ultimately, is elusive—witness how she includes herself in the "we" and thus undermines her own authority as well. She is so intent on poking fun at traditional hierarchies—masters are fearful of reprimands from servants, a husband knows better than to object to anything his wife suggests, a schoolboy jokes that the headmaster wouldn't dare go against the boys' rules with respect to sending a boy to Coventry[27]—that her subversion is dissipated.

Still, her very ambiguities open up questions that canonical authors evade. She questions the authority of antiquated schoolmasters and of mammas and papas, even lumping herself with those whose authority is called into question. Through Ernie she questions the arrangements of boys' schooling, even if he would generally seem more at fault for any mishap than any school authority is. She implicitly questions the premises of British imperialism as well, as she sends her schoolboys off on an adventure in another hemisphere and explodes the worst of their stereotypes by domesticating the presumed cannibalism of the "natives" (a move that simultaneously colonizes the Maoris). She explodes the genre by yoking it with the adventure story, and that as early as 1867—in the same year that another Englishwoman would, in effect, implode the genre, subvert it from within, within the nation, within the school, within the individual psyche, yoking it with the sensation story.

NOTES

1. See Brantlinger, *Rule* 57.

2. She lapsed from an initial support of women's suffrage, stating, in later years, "I have never been able to feel much enthusiasm about Women's Universities, Female Franchise, and the rest. Such questions from the first settled themselves in my mind as purely matters of abstract justice, unanswerable claims that must sooner or later be satisfied" (*Reminiscences* 159).

3. And in providing a "modern" portrayal of childhood in the first half of the book, then retreating to piety and moral improvement in the second half, she echoes the moral structure of the contemporaneous *Tom Brown*.

4. Together with its corollary, to do one's duty whatever one's lot might be: "We never neglect our duty without getting into trouble, and so you will find out, Charlie Steward; and not only Charlie Steward, but all the Charlies, Georges, Tommies, Johns, Lucies, Claras and Janes in the world will find it out too" (76–77). Thus does Betham-Edwards moralize as she directly addresses her readership, a readership that she construes as partly female.

5. Although Musgrave (103) and Nelson (*Boys* 73) refer to her as Ethel Kenyon, both Kirk and the *British Museum General Catalogue* list her given name as Edith.

6. For discussion of the portrayal of an increasingly internalized heroism in Victorian fiction—but that treats *Tom Brown* as an anomaly—see Merchant.

7. It's a struggle for Goddard, too, given the inevitable slippage of language. Urged, earlier, to outdo Timmins at skating, Philip bites his lip, uncomfortable with the remark, for "he had been thinking that he had quieted down his feelings against Timmins, and that he was getting schooled into bearing any advantage that Timmins might get over him. And now his indignation seemed to flame up again, and he felt

he must make an extra effort, and stand above Timmins whatever it cost him" (89). Thus Philip is to stand above Timmins by not standing above him, to suffer disadvantage by taking advantage.

8. Nelson suggests that the current had shifted by 1880 (*Boys* 29).

9. See Newton 134–135; see also J. Richards, *Happiest Days* 62–63, 97–99. Nelson finds Forsyth Grant "redolent of sentiment and androgyny" (*Boys* 73).

10. She would go on to write popular fiction for adults that grapples with the woman question, fiction that "ignored the usual clichés of morals and taste" (Mitchell, *Fallen Angel* 110).

11. As in fact is the case in *Ernie Elton, the Lazy Boy*, the precursor to *Ernie at School*. Ernie and some other boys purloin food from the larder and the fruit-room in a house where he is staying as a guest—an act that the narrator calls dishonest. Yet Eiloart has transposed this more masculine version of the transgression to the more domestic story, the one not set at school—a transposition further signaled by references to school topics in conjunction with this earlier adventure: when the boys get locked out on the roof, one thinks that "a whole day at sums" might be preferable, and we are told that another is "not the boy to turn round on his companions and tell tales" (143, 148). Eiloart incorporates the more feminine version of the transgression, the more domestic version, in her school story.

12. To the extent that a recent commentator on Brazil's schoolgirls wonders if "their creator nurtured a minor fetish for food" (Cadogan, "Eighty Years" 10).

13. In contrast with adult women in Victorian fiction for adults: as Michie points out, women are rarely shown eating in such fiction, though they are powered by hunger (13ff.). She adds that such delicacy is also associated with social class. Age would seem to be another significant variable.

14. See Kirk. Eiloart's son in effect returned his mother's crossgendered compliment by publishing, eleven years after *Ernie at School*, *The Laws Relating to Women*.

15. Eiloart's near-parody of a school story pushes her close to fantasy—though the utterly impossible never quite happens. There is no Garuda stone here, no magical switching of boy's and father's bodies, as in Anstey's *Vice Versa* (1882). Yet Eiloart achieves some of Anstey's satiric impact, though her parody is less satirically pointed.

16. Brantlinger suggests that they were in the process of shifting from class to race, that cultural themes were shifting "away from domestic class conflict toward racial and international conflict" by the end of the century (*Rule* 35).

17. A reprise, in turn, of Kilner's pigs in blankets, masquerading as master and boys, in *First Going to School* (1804)—though here a direct and humorous undermining of authority, there an implicit undermining of humanity. Like the earlier book, though, Eiloart's incorporates a thematics of bestiality, boys frequently compared to animals when they're not killing the latter, so here too is considerable slippage between human and animal.

18. See Brantlinger, *Rule* 39ff.; see also Dunae.

19. See Yuill for a discussion of the politics of *Little Black Sambo*.

20. Though this latter baby is Irish, not English. Later Ernie calls the Maori baby a "little black brat" (239), at a time when "black" was pejorative.

21. Views that crossed the Atlantic: Emerson, when casting about for an illustrative noble savage in "Self-Reliance," lights on "the naked New Zealander" (1526). See also Rowbotham 209–210.

22. A writer in *The Times*, in 1863, refers to "sagacious savages" ("Renewal"). Four months later another, after noting how Maoris make percussion caps out of marbles and wax, states, "All this is very illustrative of Maori ingenuity and would excite our admiration if we were spared from reading an adjoining paragraph headed, 'Another little boy shot by the Maories'" ("War").

23. The worst excesses of racism are, furthermore, displaced here onto Americans, as we conclude our Civil War, and, curiously, onto Northerners rather than South-

erners. Or—to cite another example—a writer in *The Times,* inclined to feel that the warlike King followers need to be sharply dealt with, can say, in the same breath, that a leader "recently regarded as the mainstay of Kingism in this province" is "by far the shrewdest and most civilized chief in New Zealand" ("New Zealand").

24. In colonial discourse, too, the trope of cannibalism similarly caps—and is made more urgent by—the missionary discourse of the cultivation of souls: see, e.g., "Settled," in which a New Zealand settler uses agricultural discourse against the missionaries, who, he says, "sowed the bitter seeds of strife in the name of the Gospel of charity. From such seeds they did not reap, even into their own garners, the fruit they desired" (310). In any case, the conjuncture of cookery and "civilization" is hardly new, as Levi-Strauss has pointed out. With respect to the Maoris, we can find it in, for example, the second sentence of a nineteenth-century British account: "The events in the colony which we had hoped to civilize according to the newest recipe are eminently vexatious" ("Maori Sketches" 498).

25. Occidentalism is an extension of—or rather a form of—what Said calls Orientalism, "a style of thought based upon an ontological and epistemological distinction made between 'the Orient' and (most of the time) 'the Occident'" (2).

26. As Marquis points out in a discussion of Aylmer's *Distant Homes; or, The Graham Family in New Zealand* (1862) and Kingston's *Waihoura; or, the New Zealand Girl* (1872).

27. It's more likely to be mistresses than masters who are fearful of servants, though, and the husband in question is an emigrating Irishman. And the schoolboy who tells of a master's subjection to the boys is presumably only joking.

8 SENSATIONALIZING THE SCHOOL STORY

ELLEN WOOD

There are secrets in canonical school stories. Schoolboys don't tell tales on other schoolboys, don't tell who broke the window or who started the fight. Yet theirs are rarely family secrets, such as whose father embezzled from whom, or whose brother one of the masters really is. Family secrets, however, are at the heart of *Orville College: A Tale* (1867), by Ellen Wood, known to her contemporaries as Mrs. Henry Wood.

Like other Victorian women, Wood signals her swerve from the canonical story by setting *Orville College* not at a public school but at a private one. It's the kind of school that Hughes's Tom Brown attended before Rugby and that he considers vastly inferior. It's the kind of school where, as in *Louis' School Days* (1850), the headmaster's personal insights into a boy's character are more important than strict adherence to formal procedures.[1]

Wood also swerves from canonical precedent by focusing as much on a master as on any boy. She does start out at the beginning of a term, as many school stories do. And there is a new boy, George Paradyne. But we remain fairly distant from him—as if to heighten his mystery.

For at the heart of the story is the issue of secrecy, Wood thus carrying over concerns from her other fiction, sensation novels like the best-selling *East Lynne* (1861). Sally Mitchell finds the essence of sensationalism in "secrets, surprises, suspense, and shocks to the nerves and emotions," its common themes including "bigamy, adultery, illegitimacy, disguise, changed names, railway accidents, poison, fire, murder, concealed identity, false reports of death, the doubling of characters and incidents" (Introduction xi–xii).[2] Jonathan Loesberg sees loss of legal and class identity as central, with suspense built by an inevitability of sequence seen simultaneously and contradictorily as circumstantial and providential (117, 126). Winifred Hughes describes sensation novels as characterized by "the violent yoking of romance and realism, traditionally the two contradictory modes of literary perception," a yoking that "deliberately strains both modes to the limit" (16).[3] *Orville College* would then derive from a merging of sensational romanticism with school-story realism, of the sensation novel with the school story.

That is, Wood could be said to translate her marginality with respect to the boys' public-school story—she was after all a woman—not into a portrayal of the racial or ethnic other but into a generic shift: she shifted the school story toward sensationalism, toward the genre where she was in effect canonical. Perhaps also Wood shifted it toward a genre particularly hospitable to women, given that the secrecy at the heart of the sensation novel was endemic to Victorian womanhood, given that the secrets "were not simply solutions to mysteries and crimes" but "were the secrets of women's dislike of their roles as daughters, wives, and mothers" (Showalter 158).

Certainly Wood does not seem to be writing too consciously in the school-story tradition; witness her sense that she has to explain things of a sort that other school-story writers did not feel compelled to. Such as why the boy Leek is called Onions—"as a sort of parody on his name 'Leek.' The college was in the habit of bestowing these nicknames" (6). Or when boys wear gowns (in chapel) and when caps (always). Wood doggedly explains what, to her nineteenth-century readers, must have been obvious or unimportant.[4]

This overexplanation of the mores of school, however it might derive from Wood's trying too hard to fit in, trying in effect to mask her humble origins as a glove manufacturer's daughter,[5] is in marked contrast to the secrecy she maintains elsewhere. Or rather both contribute to the secrecy–revelation axis, an axis central to sensation novels, where "secrets are the rule" and "passion and crime fester beneath the surface of the official ideal" (W. Hughes 190). The emphasis on passion and crime may be muted in *Orville College*—there is no sex, no bigamy, no murder. Yet this is after all a book not just about schoolboys but also perhaps for them, and during the past couple of centuries adults have commonly muted sex and violence when writing for the young. Even the worst crimes, the actions legally defined as crimes, are displaced beyond the confines of the school; and the criminals are displaced to different generations from those most closely identified with the school: from schoolboys to their fathers, from the headmaster to his son. Yet the emphasis on secrecy, and the incremental revelation of secrets, remains.

Most adults, especially the admirable ones, seem to carry some secret burden. The headmaster Dr. Brabazon, "large-hearted and large-minded," has "an upright line of secret care that sat ill upon [him], as if it had no business there" (3). He turns out to have a son who has been in prison. The admirable new master, Mr. Henry, "pale, delicate," with "a sad sort of look in his pleasant dark eyes," has "a peculiar kind of timid reticence in his manner which seemed foreign to him, for his face was a candid, open face, and his voice was frank. Dr. Brabazon put it down to the natural shyness of one who has resided abroad" (7). Yet Mr. Henry too has a family secret. And if he is not an actual ethnic other, if he is only an Englishman who has lived abroad for some years, Wood nonetheless uses the trope of foreignness, translating it into personality: "timid reticence" is somehow foreign to this nonforeign foreigner. Yet that very foreignness, like the "foreign" Mr. Henry, is somehow admirable.

A school-story trope that well accommodates Wood's concern with secrecy and revelation is that of talebearing—does one tell tales or keep secrets? Like pre-Hughesian writers of school stories, Wood foregrounds religion.[6] But with a difference. She reverses the valence of talebearing. In early nineteenth-century school stories one should tell on others for their own good, so that they can be suitably chastened and led to the paths of righteousness—as Jenny Groves does in *Robert and Frederick* (1842). Or in the anonymous "The Glutton" (1809), a boy is sent away to school to overcome his gluttony, but thanks to a pastry cook's failure to tell on him there—"Swift is the progress of vice if not early checked" (257)—he falls into ever worse ways, stealing pastry, then money. He is flogged, expelled, shipped off to the West Indies—but not before he sees his displacement, a boy who is a condemned robber, hanged, convulsing and shrieking.

Wood, however, inverts the implications of talebearing, moving to a New Testament dispensation, from justice to mercy—to sympathy, in short, with others' secrets. And in the process she extends the strictures of the code beyond those associated with it in *Tom Brown* and his ilk. In her schoolboy world, not only are boys not supposed to sneak on others (as in a canonical school story), but townspeople and relatives are not supposed to tell on boys either (uncommon but possible in a canonical story), nor are masters (a radical swerve from the canonical). The moral justification for not telling tales is not peer loyalty to other schoolboys but rather Christian compassion. Yet it has a rhetorical justification as well: to foster the aura of secrecy.

The issue of talebearing surfaces early on when various boys refer to one Edwin Lamb as a sneak. Lamb's "hair was a fiery red, and his eyes were not straight; not for that did the boys dislike him" (10)—though in this novel where faces speak volumes and gut reactions often prove more trustworthy than mere reason does, the boy's appearance is effectively the reason. The narrator continues by explaining that the boys dislike Lamb because he had been found out in one or two dishonourable false-hoods (they brought it out, "lies"), and was more than suspected of carrying private tales to Mr. Long. They called him "Le Mouton," "The Sneak," "Jackal"; in short, there was a great amount of prejudice against him, more, perhaps, than the boy really deserved. (10–11)

That final clause, though, starts to undermine the ascription of talebearing to Lamb, or perhaps the derogatory implications of sneaking. Add to that the fact that Raymond Trace, an older boy who has seemed unexceptionable, apparently defends Lamb when others assume the latter's guilt. And we have a classic setup—if this were a canonical story—whereby Lamb will be accused of talebearing and Trace will clear him. But wait. We soon learn that none of the boys particularly likes Trace, "without being able to explain why" (11). And both Trace and Lamb turn out to be reprehensible. Perhaps Wood has failed to erase the trace of an earlier direction for the story. Or perhaps she is preparing us for Trace's later perfidy by associating him with sneaking and with Lamb.

In any case, one key talebearing incident has to do with whether two older boys, Trace and Bertie Loftus, will reveal to their schoolmates who the new student, George Paradyne, is—whether they will reveal that the boy's father presumably embezzled from their fathers. Such revelation is not called talebearing. Wood has in fact reversed the valence of canonical talebearing: the issue is whether Trace and Loftus will reveal their incriminating secret not to the masters, who already know about the allegations, but to the other boys. What is at stake is thus not loyalty to one's peers but Christian forbearance and generosity.

Trace's attitude is clear from the beginning: "One can overlook some things in a fellow's antecedents; but *forgery*—that's rather too strong" (33, Wood's italics). Yet for awhile he grudgingly goes along with the urgings of the masters and of Sir Simon, a neighbor, a favorite among the schoolboys and uncle to Trace and Loftus. Trace is particularly resentful of the interference of the new master, Mr. Henry, and fosters an undercurrent of bad feeling, with the help of military discourse—referring to the man as "a regular spy" (83). Later, when some older boys are indulging in illicit smoking and they hear a cough outside, Trace says that "it's that German spy" (118–119)—taking advantage of a double slippage of meaning. As German master, Mr. Henry almost becomes German, and "spy" slips from a schoolboy meaning (a sneak) to a national one.

Trace further encourages boys to believe that Mr. Henry sneaked to

Mr. Long about the smoking—that is, that one master sneaked to another. Trace even tells Mr. Long, "I wonder you take notice of tales brought by a rat" (122). What presumption it is for him to talk this way to a master— and about another master. Such behavior would never occur in the *Tom Brown* sort of story, nor would one master be described as sneaking to another when discussing some boys' misdeeds. And if all that is not striking enough, Mr. Long decides not to tell the headmaster about the smoking, "conscious of feeling rather small himself on the subject of listening to 'a rat'—whom *he* took to mean Lamb" (122, Wood's italics)—as if reporting to the headmaster too would be ratting.

So the boys shun Mr. Henry; they send him, like a schoolboy, to Coventry. They consider his denial of guilt a lie. The accusation, by Loftus major (the older Loftus brother), is itself telling: "A gentleman could not be guilty of such an act. You have only just come among us, and in any case the matter was none of yours. Perhaps you will concern yourself in future with your own affairs, and not with ours. The first desk is not accustomed to this kind of thing . . ."—spoken with offensive "stress laid upon the word 'gentleman'" (125–126), thus underscoring how class underlies schoolboy codes. The boys feel their views are reinforced, that Mr. Henry is not quite a gentleman, when they learn how cheaply he dines—on potatoes, salt, cheese, and milk (he is putting aside money for his mother). They also assume that when he helps boys after hours with their academic difficulties he receives extra payment, and such payment somehow cancels the goodness of his acts.[7] They resent his helping the new boy Paradyne with schoolwork, especially since such help must give the boy an edge on the coveted Orville prize. Mr. Henry denies that he is in fact coaching George for the Orville—at the same time that he offers to help anyone else with schoolwork—though his hairsplitting seems rather defensive: "I am not coaching him for the Orville prize. I am not coaching him at all, for the matter of that. He reads the classics with me, and I explain away his difficulties in mathematics. It is preparatory to the Oxford [entrance] examination, not the Orville" (176–177). The boys likewise assume that Mr. Henry is guilty of stealing the headmaster's diamond-and-gold pencil. And they punish the man by giving him more work to do, making their exercises more incorrect and illegible than usual.

Yet of course Mr. Henry hasn't told, wouldn't dream of telling another master about the smoking; nor has he stolen the pencil. Even when the boys are unruly—a boy named Dick flings a rotten apple that hits Mr. Henry on the cheek, and the master has seen quite well who the culprit was— he nonetheless does not tell the headmaster who is responsible but calmly suggests that it could have been an accident. As he later explains to Dick, he would tell only if someone did something seriously wrong, certainly not "for petty spite—retaliation—revenge—oh, Dick, don't you know Who it is that has warned us against these?" (132). Thus is Mr. Henry—unlike canonical schoolmasters—ever turning the other cheek, ever ready to invoke trust in God, ever accepting all suffering since it inevitably leads to Him.

Meanwhile, Trace chafes against the prohibition against telling others what he thinks he knows about George Paradyne's father. Trace says he considers this secrecy infamous, "the first time I ever knew it was right to conceal crime" (85). Mr. Henry urges that the kindness of silence "will be repaid to you a hundredfold" (88). Then, "on a different subject," the master intimates that he knows that Trace was responsible for accidentally firing a pistol and wounding a schoolmate named Talbot. This "different subject" provides a model of how Trace should behave, by being kind, keeping secrets. But it is also implicit blackmail.

Still, "by dint of whispers and insinuations" (96), Trace fans feeling against George Paradyne. The shunning persists even when George refuses to name names in connection with a prank, though he himself is then severely caned, persists even when another boy picks a fight but George simply parries blows, proving his coolness and self-possession—either action would be sufficient excuse in a canonical story for a reversal of popular schoolboy opinion.

Thus too does Wood herself parry off fighting, that staple of the canonical school story. Or rather she eventually translates it into terms more compatible with sensation novels: into a duel. During school holidays, one boy challenges another to a duel. Their two schoolboy seconds confer about the "awful business" and decide, "We must be men for once, and do the best we can" (263)—and Wood defines manliness not as seconding a duel but as averting dire consequences, for, we eventually discover, the seconds have made sure the pistols are not loaded.

Wood further undercuts the duel through humor. The boys are uncertain of the niceties of dueling. Should they keep their hats on? A bystander named Brown suggests they might as well, adding, "What does custom signify one way or the other?" (300). Then one second tells the two principals to shake hands, "but he had no sooner spoken than [the other second] whispered to him that it was prize-fighters who shook hands, not duellists. However, the thing was done; and, as Mr. Brown remarked by the other doubt, it could not matter" (300). And it doesn't, though not perhaps in the way one might expect: it's not a matter of life and death taking precedence over mere formalities—for the pistols are not loaded. Instead, it doesn't matter because dueling itself is something that should not be treated as mattering. Discovered by Sir Simon, the two duelists are then treated "like a couple of children," made to "walk arm-in-arm, and march before him" (308)— thereby returning us metaphorically to the realm of schoolboys, deflating whatever manliness the two thought they had attained through embarking on a duel.

Back at school, pressure mounts for the Orville prize, exacerbating the tension between secrecy and revelation, especially for Trace. For the chief contenders for the prize are, of course, Trace and Paradyne.

In order to qualify, a boy first has to pass the Oxford examination— and the boys are hoping that Dr. Brabazon won't send Paradyne up for this preliminary. The headmaster presumably decides whether or not to send boys up on the basis of a Latin essay, yet the night that he is to turn in his essay, George finds it "torn, blotted, soaked in ink almost from beginning to end" (224). A rumor circulates "that Paradyne had done it himself to hide the poorness of his Latin" (225). Though of course he hasn't.

So here is another typical school-story setup, a site for playing out moral cowardice and bravery. Can George continue to act nobly? Will the perpetrator (Trace, of course) suffer pangs of remorse? Will he be found out and duly punished? Will Dr. Brabazon agonize over whether he can still send George up for the Oxford examination without seeing the boy's essay? Or might George be allowed to rewrite it? But, no, those questions do not interest Wood. For she begins the next chapter by relaying the results of the Oxford examination. Paradyne has passed. We are told, simply, "All George Paradyne's apprehensions and the school's forebodings had proved alike mistaken, for Dr. Brabazon had sent up Paradyne in spite of the damaged essay" (228). We are never told why. Perhaps Dr. Brabazon simply knows his family of boys so well that mere formalities like the essay are not what really count. In any case, Wood evades the crisis—or rather translates it into her characteristic trope of secrecy, of withholding information.

Finally, though, Trace breaks. Through him, word of the disgrace associated with Paradyne's father spreads; the boys mutter of mutiny; George is sent to Coventry; a mob of younger boys sets upon him. George, in response, becomes even more determined to win the Orville. Yet Mr. Henry urges him to withdraw, and eventually persuades the boy to do so, not so much on the grounds that one should not "hold out in opposition to the many" but out of generosity: "Withdraw from it for his sake. Let Trace get it. That past wrong upon him [the presumed embezzlement] can never be wiped out by us; but we, you and I, may do a trifle now and then of kindness to him, perform some little sacrifice or other in requital of it" (412–

413). Mr. Henry's reasoning here focuses more on responsiveness to others than on abstract principle, and more on generosity than on the expediency of yielding to the cabal. His reasoning evokes, if anything, Carol Gilligan's notions of women's moral reasoning. Yet it is a male character who reasons this way—certainly the not-altogether-admirable Mrs. Paradyne, George's mother, does not. For she at one point urges George to withdraw from the competition in "haughty resentment" of the school's treatment of him, and at another point laments "that he should have been forced to put himself out of it that young Trace might win" (428). Mr. Henry provides, in effect, the "feminine point of view" that is central to sensation novels (W. Hughes 30).

Later that day the truth comes out. Trace has been riding for a fall: it was of course his father, not Paradyne's, who was guilty of embezzlement. Trace quits the college in shame, eventually leaving with his father for America. He becomes the schoolboy that has to be eliminated, lighting out for the morally dubious territory of the United States.

What then becomes of George? When the other boys learn that his father was not guilty, they cheer and throw their caps in the air. Schoolboy favor is ever fickle in school stories, but never more so than here, as Wood forces it to reinforce her moral message. As for the loss of the Orville, which would have enabled George to afford Oxford (Mr. Henry had persuaded him to withdraw from the competition, which the worthy Talbot ends up winning)—Trace's uncle, Sir Simon, provides financial support so that George can go to Cambridge.

Meanwhile, Lamb tries to sneak out of the imputation of sneaking by displacing blame onto the absent Trace: he announces Trace's guilt in the shooting accident long before and in the destruction of Paradyne's Latin essay. Whereupon Bertie Loftus retorts, "You are the sneak. . . . Can't you let a fallen fellow alone? Trace is in misfortune, and absent" (465). The narrator adds, "Trace had never been a favourite; and perhaps he really had something of the sneak about him; but this did not make Lamb less of one" (465). Lamb functions as a partial scapegoat. If at the beginning of the book Trace's associations with Lamb hint at a kind of moral contamination—hint that Trace may not be all that he seems—then here at the end Lamb shares in some of the opprobrium directed at Trace, perhaps even deflects some. Trace may have "had something of the sneak about him," but Lamb has even more.

As for Mr. Henry, throughout it all, he is Christlike, reminding us to aim for moral virtue above all. It's as if Wood has taken to heart the animadversions of the anonymous reviewer in *Blackwood's Magazine*—Margaret Oliphant—who had called Wood's popular *East Lynne* a "dangerous and foolish work," for the central character, "who is only moderately in-teresting while she is good, becomes, as soon as she is a Magdalen, doubly a heroine": "Nothing can be more wrong and fatal than to represent the flames of vice as a purifying fiery ordeal, through which the penitent is to come elevated and sublimed" ("Sensation Novels" 567). Mr. Henry, how-ever, is not a Magdalen but a Christ.

For this paragon "seemed to have a facility for healing breaches," shedding peace "amidst warring elements" (159, 460). When boys are fight-ing and Mr. Henry appears, "It was as if magic were at work, or some mes-merist; the angry feelings subsided; the boys' passions were allayed; the fierce storm became calm" (404). His moral influence helps his students and oth-ers to become better men; he himself becomes "their dear old master, Mr. Henry—for dear in truth he had become to them" (466).

Furthermore, as with Christ, dying embodies the greatest virtue. For Mr. Henry finally dies, and seems to die for the boys, to remind them of matters beyond the earthly, to remind them to trust in God, as he has learned to. Young Dick sobs when he learns that Mr. Henry is dying, and asks for a legacy—whereupon Mr. Henry copies out "a small portion of the thirteenth chapter of St. John, in his own beautiful handwriting, and signed with his full name" (471). Thus has Mr. Henry submerged his will in a greater one, leaving a copy of the Word as a testament, not original words of his own.

Not like Wood herself—whose book functions as a testament to her husband Henry, who died shortly before she began the novel. The fictional Henry dies too, having lived not as her own had but perhaps as she wished he had. For Henry Wood's secret is a less generous one than that of Mr. Henry: Henry Wood had rather abruptly had to leave a lucrative job on the Continent as banking and shipping agent, for reasons that his son forbears revealing in his book-length memorial to his mother—his own crossgendered tribute—referring only to his father's "possessing a mind a little wanting in ballast" (C. Wood 50).

As for other tropes common in crossgendered school stories, that of laming does appear, but Wood is ambivalent about its implications. There's a tension here between stressing the importance of suffering (most of the truly good characters in this novel have been through the crucible of suffering) and stressing that of appearance (one can judge Lamb's moral worth by his physical appearance). Thus being lame could be associated with moral pu-rification or with moral debility. A boy accidentally shot at the beginning, Talbot, may end up getting the Orville prize and, with poetic justice, at the expense of the boy who had done the shooting. Yet Wood does not make us privy to any agonized soul-searching as Talbot's injury slowly heals, does not use the physical setback as a tool for moral growth—unlike Martineau earlier and Alcott later on. Perhaps Wood implicitly recognized how doing so would contradict her use of physical disability as an index of moral debility: certainly in the case of the headmaster's ex-convict son, being lame is a stigma of moral turpitude, even as it is also a way of identifying who (someone with a limp) has been lurking near the school.

This trope of physical and moral parallels, enabling intuitive knowledge of someone's real character, causes other difficulties as well. Early on, Wood wants us to believe that one can read a person's true worth through his appearance—so that the reader will know which characters to trust, which not to. Wood provides us with a parable of reading, of how to read the traces of Trace, when he reads the second lesson at the first chapel service:

> His voice was subdued; its accent to some ears almost offensively humble—offensive because there was a ring in it of affected piety that could never be genuine. No such voice as that, no such assumption of humility, ever yet proceeded from a truly honest nature.
>
> "That young man is a hypocrite!" involuntarily thought the new master, Mr. Henry. "Heaven forgive me!" he added, a moment after; "what am I, that I should judge another?" (13)

With the help of the narrator, whose perspective here increasingly merges with that of Mr. Henry, we read Trace's face, with, it would seem, increasingly greater certainty: the initial clauses are tentative ("to some ears," "almost"), followed by perhaps an overstated certainty ("never"). The second paragraph then achieves a surer certainty, a surer believability, paradoxically through its concluding tentativeness. For the final disclaimer, making the harsh conclusion seem involuntary, lends credence to Mr. Henry's judgment. Though ending with that note of tentativeness does subtly undermine this intuitive ability to judge others—reflecting perhaps Wood's own ambivalence about appearance and intuition.

For belief in intuitive judgments may help us to gauge which characters we are to trust, but what do we do when otherwise trustworthy characters judge wrong? What do we do when the virtuous Miss Brabazon believes ill of Mr. Henry—momentarily believes him capable of stealing a valuable pencil? In fact, Wood's attempts to foster trust in one's instinctive sense of a person run counter to her attempts to maintain secrecy, whether from other characters or from the reader. And Wood is hard put to reconcile herd instinct with the truth of instinctive readings. Talbot's father says of the boys' dislike of Paradyne, "There's sure to be good cause for it. These instincts are generally to be trusted" (196). Talbot then puzzles over whether the boys' instincts are really for or against Paradyne; all he can finally say is that "there is something not square, I believe, known to a few of the seniors only. The feeling against him is very strong" (196). When Mrs. Talbot then, on the next page, meets Paradyne, she is "struck with the fine character of the attractive countenance—the candour of the large grey eyes" (197) and by his alacrity in offering to run an errand. Later, another wise mother says, "I cannot think why the college should dislike [Paradyne]: it grows more and more of a puzzle to me. He is very good-looking. Did you notice his beautiful eyes and his flushed face . . . ?" (292). Do women have an instinctive ability to judge appearances?

No, not all females are reliable guides. The headmaster's daughter is spoiled. Nor is self-centered Mrs. Paradyne admirable. Nor is the neighboring Mother Butter presented in an ideal light, implicitly discredited, in part, by her lower class standing. Her refusal to make any more bullseyes, a candy treat that she has formerly sold to the boys, makes her the butt of pranks: boys send her a parcel containing a mouse; they burn an effigy outside her door. While she is not directly presented as unworthy, her serving as an occasion for boys' naughtiness and perhaps too her provision of a locale just outside the school grounds where the boys can be disorderly are not particularly commendable. If Wood is indeed portraying "the secrets of women's dislike of their roles as daughters, wives, and mothers" (Showalter 158), she is doing so through largely negative portrayals of women.

Yet women do provide important connections—not least by serving as channels of communication, as gossips, de facto telltales, people who contribute to the revelation of secrets, for good or ill. As in other boys' school stories by women, connections, especially family connections, are crucial. Not only do key family members like Mrs. Paradyne and Sir Simon live conveniently near at hand. But Loftus and Trace, two of the three boys to whom Wood devotes greatest attention, are cousins,[8] and young Dick is Bertie Loftus's younger brother. Now Wood could use the cousins the way Sherwood and other midcentury writers did, to contrast right and wrong behavior. But she does not stress differences between Loftus's and Trace's behaviors to drive home a moral point. Nor does she use the presence of the two Loftus brothers as they might be used in a more canonical story. Although brothers are fairly uncommon in canonical stories, sometimes the author of a story that details the events of a single term or year instead of the entire school career of a single boy focuses on two brothers, as Talbot Baines Reed does in *The Fifth Form at St. Dominic's* (1881–1882). Having two brothers enables one to show both the rambunctiousness of a younger boy and the steadiness of an older one, much as the single-boy stories, such as *Tom Brown,* enable one to see both rambunctiousness and steadiness in one boy over time. But Wood does not use the two brothers in this way. We hear relatively little of the pranks of young Dick. It's as if she is more devoted to the family as family, or couldn't imagine writing a story without family complications, or perhaps couldn't imagine creating an aura of secrecy without making use of secret family connections.

For family connections are implicated in most of the secrets that provide the driving force of the book. A focal secret is the identity of Mr. Henry. He turns out to be Arthur Henry Paradyne, George's older brother—Henry has promised his mother not to reveal his name, retaining the name he was called in his Heidelberg days, so as not to jeopardize his ability to support her, as the son of a presumed embezzler. But also, it would seem, to keep the secret from the reader.

Another key family secret is, of course, whose father the real embezzler was. We hear versions of the embezzlement story many times, as boy tells boy, each recounting progressively more of the secret, revealing for instance that Mr. Paradyne had not in fact committed suicide by taking poison, soon after he was arrested, but had died of a heart attack—thus he did not kill himself out of remorse but died of the shock of being arrested. And in spinning out the axis of secrecy–revelation, in the striptease that will eventually reveal the truth, Wood drops hints as to the real perpetrator. We learn of Mr. Trace losing his own and others' money in America, belying his presumed business acumen and trustworthiness. We learn of his wife's uncharacteristically thoughtful dying wish, that Sir Simon look after the Paradynes. Mr. Trace seems unduly fearful that his former clerk Hopper, though presumed drowned, might reappear. And so on.

Other school stories by women may make families central, but *Orville College* is unique in its focus on family secrets—in its sensationalizing of the relationship between family and school. The closest analogue would seem to be Margaret Oliphant's *The Story of Valentine and His Brother* (1875)—despite her own animadversions against Wood's sensation novel.[9] Oliphant's work, however, is only marginally a school story: Eton may figure in about 100 pages, but the novel is some 650 pages long. And our view of Eton is quite distant. Oliphant's comments on schoolboy lingo are emblematic of her stance toward Val's school days as a whole: someone has "spoken of poor Dick as a 'Brocas cad.' Now I am not sufficiently instructed to know what special ignominy, if any, is conveyed by this designation; but Val flamed up . . ." (1: 255). The narrator claims to lack inside knowledge of Eton, and we too tend to stay outside, on the perimeter, on the river more than on the school grounds.

Still, it's at Eton that Val re-encounters his long lost twin—here is the family secret—who has been tramping about with his gypsy mother, Val having been raised by his aristocratic grandparents. Val, sensing an affinity with Dick, helps the latter to obtain a job working on the river. But it's only much later that the two learn of their kinship: Val is running for Parliament, his parentage is impugned, he takes ill—and he is nursed to health by a woman who turns out to be his mother, someone who conveniently dies once the family is reunited so as not to be an embarrassing encumbrance. In Oliphant, then, the family plot entirely overwhelms the school story.

As for *Orville College,* the family plots shape the school story but do not altogether displace it. Rather they merge with it—the school itself, a small private school rather than a large public one, functioning as a family too. And perhaps because the school is not a public school, Wood can get away with virtually no reference to games. The closest approach to athletic endeavor occurs during the holidays, when Paradyne rescues Dick Loftus from drowning—an action that would be the perfect setup, if this were a canonical school story, for ensuring that the younger boy, the one rescued from drowning, remains steadfast to the older one, when the latter's honor is impugned. But again Wood swerves from the canonical; Dick does not stand by Paradyne.

The fact that Orville College is a private school may also be the reason why boys flout authority as much as they do. If private schools rely more on the whims of their clients, as educational historians have noted,[10] the boys—like Dickens' Steerforth—may expect to be indulged more. Or perhaps Wood simply becomes overexplanatory when, say, Mr. Henry intervenes between two boys who have been fighting and one boy says, "Move away. . . . What business is it of yours?" Mr. Henry responds, "The business of authority" (206). An admirable boy would never be that impertinent to a master in a canonical story, nor would the master need to justify himself. Perhaps too the Christian import of the book lends itself to relative egalitarianism (all are equal before God) or inversion (the last shall be first).

Look, for instance, at what happens the night before the determination of the Orville prize. The headmaster calls all the candidates except Paradyne into his study, where "the question to be decided was this: was Paradyne, with his burden of inherited disgrace, to be allowed to compete for the Orville with themselves, who had no such inheritance, and repudiated all possibility of disgrace on their own score, present and future, and for their forefathers in the past?" (410–411). Whereupon the ubiquitous Sir Simon speaks up, saying that if Paradyne is excluded his nephews Loftus and Trace will withdraw, and he persuades other boys to agree as well to allow Paradyne to compete. Is Dr. Brabazon here consulting, through the boys, the interests of the families who send their boys to the school? Or is he employing a subtle means of moral control, of showing the boys how wrong they were, in effect, to get into a row the day before?

Either way, this school and its story are enmeshed in family matters. And thus Wood's story unites the two main strands of nineteenth-century "realistic" children's fiction, boys' school stories and girls' domestic fiction. She can also be seen as reworking the norms of two kinds of school story: both the canonical and the older evangelical traditions. For in seeking sensation she focuses on family secrets and thus undermines—reorients—the norms associated with talebearing. Unlike the traditional evangelical story, talebearing is here undesirable. Yet unlike the canonical school story, the rationale for not telling tales is not the exigencies of peer loyalty but those of Christian kindness, making it undesirable, given the exigencies of the sensation plot as well, for anyone ever to tell tales on anyone. At least not until a suitably dramatic climax. These reversals start calling the norms into question, as Wood starts dismantling the canonical school story, questioning its codes, revealing its secrets, inscribing femininity. Yet the reversals do not constitute a full dismantling. That will come, four years later, in the United States.

NOTES

1. Wood may offer the panoply of an external examination—the candidates arrayed before the outside examiners, in gowns and trenchers—but the prize is awarded for reasons other than performance on the exam. Wood calls what happens at the examination a farce, but it's not the subversion of the formal occasion that is farcical. Rather the formal panoply is: "It might on the face of things, have been almost called a solemn farce, this sitting in conclave, this great examination, confined to one day and to the formal routine of questioning, but that it was known that the true adjudicator of the prize was Dr. Brabazon, who had probably decided beforehand upon the victor" (409).

2. See also Brantlinger, in "What," in which he emphasizes the salience of secrecy in his discussion of the historical, structural, and psychological dimensions of sensation fiction.

3. See also Jump, who points out that an early reviewer of Wood's work noted "that two principles, sensationalism and domesticity, were competing for the mastery of her pen" (261).

4. The critic A. H. Japp has said, though admittedly with condescension, "In Mrs. Henry Wood you have the English boy set before you precisely as he is, with all his frank honesty, with all his ingenuousness, with all his unconscious rudeness, his *insouciance,* his trickiness, and his queer mixture of unaffected affection and capacity for cruelty, in certain directions. No lady-writer, in this respect, has ever approached

her" (quoted in C. Wood 294, Japp's italics). If it is true that Wood showed unusual understanding of schoolboy characters, nevertheless her grasp of the codes, or at least of the codes of canonical school stories, seems to have been less sure—or less important to her. Brantlinger suggests that such narrative instability, such "difficulty in claiming authority," is generally characteristic of sensation novels ("What" 11).

5. See W. Hughes 119.

6. She even, like the earliest writers, indulges in some (near-)allegorical naming: Paradyne is a paragon, just short of paradise, the elder Loftus has somewhat too lofty ideas of himself, and Trace leaves traces of his misdoings, despite himself.

7. Mr. Henry would apparently agree: when offered payment for helping a boy during the holidays, he declines, saying, "It would scarcely be honourable. I am well paid by Dr. Brabazon; and any little assistance I can give them out of school is only their due" (164).

8. The third boy may not have a direct family connection with the other two, but he is connected to them, and through his family: George Paradyne's father had been a business partner of the fathers of Loftus and Trace.

9. Oliphant's work seems in part a sensation story, like Wood's, yet the sensational elements also derive from the medieval romance of Valentine and Orson, frequently retold in chapbooks from the sixteenth century and afterwards (see Carpenter and Prichard).

10. Especially their higher-class clients—see, e.g., Pedersen, "Women's" 67–68.

DOMESTICATING THE SCHOOL STORY

LOUISA MAY ALCOTT

In the late nineteenth century popular girls' stories shifted their focus from family to school—in England, from works by Charlotte Yonge to those by L. T. Meade—shifting to a setting where a measure of rebelliousness was possible, certainly not altogether out of the question. In the United States, Louisa May Alcott enacted the shift when she went from *Little Women* (1868) to *Little Men: Life at Plumfield with Jo's Boys* (1871). And in the process of turning to a school story she destabilized its conventional codes—deconstructing and regendering, even regenerating, the genre.

In effect, she affirms the genre, what had always been possibilities in the genre, by shifting genders. As Derrida has said in another context, "the masculine genre is . . . affected by the affirmation through a random drift that could always render it other" ("Law" 223). She renders the school story other. And she does so by rendering the family story other. For she shifts the gender locus of the family story—from a concern with girls, as in *Little Women,* to a concern with boys and girls, especially boys. As Ann B. Murphy notes, Alcott complexly crisscrosses gender boundaries in *Little Men:* Jo inherits the property that makes the school possible "from the ferocious paternal aunt who deprived her of a visit to the Continent because of her independence" and goes on to become "a far more powerful maternal figure than Marmee, but her new community is determinedly male" (579, n. 32).

Alcott's accomplishment can be gauged in part—can be epitomized—by her redaction of the woman writer's "apology" for writing about boys. E. J. May, you will recall, was self-deprecating when she excused her failure "to particularize the subjects for examination given by Dr. Wilkinson to the two upper classes" by noting that her "classical and mathematical ignorance might cause mistakes more amusing to the erudite reader than pleasant to the author" (*Louis* 114). Alcott is less abject: "Cricket and football the boys had, of course—but after the stirring accounts of these games in the immortal 'Tom Brown at Rugby,' no feeble female pen may venture to do more than respectfully allude to them" (135). The ironic tone here hints that it's not so much Alcott's own feebleness that needs excuse as the emphasis on sports in an influential work like Hughes's. Whereas May apologizes for leaving out something that no school-story writer bothered including anyway—details about examinations—Alcott boldly announces her omission of a major ingredient of the canonical story, the blow-by-blow account of an athletic competition. Alcott also adopts a characteristic U.S. stance of resistance to Hughes, an anxiety to differentiate Tom Bailey from Tom Brown—a resistance emblematized by what amounts to her misquotation of the English title (the book appeared in the United States variously as *Tom Brown's Schooldays, School Days at Rugby,* and *Tom Brown at Rugby*).

Which is not to say that Alcott is not apologetic in other respects. She excuses her book's lack of form, its episodic nature—"there is no particular plan to this story, except to describe a few scenes in the life at Plumfield for the amusement of certain little persons"—and protests too much that it is realistic, when she claims, "I beg leave to assure my honored readers that most of the incidents are taken from real life, and that the oddest are the truest; for no person, no matter how vivid an imagination he may have, can invent anything half so droll as the freaks and fancies that originate in the lively brains of little people" (125). Perhaps Alcott's anxiety about writing a boys' school story is displaced here. Perhaps having had great success with her "true" story of *Little Women,* she is anxious, when writing about a setting with which she has had less direct experience, to establish her claim to truth. Or perhaps, like much early children's literature, which instead of having a cumulative plot is likely to be repetitive and cyclical, the story veers toward the narrative of community.

Overall, Alcott's stance toward the genre of the school story is complex—in part because, although her book is a story of a (mostly) boys' school, it is not necessarily a boys' story. For *Little Men* is the sequel to a classic girls' story, portraying the further adventures of an adult Jo March— and Alcott even manages to infiltrate a couple of girls into the school. Alcott is thereby enabled to evade the essentializing of male and female, making possible a new gender dialectic, illuminating what had been repressed in the canonical story, its denial of the feminine.

As a sequel the book simultaneously yields precedence to the family story it follows and also replaces the earlier story (much as it takes precedence over and is replaced by the final story in the March family series, *Jo's*

Boys [1886], where the school is less salient). The position of *Little Men* as a sequel, or rather as a middle term in a series, has contributed to its relative obscurity. So too has its being a school story by a woman. Yet as a woman, a U.S. woman, and a woman writing after Hughes had stabilized the genre, clarifying what one could take an oppositional stance to—and further as a daughter of the educational pioneer Bronson Alcott—Alcott is well positioned to dissect the values of the school story. She writes as a nineteenth-century woman, committed to nurturance and domesticity, even at school—as we will see in discussions of the relationship between family and school and of the portrayal of characters. She writes, furthermore, as a nineteenth-century adult, committed to the authority of adults but willing to attempt to empower children, as long as they remain subject to adult moral authority.

Central to her endeavor is her dialectical synthesis of family and school. More than any other school-story writer, Alcott makes the home a school, the school a home.[1] To the newly arrived Nat, Plumfield "seemed more like a great family than a school" (42), headed by Mother and Father Bhaer (Jo March Bhaer and her husband Professor Bhaer). An important ingredient of this family atmosphere is the small size of the establishment: only twelve boys at first. And even this small number includes biological members of the family—the Bhaers' two sons, their three nephews—further integrating school and family.

This conflation of family and school enables Alcott to merge the two terms of the domestic feminism she espoused, a nineteenth-century feminism that focused on the family as the key to reforming society, "expanding the home to include the world, making everyone equally responsible for human nurturance" (Elbert 166).[2] As Mrs. Jo eventually exclaims, "Dear me, if men and women would only trust, understand, and help one another as my children do, what a capital place the world would be!" and her eyes "grew absent, as if she was looking at a new and charming state of society in which people lived as happily and innocently as her flock at Plumfield" (370). As Tompkins claims for *Uncle Tom's Cabin,* so does Alcott in effect claim "the power to work in, and change, the world" (130).

Not that influencing the world through the family is possible without complexity or ambiguity. Opening up Plumfield to poor children, to domesticate them—taking in the likes of Nat and Dan—was at odds with a desire to protect the family, the school, from the world outside (see C. Strickland 152). Likewise, the attempt to enlarge woman's sphere, to domesticate the world, could be tinged with anxiety over the consequent dangers to women and also over the implicit denial of a more independent mode for women. Moreover, the maternal role that Mrs. Jo here adopts is one constructed by a patriarchal society—is not perhaps sufficiently revolutionary.[3] Finally, one way in which school can empower children is by distancing them from the only authority they have hitherto known, that of the family—so if school and family are conflated, it can be more difficult for a child to triangulate to his or her own authority.

Still, the conflation does enable Alcott to question the traditional mores of boys' schooling—to introduce the ethic of a girls' school, to introduce nurturing and domestic morality to the academic and athletic. Consider, for instance, the relationship between family and school in Alcott's one work focusing on a girls' school: "Mamma's Plot" (1873). Kitty is going to a school where "madam" will not only read but correct all letters sent home—correct their sentiments as well as their spelling, check to see whether the girls "put in something about your heavenly Father, the progress of your studies, and your duty to parents and teachers" (119). Seeing Kitty's distress, her mother proposes a secret code: Kitty will write on pink paper if she is happy, blue if homesick, green if in need of goodies, and violet if not feeling well. Eventually, "finding that the pink notes made mamma very happy, she tried not to think of her 'woes' when she sat down to write. This little bit of self-denial was its own reward; for, as the woes only existed in her own imagination, when she resolutely stopped thinking of them they vanished" (122–123). Alcott thus succeeds in constraining Kitty, but in a manner that is subversive—the plot undermines school authority even as it endorses parental authority. And that cannot be. So Kitty's mother, "troubled about . . . the breaking of the rule," about setting "a bad example," writes "to madam and 'fessed,' like an honest mamma as she was" (123–124). Madam readily forgives her and even starts relaxing her supervision of the pupils' letters.

At the same time the narrator redefines what mamma's plot is. At first we may think it is simply the ruse of the color-coded notepaper—what mamma "'fesses" to madam about. But when Kitty shows that she has learned self-denial by using up the pink sheets, mamma is "quite satisfied with the success of her little plot" (123). Thus the plot is also a way of fooling Kitty into proper submission and self-denial by pretending to offer a clandestine outlet.

Yet the plotting continues to reverberate. School has in fact been undermined, even reformed: the wisest authority is not the old-fashioned preceptress of the school but Kitty's mamma. The family remains focal, to the extent that Kitty is never concerned about the honor of the school—as the hero or heroine of a canonical school story would be—but "did her best for the honor of her family" (118). And what does it mean when mamma adopts the stance of a schoolgirl, "'fessing" to her deviousness? Does she lose authority by becoming like a schoolgirl? Or does she enhance the position of schoolgirls? Alcott gets family to interact with school in a way that complexly endorses and also undermines schools and school authority, schoolgirls and their authority, parents and their authority.

As for *Little Men* and its conflation of school and family, Mrs. Jo may show some preference for "manly boys" instead of girlish ones, yet this school teaches boys "not to be ashamed of showing their emotions" nor of "own[ing] their loyalty to womankind" (60, 226, 228). In keeping with the gender oxymoron she is addressed by—the "Mrs." feminine, the "Jo(e)" then masculine—she urges the crossing of gender attributes.

It's significant, furthermore, that both Mrs. Jo and Mr. Bhaer are active in the running of the school, marrying the moral and the academic. He teaches academic lessons; she instills moral values—in this "odd school" where the important lessons are moral ones, where "self-knowledge, self-help, and self-control" are, in accordance with "Professor Bhaer's opinion," more important than Latin and Greek (28). Whether it's a matter of welcoming the newcomer Nat, finding occupations for Daisy when the boys won't play with her, helping naughty Nan to adjust, remedying the disaster of Daisy's pretend ball, welcoming back the prodigal Dan and then finding outlets for his restlessness, rounding up lost children after a huckleberry expedition, telling stories around the fireside, preparing for Thanksgiving festivities, or, more generally, throwing in a timely comment to help a perplexed child, Mrs. Jo remains central to both school and book. Rarely are scenes set in Mr. Bhaer's domain, the classroom, and he has much less of an extracurricular presence than she does.[4]

Still, even if she is the primary purveyor of moral values, his "opinion" seems to guide the school. As for her ideas, some "were so droll it was impossible to help laughing at them, though usually they were quite sensible, and he was glad to carry them out" (112). He laughs, then follows her suggestion; eventually he may even praise her for her droll idea of coeducation: "I think you were right about the good effect of having girls among the boys. Nan *has* stirred up Daisy, and Bess is teaching the little bears how to behave better than we can" (222, Alcott's italics). Alcott thus displays some anxiety about women's ideas, but she also shows the workings of women's influence in the nineteenth century, the laughter a lightning rod that makes it possible nevertheless to accept Jo's idea. In fact, despite her attentiveness to Mr. Bhaer's "opinions," Jo would seem to be the dominant influence in the school. By making the adult Jo central, Alcott is able to incorporate female views in a male world, or perhaps to integrate private and public, reproduction and production,[5] reason and emotion, feminine and masculine, so as to transform the latter terms.

Her portrayal of a central female character as the author's proxy makes Alcott's work different from all other boys' school stories I have located. Men who wrote boys' school stories seem not to have troubled themselves greatly about female characters; usually there aren't any. But women authors too seem to have had trouble imagining women in responsible positions in boys' schools. In Sherwood and Kelly's *Boys Will Be Boys* (1854), for instance, the headmaster's wife remains in the background; in Goddard's *Philip Danford* (1890), Philip may accord unusual respect to his sister and her views, but she is not an adult, nor is she active in shaping the school; in Abby Morton Diaz's *The William Henry Letters* (1870), William Henry's grandmother may be a key affective figure in the story, but she has no connection with William Henry's school; and most women authors do not provide even this prominent and responsible a female character. Unlike *Little Men*—which in this respect is reminiscent of girls' school stories by men, where there may be a responsible adult of the same sex as the author interacting with children of the opposite sex: in "Arabella Hardy" (*Mrs Leicester's School,* 1809) and "The Bamboo" (*Lessons for Girls,* 1851), Lamb and Mogridge include adult males who function as authorial representatives. Yet neither makes the man central to the school. Rather, the character seems to be a displaced embodiment of the author's anxiety about writing a girls' story, his pathway into the story. No woman writing about boys' schools seems to have felt the need to include a comparable figure. Until Alcott, that is— and she transforms the character into the guiding spirit of the school, thereby transforming both school and story.

Not only is Mrs. Jo key to Alcott's regendering of the school story, but so is the portrayal of other characters. For one thing, the school's clientele is expanded to include girls: the tomboy Nan arrives, and Daisy's role is redefined so that she seems not just to be keeping her twin Demi company but to be a part of the school. Even Bess, Amy and Laurie's daughter, is temporarily added.[6] The girls' lessons may not be identical with the boys': the former learn to ply a needle. But they also, like the boys, learn to ply their wits.

Through Daisy and Nan, Alcott explores the reaches of her domestic feminism. Daisy, who "knew nothing about woman's rights," unconsciously uses "the all-powerful right of her own influence to win from others any privilege for which she had proved her fitness" (255). Nan, on the other hand, attempts to push beyond traditional gender roles: she "clamored fiercely to be allowed to do everything that the boys did" and "had the spirit of a rampant reformer" (255, 256). She may need to be curbed, to "learn self-control, and be ready to use her freedom before she asked for it," yet Jo has the foresight to envision a future for Nan not just within the home, nor even, given the girl's "intense love and pity for the weak and suffering," in nursing, but as "a capital doctor" (256). The domestication of school is not constraining but empowering. And this empowering is quite different from that of the communities of women in Alcott's *Little Women* (early in the book) and *Work* (at the end). For Nan is to succeed in a public career as a doctor—and she evades domesticity to do so, never marrying. This domestication of a boys' school has thus repositioned domesticity, expanding its reach while simultaneously enabling at least one young woman to escape it. In no other boys' school story is a feminine principle—and principal—so much in ascendance. The only other author to approach such a stance, certainly the only one in the nineteenth century, is Harriet Martineau.

For though Martineau readily showed how girls are belittled by schoolboys in *The Crofton Boys* (1841), she still, three decades earlier, validated the feminine to an unusual degree. In part she did so by having the central character Hugh be nursed back to health by his sister: his happiness in interacting with her, even if he unconsciously exploits her as well, is more contact with femininity, certainly more favorable contact, than other writers would allow a fictional schoolboy.

Martineau also validated the feminine by the way she contextualized schoolboy belittlement of girls. It's true that a boy named Dale is teased for having a sister, especially one with such a fine name as "Amelia." Yet Martineau defuses some of the opprobrium of having a sister—paving the way for Hugh's later reliance on his sister—by deflecting the teasing to the fineness of the girl's name. For Dale and Hugh start thinking about fine names among the boys—Colin, Augustus Adolphus—and Dale realizes he can "play them off the next time they quiz Amelia" (131).

An older boy too contextualizes the dismissal of girls when he states, "You will find, in every school in England, . . . that it is not the way of boys to talk about feelings,—about anybody's feelings. That is the reason why they do not mention their sisters or their mothers,—except when two confidential friends are together, in a tree, or by themselves in the meadows" (164). Instead of dismissing the realm of feelings this boy implicitly endorses it, acknowledging it, explaining where feelings are to be discussed. Thus the feminine realm that he associates with feelings is not altogether dismissed. Even if he seems to assume the desirability of behaving in accordance with "the way of boys," his ability to talk about it as a "way of boys" slightly distances him, holding full endorsement of those ways in abeyance.

As for *Little Men,* it more fully endorses the feminine, in part by playing out the relationship between family and school, family and world—between private and public spheres. The child characters who receive the greatest attention are those who, in the past and in the present, most connect the book with the world outside the school: Nan, in part, and Nat, but especially Dan.

In many ways, Nan is a later incarnation of the Jo March of *Little Women.* Like Jo, Nan provides a middle ground for diverging tendencies: as a tomboy, both feminine and masculine; as a newcomer, like other focal characters Nat and Dan, but one who quickly becomes an insider (her social class is not in question, as theirs is); as a motherless child who needs Mrs. Jo; even in terms of the letters of her name, mediating between Nat and Dan.

Yet Nan is not at the emotional center of the work, nor, for all that she is the guiding spirit, is Mrs. Jo. Instead, the character who generates the most affect, the character through whom Alcott attempts to grapple with what remains most compelling and elusive, is the wild and difficult-to-tame Dan.[7] In providing the greatest challenge to Mrs. Jo's domesticating influence, this boy of the streets tests the limits of Alcott's domestic feminism. This boy whose looks are frequently mixed—"half-bold, half-sullen"; "half-resolute, half-reckless"; "half-fierce, half-imploring" (91, 245, 247)[8]—this boundary case for whom Alcott lacks adequate categories shows the difficulty of crossing a gender barrier and also a class one, the difficulty of transgressing the former highlighted by the superposition of the latter. Dan is, in effect, a "problem" that marks "the limits of ideological certainty," threatening "to expose the artificiality of the binary logic" that separates genders (Poovey, *Uneven Developments* 12)—and also Alcott's logic of cross-gendering transgression. Alcott wants Dan to rhyme with Nan, but he doesn't, not fully.

The only way Alcott can tame Dan sufficiently to integrate him into the world of the school, even temporarily, is to lame him. Curiously, a number of the boys at Plumfield are handicapped. One has a hump; another is feeble-minded; another stutters. In part these disabilities allow Alcott to show how the school helps those whom the rest of society has failed to. Yet the handicaps have also helped to domesticate the boys, partly unman them if you will, to make them ripe for Jo's domestic influence.

As for Dan, at first he starts fights; he worries the cow in a pretend bullfight; his introduction of drinking, gambling, swearing, and smoking precipitates a dangerous fire.[9] Sent away, he wanders back to Plumfield and, having hurt his foot, is discovered before he disappears again. In the ensuing weeks of convalescence he is slowly "tamed by pain and patience" (179). Yet Dan is not sufficiently invalided to be permanently tamed—he never becomes, in either *Little Men* or the subsequent *Jo's Boys,* a full member of the society in and around Plumfield; even an additional spell of invalidism in the sequel doesn't fit him to marry Bess. On some level, perhaps, he escapes from Jo's and Alcott's authority, succeeds in triangulating to his own.

Like Nan, Dan escapes from the web of domesticity—he too never marries. Yet he escapes not to some pinnacle of success but rather because he does not fit in, is not a suitable mate for Bess—or rather because Alcott, like Jo, doesn't quite know what to make of him. Like Bertha in *Jane Eyre,* like Christophine in *Wide Sargasso Sea,* characters whose discursive grounding Spivak explores, he remains tangential, unassimilated. Marginalized by class, he may not at first seem subject to the imperial project that Spivak describes—"a domesticated other that consolidates the imperialist self" (186), providing the grounds for nineteenth-century individualism in others. Yet he is an undomesticated other that consolidates the self privileged by class. And subsequently in *Jo's Boys* he becomes an instrument of an imperial project when—a New World echo of Brontë's St. John Rivers—he undertakes missionary work among the Indians.[10]

Alcott's attempt to tame through laming echoes a trope common in girls' fiction of the time, such as Susan Coolidge's *What Katy Did* (1872) and Alcott's own *Jack and Jill* (1880): tomboys are tamed, learn to become little women, by enduring long periods, sometimes years, as invalids. Even Nan receives a dose of such confinement: after she loses herself and little Rob on a huckleberry expedition, she is tied to a sofa with a rope. Unlike the other invalided tomboys, though, Nan is confined for only hours, and the overt purpose is to teach her not so much to live with constriction as to value her freedom: "A few hours of confinement taught Nan how precious it was" (215–216). The real point may be to learn to internalize constraint, but what the narrator emphasizes is the value of freedom.

Dan is thus perhaps treated like a tomboy, or like Jane Eyre's Mr. Rochester—another way in which Alcott incorporates some of the modes of girls and women into this story of boys.[11] Earlier women writers of boys' school stories, like Martineau and Elizabeth Sandham (*The Boys' School,* c. 1800)—and occasionally a later writer like Goddard—were able to lead boys to the paths of righteousness by laming them. Martineau's Hugh crushes his left foot when he falls off a wall, crushes it so badly that it has to be amputated.[12] After this accident that seems to preclude the traveling he had always dreamed of—he cannot now become a soldier or sailor—he learns forbearance and fortitude. And he is finally rewarded by having a friend who enables him to join the civil service and hence travel to India after all.

It's appropriate, then, that one of the ways that Mrs. Jo helps Dan to beguile his days of convalescence—he too lamed when trying to cross a wall, a metaphor for his and Alcott's (lame) attempts to cross a class barrier—is by giving him Martineau's *The Crofton Boys,* a "charming little book" that soon interested him even though he "did not love to read" (172). The book is of course meant to teach Dan the use he should make of adversity. Yet also, as one of two predecessor school stories named in the novel, it shows Alcott acknowledging not just the canonical school story but the women's tradition that preceded Hughes. And the lack of irony in the reference to Martineau's book, unlike the apologia for not providing stirring Hughesian accounts of cricket and football, suggests that Alcott finds it preferable to locate herself in this other tradition.

So too with more oblique references to school stories. One is perhaps to the school stories that could be counted among Edgeworth's tales. Demi's interest not just in *Robinson Crusoe* and *Arabian Nights* but in *Edgeworth's Tales* "opened a new world to Nat, and his eagerness to see what came next in the story helped him on till he could read as well as anybody" (55–56). What Alcott calls *Edgeworth's Tales*[13] functions like *The Crofton Boys,* as part of a desirable women's tradition, a predecessor text that usefully educates a boy to the ways of Plumfield.

Another reference is to a school story "written years ago by a dear old lady" (339), a story that Mrs. Jo retells to her school—no longer does she rely on her own powers of invention, as she had when she secretly wrote sensation stories in *Little Women.*[14] The story is about a schoolboy who admits to extracting the fruit from some gooseberry tarts and is later believed guilty of stealing a pearl-handled knife from a peddler—until the peddler returns to say he had simply misplaced the knife. Jo thereby reflects on incidents in the life of Plumfield, in particular an incident of theft, working in moral reflections for the boys to meditate on: not, for instance, to "'hit a fellow when he is down,' as they say" (342). But she herself has also in effect stolen the story, likewise the cliché that she sets off in quotation marks. Thus does Alcott underscore the extent to which she borrows from other sources in *Little Men,* including a tradition of school stories by "dear old ladies."

These borrowings from other adult authorities, other adults who addressed children, are part of Alcott's cross-generational project. For she is not just crossing genders and gendered literary traditions but also working across generations, an adult writing of and for children. As Jacqueline Rose points out, children's literature is always written across this gap, this rupture between the writer and the addressee, this rupture through which we adults attempt to regulate our relationship with language as well, associating the child, as we do, with the origins of language.

Alcott's generational crossing in *Little Men* is particularly salient, for not only does she include an adult proxy, but this proxy has herself crossed generations since *Little Women*. Not only does the relationship between Jo and her young people become a map of the relationship between Alcott and her child readers, but so does the relationship between Jo and her earlier textual self. The point of origin is no longer *Pilgrim's Progress,* as it was in *Little Women,* where Jo encountered her Apollyon and Meg dallied with *Vanity Fair,* but rather a book by a woman: *Little Women.* And in this self-referential process Alcott maps the younger generation onto the older, the characters of *Little Men* onto the characters of *Little Women.* Nan and Dan, in particular, are versions of Jo, both playing out Jo's urges to escape domesticity, both succeeding in ways that Jo did not.

In fact, this complex give and take between books blurs the generational focus, rather like the genre dialectic between school and family stories—and it blurs the focus more than in any contemporary boys' school story. Is this a story about children, or do we still have a strong interest in the latter-day Jo March? Or rather, does the author continue identifying with Jo, inviting the reader to do so too? Alcott is, in effect, playing out the implications of the double audience, both children and adults, to which children's literature is addressed, Jo thus functioning as proxy not just for Alcott but for adult (and adult-identified) readers. The mapping of one generation onto another prevents either from gaining priority.

Yet another kind of generational mapping figures in this book's genesis as well. For much as Edgeworth honors her father's ideas in *The Parent's Assistant* (1796), *Little Men* in many ways honors Bronson Alcott's philosophy of education. Both women seem to have been enabled to write of boys in part because of their relationships with their fathers. Edgeworth drew directly and uncritically on her father's experiences as well as on his philosophical approach. Alcott, though not particularly critical of her father's philosophy of education, with its emphasis on nurturing the child's innate qualities and on fostering self-control, does implicitly criticize the realization of some of his ideas. For Plumfield can be seen as a commentary on

Bronson's failed attempt to achieve utopia at Fruitlands.[15] More significantly, Alcott adds an emphasis on self-help, on educating a child for a practical vocation (see McCurry 84–90).

Like Bronson, Jo keeps careful records of each pupil, but she discusses them in private rather than in public, and the fictional Plumfield makes more use of peer pressure than Bronson's Temple School did (see Elbert 29, 186). Alcott further derived from her father such ideas as the stress on physical exercise, on not cramming the mind too much, on valuing the spiritual, on opposing corporal punishment, even on being open to coeducation—though the daughter seems to have been more enthusiastic about this last than the father was.[16] Thus Alcott charts her own way, her father's views perhaps helping to distance her from traditional ones, yet she also differentiates her own views from her father's.

Like Bronson Alcott, Jo believes that children are "more tamed by kindness" than by whippings (104).[17] She keeps rules to a minimum, and when rules don't work—when it proves impossible to contain the boys' high spirits—she modifies the rules, allowing "a fifteen-minute pillow fight every Saturday night" if the boys "go properly to bed every other night" (17). Professor Bhaer too is more gentle than stern, giving "a boost over the hard places" rather than "raps on the head" (40). When the musician Nat needs to be punished for neglecting lessons, he has "to hang up the fiddle and the bow for a day" (58). Alcott even indulges, in *Little Men,* in a kind of generational inversion—in a way that simultaneously counters and echoes her father. When Nat has trouble giving up his habit of lying, Mr. Bhaer tells of his similar difficulties as a child and how his grandmother cured him—by snipping the end of his tongue. Mr. Bhaer's approach, however, is to get Nat to strike his elder with a ferule, rather than vice versa, a measure that apparently works. Thus does Mr. Bhaer invert the approach of an earlier generation, inverting the direction of punitive action. And by granting agency to the child, Alcott starts to question traditional sources of authority—though she simultaneously endorses her own father's authority, for he too used this inverted punishment (see McCurry 93).

Alcott does not assume that adults are the only sources of knowledge: as Jo notes, "Half the science of teaching is knowing how much children do for one another, and when to mix them" (114). That becomes her justification for her experiment in coeducation. Mr. Bhaer even avers that the children "teach us quite as much as we teach them" (222). Though Mrs. Jo quickly circumscribes this teaching, limiting it to teaching the adults about childrearing, prefacing her remarks with a condescending direct address of the little darlings: "Bless the dears! They never guess how many hints they give us as to the best way of managing them" (222). In short, where canonical boys' school stories tended to pay lip service to the authority of adults yet actually acceded to schoolboys' priorities—such as sports—Alcott pays lip service to the authority of children while nonetheless steering them toward the views of adult authorities. Mrs. Jo's moral presence dominates, even if she governs more by suasion than with a switch.

And she governs by emphasizing cooperation (with peers, with adults) over competition. That too is part of her cross-generational project, likewise one of the ways she differentiates her work from canonical school stories. I have already noted her disclaimer with respect to cricket and football and stirring accounts thereof. She doesn't altogether deny her schoolboys the competition provided by sports; she simply forbears describing it.

Nor does she translate competition into the classroom, as other women authors of boys' stories have done, women like the American Mary Densel. Although Densel's *Tel Tyler at School* (1872) is, like Alcott's book, part of a series, it stays with the first generation of children, simply branching out to a different sibling. There is then less compulsion to adopt the adult's perspective, or to complicate the child's: Densel sticks closer to the Hughesian model. There is some discussion of baseball, for instance, when the eponymous Tel first arrives at his military academy, even if we never witness a practice or wait breathlessly for the outcome of a game.[18] More importantly, Densel devotes considerable attention to a declamation competition. Tel eventually succeeds in winning it, only to question his reasons for wanting to win—had he wanted to because it was right to do one's best and winning would please his father and sister, or because he wanted to show himself superior to the other boys? And then he disavows competition, selflessly supporting another boy's election to sergeant. This self-sacrifice is not in vain, however, for Tel goes on to win the school's highest prize, for "conduct, scholarship, and military standing" (184). Densel complexly endorses and disavows competition—ultimately, it seems, endorsing it.

Alcott, however, opts not to include any such competitions—not baseball, not declamation, not the good conduct prize. The closest analogue is Composition Day, when pupils recite compositions based on natural history, telling about sponges and cats and dragonflies. In doing so they reinforce our sense of their characters, rather like the storytelling game of Rigmarole in *Little Women*. But also we can see the humor in—and feel superior to—their efforts.[19] Nan has written an essay on the sponge, with special attention to its use as a repository for ether held "to people's noses when they have teeth out": "*I* shall do this when I am bigger, and give ether to the sick, so they will go to sleep and not feel me cut off their legs and arms" (288,

Alcott's italics). The boy with a hunchback tells of his observations of drag-onflies, especially how they burst out of their old skins—and thereby sug-gests, "to the minds of the elder listeners," how he would some day, "leav-ing his poor little body behind him, find a new and lovely shape in a fairer world than this" (295). Composition Day is, in short, an occasion for fun, for revealing character, for teaching the reader how to read character alle-gorically—and for replicating Alcott's own activity as author. It is not an occasion for competition and conflict.

Alcott likewise avoids conflict between children and adults—likewise blurs the generational dialectic—in her treatment of the code against talebearing. Again she provides new perspectives, though her elaborate dis-placements of the trope are also evasive. Like writers of girls' school stories and of other U.S. boys' school stories, Alcott does not draw a sharp line between boys and masters: her complex treatment of talebearing sets into relief the contradictions that permeate the trope, contradictions between loy-alty to peers and loyalty to adults and the religious and moral authority that the latter represent.

In *Little Men* Alcott sets up a conventional test of the talebearing ethic: the wrongful accusation. Nat is accused of stealing some money. He knew where it had been left and has a dubious background as a street mu-sician, not to mention a lingering propensity for lying. He steadfastly de-nies guilt and accepts punishment, but not to protect someone else, as would be the case in a canonical school story. Instead he is himself pro-tected by a more recent newcomer with an even more dubious background: Dan claims to be guilty. Only by inverting the significance of the phrase, making it an expression of peer solidarity rather than a violation of it, can Dan be said to tell a tale—he tells a lie. Just as Alcott subtly redefines the terms of the classic ingredient of the British school story, the wrongful ac-cusation: she displaces the supreme sign of friendship from not telling the truth to (unspeakably un-British)[20] telling a lie—anticipating Tom Sawyer's claim, five years later, to having committed a misdeed actually perpetrated by Becky Thatcher. Furthermore, Alcott gets Dan to insert himself into Nat's position not just by taking the blame but by using Nat's character-istic tool of lying. Still, as in other school stories, Dan is eventually cleared—after he saves the real culprit's life and the boy duly repents (this latter a plot move reminiscent of pre-Hughesian stories). Overall, Alcott redefines the grounds of the conventional, implicitly questioning its prov-enance—only to capitulate to a standard ending, the improbable self-rev-elation of the culprit. At the same time, since there is no tale for Nat to tell, she could be said to evade the issue of talebearing—she protects her boys, as Mrs. Jo does, making it impossible for them to tell tales.

The plotting of Nat's wrongful accusation does, however, bring the boy to the verge of a more straightforward adumbration of the trope. Though here too talebearing is displaced. When a schoolmate named Ned belittles the self-accused Dan, Nat hotly retorts, "I don't want to tell tales, but, by George! I will, if you don't let Dan alone" (237). Whereupon Dan appears and tosses the boy in a brook—thereby abrogating the need for Nat to seek a reprisal by telling tales, and again evading the conflict between talebearing and loyalty to peers.

At the same time, in the same scene, Alcott redefines what it means to be a sneak. For when Nat threatens to tell, Ned jeers, "Then you'll be a sneak . . ." (237)—using *sneak* as nineteenth-century schoolboys did, to refer to someone who tells tales. Dan subsequently retorts, "You are a sneak yourself to badger Nat round the corner" (237)—out of sight of Mr. Bhaer, who has forbidden the boys to tax Nat about the theft. Thus Dan reinstates an older meaning of *sneak,* referring to anyone who acts in a clandestine manner. He trips Ned up verbally as well as physically, enabling Alcott to submerge talebearing, subordinate it, reorient it.

Alcott's first reference to telling tales in *Little Men* is also in connection with Ned, a reference that draws on the more typical associations of the trope, though it too starts unraveling the canonical. She introduces this minor character as someone who, "without being at all bad, was just the sort of fellow who could very easily be led astray" (24). She buttresses this statement by alluding to two standard school-story tropes: Ned "was apt to bully the small boys" and was "a little given to taletelling" (24). Yet even here she subverts the stereotypical, since a tendency toward either bullying or taletelling would brand a boy, usually irredeemably, in a canonical school story. But Ned, we have just been told, is not "at all bad." Perhaps she also subverts the expected when, as the story unfolds, we see what a minor role he plays: in a canonical story the bully or telltale would be a major focus.

A final reference to telling tales in *Little Men* is more metaphoric—or perhaps more literal. When the visiting Mr. Laurie proposes to make a museum for the boys' natural history collections and, "with a merry look in his eyes," itemizes the inconvenient doorbugs, dead bats, and wasps' nests that Mrs. Jo has been stumbling over, it's clear to the boys "that someone told tales out of school, else how could he know of the existence of these inconvenient treasures" (179–180). Quite literally, the tales have been told out of school—someone, presumably Jo, has been talking to Laurie. This literalization of the trope neutralizes the baggage of its customary significance, the conflict in loyalty for which it is a nexus, as does the ascription to an adult authority of telling "tales out of school." If a child's telling on another has by now become negative in school stories, something that at least requires an apologetic excuse, what does it mean for an adult authority to tell tales—someone, in short, who is not bound by the strictures of the code, has in fact been the "other" that the code excludes? True, this adult is guilty of violating the code, but in a context where it is made to seem applicable to her, not just to schoolchildren. Alcott reorients the schoolchild code against talebearing, making light of it, as if telling tales is not just benign but even rather jolly. She appropriates the trope for her own moral economy—using it to connect adults and schoolchildren rather than to demarcate their separation.

Alcott further connects adult and child, male and female, further advocates cooperation over conflict, through her deployment of discursive registers. Her discursive field is not a playing or battle field but a horticultural one. Canonical school stories bolster competition through the metaphorical subtext of war. In describing the Doctor's sermon in *Tom Brown's Schooldays,* Hughes stresses how this headmaster enlists his boys in a moral "battle-field ordained from of old," explaining "how that battle was to be fought; and stood there before them their fellow-soldier and captain of their band" (118). Girls' stories, and also other stories that emphasize an adult perspective (especially if they're not set during the Civil War), tend instead to describe the students as plants to be nurtured. In *The Governess* (1749) we learn that most of the girls "had in them the Seeds of Good-will to each other, altho' those Seeds were choaked and over-run with the Weeds of Envy and Pride" (11). Or if garden imagery appears in a more canonical story like *Stalky & Co.* (1899)—a housemaster "lurched out with some hazy impression that he had sown good seed on poor ground" (73)—we can be certain that its application is undermined, Stalky and his friends sure to outflank any such attempt at moral cultivation.

So it's not surprising, given the traditions that Alcott prefers to draw on, to find that she suppresses the discourse of war and cultivates that of gardening. On the rare occasions when the word "battle" appears it is likely to be distanced through miniaturization and humor—little Rob gets "the best of the battle" with some squirrels over nuts (312). Or the hired hand Silas may tell of a war experience, yet he emphasizes not the fighting but his devotion to his horse (who seemed in fact the more bellicose of the two) and how he and a Confederate soldier, both wounded, "helped one another like brothers" (336). If, during the Civil War, fiction sometimes symbolically enacted the national rift by portraying two antagonistic brothers, one in blue and the other in gray (Alcott's version of such a story, "The Brothers" [1863], makes the brothers black and white and thus grapples more directly with race than others do),[21] then in the following decade Alcott offers a vignette that symbolically heals the nation's wounds, making enemies into brothers, domesticating the nation as she has domesticated the school. Or alternatively, if in *Little Women* the Civil War makes possible a community of women by taking away the father (much as wars generally seem to have empowered women, opened doors to nontraditional activity for both Scarlett O'Haras and Rosie the Riveters), then in a postbellum world Alcott attempts to enlarge her community to include men—and to domesticate them.

Or to cultivate them. For *Little Men* is pervaded by the discourse of agriculture.[22] The most extended example is Professor Bhaer's self-conscious allegory about "a great and wise gardener," some of whose undergardeners "did their duty and earned the rich wages he gave them; but others neglected their parts and let them run to waste, which displeased him much" (43). Each member of the school then goes on to pledge what moral virtues he or she will cultivate. And much as the male-generated allegory of *Pilgrim's Progress* provides a moral and discursive framework for *Little Women,* so does this putatively male-generated allegory in *Little Men,* finally culminating—during the harvest celebration of Thanksgiving—in "the bouquet of laughing young faces" that surround Jo and the Professor, love having "taken root and blossomed beautifully in all the little gardens" (372).

Yet in this bouquet that closes the book, "the good professor and his wife were taken prisoner by many arms" (372). Jo makes her last textual appearance not as Mrs. Jo, nor even as Mother Bhaer, but simply as the professor's wife. And imprisonment intrudes in this paragraph of love and flowers, an eruption of the effects of armed battle. Even Alcott's domestication of the school story cannot repress all traces of the canonical, as it hints not just at the joys but at the perils of domestication.

Another subtext that runs through the book and subverts the canonical, a subtext supporting Alcott's emphasis on self-help, is that of wages and payment. Alcott's intention is to encourage these boys who will have to work for their livings to start being independent: to keep hens whose eggs they sell to the Bhaers, likewise vegetables they have grown, to sell worms to one another or the fruits of their carpentry. Such endorsement of the bourgeois would be unthinkable for the public-school boys of canonical stories, for whom having a family in trade was even worse than having a sister. In the United States, however, the myth of the self-made man made class boundaries seem more permeable. Alcott is, in effect, encouraging her boys to become Ben Franklins (at least as his life was interpreted in the nineteenth century). Yet her vision remains eighteenth century, preindustrial, as Jean Fagan

Yellin has noted in another context (535–538). The closest Alcott comes to acknowledging misgivings is in her portrayal of Jack, the most despicable boy, a sharp dealer like his Yankee trader of an uncle: hyperacquisitive, Jack turns out to be the thief that Nat had been accused of being. Or rather he marks the cleavage between two of the strands that can be seen as comprising the myth of the self-made man: one, middle class and Protestant, stressed industry, frugality, honesty, and piety, leading to "a respectable competence in this world and eternal salvation in the world to come"; the other, emphasizing getting ahead, stressed initiative, aggressiveness, and competitiveness (Cawelti 4–5). Jack reveals the slippage of the former into the latter, a slippage that, Alcott feels, must be sharply dealt with.

Whether Alcott is trying to appeal to the interests she envisions her readers as having, or is trying to steer them into what she sees as worthy versions of the self-made, or is simply spoken by the discourse of emergent industrialism, the language of the marketplace permeates *Little Men*. Not only do boys get others to do tasks for them by offering payment (one gets others to collect grasshoppers for a prank and then "pays" them with peppermints) but one boy "pays" another for morally uplifting talk by sharing his knowledge of natural history, boys "pay" Dan for his sufferings when accused of theft by pooling their resources and buying him a microscope, and Jo is confident that the "wages" Dan needs for service are simply love and confidence. Even in his garden allegory Professor Bhaer speaks of earning "rich wages." So despite some attention to giving instead of paying—the punishment that Jack suffers is to give away his possessions (yet even here giving becomes punishment)—the discourse of the marketplace starts invading the spiritual economy that Alcott is attempting to endorse. Jack's giving away of his worldly goods, for instance, is described in terms of "buy[ing] up a little integrity, even at a high price, and secur[ing] the respect of his playmates, though it was not a salable article" (273). The monetary language—"buy up," "high price," "secure," "salable"—is presumably translating Jack's favorite trope into spiritual coin. Yet the humorous breeziness of the sentence, its patness as it addresses the moral and the spiritual, starts unraveling the sentiment: the language shows that we can make a calculus of the spirit that attends to profit and loss. In her attempt to enter Jack's perspective, Alcott sullies—or reveals the contradictions underlying—her own. She may, through her mercantile discourse, subvert the class privilege underlying canonical stories, but she also subverts her own moral import. Like other writers in the second half of the nineteenth century, writers attempting to interpret an industrializing society through the lens of traditional religious views, she "tended to confuse economic success and moral merit"

(Cawelti 53). Or rather she hints at the workings of the Protestant ethic, the mutual implication of Protestantism and capitalism.

All together, Alcott domesticates the school story through reworking tropes and resituating the school, thereby regendering a genre. Her reworking carries a conscious gender valence: she is a woman reworking the boys' school story by writing about a woman central to a (mostly) boys' school. And in doing so she excavates the femininity suppressed by canonical stories. In bringing together family and school, school and world, Alcott voices tensions and conflicts and contradictions: between British and U.S. schools, the latter more likely to be coeducational; between British and U.S. literary traditions, the latter anxious to differentiate itself from the *Tom Brown* strand of boys' story; between, perhaps, "real" (U.S.) schools and an established genre. Alcott may be writing about her own experiences as a girl at school, about her father's as the creator of the experimental Temple School, about the experiences of her nieces and nephews. Yet, less committed to the systems espoused by the writers of the canonical school story—to their gender, to the system of the genre, to the educational system, to Britain, to the imperialism that the educational system buttressed, to the military discourse undergirding and implicated in all the rest—she felt less need to tidy their contradictions.

In crossing generations, too, Alcott unearths hidden truths. At the end of the book, in a chapter devoted to thanksgiving and Thanksgiving, young Demi gives a history of the holiday that situates the moment and the book more truly than he knows: "The Pilgrims killed all the Indians, and got rich; and hung the witches, and were very good . . ." (358). Alcott here points to truths that elude the consciousnesses of her adult personae, showing how her forefathers had erected barriers: racial barriers that enabled them to get rich, gender barriers that enabled them to feel righteous. At the same time women and Indians, wealth and goodness, are curiously confounded—the leveling *and*'s implicitly equate them. In *Little Men* as a whole, she similarly crosses the barriers of generations and genders, even of wealth and goodness—though race eludes her. Yet still in regendering the genre of the school story—attending to what it marginalized—she reveals how it displaced and suppressed contradictions. Her regendering regenerates the genre.

NOTES

1. Blackburn has also commented on this conjunction yet does not go on to discuss its implications. I. Martin has discussed possible mergings of school and home yet does not discuss *Little Men*.

2. Alcott herself may have supported women's suffrage, but she constantly subordinated her rights as an individual to her duties as a family member—her writ-

ing was a way of supporting her family, at the same time that it extolled devotion to the family. Keyser argues that in the subsequent *Jo's Boys* (1886) Jo moves beyond domestic feminism to a sense "that women's sphere exists wherever she chooses to make it"—albeit not without ambivalence (458). For the earliest working out of the concept of domestic feminism—not specifically with respect to Alcott—see D. S. Smith.

3. As Zwinger suggests, "Sentimentalizing the mother is always already a patriarchal ploy . . ." (64): where, in short, can we find a mother tongue that does not speak the Law of the Father? Alcott's writing here is not particularly traversed by a Kristevan semiotic and hence may simply reinscribe the patriarchal.

4. But see Keyser, who argues that Plumfield is a society where "women still nurse the body and nurture the emotions while men stimulate the mind and foster, as well as pursue, careers" (88). Yet I see the key purpose of Plumfield as not so much to stimulate the intellect as to foster moral growth (as in other contemporary school stories), and in this realm Jo is paramount, assuming the role played, in *Tom Brown*, by the headmaster.

5. See Laird 282–288.

6. Though her addition, in particular, would seem if anything to sharpen gender distinctions: her refined femininity may inspire the boys to behave more politely, but it's by appealing "to the chivalrous instinct in them as something to love, admire, and protect with a tender sort of reverence," and Nan, in turn, is inspired to toil over the feminine activity of sewing "for love of Bess" (228, 224).

7. As such critics as Black (16–17), Hamblen ("Divided World" 63–64), Keyser (94–96), and MacDonald (35–36) have found.

8. He likewise generates mixed looks in others, making Jo "half-merry, half-reproachful" (159).

9. A similar dangerous fire appears in Alcott's adult novel *Work: A Story of Experience* (1873): there the fire, caused by the heroine's staying up late to read, functions primarily as a reminder of "the searing dangers of books to women" (Clark, "Portrait" 82). Yet there is something to be said for books; there is something to be said for their attractiveness—for Alcott is after all writing books herself, and books that flirt with the dangerously fictive, for all that she attempts to emphasize the "truthfulness" of her books for children. The fire in *Little Men* is likewise meant to be a reminder of searing dangers—as perhaps is the other significant fire in the book, the one to the Kitty-mouse, where Demi Brooke gets his sister Daisy and little Rob and Teddy to "sackerryfice" their favorite toys, this latter fire perhaps hinting at the dangers of self-sacrifice. But these fires also hint at attractions, the attractiveness of Dan's misdemeanors, the attractiveness of sacrifice to others.

10. Race is even more tangential than class in *Little Men*. All of the boys at Plumfield are white—even though in *Little Women* Plumfield had admitted a quadroon. Crossing racial boundaries was not unthinkable for Alcott, since her father had once admitted a black child to his Temple School, though the upshot of that action underscores the difficulty of imagining a viable interracial school: admitting this child was the final straw that caused the school to fail. And the Bhaers' black cook figures very little in the text—this black cook clled Asia, one race conflated with the appurtenances of another. Alcott tended to ignore race in her children's literature.   ·

11. For discussion of nineteenth-century attitudes toward tomboyism see O'Brien. For discussion of "the blinding, maiming, or blighting motif" that appears in *Jane Eyre* and other novels when women write of men, see Showalter 150.

12. Postlethwaite argues that Martineau "transforms the rage she felt at the restrictions of gender into a parable of suffering and redemption" (596). Hugh's disability is simultaneously a punishment for his aspirations, a metaphor for Martineau's gender handicap, and an agent of growth. The book thus provides "a vision of a male world transformed by the female sensibilities of suffering and sympathy" (601)—at a time when Martineau was herself an invalid, lacking mothering. For discussion of handicaps as instruments of moral growth in children's literature, see Pickering, *Moral*

Instruction 90; and Nelson, *Boys* 21ff.

13. *Edgeworth's Tales* could refer to any of a number of volumes by Edgeworth printed and reprinted during the nineteenth century: *Moral Tales, Popular Tales, Tales of Fashionable Life,* not to mention the eighteen-volume *Tales and Novels.* None of these appears to have included the school stories "Tarlton," "The Barring-Out," or "Eton Montem," yet Alcott could also be referring to Edgeworth's tales more generally.

14. For all that she says, though specifically in connection with writing about each boy in her "conscience book," "I really don't know which I like best, writing or boys" (32). Furthermore, plagiarism—if Mrs. Jo's retelling could be considered plagiarism—is implicitly condemned in *Little Women* in the storytelling game of Rigmarole. I have been unable to locate the story by the "dear old lady."

15. See Elbert 166. Alcott's direct commentary on Fruitlands appears in "Transcendental Wild Oats" (1874).

16. See MacDonald 31–34; see also Hamblen, "Louisa May Alcott."

17. The success of which method is somewhat belied by the fact that Dan, the boy discussed in this connection, is only temporarily tamed, not fully tamed, by kindness.

18. Rather, we learn that his skill at it throws him in with an undesirable lot of boys. Thus perhaps does Densel metonymically put down the *Tom Brown* type of school story, by putting down athletes.

19. It's only the younger pupils who recite, the ones most likely to be "quaint," the reader thereby invited to collude in condescending spectatorship, watching from an adult perspective.

20. See, e.g., Avery, *Childhood's Pattern* 141. But see also Newsome (46), who suggests that it was headmasters like Dr. Arnold who were most severely opposed to lying, not the boys themselves, and in fact reminiscences show that boys often indulged in lying. Perhaps strictures against lying were adopted by schoolchildren in accordance with adult wishes; perhaps British writers of children's stories projected onto children their own horror of childhood lies.

21. See Diffley 649–652.

22. McCurry traces imagery of organic growth back through Bronson Alcott's discussions of education to Pestalozzi and Rousseau (83). Wallace finds a similar horticultural discourse in Alcott's *Work,* a language of flowers, yet reads it as erotic.

10 ENGENDERING THE SCHOOL STORY

JULIA A. MATHEWS

If Hale and Eiloart translated their project of crossing genders into a crossing of racial barriers, and if Wood and Alcott translated it into a crossing of genres, several late-nineteenth-century writers addressed gender itself. But only one such crossgendering writer makes gender difference central, along with sexuality, struggling to define masculinity by contrasting it with femininity, a struggle intensified by a constant sense of slippage.

The story is Julia A. Mathews' *Jack Granger's Cousin* (1877). Like many nineteenth-century U.S. writers who wrote primarily for children, Mathews is not now well known. Nor did her works ever achieve the popularity of, say, Alcott's. Yet *Jack Granger's Cousin*—"one of the best of Julia Mathew[s'] stories," according to a review in *Harper's* ("Editor's Literary Record" 311)[1]—was sufficiently resonant that it was immediately reprinted in England and was still in print in the United States as late as 1903. Whether or not the book was hugely popular, though, it is important because it captures the complexities of gender—in dialogue with class, ethnicity, sexuality, and age—in a way that few contemporary works did. In engendering the school story this text more fully acknowledges the pivotal role of gender than other school stories do. It richly embodies the contradictions circulating among and within discourses of masculinity in the late-nineteenth-century American middle class.

Mathews' gender slippage is associated with genre slippage as well, for *Jack Granger's Cousin* is not just a school story but a conversion story, a bad-boy story, and a family story. Mathews had made her name by writing what many would call Sunday-school literature. She is listed in the 1904 edition of Oscar Fay Adams' *A Dictionary of American Authors*, for instance, as "a writer of Sunday-school fiction," though two of the three works there listed, including *Jack Granger's Cousin*, are the least Sunday-schoolish of her fiction. Such a label is, in fact, rather loose and misleading, including as it does both stories of angelic children whose early deaths spread conversion like wildfire, published by the American Sunday School Union, the American Tract Society, and various denominational societies,[2] and also less stereotyped and more lively books that were simply acceptable to Sunday-school boards. Such boards might in fact welcome, as the highly respected and influential Ladies' Commission on Sunday School Books of the American Unitarian Association did, not only books that upheld denominational doctrine as well as books that were religious but not strictly doctrinal, but also books that were good even if not expressly religious[3]—though all would be implicated in the "disciplinary intimacy," the moral educating, that Richard H. Brodhead finds structuring much antebellum fiction. All would also take children seriously, not trivializing their relationship to society, as some better-remembered children's literature has, literature that places children in a world apart (see MacLeod, *American Childhood* 76). Whatever its merits, though, Mathews never did escape the Sunday-school label. And *Jack Granger's Cousin* can in fact be read as a conversion story, the boy Paul increasingly converted to his cousin Jack's Christian manliness—though to a latter-day reader the emphasis may fall less on the "Christian" than on the "manliness."

Certainly contemporary reviewers seem to have read the novel primarily in the context of moral improvement—which was how most nineteenth-century American school stories were framed, marking their difference from their better-known British equivalents, from *Tom Brown* to *Stalky*. Susan Coolidge, author of *What Katy Did* (1872), parallels *Jack Granger's Cousin* with Sherwood's *Robert and Frederick* (1842). And the language with which she goes on to praise Mathews' book is largely in the register of evangelical discourse: this "hearty, sweet-natured book" is "full of good lessons" and "is recommendable as pleasant and wholesome reading for boys" (143)[4]—even if "hearty" and "pleasant" hint at something beyond the purely evangelical, something more rugged and entertaining. If Coolidge's style effects at least a temporary resolution of the shifting currents that run through Mathews' book, by joining "hearty" and "sweet-natured," the reviewer in *Publishers' Weekly* hints at the same currents with less resolution. This reviewer concludes with pietistic language, describing the book as "one that both parents and children may derive instruction from," setting forth "the very highest ideal for the young people's imitation" (Review of *Jack Granger's Cousin* 492). Yet earlier the reviewer has stressed the ways in which the character Paul, a "Miss Nancy," "a thorough prig in his talk and manners," is thrown into contact with "rough, hearty school-boys" and reveals his cowardice (492)—terms that suggest more of a bad-boy framework.

So compellingly, in fact, that in the transitional sentence between the two readings—"The book winds up with a charming episode showing all the boys in their noblest guise, and reinstating Paul in the reader's respect"—the words *charming* and *noblest* seem, following all the talk of hearty schoolboys, rather discordant. Such discord marks the uneasiness with which the two genres—and their attendant ways of constructing masculinity—conjoin.

Yet the reviewer's language does hint that Mathews' book is influenced not only by the conversion story but by the bad-boy book. This influence is further signaled by Mathews shift in publisher from the religious-oriented Robert Carter and Brothers, who had published her work between 1865 and 1876, to the more secular and literary Roberts Brothers.[5] Mathews' image as a Sunday-school writer was certainly reinforced by her usual choice of publisher: Carter published the most extensive "series of children's books and Sunday school library titles . . . ever issued by a single house" (Tebbel 331). Her identification with Carter was strong enough—and Mathews work was prominent enough—that she is one of four authors, along with Susan Warner, named in connection with the firm by publishing historian Richard L. Darling ("Children's Books" 67).[6] *Jack Granger's Cousin,* however, was published by a firm more noted for the literary quality of its list: Roberts Brothers "could probably claim the most distinguished list of writers for children in America" (Darling, "Children's Books" 69), including Alcott, Coolidge, Juliana Horatia Ewing, and Robert Louis Stevenson—not to mention such other authors as the Rossettis, Swinburne, Morris, Channing, Dickinson, Wilde, Meredith, Schreiner, Balzac, Molière (Tebbel 429; Kilgour 1–2, 281).

Possibly, as I have suggested, Mathews switched to Roberts Brothers because she was responding to more secular influences, in particular, the bad-boy book, emerging with the publication of Aldrich's *The Story of a Bad Boy* (1869) and Twain's *The Adventures of Tom Sawyer* (1876). Certainly Jack Granger would seem to embody the characteristics of the bad boy as outlined by critic Anne Trensky: he is "typically rough and tough, quick to play and quick to fight" ("Bad Boy" 508). If Jack is not as disobedient as Tom Bailey or Tom Sawyer, he is nonetheless ultimately adored, as they are, by adults. And as a woman attempting a version of the bad-boy book—a genre generally attempted only by men—Mathews is not so much reacting against previous pious literature as integrating the two genres, the effeminate boy no longer the good boy who must be ignored or eliminated but in effect a bad boy who must be converted—and perhaps adored, as Becky Thatcher is.

Finally, like other women writers of boys' school stories, including

Alcott and Martineau, and like other authors of conversion stories—though unlike most authors of bad-boy books and of canonical British school stories—Mathews devotes considerable favorable attention to her boys' family context: the two central characters are cousins, living in the same household. The fourth genre that Mathews seems to draw on is that of domestic fiction, especially the strand described by Ann Douglas as the family journal rather than the courtship tale, the former providing "a settled and large fictive arena in which to explore a wide spectrum of situations and emotions engendered by sibling rivalry and parent–child relations as well as by romantic feelings" (Introduction xx)—not, in other words, that romantic feelings are altogether expunged. In fact, Mathews would seem to draw on a romantic plotting that had emerged half a century earlier, one that opposes two girls, one fashionable and gay, the other modest and kindly (see Bushman 302–303)—only Mathews effects a sex change. And unlike other women writing of boys at home and at school, Mathews addresses the contradictions between family and school through a focus on gender. And through contradicting herself, placing biological essence against linguistic construction: Mathews linguistically embodies the opposition of masculine and feminine in two boys, an opposition that nonetheless keeps slipping away, given their biology.

Much like genre conventions, constructions of gender, class, race, ethnicity, sexuality, and age intertwine complexly, and they are often defined through one another, in constellations that shift over time. Before the Civil War middle-class American men seem to have defined themselves more in terms of class and ethnicity than in terms of gender, and they seem not to have been particularly anxious about any feminization of society—even if subsequent commentators like Leslie A. Fiedler and Ann Douglas have been anxious for them.[7] Yet by the 1870s, the decade of *Jack Granger's Cousin*, it was easy for politicians to cast aspersions on patrician reformers and the stalwarts of high culture by calling them effeminate. It may have been that the Civil War effected a revaluation of physical toughness and courage (though England was going through a similar shift without having had a civil war); it may have been that a way of accommodating an increasingly bureaucratized capitalism was by turning to compensatory male fantasies of independence and adventure.[8] In any case, one way of charting the history of masculinity is by saying that an ideal of gentility (masculinity defined through class) was largely superseded by, or at least overlaid with, the rugged independence of what came to be seen as—and still is seen as—the stereotypically masculine.[9]

Another way of charting masculinity is to focus less on what super-seded what and more on a cross-section of available codes. By the late nine-teenth century the norms of gentility continued to hold sway in cultural in-stitutions, the gentry continuing to be the bearers and definers of culture.[10] And given their prominence in both publishing and education, it's not sur-prising that in the conjunction of the two realms—in literature for children—the norms of the genteel, specifically the ideal of the Christian gentleman, dominated. Yet these norms, which included self-control, service to others, courtesy, and sincerity, were in dialogue with other norms for masculinity.[11]

Some of these other norms can be associated with the social-economic elite, the new upper classes, an alternate construction of gentility, if you will, except that by now "gentility" had largely been claimed—and domesti-cated—by the middle class. The elite's norms included responsiveness to fash-ion, to conspicuous display—what the Christian genteel would brand as superficial instead of sincere. This fashionable elite modeled itself on the European aristocracy and tried to endorse hereditary privilege, whereas members of the cultural elite considered themselves democratic: anyone with the right education could enter the cultural elite (assuming of course that "anyone" could get access to an elite education).

A third strand of norms is associated with the middle-class ideal of the self-made man, with its valuing of industry, frugality, initiative—and getting ahead. Although its lip service to democracy allies it with Christian gentility, the emphasis on individual advancement over service to others sharply differentiates it.[12] And although the genteel ideals could by and large be unisex, those of the self-made man could not; if the opposites of genteel were defined primarily through class ("vulgar") and age ("childish"), the opposite of the self-made man, that which was most to be feared, was de-fined through gender ("sissy").[13]

Julia Mathews addresses values from these three strands. Like other nineteenth-century U.S. writers for children, she is particularly attuned to the values of Christian gentility. Her father had, after all, been a minister and an educator: the little biographical information available indicates that Mathews was born about 1836, that she started publishing stories for chil-dren in 1855, that her sister Joanna wrote too, that her father was a minis-ter in the Dutch Reformed Church and the first chancellor of the University of the City of New York, later New York University, that her maternal grand-father had been a leading New York merchant.[14] After *Jack Granger's Cousin* and her venture into literature for adults, *Bessie Harrington's Venture* (1878), Mathews seems to have published very little, and that little seems not to have pursued the more secular cast that emerged for her in the 1870s. The only subsequent new items attributed to her in the *National Union Catalog*—if indeed the attributions are correct—would seem to be *Harry Moore's Choice, with Other Missionary Stories,* published by the Presbyterian Board of Publication in 1882, and *A Message from the Woodland,* published in Beaver Falls in 1892.

Certainly Mathews' earliest work is very much in the tradition of pious gentility. Witness a sampling of titles: *Lily Hudson; or, Early Struggles 'midst Continual Hope* (1855); the six titles in the Golden Ladder series (1866), illustrating the Lord's Prayer, including *The Crossing-Sweeper* and *Nettie's Mission;* the six titles in the Drayton Hall series (1871), illustrating the Beatitudes, including *Laurence Bronson's Victory;* the five titles in the Dare to Do Right Series (1872–1874), including *Grandfather's Faith.* Witness, more particularly, *Drayton Hall, and Other Tales, Illustrating the Beatitudes,* published shortly before *Jack Granger's Cousin* and dedicated to the memory of Mathews' recently deceased father—and one of her last volumes to appear anonymously or pseudonymously. The title itself reveals its exemplary intent. This pious book proffers a plenitude of conversion experiences, including numerous deathbed repentances. By the last story, though, Mathews is moving toward the themes and language of *Jack Granger's Cousin*—as if she is starting to move out of her father's shadow.

The earlier stories in the volume deal largely in stock evangelical clichés: a wrongful accusation brings on a boy's death; a boy rescues his worst enemy from a fall off a cliff; a street urchin is reunited with his pious grandfather; a boy's missionary work reunites a repentant ruffian with his mother. The resolution of the final story, too, is a melodramatic cliché, yet its premise is unusual for a school story; rarely is adult authority so thoroughly undermined. For the hero of "True to His Flag," the pious Frank Austin, has to resist the overtures and commands of his impious parents. His father has wagered that Frank can beat another boy at cards; Frank, of course, cannot be party to such a wager. Resisting both his father's commands and his mother's entreaties, Frank remains "true to his flag" and is sent off to a stern military academy but (will his father relent?) is recalled when his ailing mother seems to be at death's door (will she die before he can return?). He makes it back in time, and his father is duly contrite.

Here, more than in the other stories, Mathews starts using language that crosses gender and age, that hints at physical touching and yet is militaristic. Her language is, in short, starting to echo her subject: the transgressive language echoes the piety that transgresses boundaries between this world and the next. It is acceptable here, even desirable, for a man to become a child again, for a schoolboy to behave with womanly tenderness, for one boy to embrace or even kiss another. Yet as if recognizing that her boys' masculinity might be impugned, her language is more militaristic as well: Frank soldiers on, fighting "like a man" and remaining true to his flag—yet thereby, as if to show the limits of the metaphor, evading a return to military school.[15]

It is noteworthy, furthermore, that both here and in her subsequent novel Mathews is attentive to family context. In fact, one of the ways the literature of Christian gentility invited feminine participation was by being hospitable to the family, and the source of values in such a story is likely to be a woman.[16] Yet Mathews manages to accommodate emerging notions of manliness—by abrogating females, even if not femininity. She attempts, in *Jack Granger's Cousin,* to accommodate patrician gentility to emerging norms for middle-class manliness in the persons of Paul Stuyvesant and Jack Granger (eventually expelling a third party, in the person of Philip Ward).[17]

The first encounter of the two cousins, when Jack's father, Dr. Granger, arrives home with Paul, is an encounter between two registers of masculinity: for one, the opposite that defines masculinity is childishness; for the other, it is femininity. From the perspective of someone with the genteel Paul's values, Paul is a man and Jack a mere child: Paul's elegant formality—he offers an arm to Mrs. Granger to take her in to supper—gives him "the air of a thorough man of the world" (7). When Mrs. Granger offers to greet Paul with a kiss, he declines by rising and formally extending his hand. Paul values formality over spontaneity, the former defined as restrained and manly, or better yet gentlemanly, the latter as childish.

The Granger family, on the other hand, values childlike informality: Jack greets his father by kissing him, "big fellow that he was, like any loving child" (4). In their register Paul lacks manliness—is not yet "a manly, healthy boy" (5). Paul is, rather, effeminate: this "Miss Nancy," this "awful muff," "looks like a pretty girl" to Jack (4, 7). Manliness is here associated with spontaneity and—no longer is a "manly boy" an oxymoron, no longer is it insulting to consider a thirteen-year-old boy a child—its opposite is girlishness.

By the end of the chapter Dr. Granger may piously hope that each boy will learn from the other, yet while Paul will learn directly from Jack how to be a manly boy, Jack learns from Paul only indirectly—he is toughened by the trial of dealing with Paul, learning self-control, becoming what could be called a Christian gentleman. Certainly, by the end of the first chapter, only Paul thinks that his cousin "seems almost a man compared to me"

(14); Jack doesn't think the same of Paul. And rarely, in subsequent chapters, is Paul's mode of behavior associated with manliness. Instead this effete boy continues to be associated with femininity, and Jack's values, modified only slightly in the course of the novel, take precedence. The novel thus enacts a crucial nineteenth-century shift in notions of masculinity, from one that opposes it to childishness to one that opposes it to femininity. Yet Mathews is reluctant to abandon Christian gentility. She tries, in effect, to rescue the concept of the Christian gentleman by redefining it not in opposition to childishness but in opposition to femininity—by redefining it so that it parallels the emerging notion of the self-made man. Or to put it another way, Paul's pseudogentility is disparaged, associated with the effete fashionable elite, so that the true gentleman can turn out to be the boyish Jack.

Paul continues, for instance, to be disparaged for being girlish: a spoon, a spoony, a Miss Nancy, a Miss Pauline.[18] He is usually disparaged, that is, in accordance with Jack's register of masculinity. And by the end of the book being a child is, for him, revalued. Paul's eventual change of heart is signaled by "a fit of sobbing, as if he were a little child" (192)—and being childish here is good. He must become a child again in order to become a man: he must become the child that he actually is, no longer effeminately aping manliness, in order paradoxically to become manly. In the final paragraph Jack's friend Tom, an exponent of sanity throughout, offers a parody of an ending, spoken through the language of both childhood and religion: after he clasps Jack's and Paul's hands and joins theirs together, he says merrily, "That's the way they do it in books . . . Then they say, 'Bless you, my children,' and that's the end" (208). This mock benediction—a mock marriage too, but more on that later—may self-consciously start to distance us from the book, reminding us that it is a book: it may ironize the references to children and to religion. But it does not disparage them. Instead it enables us to look at both anew, enables us to join boyhood and Christianity while yet acknowledging the provisionality of the yoking.

Early on, Paul defines the emerging masculine ideal by opposing it—being what it is not supposed to be, and thus paradoxically also embodying it if, as we shall see, boys are supposed to do what they're not supposed to do—if, more generally, opposites inscribe themselves in what they oppose. He embodies a kind of femininity, or better yet androgyny, against which masculinity can be defined. Mathews establishes a masculine–feminine dichotomy that will be dissipated, over time, by the individual, only to reinforce the abstract polarization even more since the two poles of the dichotomy demarcate Paul's progress—an itinerary that blurs essentialism only to reinscribe it.

When Dr. Granger arrives home with Paul, who has been living with some aunts, he tells his wife, "There are about ninety pounds of bottled-up boy, kept tightly corked for the last three years; and if you and I, with Jack's help, don't succeed in drawing the cork, he will grow up into the veriest Miss Nancy that ever wore coat tails. They've almost crushed his boyhood out of him, among them" (3). Paul's essence may be boyish, but it has been tightly corked, tightly corseted. And the narrator constantly iterates Paul's effeminate lack of masculinity. Paul has "womanish ways" and an "utter lack of strength and courage, boyish freedom, and love for fun" (19). Jack figures that Paul can be persuaded to join a long walk to a railroad bridge only because several girls are going too. Paul likes nothing better than to accompany Jack's mother shopping, "wonderfully versed," as he is, "in the merits of this and that make of muslin, or print, or lace" (31). And when she tells Paul he is "as good as a girl," he remarks, "I have often wished that I were a girl" (32).

Jack, on the other hand, is "rough to a fault, daring to recklessness, frank almost to rudeness" (19). He is not afraid to fight. Nor is he one to cry, even when exasperated with Paul: as the narrator tells us, "If Jack had been a girl, a hearty burst of crying would probably have calmed his feelings, and taken off the keenest edge of his disappointment; but being a boy, that relief was out of the question" (114). Or rather, if crying is defined as girlish, then Jack would be the last person to indulge, though, as we have seen, it is later acceptable for Paul to indulge—as long as crying is then defined as childish. Overall, Jack is honest and steadfast and daring, with a stern sense of what is right.

Yet the ideal of manly boyishness that he represents is subject to constant slippage. Jack admonishes Paul that boys "don't read 'Tupper's Proverbial Philosophy,' and such things; and they're not afraid of tanning their skin, or blistering their hands, or soiling their boots, or any of those things. But they do tease, and chaff, and play tricks, and do lots of things they've no business to do . . ." (52). Starting with a trope that adverts to reading, defining our reading for us, and implicitly questioning the masculinity of reading itself (and thus of reading Mathews' book), we learn that boys are supposed to do what they're not supposed to do—boys break through codified boundaries, embodying slippage among categories (with the help of a "business" metaphor that hints at an underlying mercantile norm, a whiff of the norms of the self-made).

There is also slippage in Jack's antifemininity. In keeping with the ideal of Christian gentility, which lauds domestic affections and Christian kindness and forbearance, Jack is "tender-hearted as a woman toward anything weak and helpless; and generous to lavishness, not only in giving but in doing for any who needed his help" (19). To be boyish is also to be womanly. Yet when asked to stand by his cousin Paul, Jack at first responds, "Take Miss Nancy under my protection, you mean, sir. . . . Not I. If he were really a girl, that would be all well enough; but I don't think I'll undertake to mother a boy of my own age. He can take care of himself, I should think" (4). A curious use of "mother," this: he is not about to mother Paul, but he would if his cousin were a girl. Mothering a boy is somehow too threatening to the masculine ideal—unless, as happens later, Paul is defined not as a boy but as "a tired baby, who lifts its pretty hands to be taken into some strong, restful arms" (20).[19]

Another key site for slippage in the portrayal of masculinity, another node of contested meaning, is that of self-control, which both Jack and Paul need to develop.[20] Mathews does not directly confront the contrary implications of Christianity and Jack's version of hearty masculinity—unlike, say, Louisa C. Tuthill several decades earlier in *The Boy of Spirit: A Story for the Young* (1845), partly set at school. The good-hearted but essentially unworthy Frank indulges in fights and pranks and even drinking, because he is spirited, boyish, eager to be "manly." Unlike the worthy James. Yet even James is at first reluctant to attend a Sunday school taught by a woman, belittling the woman in question—"I hate old maids"—until his mother suggests it would be "not only unmanly, but very ill-bred to speak slightingly of any class of women" (25, 26). Tuthill confronts gender stereotypes, eager to show that true manliness is congruent with Christianity. She wants to show, in effect, that truly being a man of spirit means being a man of the spirit, or rather the latter should supersede the former. Or perhaps kill it off: Frank comes to repentance only on his deathbed, after he has killed a man in a duel—as if to demonstrate that the stereotypically manly and the Christian can be yoked together only with violence.

Mathews is less direct, hence allowing slippage—and perhaps accommodation—between Christianity and masculinity. Jack needs to learn Christian forbearance, for instance, when Philip Ward destroys the drawing Jack has prepared for a competition.[21] In describing Jack's struggle here with himself, the narrator keeps tossing in the word *gentleman,* a term rarely used elsewhere in connection with the boy—as if she is anxious to buttress the masculinity of Jack's forbearance. And she quickly goes on to bolster any weakness in the ideal by invoking the imagery of battle (as had earlier genteel writers like Warner and Hale): "Perhaps Jack Granger, boy or man, never fought such a battle in his life as he waged with himself that afternoon" (189).[22]

Yet another node of contested meanings is the ideal of consistency[23]—an ideal whose insistence registers anxiety about competing norms. Jack ought to be consistent. He ought to be consistently masculine. He ought further to be consistent in his relationship with Paul—or at least to change only gradually and incrementally. Yet Jack's attitude toward his cousin does not progress neatly from resistance to acceptance. Nor does he display the erratic attraction and repulsion that might now be considered psychologically realistic in fiction. Instead, as in Adams' *Edgar Clifton* (1852), the process is more cyclical: a repeated iteration of change, each time starting from the same place. At one point, after Jack has returned to hating Paul, despising him for not being able to "think and feel the same way two days in succession," Jack's father responds, "Such weak people as Paul . . . are almost invariably vacillating and uncertain. Don't stand up there, as if you were going to start out the next minute" (60). Dr. Granger goes on to stress that "that which is vacillation in one of my boys is scarcely strength of purpose in the other" (61). Jack is trying, in short, to displace his own inconsistency onto Paul, his own tendency "to start out the next minute," much as, in effect, he tries to displace femininity onto the latter.

Even more inconsistent—more subject to slippage—is Paul, at least from the narrator's perspective. She accuses Paul of being "governed always by the passing emotion of the moment, and led by any stronger nature than his own"; Jack of mere shortness of temper, of outbursts that are "quickly repented of, and, as far as possible, atoned for" (117). Jack's changes are glossed as Christian repentance, Paul's as the product of another's manipulation.

Or when Paul is consistent, it is defined as stubbornness. We learn that, "indulged and spoiled from his very babyhood, he had never learned self-control, nor gained the power to submit gracefully and pleasantly to contradiction of any kind" (57–58). Yet even here—congruent with Jack's moral economy—Paul's stubbornness is opposed to graceful submission, that ideal of femininity. And a moment later the doctor perceives "an underlying tone of obstinacy" that reveals that "there was something that was not very soft and yielding in this strange boy's composition" (58). Here is the seed then of Paul's subsequent manliness, the strength that eventually enables him to stand up to Philip. In contrast with his feminine qualities? In part. Yet given that femininity too embodied contradictions, encompassing both the compliant wife and the hysteric,[24] Paul's stubbornness can still be recuperated as femininity, especially since he expresses it is not forthrightly but sulkily, through passive aggression. His subsequent refusal to acknowledge Jack's heroism in rescuing him from a railroad bridge defines Paul as mentally "immovable" (87), reiterating his physical immovability on the bridge—and adumbrates the lack of mobility generally accorded females. The valence of stubbornness, of immovability, remains ambiguous, movable after all, subject to slippage and contradiction. A slippage and contradiction further heightened by hyphens and "half" prefixes: Paul is what Dr. Granger calls his girl-boy, what Jack considers "more than half-girl" (170).

While some of Paul's slippage is an ambiguity present until the end, some is naturalized as a progression from feminine to more masculine, as he learns a more fitting manliness. Even early on there is "promise of better things, if he could be lifted out of the softly curved channels of his hitherto pulseless existence" (18). He then proceeds to shift in allegiance from the effete gentility of a world of women (having lived with four aunts) to a world of boys. Early on this dapper young boy carries a cane and wears gloves, the picture of genteel refinement—or perhaps of what Marjorie Garber might call unmarked transvestism, the "synecdochic quotation of transvestism," symptomatic of "a category crisis of male and female," indeed of "the crisis of category itself" (356, 275, 17). Later he in effect removes the gloves, as Mathews indulges in that favorite Victorian trope for synecdochically representing the female body, the trope of hands[25]—hands here variously gloved, blistered, extended, shaking, striking, trembling, "hand-in-glove," "open-handed," "having a hand in." The progression culminates on the last page with Tom's offering a hand to both Jack and Paul, "and as their two right hands grasped his, he laid them together in his own" (208). Paul advances from gloved reserve to a manly clasp—or perhaps to having his hand joined with Jack's in a metaphoric marriage.

When Paul finally addresses a confession to the assembled boys at school, he recounts the moral and gendered progress he has made in the previous months: he stresses that though he was happy at school from the start, "In my home I was not so content; for instead of doing always as I pleased, being petted and spoiled, and excused in every wrong thing that I did, as I had been in the past, I was taught to do right simply because it was right; to be manly, and firm, and earnest, because unmanliness, and vacillation, and half-heartedness were weak and wrong" (199). What makes him masculine is thus home, not school, thereby devaluing school and endorsing the family context, where, paradoxically, feminine influence exists. The academy was in fact often linked by the self-made man with femininity, its associations with enervation and impracticality making it a "'feminine' dream world" (Catano 424)[26]—though it was not usually more associated with femininity than the family was. In reversing the valence of home and family (the revered Doctor of school stories here affiliated not with the school but with the family), and in effect the typical boy's trajectory from family to school, it would have been possible to domesticate boy and school, to extend feminine influence, as Alcott had in *Little Men* six years earlier; but instead Mathews attempts, by and large, to contain eruptions of the feminine, masculinizing the home.

The interplay of masculine and feminine continues, at the assembly, when Paul silences Jack's objections by speaking "in a tone of decision and command that surprised Jack into silence" yet restrains comments from his schoolmates with a "small, girlish-looking hand" (200, 201). Jack then says to the school at large, arm about Paul's neck, that "the chap who dubs Paul Stuyvesant 'Miss Pauline' after this, will prove that he don't know real courage or true manliness when he sees it" (203). Tom reaches a hand to Paul, and the latter "rose to take it, his great brown eyes full to overflowing with the tears which he was manfully striving to restrain" (204). The hints of the laudatory imply that Paul has somehow proved his manhood, or at least his boyhood. Yet hints of the feminine remain: the tears (childish or girlish?), the girlish hand, possibly the touching (Mathews does not treat touching as unmanly), certainly the mention of "Miss Pauline" (even while—or especially while—denying the invocation). The emphasis on behaving manfully, on "true manliness," has the effect of protesting too much.

Yet it's this constant slippage that, in effect, enables Paul to survive—to become acceptably masculine. It's worthwhile contrasting the gendering of this novel with two other works of this half century, both evangelical, both at least marginally school stories, and both addressing issues of gender. A decade later, in the American Mary R. Baldwin's *The New Boy at Southcott* (1887), the weak but virtuous Jamie is frequently associated with the feminine and is accorded so little slippage that he must die. He is like the permanent invalids in George MacDonald's *At the Back of the North Wind* (1871) and Kate Douglas Wiggin's *The Birds' Christmas Carol* (1887). Like Beth of *Little Women* (1868) too, Jamie tends to be a static symbol representing a connection to an other, better world: we do not see him being tamed, and the apotheosis of his invalidism is not adulthood but death. Jamie also resembles characters in evangelical school stories, a tradition that Hughes flirted with but then flouted when the exemplary Arthur's near-death has an impact on Tom Brown but Hughes allows Arthur to live. Here, however, Jamie Mason dies.

Jamie's main failing, aside from being sickly, is that he would like to go to heaven more to be with his parents than for Christ's sake. He is unremittingly kind—to the extent that, as another boy notes, "I've actually seen him take a spider up that he knew our housekeeper would kill if she got the chance—I've seen him take it up and say, 'Poor spider, why shouldn't you live!'" (201). In this book where the feminine is often desirable, at least as a touchstone, Jamie is sensitive to the feelings of a girl named Florrie, recognizing, for instance, her discomfort with her brother's exaggerations. He is also someone who believes in webs of connection with others and in turning to women as moral guides. He counters one boy's proclamation of a kind of manly independence, a competitive distrust of others, by saying, "But I thought every body needed friends; mother used to say so, and she used to tell me that we ourselves must show that we want to make friends of people" (230–231).

Like Mathews' Paul, who falls off a boat early on, thanks to Philip Ward, Jamie is subjected to a dunking at the hands of a not-altogether-admirable boy. For Baldwin the episode looms importantly throughout. The central agon of the book is a rowing contest, a contest that boys plan and train for but that never finally materializes, as if to signal Baldwin's swerve from the canonical focus on athletic competition: if Hughes swerves from the evangelical school story by letting the virtuous Arthur live, Baldwin swerves from the Hughesian story by having boys prepare for an athletic contest that they never compete in. Instead, the associations with water and with rowing coalesce in a trope of spiritual travel. Jamie tells of a dream, for instance, in which the voice of his dead mother calls him to row across the water to her. He recounts this dream of transition in a suitably marginal setting, in a winter wigwam his schoolmates have built—the wigwam a borrowing from a nonwhite culture, metaphoric for the otherness that Jamie is approaching. And Jamie's translation to spiritual realms is coordinated with the moral reformation of Ned, the boy responsible for pushing Jamie overboard—so that Ned can eventually win the girl Florrie. Thus the feminine boy must die, in Baldwin's work, so that the bad boy can get access to the feminine.

On the other hand, in the British Mrs. S. C. (Anna Maria) Hall's earlier *Daddy Dacre's School: A Story for the Young* (1858), the invalid Edward, considered girlish, is contrasted with the rough-and-tumble Octavius, an orphan who occasionally laments the loss of a mother's kiss but is otherwise loudly antifeminine. Octavius then misbehaves and is suitably invalided in a fall off a crag, so that by the end of the book Octavius and Edward have effectively changed places: it's finally Octavius more than Edward who seems feminine. Octavius has never been stoic about illness, we are told—he is "worse than any girl" in this respect (175). Once he encounters serious injury, then, he is effectively feminized. The net effect is that Edward's grandfather is educated to an appreciation of Edward's virtues and God's ways.

If in Baldwin's book the feminine boy must die to enable the reform of the bad boy, and in Hall's the feminine boy must be appreciated to enable the improvement of his grandfather, in *Jack Granger's Cousin* the feminine boy is not particularly the means whereby others improve (though in providing trials to Jack he presumably fosters some improvement). Instead he is himself assimilated, once the bad boy is purged. For the bad boy Philip Ward constitutes a crucial third term in Mathews' scheme—allowing the Christian polarities of good and evil to overlay and partly mask the gender oppositions (gender partly neutralized by Christianity, as in the notion of the Christian gentleman), allowing the feminine Paul to be redeemed as long as the selfish and conceited Philip is effectively expelled.

In part Paul, Philip, and Jack embody competing strands of masculinity—the fashionable snob, the self-made man, the Christian genteel—thus dramatizing the contradictions then circulating in society. But only in part. For the correspondence between each boy and a given ideal remains imperfect. Paul embodies some of the values of the fashionable elite, with his impeccable clothes and jealousy of privilege. Yet he is not accorded particular wealth, nor would he and his seem to have been active in any social whirl— his aunts leave him to attend to an inheritance in Florida, not to socialize in Newport.

Nor does Philip comfortably fit the idea of the self-made man. He may be highly competitive (even resorting to underhanded means to win a school prize) and acquisitive (he desperately wants the gold watch that his father will give him if he wins the prize). But he is not particularly frugal or industrious. Nor is he—or anyone in the book—particularly associated with metaphors of profit and loss; though he does retain some measure of popularity through his liberality with money—and is in fact the character most associated with, most defined by, money (Mathews describes him as selfish and, in the next breath, as openhanded, her contradictions signaling contested terrain). He may, furthermore, be the one boy in the book who leaves the academy, a site that the self-made man is likely to absent himself from, but it's only to be sent to a different school. In part, Mathews would seem to be disposing of the concept of the self-made man by stressing his negative qualities, his selfishness more than his enterprise.

As for Jack, his embodiment of the Christian gentleman—with its norms of self-control, service, courtesy, and sincerity—is similarly uneasy. He may be progressively schooled in the self-control that is at the heart of the ideal. He may enact the ideal of service through his attempts to help Paul.

And he has always been sincere, if anything too frank. But his rough-and-tumble boyishness resists assimilation to gentlemanliness, and rarely is the latter term applied to him. The uneasiness with which manliness and Christianity and gentility conjoin in Jack testifies to the uneasiness of their juncture in society at large.

In short, if Mathews is doing the cultural work of playing out the contradictions associated with masculinity, it's not by creating characters who reify key abstractions, such as Hale's white Rachel and black Tirah, but by creating permeable characters through whom abstractions circulate. Or rather, the important cultural work that Mathews undertakes is not to consolidate norms and resolve the contradictions in prevailing notions of masculinity. It's rather to define what masculinity is not: she defines masculinity against femininity and subordinates the latter. She portrays what Eve Kosofsky Sedgwick has described, in *Between Men,* as the homosocial bonding that consolidates male power over women, a bonding acted out through both homophobia and homophilia—in this case, hatred of Philip, both hatred and love of Paul. A bonding so effective that females are no longer necessary to enact the feminine.

For both Jack and Philip desire Paul, use Paul to play out their conflicted desires for each other, desires homophobically translated into hatred. Even before Paul arrives, Jack has felt "almost bound to oppose anything that Philip suggested" (37). And Philip is more transparently described as using Paul, taking advantage of the "one point on which Jack could easily be wounded," to enforce his hatred of Jack (96). The relationships among these three characters are brought into high relief by two crises in the book, the first adumbrating Jack's physical courage, the second his moral courage, both defining him against Philip, and in both Paul functions as counter.

The first crisis culminates in Jack's daring rescue of Paul from the Tiverton Bridge—the bridge an appropriate trope for the crossovers that erode polarities in this book. Or perhaps rescue from a bridge, particularly Jack's rescue of Paul, is a metaphor for Jack's eventual rescue of Paul from femininity—and hence a reinforcement of polarity. In any case, a group of young people makes a trek to a little-used railroad bridge when a special excursion train appears. Philip quickly runs off and saves himself, other boys help various girls down, and only Jack and Paul remain. Paul, more of a girl than the girls are, is "paralysed with terror. Imploring, entreating, commanding, were all in vain. Paul would not, could not, move" (77). So with one arm Jack seizes "the shaking, helpless figure which clung to him like a drowning man" (78), and with the other he grasps an outer beam and hangs from it till the train passes. Philip is thus shown up for the coward he is, the narrator valiantly trying to make him worse than Paul by having Tom say, "I had rather have stood shivering with terror on the track, like Stuyvesant, than to have saved myself with you, leaving weak girls to take care of themselves" (79). Paul will then acknowledge that Jack saved him, but only petulantly: "I cannot conceive how any one could think of going to such a place when there was a possibility of a train passing over the road. Even Philip Ward says that he would not have thought of going except to be of assistance to me" (83). Which of course Philip wasn't. Given that Philip has earlier been responsible for ducking and nearly drowning Paul in a boating mishap, then on the bridge, where Paul clings "like a drowning man," Jack metaphorically—though only temporarily—saves Paul from Philip.

The later, more extended crisis entails competition for a school prize: not the prize for "general excellence" but rather that for drawing, pitting Jack against Philip, the competition a translation of their rivalry for Paul's allegiance, the drawings displaced adumbrations of Paul, also adumbrations of the crisis of representation that engenders the book. In these contests Paul becomes the desired, not the sissy outcast: he is simultaneously drawn into the masculine realm and feminized.

Now drawing is a curiously gendered site for playing out Jack and Philip's rivalry. For drawing, when not linked to utility, was often a pastime for leisured ladies. And what do we make of the implication that Philip is somehow a sneak to propose that each contestant draw a dog, given that animals are Jack's weakness and Philip's strength? Jack intends nonetheless "to beat him on his own ground" (112). Mathews attempts to translate the rivalry into more typical boys' school terms—sneaking, fighting—even though the former term, at least, fits the situation only imperfectly, and the gendering of drawing lingers.

As for the content of the drawings, Philip's predilection for animals is of course a projection of his nature: he is someone who can lose self-control and "with a roar like an enraged animal" strike another boy (133). Jack could then perhaps be seen as taming bestial proclivities when he undertakes to master the drawing of an animal—much as Mathews might be seen as trying to tame the bestial proclivities of the literary bad boy, so often associated with nature,[27] in her domesticated portrait. Yet what Philip and Jack draw is on some level Paul. Early on, Jack's treatment of Paul is explicitly compared to the way he would treat a dog or horse, with care or caresses as well as stern punishment; later Paul thinks, with respect to his rescue from the bridge by Jack, "He would have done as much for a dog, I daresay" (149). Paul is not just a dog but variously a calf, an ape, "a perfect jackass," "a most curious, incomprehensible animal," a donkey, a deer—one time for Philip, the rest for Jack, and for both mostly in moments of passion. As other, Paul is animal as well as female, especially to Jack, and especially when Jack is himself being beastly. Paul is both projected upon and desired, and Jack and Philip act out their passionate feelings by physically mauling (or seeming to) each other's displaced representations of Paul, each other's drawings.

The ambiguous gendering of the competition is underscored when Philip brings his picture to the Granger household. Dr. Granger comments, "It will take some manliness and some sweet-heartedness on both sides to carry it off gracefully, whichever wins . . ." (128). Winning and losing require both manliness and sweet-heartedness, yet the need to name both implies that manliness does not necessarily include sweet-heartedness, that notions of manliness and Christian self-sacrifice do not easily conjoin.

The gathering breaks up because of a downpour (yet another dunking), which necessitates that some ladies be accompanied home: as at the Tiverton Bridge, females help to precipitate the crisis, serving as a catalyst, not unlike Paul. Then Philip's picture is discovered torn. He accuses Jack, calls him a thief, and impulsively throws Jack's picture into the fire, though only the back is then scorched. But of course Jack could never have harmed Philip's picture; no one manly could have done so. Rather, a child did, by accident, little Frank Brewster—thus is unmanliness displaced onto a child, reinscribing the man–child duality that most of the book has rewritten as man–woman. Or rather, given that before he confesses to his guilt Frank is subject to a "feverishness . . . more like that induced by mental distress in a grown person than like the symptoms of a sick child" (179), the man-child duality is questioned, this man–child more adult than childish when he does a childish action.

The crisis is then effectively reiterated the next day, Philip enacting what he had accused Jack of. Philip gets Paul to take Jack's picture, presumably just to hide it for a day or two. Yet overcome by "the same impulse of revenge which had overcome him on the previous evening" (154)—in short, lacking the self-control that Mathews has been at pains to define as manly— Philip tears up Jack's picture, then burns the pieces. When Paul eventually announces that he will confess his own role in the disappearance of Jack's picture, Philip is dismissive of Jack, and suddenly Paul's "slim, white hand had struck Philip a stinging blow across the face" (177). Furthermore, we learn, when Paul ignores Philip's threat of a drubbing, "All the little manhood that was in him rose in resistance to the tyrannical command of one whose falseness and baseness at last stood out before him, revealed by the light of the strong contrast thrown upon them. The patient lessons, the strong helpfulness, and the manly example of the past six months had not been for naught" (177). Manliness thus follows on—is predicated on—violence. Manliness is also associated with patience—or is it so little associated that the narrator has to insist that "patient lessons" are a "manly example"? Is such manliness nonetheless belittled by the phrase "little manhood"? And is it "strong contrast" that is revelatory, the contrast between Philip and Jack—or is it slippage? For Paul has now been converted to Jack's party.

And speaking of slippage, remember that prize for general excellence? It turns out that it is awarded by vote of the students for "generosity and courtesy" (196)—that is, genteel selflessness and polite formality. Paul snatches an opportunity to explain Jack's goodness to the assembled school, and Jack wins the prize to great acclaim. So the real contest between Jack and Philip is not for the drawing prize (too feminine after all?) but for the prize for gentility (or is this one feminine?). Jack wins, and Philip loses so badly that he is effectively expelled, withdrawn from the school by his father—as family once again impinges on school. Jack wins then by not competing, by withdrawing from the drawing competition and by not overtly competing for the other prize: he who is aggressively competitive, like a self-made man, loses; he who more demurely behaves like a Christian gentleman wins. Jack even gets the prize drawing materials that were to have been awarded the winner of the drawing competition, though the real prize is, of course, Paul.

And in a way that is sexualized. Perhaps we can put aside Paul's eventual declaration that he does not just think well of Jack, does not just care for him, but "I do more—I love you" (186), likewise Jack's accusation that "I saw that [Philip] was making love to you all day" at school (55). Nineteenth-century women and also some nineteenth-century men tended to express their liking for one another with an excess that we now read as sexual.[28] It is harder, though, to put aside the image that follows Mathews' description of Paul's "little manhood" rising in resistance to Philip, whose actions suddenly appear base compared to Jack's "manly example" (not to mention that rising "little manhood" itself): "The seed had not fallen on barren ground; the soil had not been rich, but it had some elements of fruitfulness in it; and the seeds had taken root, and now they were beginning to bear" (177). Earlier school stories from *The Governess* (1749) to *Little Men* (1871), and evangelical stories more generally, may often have used agricultural metaphors, yet they did not provide contexts that made the seed into semen. It's hard, too, to dismiss the sexualizing implicit throughout in the language of eyes, how Jack's sympathy is always ignited by a look from Paul—whether Paul "looked up wistfully into his cousin's handsome, sunbrowned face" and then "the appealing look" in Paul's eyes, "quite too soft and sweet for a boy's face," "went straight to Jack's big, honest heart"; or else Paul turns on Jack "his beautiful brown eyes all alight with pleasure" (14, 116).[29] And it's hard to dismiss Jack's description of Philip as a "thorn in the flesh," and as having "the stiffest prickers of any thorn I ever saw" (105). So when Jack eventually claims, "If, by losing my poor little [drawing of] Snap, and my hope of the prize, I have won you, Paul, I'm almost willing to let them go" (191), we might piously read him as having won Paul over to the righteous side, in his struggle with Philip. That's undoubtedly how nineteenth-century Sunday-school readers would have read the passage. But—just as their concluding handclasp, ministered by Tom, can signal not just a brotherly benediction but a wedding—that is not the only way in which Jack has won Paul. Paul is not just Jack's Huck but also his Becky Thatcher.

In short, with what now seems surprising frankness, Mathews charts the parameters of a homoerotic triangle. Children's literature generally steers clear of sex; to take just one example, the twentieth-century classic *Charlotte's Web* (1952), for all its refreshing frankness on the matter of death, is notably reticent about the provenance of Charlotte's eggs. Yet maybe to the extent that we are dealing with children, after all, homoeroticism can emerge in *Jack Granger's Cousin*; to the extent that homosexual activity can be seen as simply a stage in adolescence, it can be permitted. Freud, for instance, would shortly talk of "the regularity of enthusiastic friendships formed by boys and girls with their own sex," in the context of discussing how "the first feelings after puberty often enough go astray, though not with any permanent injury" ("Three Contributions" 619).[30] Or, drawing on nineteenth-century ideas that associated childhood with bisexuality, he would say that homosexuality scarcely deserves to be called a perversion: "It can be traced back to the constitutional bisexuality of all human beings . . ." (quoted in Weeks, *Sexuality* 151).[31] Or, nineteenth-century educated Englishmen, as Sedgwick among others has noted, accepted some homosexual activity in their public schools but were expected to outgrow it—leading to associations of the homoerotic with childishness (*Between Men* 176–177). Perhaps Mathews too can accept the homoeroticism she depicts as just an adolescent fancy, can allow it precisely because she is writing children's literature. Perhaps if children are innocent, one can say almost anything to them—especially at a time when the idea of homosexuality was only beginning to emerge.[32] Perhaps our constructions of childhood can allow space for creating a gay neverland, somewhere over the rainbow.

Mathews anticipates the shift that Sedgwick documents about the turn of the century, "by which the exemplary instance of the sentimental ceases to be a woman per se, but instead becomes the body of a man who . . . physically dramatizes, *embodies* for an audience that both desires and cathartically identifies with him, a struggle of masculine identity with emotions or physical stigmata stereotyped as feminine" (*Epistemology* 146, Sedgwick's italics). Yet—perhaps because she was writing for children, perhaps because she didn't yet have to label the relationship she was describing as homosexual, perhaps because she could still rationalize it as genteel Christian brotherhood[33]—Mathews manages to portray the homoerotic without the usual nineteenth-century panic, without the homophobic anxiety to deny homosexuality, or rather with such panic channeled, expelled via Philip.

In winning Paul, Jack also plays out another cultural myth. If Paul's aristocratic gentility (with his elegant formality, his gloves and cane) is defined against Jack's egalitarianism, Europe against America, then Paul's defeat is another victory for the American Revolution. In response to Paul's stating, right off, that his "aunts did not wish me to associate with the mixed crowd at school," Jack says of his own school, "There is scarcely a chap in the school that I don't like, and don't call my friend, rich or poor, big bug or little bug" (11). Jack goes on, more clearly endowing his egalitarian values with masculinity: "If a fellow is true and brave, and stands to his colours, and to his friends as a chap ought to do, it don't make any difference to me if he don't walk in my tracks, or buy his coats of my tailor. That's none of my business. I'm no better than he is, because my father happens to carry an old name, and to own a few acres of ground" (12). That is, masculinity, standing to colors, takes precedence over birth, or perhaps compensates for lack of birth. Though it doesn't hurt if one also, like Jack, "happens to carry an old name."

Jack then starts to admonish Paul: "If you think that those aristocratic notions will go down here"—but "recollecting himself, he paused. 'I beg your pardon,' he said, with a manly frankness of tone and manner which Paul thought quite atoned for the sharpness of his first words. 'I had no right to speak to you in that way. But I tell you what it is, I spoke the truth, if I did speak it rudely' (12). Thus manliness should not be too rude—or perhaps it should be, so that it can be apologized for—or perhaps an apology is not really manly, given that the narrator has to stress its manliness. Yet even this early in the book, such "manly frankness" appeals to Paul. Paul, in short, learns to devalue the effete attitudes of an aristocratic Stuyvesant in favor of those of a more democratic Granger.[34]

The mapping of class onto gender further reinforces the cultural myth. As Sedgwick has noted of the Victorian novel, women may be equated with aristocratic power, both granted a metaphysical and ungrounded status, and "the *displacement* of power relations onto a historical fiction of class relations, and their temporal *condensation* in an erotic narrative, was a way of rationalizing gender inequality, and other inequalities, in the face of an egalitarian public rhetoric" (*Between Men* 158, Sedgwick's italics). Jack's winning of Paul represents the winning out of the bourgeoisie over the aristocratic/feminine, the winning over of the aristocratic/feminine, with the submission of the latter masked by the rhetoric of egalitarianism.

All this winning and wooing are, however, at the expense of the biological females of the story. As Garber has said in another context, "A man may be (or rather, make) a more successful 'woman' than a woman can" (234). If Mathews does not particularly validate Paul's femininity, if she is at best conflicted about it, she validates women and girls even less.[35] In embodying her feminine principle not in a female but in a male, she may make the ideal of Christian gentility more acceptable to males. She may also avoid essentializing women. But at what cost. And even if she avoids essentializing gender biologically, she does so ideologically, by dichotomizing masculine and feminine, however elusive strict dichotomy remains. By making gender so central to her tale she insists on male–female polarity even as she erases the female.

Jack's mother may be pretty and graceful, and her house may be tasteful and elegant, but she and her furnishings remain a backdrop, one that somehow enables Jack to become red-blooded, whether through opposition and complementarity (the feminine supporting, enabling the masculine, enabling anything "feminine" to be relegated to a realm defined as other) or through his father's counteracting influence. Certainly the household where Paul stayed previously, with his aunts, does not seem to have had a beneficent influence. The issue of gender is more directly addressed when Paul admits that he has wished he were a girl, and Aunt Nellie, Jack's mother, responds that not only should he avoid mentioning such a thing in front of the boys, but

> I do not like to hear you say so, myself. I am very far from depreciating a woman's power, when it is rightly used, and would not exchange my place, as wife and mother, for that of the greatest man in the land; and yet I feel sorry to hear you say that you would like to give up the more extended power for good, and the grander oppor-

tunities, which must always belong to a man. It seems like selling your birthright. (32)

But we may well wonder whose birthright has been sold. A far cry this from Mrs. Jo's pronouncements in *Little Men.*

Mathews also uses a female as a scapegoat, when Jack is being manly and patient in the face of Paul's unjust imputations. After Tom's sister Clara has told Paul off for thinking Jack guilty of harming Philip's drawing, the doctor is more inclined to chide her than Paul or indeed anyone else. Clara is the most outspoken of the few girls mentioned in the novel, likewise the most independent; she is something of an artist, and a girl who can be counted on to rescue herself from the Tiverton Bridge. She would thus seem, in her rare appearances, to be allowed some of the gender slippage allowed to Paul. Yet by making Clara a scapegoat, the young person most chided for being at fault—by reprimanding a girl who would be boyish—Mathews enforces gender boundaries, excluding Clara from the masculine. And given that Clara generally feels animosity toward Paul, given that she seems jealous of Jack's interest in Paul, Mathews likewise excludes Clara from the homoerotic economy of the novel.

Certainly the one documented contemporary girl reader of the novel, reviewing the book for *The Literary World,* resorts, like Clara, to some interesting shifts in reading. In the midst of her one-paragraph review she states the story's suitability "for older boys and girls"—unlike Susan Coolidge, who will unabashedly refer to it as "reading for boys" (143)—though she concludes by focusing only on what the book teaches boys: it "teaches boys not to fight" ("Books" 94).[36] The slight eccentricity of her conclusion—I'd have been tempted to say something more like "not to be a sissy," but that probably reflects my greater familiarity with the then-emerging bad-boy genre— suggests some of the difficulty in pigeonholing *Jack Granger's Cousin,* which perches only uneasily in the pietistic tradition in which she tries to read it. Also striking to me is the eccentricity of her choice of favorite character, or "rather the nicest boy in the book": not one of the three main characters, but Tom Brewster. On the one hand she appropriately acknowledges his role as the voice of sanity among the boys, but her choice of a peripheral, enabling character is related, I think, to the peripheral, enabling character of the roles here allotted to girls. Tom's sister Clara is even more marginal than Becky Thatcher in *The Adventures of Tom Sawyer* (1876)—leading perhaps to less need for her forcible expulsion or for the hero's concomitant accession to the middle-class masculine virtues of "stability, autonomy, and self-possession" (Hendler 48). Jack and Paul remain rather more fluid with respect to gender, and that which must be forcibly expelled is not the female but the exemplar of male acquisitiveness.

Mathews' portrayal of women and girls is thus quite different from Alcott's. For Alcott domesticated the school, extending Mrs. Jo's familial influence. Similarly, Southcott Home is a family enterprise in Baldwin's *The New Boy at Southcott,* even if Mrs. Morrell is much less of a presence than Mrs. Jo. In *Jack Granger's Cousin,* however, the family and the feminine do not metaphorically infiltrate school. Nor does schooling infiltrate the family, as in Hall's *Daddy Dacre's School,* where two boys, home from school, receive instruction from a former servant: Hall displaces schooling to a quasi-familial context, taught by someone called Daddy. Unlike Baldwin, who makes the school a home, and unlike Hall, who makes the home a school, Mathews enforces the separation of school and home. Yet school and home are dialectically engaged with each other, in this book whose title underscores the importance of family relations yet whose key conflict centers on a school prize (which is in turn a displacement of family rivalry and attachment). If the emergence of the genre of the school story symbolically enacts the separating of "public" from "private," of "public" schooling from "private" family, then Mathews shows the implicature of each realm in the other. And the medium for this interaction is the family connection of Jack and Paul: two classmates and cousins who need to become like brothers,[37] if not spouses.

The emphasis on family is reinforced by Mathews' allusions to predecessor texts. She does not allude to *Tom Brown*; she does not make an Alcottian put-down of Hughes's book or his ideals of manliness. But Mathews does allude frequently to predecessor texts by women, works that often privilege family. Paul has spent the previous decade with his elderly genteel aunts, in a community known as Crawford—an allusion, it would seem, to Elizabeth Gaskell's *Cranford* (1853), with its genteel community of women. This British realm against which Mathews defines her independent Americans is feminine, underscoring Paul's aristocratic effeminacy—reserving the masculine for things American.[38] On the other hand, when Jack pooh-poohs Paul's reading, it's not reading per se that he belittles (or at least not overtly) but the choice of reading matter: Tupper's *Proverbial Philosophy* instead of more exciting works like Marryat's or Stockton's or *Little Men* or *Eight Cousins.* Thus the gauge of manliness is, in part, works by a woman, works exploring the relationship between domesticity and masculinity. Though is it significant that Alcott isn't named, thereby allowing her feminine presence to be hidden? Or is not naming her an act of homage, an assumption that everyone would be familiar with the books? Furthermore, one of the titles focuses on cousins, and the book addresses the introduction of a child to her cousins, making Mathews' book a metaphoric reworking of *Eight Cousins* (1875), with Paul playing the role of Rose.

Mathews, in sum, keeps her boys at both home and school. And she constantly reverts to the feminine. The trope of femininity helps to define masculinity, mostly opposing it, mostly suggesting what boys should not do or be. Any reconciliation between the two is tenuous at best. As Tom notes, "Girls are awfully queer, Jack. They think that boys are funny; but if they could see their own streaks as plainly as they can see ours, they'd be surprised at themselves, I think" (103–104). The two genders remain at odds, each thinking the other queer (how prescient), though Tom has the grace to recognize not just what boys think of girls but what girls think of boys, and to qualify the statement with a tentative "I think." Yet for all that masculinity appears to be the desired norm in the book, it is constantly checked, infiltrated, by femininity. Mathews would seem to assume some underlying feminine principle, much as Tom's comment on girls seems to assume a readership including girls—like that girl reviewer for *The Literary World*. Writing as a woman, Mathews seems uneasily to assume such underlying femininity even while disavowing it, as she both essentializes and deconstructs it. Her novel richly orchestrates the contradictory interplay of late-nineteenth-century masculine discourses, their homosocial implication in one another, and the emerging ascendance of masculine–feminine polarity.

NOTES

1. The reviewer also states that Mathews and her sister "are always entertaining storytellers" (311).

2. Darling finds little evidence of the metastacizing angel after 1871 (*Rise* 29).

3. See Darling, *Rise* 53. For a good discussion of books that were explicitly published for American Sunday schools, see Gillespie, "Schooling." For a good discussion of books that would fit under a broadly defined Sunday-school rubric—a discussion that acknowledges that "there is little useful distinction to be made between most Sunday stories and those produced for children by secular publishing companies" (23) before the Civil War—see MacLeod, *Moral Tale;* see also Trensky, "Saintly Child."

4. The reviewer in *Harper's* too concludes that "the interest of the story lies rather in its power over the moral feelings than in any remarkable adventures or interesting plot" ("Editor's Literary Record" 311).

5. A switch mediated by the Sunday-school publisher Anson D. F. Randolph, who seems to have been the first publisher of both of her Roberts Brothers books.

6. Much of this essay is incorporated in Darling's *Rise* 13–25. Another sign of the strong association is that one reviewer lists *Jack Granger's Cousin* as being published by Carter ("Editor's Literary Record" 311), though I can find no other evidence that Carter had anything to do with the book; the three other reviews that I have been able to locate ("Books"; Coolidge; Review of *Jack Granger's Cousin*) list the publisher as Roberts Brothers.

7. Both Fiedler *(Love and Death)* and Douglas *(Feminization)* castigate nine-

teenth-century sentimentalism. Not that the Civil War marked a sudden shift; even in 1841 Emerson could make a negative association between "the cultivated classes" and "feminine rage" (1516). See Griffen 189–196, for a discussion of this mid-nineteenth-century shift, a discussion that informs the rest of this paragraph; see also Demos 103–104; Pleck and Pleck, Introduction 22; and Rotundo, *American Manhood*.

8. For in reality, by the end of the century, there was an increasing emphasis on what has been called "domestic masculinity," with men participating more than before in the family, in suburban companionate marriages, playing ball with the kids—creating, in effect, all the more to be compensated for (see Marsh 112ff.; see also Rotundo, *American Manhood* 262–274).

9. See, e.g., Cawelti 4ff. Rosenberg sees the latter ideal as older (224); Rotundo sees them as having arisen more or less simultaneously—both being visible at the beginning of the nineteenth century—and as dialectically related ("Learning" 42). G. Wood, however, sees the radical notion of the self-made man as rejecting eighteenth-century republican gentility (which stressed service even if it did not yet dignify work), especially the latter's stress on the values of "knowledge," "character," and "extensive connections" (e.g., 341). Bushman finds the origins of genteel culture in the Renaissance court and sees it competing—at times amalgamating—with republican, capitalist, and Christian cultures (e.g., xvi–xvii, 403, 446). Moon, on the other hand, stresses the "constantly shifting meanings" of *gentle* and *gentleman* and their function as terms of exclusion, demarcating status, over any substantive meanings (92–93).

10. See R. G. Kelly 58ff. His discussion (56–85) informs this and the two succeeding paragraphs.

11. And with themselves—as Halttunen has pointed out, the emphasis on self-restraint was at odds with the emphasis on sincerity (92), genteel decorum with Christian transparency. Bushman would add humility (stronger in more Christian contexts) and taste to the norms of Christian gentility (80–81).

12. As a proponent of the genteel ideal would say, "The habit of acquisitive eagerness, of buying as cheap and selling as dear as possible, eats into the marrow of manliness; and overreaching and crafty trafficking are as incompatible with gentlemanhood as perjury is with piety" (Calvert 110–111).

13. See, e.g., Catano 426, for discussion of how the myth of the self-made man defines the masculine against the feminine, partly with the help of battle imagery. Another strand, invisible in most discussions of nineteenth-century society and in most products of genteel culture—including *Jack Granger's Cousin*—is that associated with the working class. This strand emphasized mutualism more than—or in dialogue with—self-advancement; it stressed the dignity of work and favored physical action and violence; its adumbrations are relatively free of expressions of Christian piety (see Denning 172, 193). Yet another would seem to be what Rotundo calls the Masculine Primitive, an ideal whose norms stress the instinctual, physical strength, and personal force ("Learning" 40–42).

14. See Allibone; Kirk; Obituary; and *Population Schedules 1860,* New York 56: 29.21. Her date of death is unknown. The 1898 Summit, New Jersey, Directory lists her sisters Joanna, Elizabeth, and Sarah as residing in a household in that community, but not Julia.

15. Not that military metaphors were all that unusual in evangelical stories—see Gillespie, "Enginery" 7.

16. To the extent that it became increasingly difficult, toward the end of the century, to portray effective men who were gentlemen—see R. G. Kelly 72, 76, 78; also Bushman 281.

17. My argument parallels that of Hendler with respect to *Tom Sawyer* and other bad-boy books, yet where he focuses on the heterogeneity of the focal boy character, his plural subjectivity (35–44), I attempt to trace the trajectories of competing strands of manliness. It also intersects with that of Richardson, who argues that nineteenth-century alternative stories of the development of masculinity, ones that allow

for femininity as well *(The Little Lame Prince, Little Lord Fauntleroy)*, nonetheless tend to fragment identity—and ultimately reinscribe patriarchal values ("Reluctant Lords").

18. Then again, in a Christian context, it is not necessarily reprehensible to be Pauline. A crux in recent Pauline scholarship is, appropriately, Paul's contradictory messages about gender—see, e.g., Boyarin.

19. Other sites for gender slippage include Jack's special relationship with his father—a family connection, but a masculine one. Also perhaps Jack's greeting his father, you will recall, by kissing him, "big fellow that he was, like any loving child" (4). Kissing is thus childish, yet it's good to be straightforwardly affectionate, manly to be direct—manly to be childish. Jack further ironizes the act when he explains why his father took him aside (actually to admonish him), by saying that they "had more hugging and kissing to do than we cared to practice in public" (8). Jack here derides hugging and kissing, or at least excessive amounts, by mockingly pretending to endorse them. Yet his irony also mocks the stereotype that dissociates boys from kissing. Later Jack is so grateful for the way Tom comfortably introduces the dandified Paul to other boys that "Jack could almost have kissed his ready friend" (35). The "almost" here functions like the mockery of Jack's earlier statement: it enables evasion of both the stereotype of masculine behavior and its inverse.

20. Like Jo March in *Little Women*. Self-control, especially as embodied in selflessness, is central to the nineteenth-century Calvert's ideal of the Christian gentleman (26ff.). See also Godkin's emphasis on discipline and self-denial (202).

21. Mathews' contemporary Godkin notes the conflict between Christian forgiveness and a kind of clubhouse code of gentlemanly honor that would seek revenge for a wrong (198). It's tempting to find significance in the fact that Godkin is discussing a much-publicized case of adultery—to note that the conflict is particularly acute in a sexually charged context. But more on sexually charged contexts later.

22. As if not entirely comfortable with the ideal of the Christian gentleman, the narrator takes pains to emphasize that even at his most Christian generous Jack remains manly. Before he knows that his own drawing has been destroyed, Jack tells an alienated Paul of his generous intent to withdraw from competition for the drawing prize. Jack deprecatingly asks his father,

> "Do you think it was spooney? I didn't want to tell him, father; and I had the biggest kind of a fight with myself before I made up my mind to do it; but I thought it might help Paul—might help me"—
>
> Jack paused, confused and abashed by the thought, that after his hard-fought battle, his father considered that he had gone too far for his own self-respect. But the doctor took up his words, and finished his sentence for him.
>
> "Might help you to show Paul what a noble, pure-hearted fellow he was accusing of dishonour, and turning his back upon for the sake of an unworthy friend. God bless you, my boy. I thank Him with all my heart that you are my son. Your mother ought to be a proud and happy woman." (161–162)

Jack's uncertainty as to whether he may have been "spooney" anticipates and partly disarms a reader's potential resistance to his behavior. But the uncertainty also reinforces such resistance both by naming it and by having so reliable a character as Jack consider it. Still, his struggle and sacrifice are dignified by the manly metaphor of battle, and his father reinforces the Christian view—though, curiously (given her general invisibility), he refers to Jack's mother as arbiter, the arbiter of the Christian thus a woman.

23. As Calvert notes, "There is no sinister or even wayward shifting in the true gentleman. You know where to have him" (148).

24. For discussion of the role and image of the hysteric, see Smith-Rosenberg 197–216.

25. See Michie 98ff.; Bushman 295.

26. Pleck and Pleck suggest that "anti-intellec[tu]alism had become associated with masculinity in the 1870s" (Introduction 21).

27. See Trensky, "Bad Boy" 511–515. Though not perhaps, to use British schoolboy slang, all their beastliness.

28. See Smith-Rosenberg 53–76; Yacovone; Duberman, "'Writhing Bedfellows.'"

29. R. Martin suggests the importance of eye contact—"a kind of cruising"—in nineteenth-century literature that broaches homosexuality (181).

30. See also Ellis 75–83.

31. For discussion of the currency of the idea in nineteenth-century Europe, see Weeks, *Coming Out* 66.

32. As Nelson says of the savage reviews Oscar Wilde's second volume of fairy tales received after he claimed that they were not addressed to children, "What had leaped into the foreground on the stories' redefinition as adult reading was their homoeroticism. . . . Certainly children's fantasy had mixed eroticism and Angelic ethics before Wilde came along, but adult fantasy couldn't afford this luxury" (*Boys* 165). Martin suggests that by the 1880s homosexuality had emerged sufficiently to have a public profile (180–181). Or rather, "from the 1840s to the 1880s a range of possibilities existed that could run from boyhood 'chums' to an idealized comradeship of 'knights-errant' to an anguished and guilt-ridden projection of the self onto figures of Gothic evil. The very range of these possibilities may suggest the extent to which the categories that we now take for granted, such as an absolute split between homo- and heterosexual based on genital behavior, were nascent and fluid" (182). For other discussions of the emergence of gay identity, see Weeks, *Coming Out*; and D'Emilio.

33. See Moon (88) for a brief discussion of the homoerotic language with which evangelical fervor was often expressed.

34. Paul learns, for instance, to seek gentility not in birth but in breeding. But of course "breeding" refers ambiguously to either pedigree or training, though Mathews does not overtly play with the disjunction. Dr. Granger tells Paul that Tom Brewster is "a thoroughly well-bred young fellow," even though his "pedigree is but short" (29). The doctor goes on, "No one values gentle blood, and high standing won by real worth, more than I; but a gentleman is never so little a gentleman as when he condescends to plume himself upon the accident of his birth" (30). This statement captures some of the slippage encoded in "breeding." "Blood" of course refers to pedigree, though the winning of "real worth" to which it is conjoined by "and" may have more to do with training—with, that is, how well bred Tom is. The second independent clause of the statement, meant (via "but") to counter the first (if indeed so contradictory a clause as the first can be countered), would seem to endorse training over birth. Yet by assuming that a gentleman born is indeed a gentleman (even if only, at times, little a gentleman), and by having such a gentleman condescend—never mind the murkiness of the "never so little" construction—the doctor belies the overt message. Dr. Granger would seem to be urging less attention to birth even as his syntax reveals that he sneakingly admires it—much as Mathews' choice to give Paul an impressive "old name" (29) allows her to ridicule his effeteness at the same time that she counts upon his snob appeal.

35. She similarly marginalizes females in another work—not a school story—published earlier in the decade, *Our Four Boys* (1872). It's not just by chance, for instance, that the horse that becomes a counter in the conflict between adult male and boy, dying in the struggle, is female. At the same time Mathews provides a largely positive portrayal—only faintly ludicrous—of a "strong, masculine woman" (145) who runs a farm while also caring for an invalid husband and an idiot son, even if this figure remains peripheral to the main action of the story.

36. A more polished acknowledgment of the multiple readership appeared in *Harper's*: "It is intended especially for boys, but it is equally good reading for girls,

and the mothers will find it fascinating if they once begin it" ("Editor's Literary Record" 311).

37. As Tom states at the end, "You are real brothers now; let's all forget that you were ever anything else" (208).

38. Or on another level, Mathews plays the literary Cranford off against the mythic Camelot, Paul's Crawford against Jack's town of Camlot Falls. Paul is associated with a feminine realm of little physical activity, Jack with a more hearty fighting crowd that at least had the egalitarianism afforded by a round table.

PART III
IN THE TWENTIETH CENTURY

Policing the Borders, Satirizing the State

H. G. Wells and Other Female Impersonators

The school story changed in the twentieth century. The canonical story split into two main streams, one for adults and one for children perhaps, or at least one for elites and one for nonelites. Some date the change to the turn of the century and Kipling's *Stalky & Co.* (1899), others to the First World War and perhaps Alec Waugh's *Loom of Youth* (1917).[1] Soon after the turn of the century, in any case, the more elite stories started becoming more critical of school, more cynical, sardonic, subversive—also, in a sense, returning to the didactic as they criticized schooling. At the same time, pulp magazines started producing school stories, the best known being those by Frank Richards (Charles Hamilton), the creator of the fat Billy Bunter, a British cult figure.

School stories outside what had been the mainstream, those other than the British boys' school story, were changing too. British girls' stories were becoming more popular and jocular, acquiring a tone close to that of nineteenth-century canonical boys' stories—with the advent of Angela Brazil and other writers, culminating in the least-common-denominator popularity of Enid Blyton's Naughtiest Girl, St. Clare's, and Malory Towers series. U.S. stories were splitting into different strands as well: boys' prep-school stories, similar in tone to the earlier canonical British stories; boys' sports stories, addressed to a less elite audience;[2] and girls' college stories, such as Jean Webster's *Daddy Long-Legs* (1912).

And in the context of these changes British men returned to crossgendering. Their return in the twentieth century did not happen all of a sudden. It's hard to point to one author as the first. Is it Desmond Coke, who in 1913 published a boys' school story but under the pseudonym of Belinda Blinders? Is it H. G. Wells, who includes some description of Joan's education as well as Peter's, in his 1918 fictionalized treatise *Joan and Peter*? Is it Charles Hamilton, who, as Hilda Richards, started writing of Bessie Bunter at school in 1919 but didn't publish a book-length version of her adventures until 1949?[3] Or do we wait till 1937 when Gerald Lord Berners, under the name Adela Quebec, privately published *The Girls of Radcliff Hall*? In any case, a common theme in these works echoes a theme in some of the brief treatments of schooling, especially portraits of private schools, that appeared in nineteenth-century mainstream fiction. Fiction ranging from Thackeray's brief satiric portrayal of Miss Pinkerton's academy for young ladies in *Vanity Fair* (1847–1848), to Dickens' galleries of schools in such works as *Nicholas Nickleby* (1838–1839) and *David Copperfield* (1849–1850), to Eliot's account of Tom's schooling—and Maggie's education, "shreds and patches of feeble literature and false history" (306)—in *The Mill on the Floss* (1860). This theme is a concern for social criticism, a criticism generally heightened in the twentieth-century works by way of parody or treatise.

When Desmond Coke published *The Chaps of Harton: A Tale of Frolic, Sport and Mystery at Public School* (1913) under the pseudonym Belinda Blinders, he wrote as a man crossdressing to write about a boys' school. He achieved a double cross that rereverses back to a man writing a boys' school story. But he does so as a female impersonator and for the sake of parody. Parody not so much by a woman as by a parody of one: Blinders—a tattling tomboy if there ever was one—cannot seem to prevent occasional outbursts that reveal what Coke hopes we will see as her rather ridiculous feminism. Still, he also parodies the male school story, especially popular magazine versions—such as Bracebridge Hemyng's rollicking tales of Jack Harkaway, which begin at school—and also the endeavors of crossgendering women like Forsyth Grant and especially Kenyon. It's as if Coke is defending his turf from interlopers, enforcing the authority and authorship of his own gender and class, policing the borders.

Most obviously, he is parodying the woman author. Coke misses out on what seems genuinely to characterize a woman author of school stories, the provision of a family context. Instead he constructs a straw woman— the construction of which he hints at on the title page, where, unable to omit his own name entirely, he lists himself as editor. Belinda Blinders is a militant suffragist, someone unable to stifle non sequiturs that presumably undermine her credibility. Early on, the narrator describes a gauntlet that our hero Ralph Sandford is forced to run (what Blinders has the boys term "running to Coventry," one of her many misconstruals of schoolboy language and norms), other boys having been angered by his talebearing. The narrator laments that such miscarriages of justice "are *bound* to happen until Woman gets her vote" (88, author's italics).

Later, as the boys try Ralph in an improvised court martial, the boy who serves as prosecutor reasons syllogistically, if from unverified premises, like Carroll's King of Hearts at the trial of the Knave: "You have all seen what happened, and you know what's got to . . . Sandford here has stolen marked exercises, and that is against the Public School Tradition. Now he denies it. Therefore I say he is a low cad" (105). The narrator comments,

> There was no cogency about his argument.
> Those Women, however, who have done any work at interrupting meetings will know that logic is of small use to a male. (105)

Later the boy acting for the defense assumes the proof of what he states before he has proved it: "Note the calm disdain of virtue, and then compare it with your unjust clamours! I tell you there stands there a wrongly accused chap. Will you brand him and his parents with disgrace? See how already, innocent, he is held captive and disgraced! No, I cannot believe that Harton will do such a thing" (106–107). The narrator comments, "It was a closely-reasoned, cogent, proof of Ralph's innocence, but it availed nothing" (107). Much later, Ralph restores the headmaster's daughter, whom he has unwittingly helped to abduct, and the "real" culprit is caned with a birch rod; the narrator castigates the brutality—"males are brutal things"—but then states, "This is the medicine for those riotous brutes who do not scruple to ill-treat a woman quietly occupied in interrupting speeches" (154, 155). So much for the tactics and logic of suffragists.[4]

On the other hand, to put the writers of pop-culture stories in their place, Blinders writes at times the kind of gosh-wow, overexplanatory, overexclamatory dialogue characteristic of the pulp stories. When Jack quite literally bumps into an older boy named Dick at the Harton train station, the latter asks the former his name:

> "Jack," replied the other, truly.
> "And I'm Dick!" whistled his new friend in surprise.
> "We're quite certain to get on, then," Jack responded, forwardly. . . .
> "What! Are you going to Harton College?" gasped the other.
> "Yes," answered Jack. "Are you?"
> "I am there already," Dick replied.
> "What, both Hartonians?" exclaimed Jack. "Well, that is a rum go!" (5–6)

Then there is some moralizing, courtesy of the early pious strand of school story: after Jack has persuaded Ralph to change places and pretend to be Jack and hence a fag, the narrator abjures, *"Ah now, Ralph, have a care indeed!* This 'friend' has led you far enough along the down-grade hill of Sin!" (19, author's italics).

The narrator is also guilty of frequent malapropisms. In part they parody schools and school stories and the vagaries of schoolboy invention, but they also presumably satirize the ignorance and presumption of the presumed authoress. For she writes "Prefix" for "Prefect," "Zenophone" for "Xenophon," "Alpha and Bodega" for "Alpha and Omega," "Alma Mata" for "Alma Mater," among many others. Take that in the context of her other gaffes, such as indicating that Italian is taught along with Greek, that the sixth is the lowest form, that schoolboys would be reading Epicurus. Take it further in the context of such felicitous phrasing as "The school clock was striking almost five . . ." and "with sandwiches or champagne flowing on all sides" (94, 130). And we may begin to wonder about the extent to which "Harton" is, on her part, an intentional portmanteau—its rival of course "Erow"—or whether she was in fact attempting to write of Eton and Harrow but simply got their names wrong.

The feminine continues to erupt in allusions to the headmaster's abducted daughter Muriel—much as the girl continues to erupt, to surface, in Ralph's and the narrator's consciousness. Muriel is treated pretty simply as a damsel in distress, but with special attention to her dress: "I regretfully refrain from dwelling upon her distress, the million missed luxuries, the absent caresses, the gradual loss of freshness in her white print costume with just the touch of needed colour—a pink moiré bow—up at the neck and a sash of the same fresh hue—all of the horrors incidental to so terrible indeed a case" (115). On the other hand, Coke also allows something of his own attitude to erupt in the stock melodrama allusion to the family of a villainous usher: "He would seek other work, were it not for his wife, mother, and children: curse them!" (85). Yet perhaps the usher is not so heartless after all—for all that he curses his family, he nevertheless supports them? But we need to reread the allusion in light of his later thoughts: "Defy Jack Dashaway, his secret would be out and he in Holloway: defy the Master, he would have to go back to his wife and mother. . . ." (91, author's ellipses).[5] In short, teaching is desirable because it enables the man, villain though he may be, to avoid family connection, to avoid females—an attitude not unlike Coke's, in his efforts to bar women from his terrain. Yet even while barring women Coke also in effect invites them, as he allows Belinda Blinders, his conception of a feminine consciousness, to write a school story.

And, furthermore, by allowing the presence of the feminine he is able to question standard themes. The questioning may remain largely at a literary level, questioning the tropes of school stories more than the issues they may be tropes for, yet Coke cannot avoid addressing at least some of the latter. With respect to standard school-story tropes, Ralph, like other new boys, learns "the exact angle at which to wear a mortar-cap," is "tossed in a blanket for saying . . . prayers," is "shown the School dandy and School twins," and "thrashe[s] the school bully" (14–15). Ralph is placed in a high enough class that he doesn't have to become a fag, but that seems unfair to him, so he agrees to change places with Jack. Yet, fearful that the exchange may not be quite honest, he sobs out this "shameful story" to his fag-master, leading to the first of many floggings, cruel cuts on the hands, five "divided equally between the hands," Ralph bravely choking back his shrieks— at least until the third cut (20). Thus does he, unlike the virtuous hero of the pious school story, "bend to the iron system, and he went out broken" (22). Finding that meek virtue—not to mention talebearing—does not lead to popularity, Ralph agrees to show he is ready for fun by helping a lady feel what it's like to come down a ladder at night, hence "innocently" participating in Jack and Dick's abduction of the headmaster's daughter.

Once he discovers what dastardy he has been party to, Ralph decides to do something for the College in atonement. But first he needs some money. So he decides to win the prize for the Cycle Championship, racing against the school bully Bossett. And here Coke, like Ralph, is in rare form. Ralph dutifully practices "all that early afternoon, till lunch" (52), but Bossett succeeds in drugging the boy and tying him up. Rescued by a friend, Ralph makes it to the starting line just in time—he doesn't even have to stop to wait for the starting signal—but then, alack, he has a slight accident, so that he has to pedal with his left foot and right hand. So of course Bossett is gaining on him, until Ralph has the foresight to crash into Bossett, and Ralph would seem to be home free. But wait, the referee, Bossett's crony, has tossed some tacks onto the course. Ralph of course manages to pull back on the handlebar (he is now pedaling with just one foot) so that the bicycle leaps over the trap and crosses the finish line. Bossett then tries to disqualify Ralph as having crossed the starting line before the referee dropped his flag, but lo, the flagstick shows the imprint of Ralph's tires, proving that the flag had fallen before Ralph crossed the line.

I won't go into detail about how Ralph inadvertently plagiarizes from Tennyson—his punishment is to "write an apology to the author" (90) and to help the editor of the *Hartonian Herald* with the book reviews. Or how Ralph is accused, and convicted by a student-run court-martial, of stealing the examination papers that Jack has secreted in Ralph's desk—only to be saved by the Captain of the School, on the grounds of the eloquence of Ralph's face. Or how Ralph's friend Nightingale doesn't die, even though no one has died yet this term, and, "casting his mind back across the many tales that he had read of Harton life, remembering the sad rate of mortality, especially among the good, [Ralph] could not deny that by all mathematic laws the time was ripe; and, looking around, no one seemed more like it than this limp, coughing, virtuous Nightingale . . ." (123). Or how Ralph uses his prize money to buy cricket flannels and a ticket to the great match with Erow, where he waits near the rails until one of the Harton men is injured, and the cricket captain having forgotten to bring a twelfth, Ralph comes forward, and despite never having played before, he makes the ten runs necessary to save the day.

In playing with the tropes of school stories, Coke hints at deeper matters. He conflates the sneak and the hero, for instance: a classic sneak, Ralph tattles to Dr. Horton about Jack's use of a crib (cheating) and threat to steal examination papers; yet also (according to the parodic errata page preceding the table of contents) it seems that Ralph becomes the hero of the College by acclamation. And Coke is thereby able to put in bold relief some cruxes evaded in canonical stories—how to make the hero acceptable to both masters and boys, and how troublesome the code against talebearing is, how unwieldy, how difficult to accommodate to the powers that be.

Or, to go back to the cricket match, consider the narrator's feminine dismissals of sport. She tells us that "our hero, like all sensible women who have ever applied intellect to the same question, decided soon enough that the sole reason why fools so obviously win success in sport is that the wise man does not worry with it" (126). And she cannot help exclaiming at the cricket match, during the climactic moments while Ralph is at bat: "(Oh what a foolish hobby for grown boys or even men!)" (140). Her aside is meant to seem foolish. Yet this match, with its intentional incapacitation of a player and its last-minute rescue when our hero emerges from the sidelines, is indeed foolish. Coke's stance remains complex. Take the following comment on the spectators: "There is no kind of man, in brief—for Ralph still waits the bowl—that is not for the nonce again a boy. And some, too, of the women are not far removed from it" (142). Coke is satirizing Blinders's control of language, yet her slippage erodes the gender boundaries that Coke is trying to enforce. In some sense women are in fact not far from boys, both groups marginal to adult male reality.

And one of Coke's complex purposes is also to question the worship of sport by showing its absurdity—much as he does in his more serious boys' school story, *The Bending of a Twig* (1906), written under his own name. The hero of the latter, Lycidas Marsh, is not much of an athlete; he does cox his House's winning boat in the annual Bumping Race, but his coxing isn't quite cricket—he melodramatically delays the crucial bump—and no one is eager to give him an opportunity to repeat the exploit. Later, as Head of his House, Lycidas faces down a popular, rule-breaking athlete, even imposing lines for the boy to write as punishment. Though at the cost of considerable popularity: Lycidas assumes that he has lost all standing with the other boys; only four years later does he learn that much of the house had in fact sympathized with him. Thus, with a qualified victory over the athlete, Coke tries to redress the imbalance of canonical stories. His treatment of the cricket match in *The Chaps of Harton,* too, does not just undermine the authoress but undermines, a little, the worship of sports.

On the other hand, Coke does not do much with the possibilities for latent and not-so-latent homosexuality, as men writing boys' school stories were beginning to do, in works like H. O. Sturgis's *Tim* (1891) and Horace A. Vachell's *The Hill* (1906). He seems to steer clear even of implicit homosexuality—boys like Jack Dashaway in *The Chaps of Harton* "always go in threes" (6), like Stalky and Co., like convent schoolgirls. Yet by transporting some of the tropes of girls' school stories to this one, in particular some of the fondness and hugging—or if you wish, the tropes of early pious school stories, in which a boy may put an arm about another in the name of moral uplift—Coke seems to hint at what was starting to be recognized in boys' schools. For Nightingale (pet name, "Nightie") has been known to pass an arm around Ralph's waist.

And what do we make of the erasure afforded by the errata (or "erratae," as Blinders has it) page? Do the assembled boys allow Ralph to stay on at Harton, once he has become the hero of the cricket match and has confessed to his unintended culpability in the kidnapping of the headmaster's daughter? Their resounding "No" is to be changed to "Yes," according to the errata. This emendation enables Coke to offer contradictory endings, to put part of his text under erasure, much as he has put his own name under erasure as author of the book.

In short, like real woman authors, Blinders questions standard themes, not only those of the pulp magazine stories but also those of the more pious type of story, the type represented for Coke by Thomas Day's *Sandford and Merton* (1783–1789): for Coke's hero's name is Sandford, the boy rescues the headmaster's daughter from Merton Street, and the sequel, describing Ralph's further adventures when he goes on to Camford, is, as the narrator makes sure to mention in a footnote puffing the book, *Sandford of*

Merton. Though also Coke is questioning all previous school stories, including canonical ones, clearing a niche for himself in this much traversed terrain, as in fact he does in *The Bending of a Twig,* which begins with parody. Lycidas prepares for school by reading some school stories chosen by his mother: *Stalky & Co., Eric, Tom Brown, The Hill,* and the joker in the pack, *Jack Joker, or, A Real Good Time: A Rollicking Tale of Real Life, Mystery and Fun at School,* in which the headmaster turns out to be Jack the Ripper. The boy's attempts to apply this feminine-sponsored reading get him, of course, into endless trouble, whether he uses the wrong slang or tries to find the School Bully to beat up so he can become popular. Yet soon the book shifts out of parody to become that which it has been parodying: a traditional school tale. Lycidas plugs away, at schoolwork and sports, and eventually becomes the Head of his House. A measure of how much the book has shifted is Lycidas' attitude toward the earlier school stories when he eventually rereads them: he recognizes "that underneath these stories, whether of sentiment or of melodrama, there lay one and the same emotion which inspired them, the author's great love and enthusiasm for his school"; henceforth, "inspired by authors who had loved their own, he felt the spirit of the Public School thrill through him, he became every term a firmer lover . . . of Shrewsbury" (264).

Overall, Coke seems to want to satirize pulp school stories, pious stories, and women writers, but he also creates a vehicle that begins to criticize the kind of school story Coke himself had written in earnest.

Other men who wrote girls' school stories in the twentieth century, or who briefly addressed girls' schools in their fiction, more directly undertook social criticism. George Orwell devotes a small portion of *A Clergyman's Daughter* (1935) to the experiences of the eponymous Dorothy teaching in a fourth-rate private school. She tries some creative ideas—getting the girls to make a plasticine contour map, marking off a roll of wallpaper as an historical time line, encouraging them generally to think—only to be put down, by the parents, through the owner Mrs. Creevy. So Dorothy returns to the monotonous rote learning, the emphasis on handwriting and sums. Orwell cannot resist telling us the point of all this (in addition to the way it highlights the limited opportunities for an educated woman who needs to support herself) in case we have missed it: he rattles on about the "vast numbers of private schools in England," some ten thousand, at any moment, "of which less than a thousand are subject to Government inspection"; worse, though, is that their sole purpose is to make money—"they are started in exactly the same spirit as one would start a brothel or a bucket shop" (259–260).

H. G. Wells too undertakes social criticism, in *Joan and Peter: The Story of an Education* (1918), a treatise more or less fictionalized—what a critic describes as one of Wells's last novels "to pledge even token allegiance to non-doctrinal art," part of Wells's project, in his last three decades, to educate the world (Costa 133). Wells himself considered it and two other novels—of his dozens of fictional works—"as near to being full-dress novels as anything I have written" (*Experiment* 423). Yet as Woolf noted in a review, Wells here "throws off the trammels of fiction as lightly as he would throw off a coat in running a race," even if no one else "can make an inquiry of this sort so vivid, so pressing, so teeming and sprouting with suggestions and ideas and possibilities as he does" (246). She concludes, "But if he is one of those writers who snap their fingers in the face of the future, the roar of genuine applause which salutes every new work of his more than makes up, we are sure, for the dubious silence, and possibly the unconcealed boredom, of posterity" (247).[6]

Wells writes in *Joan and Peter* about both a boy and a girl. Yet it's clear that his main interest is boys' education (and the one school story he alludes to is *Stalky & Co.*). The central consciousness of the book, the children's guardian Oswald, admits that at first he was more interested in Peter's education; later he says that his interest in Joan's increases, though even then he seems somewhat more interested in Joan romantically than educationally.[7] And he never devotes anywhere near as much space to the girl's education as he does to Peter's; nor can he manage to discuss her education, or even the less explicitly educational aspects of her life, without putting down women. Wells may acknowledge that during the war Joan became an exceptionally good driver, skidding corners marvelously, yet when the Ministry of Munitions remarks that "all our girls drive like this," Wells qualifies the assertion by describing the remark as being made "carelessly, loyally, but untruthfully" (458). Joan's skill makes her unlike other women—and those marvelously skidded corners are all the war excitement she gets, in contrast with Peter's flying and getting shot down.

Wells also allows a sexual double standard: Joan remains a virgin until she and Peter are reunited and eventually marry (fortunately they are neither biological nor adoptive siblings, even though they share a guardian), while Peter has been sowing wild oats. Nor does Wells satisfactorily resolve the problem of Peter's being accustomed to getting his own way with Joan's later willingness to marry him: apparently once she realizes her love for him, getting her own way—beyond getting him—doesn't matter. She may be allowed to dream of some kind of career in building—in making "a cottage or a flat that won't turn a young woman into an old one in ten years' time"

(581)—but it's an end that does not grow out of earlier aptitudes or studies, unlike Peter's career. Overall, Wells uses traditional novelistic plotting—a love story—to put the woman in her place.

As for the traditional trappings of the school story, the few that appear in *Joan and Peter* are subordinated to the satire. When Joan and Peter are small, they attend a crank school called the School of Saint George and the Venerable Bede. The two aunts then overseeing them want the children to be "'free and simple, but fearlessly advanced, unbiassed and yet exquisitely cultivated, inheritors of the treasure of the past purged of all ancient defilement, sensuous, passionate, determined, forerunners of a super-humanity'—for already the phrases at least of Nietzsche were trickling into the restricted but turbid current of British thought" (112). The Miss Murgatroyd who runs the establishment is undiscriminatingly entranced by new educational ideas. The instructor Miss Mills teaches Joan and Peter to "read" according to some inventive new method, so inventive that she never discovers that they already know how. As for Miss Mills's mathematics, "She was not clear about seven sevens and eight eights; she had a confused, irregular tendency to think that they might amount in either case to fifty-six, and also she had a trick of adding seven to nine as fifteen, although she always got from nine to seven correctly as sixteen" (123). She infects Joan with her mathematical convictions, Joan becoming "a mathematical gambler of the wildest description" (123).

There is a fight between schoolchildren at the crank school, but it serves primarily as an occasion for satire of the headmistress. Peter doesn't get to fight the school bully, exactly—instead he fights the school philistine, the boy who belittles others' bicycles and clothes, his own clothes having been "made by Samuelson's, the best boys' tailor in London; there was no disputing it because there was an advertisement in *The Daily Telegraph* that said as much" (136). The two fight about Joan: Winterbaum claims her as his girlfriend, and Peter, though he himself claims another, won't have it. So they fight a duel with sticks, which Miss Murgatroyd stops; she then addresses the school by droning on about how she hoped she'd never again have "to reprove any of her pupils for fighting," since nothing is "quite so wicked as fighting because nothing was so flatly contradictory to our Lord's commandment that we should love one another," unless of course we fight "the good fight," in which case both boys and girls can be warriors, since "Earth was a battlefield, and none of us must be dumb driven cattle or submit to injustice or cruelty," so "let us think . . . of the Red Indian perpetually in training for conflict, lean and vigorous and breathing only through his nose. No one who breathed through his or her open mouth would ever be a fighter" (139). So much for the battle discourse of canonical school stories.

The other school that receives extended satirical treatment is the private preparatory school that Peter briefly attends after one of his then guardians, Lady Charlotte, kidnaps him. Almost immediately he is embroiled in a fight with a bully's lackey. The lackey bobs and weaves, taunting Peter, whereupon Peter lands a blow, and then the other boy makes sure to bob and weave out of range of Peter's fist. Whereupon the bell rings for tea, and the continuation of the fight, though frequently promised, never materializes.

As for the school's philosophy, there is none. Mr. Mainwearing and his teachers simply teach the way they had themselves been taught, thus comprising "the last link of a long chain of tradition that had perhaps in the beginning had some element of intention in it as to what was to be made of the pupil. Schools, like religions, tend perpetually to forget what they are for" (172). The school concentrates on preparing boys for examinations, which are prepared in their turn by experienced teachers, who "had, at best, Babu Latin and less Greek, and so they knew quite well how to set a paper that would enable the intelligent candidate to conceal an entire incapacity for reading, writing, or speaking a classical language" (172); similarly with other subjects. The masters cane more or less arbitrarily. They censor letters. They allow the boys largely to take care of themselves outside the classroom and herd boys of disparate ages indiscriminately together, so of course, for lack of anything else to do, the older ones bully the younger. High Cross School may not be a sterling example of the English private school, the narrator admits, but neither is it the worst.

I'll go into less detail about the various other schools Joan and Peter attend, tempting though it is to repeat Wells's chestnuts, as he delights in weak-minded gentlemen arguing that Latin strengthens the mind; in an imprecise writer urging that Greek teaches one to write precisely; and so on. Joan is first farmed out to the widowed sister of Lady Charlotte's personal maid, someone who needs a little income. Then, under Oswald's aegis, she attends a modern school a convenient ten miles away from a school that Peter is attending; her education continues to be an addendum. Joan's school teaches "the revolt of women from the love of men—in favour of the love of women" (294). Not a love that Wells wants to encourage. The teachers are of course suffragists and enthusiastic hockey players, but Joan is immune from the worst effects: she so far fails to idolize her headmistress and the other instructors that "their enthusiasm for the vote . . . prevented hers" (295).[8]

Meanwhile Peter attends a preparatory school where the proprietor does what he can for boys, given the constraints of parents and examinations and the expectations of the public schools to which his boys will proceed: he has languages taught comparatively; he teaches logic, to improve English expression; he cultivates characters and souls, tries to avoid "crushing out individuality and imagination as most schools do" (278). That such a man would choose teaching is explained by a disability, a "slender and delicate physique," which led him to choose "some field where his weak and undersized body would be at no great disadvantage" (279, 280). Yet given the cult of athleticism, it is hard to imagine that he is not at a disadvantage. The narrator goes on to lament that "in Great Britain, in the schools of the classes that will own and rule the country, ninety-nine per cent of the work was done by unskilled workmen, by low-grade, genteel women and young men. In America the teachers were nearly all women. 'How can we expect to raise a nation nearly as good as we might do under such a handicap?'" (280). How indeed. Unless one physically handicaps male teachers. If in earlier school stories some boys could be sufficiently tamed to be educated only through laming, in Wells's book it's the teacher who is physically cut down to a suitable size.

Then Peter goes on to a public school called Caxton. It is imperfect but does offer some reasonable science instruction, not insisting on an exclusively classical education; thus it interests the boys in academic work "enough to put games into a secondary place. At Caxton one did not see boys playing games as old ladies in hydropaths play patience, desperately and excessively and with a forced enthusiasm, because they had nothing better to do. Even the Caxton school magazine did not give much more than two-thirds of its space to games" (263–264).

Nor is university education much better. Joan and Peter's instructors at Cambridge are uninspiring, "for the most part little-spirited, gossiping men," who know little of the world outside the ivory tower (323)—the women, if anything, worse. Little of use is taught. Real education—"the discussion of God, of the state and of sex, of all the great issues in life" (271)—takes place informally, unsatisfactorily, the students unsystematically picking up ideas from one another, from "chance acquaintances, and more particularly a number of irresponsible journalists and literary men" (271–272).[9]

In the latter half of the book Wells is increasingly given to long-winded philosophical pronouncements. He extends the meaning of education—nations as education, war as education, educating as education. For Oswald finally realizes that in educating Joan and Peter he has been educating himself. He talks of these ideas with Peter more than with Joan: not that he doesn't talk with her, but their talk tends to be more concrete. In the last extended discussion of ideas in the book, Oswald and Peter go on for pages and pages, while Joan, present, remains silent.

For Wells largely ignores the affective. He may mention that sex should be addressed in education, but he never explores how, unlike his exhaustive dissections of the teaching of God and country and various other practical affairs. His attitude is not unlike that of Oswald toward his housekeepers, whom he keeps having to dismiss because of their matrimonial hints, until eventually he happens upon Mrs. Moxton, someone who insists she is not a "lady"—does not aspire to become one—but a housekeeper: "incapable of tenderness, dissimulation, or any personal relationship," she is "a woman with a pride in her work, a woman to be trusted" (287). A woman who can therefore conveniently remain in the background during the rest of the story, keeping the household together, pretending when necessary that Joan is doing it, a woman who has excised the affective, a woman who knows woman's place—thereby solving the servant problem for Oswald and Wells.[10]

Wells does, however, do some curious maneuvers with his more admirable male characters—showing some of the anxiety perhaps that Mogridge and Lamb show when they create authorial proxies, but also echoing women writers' treatment of educable males. For Wells gives both Oswald and Peter physical disabilities, much as he has given the admirable schoolmaster an undersized physique, like Wells's own. Wells was fond of emphasizing his own disabilities and how much they had benefited him— his own personal mythology of the fortunate fall. A broken leg at age seven introduced him to a world of reading; his father's fall a few years later dispersed the household and made little Bertie's lower-middle-class future less certain: "I became one of the intelligentsia and was saved from a limited life behind a draper's counter by two broken legs, my own first, and then my father's" (*Experiment* 237). And then, "I was guided to mental emancipation and real prosperity by a smashed kidney, a ruptured pulmonary blood vessel, an unsuccessful marriage and an uncontrollable love affair" (*Experiment* 237). Men need adversity, need to be a little out of the main ruts of society; Wells's physical nonconformities become a metaphor for his social nonconformity.

As for *Joan and Peter*, Oswald's disability is clearly educational for him: half his face is disfigured, so he learns to cope with his presumed undesirability to women, to submerge vanity, to submerge himself in "good" work (which he eventually learns to define as something other than colonizing—what he once considered educating—Africa). It also enables him to become the ideal guardian for Joan and Peter. He has of course loved their mother (Joan's foster mother), to no avail. So he is unencumbered by the long-term distractions of womankind, or even by the ties of biological paternity. And illness has conveniently unfitted him for continued work in Africa. So, given that he is independently wealthy, he can devote himself wholeheartedly to finding the best possible educations for Joan and Peter. He is perhaps a twentieth-century echo of the disinterested tutor that Rousseau memorializes in *Emile*—not that Wells endorses "extreme Rousseauism," which he associates with running wild until twelve and eating fruit and nuts (22). As a guardian rather than a parent, Oswald is a "disinterested" educator: Wells retains a shadow of the family connection but attenuates it, cutting some of the affective ties, metaphorically reflecting Wells's own distancing from his characters, his tendency to retreat to ideas. Even "family" becomes an abstraction for Wells, when he suggests that "education is a prolongation and elaboration of family association, forced upon us by the continually growing danger of the continually growing destructiveness of our kind" (399)—a metaphor that may slightly domesticate mankind but also succeeds in dispersing the family.

Yet for all that he is disabled and thereby removed from the masculine mainstream, Oswald has acquired his disabilities not as de facto punishment for schoolboy lapses, as happens in school stories by Martineau and others, but in the manly occupation of battle. The disfiguration may make him marginal, positioning him for suitably disinterested consideration of the British educational establishment, much as Wells's shopkeeper origins made him marginal. It may tame Oswald some, make him receptive, excuse him from the performance of other manly duties, but his disability is in part a badge of honor, an enduring trace of the once-active man.

Even more manly, without being debilitating, is Peter's disability, if it can be called one. He is twice wounded in the Great War. In part the wounding may tame him sufficiently to be able to marry Joan: it's while he's recovering from the second injury, the one that lames him, that he becomes engaged to her. But we see so little of him after the injury, and have seen so much of him before—and his disability will not deter him from a proposed career in medical research—that the effect of being shot down, first in a plane, then in a balloon, primarily validates his manliness. He may thereby gain another connection to Oswald, his masculinity too partly erased—or perhaps he is scarred by his masculinity—but he is more emphatically a war hero.

Still, the disability metaphor remains complex, continuing to hint at more general debilitation. Oswald, for example, reflects on the stupidity and class jealousy "that had crippled Britain through three and a half bitter years" (551). A country would not seem to benefit from a little laming. Yet given that the war sets Joan's mind to rights, apparently enabling her to avoid seduction by a predatory male, the crippling of a country during wartime does have its uses—a situation that Wells personalizes in Joan, instead of acknowledging that women's status in the workforce is generally enhanced by war.

The metaphor of disability may thus allow Wells to address some of the complexity of gender, and he also chooses to address women's education, but the topics are not ones he could fully embrace—he could only romanticize them, not give them his full attention.

Not until 1937 can I find a man in the elite tradition who allows himself to write a full-fledged school story about girls—and then only as a parody, only under a pseudonym, and only for private circulation. Like Desmond Coke, Gerald Lord Berners adopts a female pseudonym—Adela Quebec—but Berners then goes on to write a school story about girls.[11]

Berners was not just a writer but also a painter and composer, a composer fond of musical practical jokes, as in his *Three Funeral Marches* for piano: *For a Statesman, For a Canary,* and *For a Rich Aunt,* the last "in raucous dissonances" (Baker) but with "a note of happy expectation" (Girouard 14). He also collaborated with Gertrude Stein on the ballet *A Wedding Bouquet.*[12]

Berners was a notable eccentric. His Palladian villa sported doves dyed rainbow colors and whippets with diamond collars (Girouard 9). Every year he would receive a white horse in his drawing room, the horse having been trained to walk in and "kneel there, where he would be given his tea when we had ours. All this without disturbing in the least the many lovely flowers and objects in the room" (Toklas 159). Berners would give a fireworks party to which "guests were encouraged to bring effigies of their worst enemies to burn—not more than six each" (Girouard 18). He was gifted too with "a superb power of retort, which his adversary would, in self-defence, ascribe to eccentricity": when a pompous acquaintance complained that she and her husband had had to tell a remiss headwaiter who they were, a concerned Berners inquired, "And who were you?" (Sitwell 146–147). Perhaps not least of his eccentricities was that, as Stein notes, his was "the only house in England where the corridors where the halls are warm" (265). Beverley Nichols sums him up thus: "Apart from his generosity, his occasional flashes of genius, and his very genuine passion for the arts, he was a sort of poltergeist, playing amiable tricks on the pompous; and his ghost will always walk with laughter" (163–164).

As for *The Girls of Radcliff Hall* (1937), it parodies the gushing enthusiasms of popular twentieth-century girls' school stories, with their underpinnings of privilege and materialism and latent lesbianism. He plumbs the undercurrents that popular writers like Angela Brazil blithely ignore: in the early 1920s she seems to have named one of her schoolgirls Lesbia for the sake of the name's exoticism, unaware of what else it could imply (see Freeman 118). Quebec, on the other hand, pushes stereotypes and preconceptions to their limits. He includes the unsettling foreigner, in this case an American girl; the attractive tomboy; and of course the admirable headmistress, the rich Miss Carfax, who has been unlucky in her love for a man and who now works only because of her love for the girls (but such love). Not unlike Berners himself, this polymath is a musician, painter, and writer—she "had even written a novel that had not been recommended by the Book Society" (16).

Then there is the spelling out of the name of a rave on her pillow with chocolate drops, the claiming that one needs to go to London to visit the dentist as a cover for an assignation, the bags-I-isn't-it-swell slang, the poisoning of a rival's toothpaste so that she comes down with trench mouth, the hiring of an American mistress since so many girls intended to become film stars and so needed to be "taught to speak American properly" (80). Or take the trope of the thrown book, usually a sign, in canonical school stories like Farrar's *Eric* (1858) or Reed's *Fifth Form at St. Dominic's* (1881–1882), of how children misapply the instruments of learning; or in *Vanity Fair* (1847–1848) it is a sign of Becky Sharp's relationship to traditional authorities and also a critique of Miss Pinkerton's academy. Here it is the headmistress who throws it: she has been spying on two girls who have been fondling each other in the infirmary annex, and by throwing a medical dictionary she succeeds in interrupting their rapture—and in reversing the valence of the trope. For in no other school story would the book be thrown by an adult.[13] Throwing a book reveals a disrespect for learning—for, in this case, academic as opposed to practical knowledge of anatomy. Yet the book also interrupts the acquisition of the latter kind of knowledge. What the multiple reversals achieved by the headmistress do, in effect, is what Quebec does, metaphorically, with respect to the school story.

Particularly prominent in his story is materialism. Lizzie is rich—her Rolls has mauve corduroy, a wireless set, a cocktail bar, and artificial flowers in a silver vase. So of course everyone likes her. Especially because of her lavish presents, including cars—even Miss Carfax starts calculating how to squeeze one out of the girl. It's only fitting that when Lizzie leaves for a convent, a former flame gives her "a lovely miniature scourge made of seed pearls and garnished with tiny spikes of blue enamel" (94). One character, discoursing on how she wouldn't allow strangers to kiss her, eventually admits that she might if offered ten pounds. The mother of another, alarmed by the passionate tone of Lizzie's letters, finally decides that "if Lizzie really were rich it might be unwise to discourage the friendship" (35). Quebec thus highlights the materialism, emphasizes the crassness, implicit in works by Brazil and the like—as a way of debunking the values purveyed by such works. Yet there are complexities to his attitude—he revels in the materialism too, the luxurious details. Not for nothing did he go Lizzie one better in the furbishing of his own Rolls: he had a tiny piano built in (see Brinnin 354).

Also prominent is lesbianism. As Berners has said elsewhere, lamenting that it is no longer possible to write innocently of a friendship between an older and a younger boy at school, "In those innocent, pre-Freudian, pre-Havelock Ellis generations how lucky were the authors of school stories! They could write of such things quite naïvely, without any fear that their readers would automatically place their tongues in their cheeks and indulge in a knowing leer" (*First Childhood* 228). Quebec is hardly naive in *The Girls of Radcliff Hall,* though he describes little physical lovemaking beyond some general fondling—and whatever we want to read into the ecstatic expressions of girls who have fallen asleep in the same bed. He works through implication. Such as the implications of the descriptions of the headmistress: her fondness of girls has only rarely led to slander. And the implications of the title, alluding to the well-known lesbian novelist Radclyffe Hall. Or the titillations of displacement, such as Millie's "almost morbid interest in the sex life of the hens" (97) at the poultry farm to which she retires with Miss Carfax. Or of double entendre: Miss Carfax is said to keep a photograph of Millie in her drawers—no, we're reprimanded, not her underwear; Millie announces that "Lizzie has promised to give me a Baby!" (56)—a Baby Austin, that is.

The effect of portraying rampant lesbianism is in part to debunk the implicit values of popular girls' school stories. But not just to debunk. For by highlighting the raves and making them so widespread, so ordinary, Quebec also to some degree normalizes lesbianism—making it appropriate that the copy that I read had been in Gertrude Stein's library, presented to her by Berners. Certainly, compared to Clemence Dane's *Regiment of Women* (1917), the British school story that is most infamous for unearthing lesbianism, *The Girls of Radcliff Hall* portrays the mutual attractions of women as normal and healthy. Dane limits the potential lesbianism, centers it on a power-hungry mistress, someone whose manipulations lead to a girl's suicide, and thus discredits the attractions of these "perverse impulses" (344). Quebec, on the other hand, does not particularly punish lesbian behavior. Nor does he luxuriate in an opulent and prurient decadence. He is instead matter of fact. Of various predecessors, his tone seems closest to that of Colette, who portrayed the crisscrossing fields of erotic desire, same-sex and otherwise, in *Claudine at School* (1900)—in a work initially published, crossgendered, under her husband's pen name, Willy. None of Quebec's characters may have particularly attractive personalities, yet he makes the passion of one woman for another appear unexceptional if not quite unexceptionable.

Berners is, after all, someone who has written that manliness "did not seem to correspond with the natural instincts of the human being" (*First Childhood* 96). Someone who could talk of what homosexuality he observed at Eton with some equanimity, as "merely the ebullition of puberty" (*Distant Prospect* 49). Yet not without uneasiness—"It is of course advisable that these juvenile aberrations should be discouraged, just as are the other excesses of drinking, smoking and gambling" (49). And he goes on to suggest, with respect to those who are "genuinely homosexual," that "their pathological peculiarities will have to be dealt with by psycho-analysts or, if they are unlucky, by the police, while those who are sexually normal will soon abandon this kind of nonsense for the real thing" (50).

His writing of lesbianism is of course different still. When a Baudelaire or a Lawrence writes of lesbianism, he indulges "in a controlling, sophisticated kind of voyeurism: he can penetrate the intimacy of women's bodies, be where in life he is not, gain access to a holy of holies" (Ward Jouve 85). Though less voyeuristic than other men, and lacking Lawrence's acute fear of lesbians, Berners doesn't escape some distancing and discomfort. If real girls in real boarding schools, in the early twentieth century, seem to have maintained a balance between distance and desire, desire heightened by sacrifice and physical distance,[14] Berners has collapsed the physical distance between his characters, thereby flattening desire—and also distancing us from the characters. For like other men he sexualizes lesbianism: he ignores (some) lesbians' own emphasis on a more encompassing sensuality (not just genital) and on other aspects of intimacy, not to mention, often, their concern for the politics of women's independence and equality (see Faderman 328). He effectively sexualizes the romantic friendships immortalized in popular girls' school stories.

A sign of his discomfort with the lesbianism he portrays in *The Girls of Radcliff Hall*, and perhaps of his discomfort with writing a girls' school story, is that he resorts both to a (female) pseudonym and to private publication. True, a woman like Djuna Barnes could let herself be less tortured in her depiction of lesbianism if she printed a work like *Ladies Almanack* (1928) privately (see Faderman 369). Yet resorting to both private publication and a pseudonym seems excessive. Or rather it multiplies the ironies of the undertaking. Berners' ironic play with the sexualized language with which men had attempted to control the New Woman may resemble that of women like Woolf and Barnes, yet if their attempts to invert language ultimately failed to shake the status quo and wrest economic power from men, as Carroll Smith-Rosenberg has argued (296), so too does Berners'. Even more so. His ironic stance consistently eludes attempts to pin down meaning. It thus marks, in effect, the mid-twentieth-century dissolution and decline of the school story, especially the girls' school story: Angela Brazil may have continued writing school stories until her death a decade later, but schoolgirls in the second half of the century no longer read her works, no longer know quite what to make of—or think they know exactly what to make of— the romantic friendships of girls with names like Lesbia.

After *The Girls of Radcliff Hall,* most of the male crossgendered works that I have been able to locate are from the realms of popular culture, works that are not overtly attempting social criticism or parody.[15] I'll briefly discuss two examples, one that could be considered metaphoric with respect to latter-day crossgendering of the genre, the other more representative.

The metaphoric example is a detective story by Colin Wilson, *The Schoolgirl Murder Case* (1974). It is metaphoric with respect to twentieth-century male crossgendering because of the way it registers displacement and avoidance. It is not about a school. Nor is it even about a schoolgirl—but rather about the erasure and displacement of one. For the "schoolgirl" has been murdered before the book begins. What is more, she turns out not to have been a schoolgirl after all, but a prostitute in costume—a metaphor for crossgendering but also for the displacements (things are not what they seem) endemic in detective fiction. Still, despite the evasions, the schoolgirl trope reverberates throughout the book, providing not just the book's title but its ambience. A minor plot comprises the tracking down of a serial rapist of schoolchildren; these crimes are solved at the same time as the murder, by the immediate subordinate of Saltfleet, the chief superintendent featured in the book. And the victim of a related murder has written pornography featuring schoolgirls, with a protagonist who watches the weekly flogging at a girls' school, then is himself "birched by the headmistress, while two sixth-form girls trample on him with high-heeled shoes" (49). Wilson evades crossgendering, focusing on the male detective, even as he flirts with it. And even as he hints at subtle connections—is it coincidental that a male murder victim is described by one character as like a schoolboy, or that Saltfleet himself feels like one in the presence of the victim's aunt? Yet ultimately Wilson hasn't a clue what to do with schoolgirls. Like his character Saltfleet, whose interactions with his schoolgirl daughter are constantly aborted: she picks up the phone only to be told to get off the line; he cancels a boating expedition with her; nor is she allowed to accompany him on a fact-finding trip even when his wife does.

The representative example of male crossgendering is the work of Charles Hamilton—representative of a number of male authors who wrote girls' school stories for pulp magazines in the first half of the century—and the most prolific (children's) author ever.[16] He is the most popular of the pop-culture writers, as the creator of Billy Bunter: "the overweight anti-hero whose name has become an addition to the language" (Cadogan and Craig 227), in England at least; a figure who "has become a part of English kitsch, beloved while sneered at, like garden gnomes or plaster ducks on the wall" (Quigly 25). In 1919 Hamilton started writing stories about Billy's sister for a pulp magazine, though he soon gave up the field to other writers; thirty years later he published a book about her. What results, in the book, is not so much intentional satire or parody, as was the case with other crossgendering men in the twentieth century, but *Bessie Bunter of Cliff House School* (1949), by the pseudonymous Hilda Richards, does function as unconscious parody of school stories and their values.

Like her brother, the bespectacled Bessie is fat—"the happy possessor of the fattest figure and the fattest head at Cliff House" (16). She is someone who can't stop eating. Someone who is willing to lie if it will get her out of a punishment. Someone whose knowledge of French is so acute that when her French teacher calls out, "Assez!", Bessie thinks she is being called a name derived from a large part of her anatomy.

Yet perhaps it's a sign of Richards' uneasiness in writing about girls that he involves the boys from the neighboring Greyfriars so extensively in the plot, setting seven of his thirty-seven chapters at the boys' school and several others in neutral territory in the town. The main plot focuses on the admirable and popular Marjorie Hazeldene and her less admirable brother, called Hazel. Hazel has run away from school and hides out at Cliff House, in the gardener's shed.[17] Accused of having taken money belonging to the master Quelch, the boy is fearful to return to Greyfriars—until Marjorie, with a little assistance from her admirer Bob Cherry, discovers that the money has simply been misplaced. It turns out that Bessie, angry with Quelch for not letting Billy accompany her to the circus, had gone to the man's empty study and hidden the letter containing the money.

If there is an author's proxy in this story, a male character who intrudes into the precincts of girls, it's Hazel. Yet unlike Mogridge's Old Humphrey or Wells's Oswald, the boy is not an admirable figure. We learn that "often enough, when his weakness or folly had landed him in trouble, he had come to Marjorie for help, and her quiet calmness and steadiness had helped him" (72). And receiving such help from a sister, as Philip did from Gabrielle in Goddard's *Philip Danford* (1890), is not admirable here. It's not desirable to be "the sort of chap to land his troubles on a girl!" (106). It's not desirable to look a bit like a girl, with an "almost effeminately good-looking face" (85). Thus does Richards, through Hazel, castigate his associating here with femininity.

On the other hand, Hazel is wrong to consider himself vastly superior to girls, to be "openly amused at the idea of a girl being able to talk sense, or to do anything worth doing" (143–144). For Marjorie does, after all, solve the mystery of the missing money—even if she does so with Bob's help and gives him most of the credit. Richards is ambivalent about girls and femininity. He portrays girls who are admirable, girls with the public-school values of boys: as one ironically says to Hazel, "Catch me running away! But then, of course, I'm only a girl! Boys know best, no doubt" (171). Yet Richards does use boys as a crutch—as if he cannot quite give girls all the credit. And associations with femininity are undesirable, unmanly.

Then of course there is Bessie. She's hardly an admirable exponent of femininity. And her presence shapes the tropes of the story. Feasting here is not as festive as it is in other girls' stories—thanks to the associations of eating with fat Bessie, her fingers sticky with toffee, herself intruding on others when she thinks they have laid in something good for tea. Instead of providing the thrill of the mildly forbidden, the one outlet available to girls for shaping the self, eating is associated with grossness. Perhaps one reason why Bessie didn't catch on with the public as Billy did—aside from Richards' lack of sureness in writing about girls[18]—is the cultural significance of what it means for a girl to be fat. A fat boy can be deliciously repulsive. A fat girl is simply repulsive.[19] A greedy fat boy can subvert the straight-arrow, stiff-upper-lip values of a proper boys' school, a subversion particularly valued by a readership comprised of boys who were not themselves attending public school, whether because they were still too young or because they were from the wrong social class.[20] A greedy fat girl subverts what?—the values of a girls' school, which already subvert, or at least provide a new perspective on, those of a boys' school? It's suggestive that the magazine featuring Cliff

House stories became financially viable only once Bessie was toned down and a scholarship girl appeared[21]—as if girl have-nots wanted the fantasy not of someone who is bumblingly at odds with the system but of someone who succeeds against the odds.

NOTES

1. For the positing of the former as the turning point, see Eyre 82; for the positing of the latter, see Howarth 71.

2. Saul and Kelly see both as essentially sports stories, one more Brahmin than the other (237).

3. Other men too were writing pop-culture stories for girls in the 1920s and thereafter. One influential editor "was convinced that men were more sympathetic than women with the aspirations of pubescent girls. He saw every woman writer as a potential mother whose protective and occasionally repressive attitude might colour her stories . . ." (quoted in Cadogan and Craig 230).

4. Another such feminist outburst occurs in the middle of a sentence, its syntactical positioning presumably rendering it even more absurd:

> It is now time to relieve the reader's suspense as to Ralph's long-projected scheme and tell him or her—for that is the ungallant order of the sexes arranged by grammarians, a male class, and I hope this story (rough and indeed villainous as it must be from its very setting, if not also from the need to let Ralph's later virtues stand out in relief against an earlier set screen of black) may yet not fail of its appeal to some among my gentle comsexuals—what the brave lad had resolved to do with the ten shillings won in so dramatic a way at the School Gala Cycling Race, narrated in an earlier chapter. (124)

So much for Blinders' mastery of style.

5. Holloway is, of course, a woman's prison, where suffragists were force-fed.

6. She went on to express her reservations more generally about Wells's writing in her celebrated "Mr. Bennett and Mrs. Brown" (see 327).

7. Like Wells himself—a recent biographer notes that Wells "confessed to falling in love with Joan as the story grew . . ." (D. C. Smith 248). In his autobiography Wells states, "Joan I like as a character; A. A. Milne has said nice things about her, but nobody else has had a good word for her—or indeed a bad one" (*Experiment* 420–421).

8. Later Joan "was to find in the vote a symbol of personal freedom—and an excellent excuse for undergraduate misbehaviour" (295)—though we never directly witness this enthusiasm. Later still the outrages of militant suffragists are described as ridiculous, though Oswald realizes that they are expressing "a vast confused insurgence of energy that could as yet find no other acceptable means of expression" (402). In short, Wells keeps some distance from the goals of feminists. A recent biographer stresses that Wells "was a feminist in the sense that he crusaded for equality for women and believed in an androgynous life"—while yet stressing that there are certain insuperable biological differences (D. C. Smith 178). Certainly, Smith notes, women loved Wells and the way he treated them. And they hardly ever got suicidal after he was through with them.

9. Among the "school of irresponsible contemporary teachers" that Joan and Peter ferret out are the Belloc-Chesterton group, the suffragettes, and Wells and other Fabians (272). These are not people that particularly appeal to Oswald, given the social origins of such as Wells, that "counter-jumper," not to mention their looks: Oswald has seen a picture of Wells that shows "a pasty face . . . with a sly, conceited expres-

sion," a "crumpled frock coat," and "large, clammy, white misshapen hands" (273).

10. Not unlike Wells's own wife of many years, Amy Catherine, whom he re-named Jane. In his autobiography Wells stresses the importance, for him and for others who labor "in preparing that new world, that greater human life, which all art, science and literature have foreshadowed," of having helpers who will take care of life's petty cares (*Experiment* 5–6).

11. Another midcentury parodist who echoes—in 1949—some of the themes discussed below is Marshall; witness the following from his brief epistolary story "Look Out King Wenceslas!": "The American girl has made a great hit. I feared that her name (Gloria Milton Zimmermann) might be against her, but when she announced that she came from Chicago they were all over her. She has been most generous: nylons for the Sixth (and yours truly!), refrigerated steaks all round, and fearsome concoctions called Rye and Bourbon which have caused much merriment in the studies" (31).

12. She commented of his music, at the opening performance, that "each time a musician does something with the words it makes it do what they never did do, this time it made them do as if the last word had heard the next word and the next word had heard not the last word but the next word" (277).

13. Though in factual reminiscences masters may throw books at yawning boys (see Mack, *1780 to 1860* 164). Berners himself, in his autobiography, writes of a master whacking a boy with a Greek Primer—though he himself was the one responsible for actually throwing a book, in this case the Bible, narrowly missing the Headmaster (*First Childhood* 142, 247).

14. See Vicinus, "Distance."

15. But see William Trevor's "Nice Day at School," which undermines the conventions of twentieth-century girls' school stories by being set at a comprehensive day school rather than a boarding school, with a heroine living in a council estate; it overtly addresses heterosexual sex, only to have the heroine retreat from it—in a way that implies a critique of class and gender privilege. Trevor's boys' school story, "A School Story," plays with the eighteenth-century girls' trope of storytelling and ends in parricide—implying a critique of the patriarchal underpinnings of school and society.

16. He invented at least 107 fictional schools, wrote some 7,000 stories, and has made it into the *Guinness Book of Records* for having produced a lifetime total of more than 72,000,000 words (Lofts and Adley, *Men* 15; Carpenter and Prichard).

17. In the terrain, that is, of the one other male allowed full-time access to the girls' school—though Potts may be excused (or at least does not matter so much) because his class is lower, his speech ungrammatical.

18. He wrote only the first few of the Cliff House episodes for the new girls' journal *School Friend* in 1919. Some have said that he stopped because "his characterization of Bessie was too crude for girls' tastes" (Carpenter and Prichard; see also Wernham and Cadogan 116), others that it was because the editor of the boys' journals *The Magnet* and *Gem* forbade him, given that Richards was already committed to producing some 70,000 words a week (Lofts and Adley, *World* 63–64). In any case, the editor of *School Friend* stated that "whilst Frank Richards was the greatest writer for boys, his girls' stories were simply boys' stories with girls' names," and that many girls wrote in "complaining that Bessie was too fat, and many on the plump side complained of being tagged 'Bessie Bunter'" (quoted in Lofts and Adley, *World* 65, 64); subsequent writers using the penname Hilda Richards gradually altered her, making her plump rather than obese, a "lovable duffer" (Cadogan, "Absolute Mascots" 35). Hamilton himself remains decorously silent on the matter, in his autobiography, saying only, "But there were some spots of bother about the series in the 'School Friend,' which Frank will not particularize—he will, in fact, say nothing more about it" (162).

19. Or perhaps becomes "a subject for sympathy rather than amusement" (Cadogan, "Eighty Years" 14).

20. Even if the subversion is ultimately recuperated by this "comedic anti-hero

who is the antithesis of the system and whose discomfiture affirms its virtues" (J. Richards, *Happiest Days* 272). Regarding the "wrong" social class, an historian has suggested "that Frank Richards during the first quarter of the twentieth century [may have] had more influence on the mind and outlook of young working-class England than any other single person, not excluding Baden-Powell" (Robert Roberts, quoted in Wernham and Cadogan 182).

21. See Lofts and Adley, *World* 65. Not that boys reading about Bunter actively liked him: he was "an also-ran in the popularity stakes" (quoted in J. Richards, *Happiest Days* 283), far behind the cheerful and spirited Bob Cherry and a scholarship boy called Mark Linley. Yet although readers may have claimed not to like Bunter, the popularity of this series, even compared to others propagated by Hamilton, belies their claims. At the very least his presence seems to have created a milieu—with possibilities for scapegoating—that struck a popular chord.

The final flowering of the crossgendered school story came in the mid-twentieth century, in the 1930s and 1950s, in boys' stories by British women, in stories of consciousness and human connection. But first let's consider two women who, like twentieth-century men, became didactic when they crossgendered school stories.

One was the journalist Elizabeth Banks, an expatriate American—in fact, the only twentieth-century American I have located who could be said to crossgender a school story. It may be that once a kind of school story became popular in the United States, as in nineteenth-century England after *Tom Brown's Schooldays*, it became difficult, or unnecessary, to crossgender such a story. Once the prep-school and sports stories became dominant, and the college stories, few writers felt the need to crossgender. Men like Claude Moore Fuess and Owen Johnson could write lucrative stories about Andover or Lawrenceville, prep-school stories with some of the mystique of the British public-school stories of earlier decades, similarly women like Grace Margaret Gallaher and Grace Louise Cook, writing about Vassar or Wellesley. Or men and women could write pop-culture series stories, following a character such as Marjorie Dean or Dave Darrin through each year of school. With all these outlets, perhaps it became unnecessary to cross gender boundaries. And perhaps the decline of the religious-didactic story made it less acceptable for men to write of girls, less justifiable: if earlier a man could in some sense write for girls, preaching to them, he would now need to write as a girl, and that was more hazardous. Perhaps too the rise of women's colleges, in conjunction with the women's movement, provided a suitably prestigious and urgent setting for women writers. So the only crossgendering American I have found is, appropriately, an expatriate in Britain.

Banks's fictionalized treatise *School for John and Mary* (1924) is modeled on Wells's *Joan and Peter*.[1] Maybe she hewed so closely to a male model because she was not just a woman but an American in Britain: doubly marginal, she may have tried all the harder to be what she considered mainstream.[2] Or perhaps her distance from the British educational system is akin to Wells's, her distancing caused by nationality as well as class background. Or perhaps, as a journalist who had "worked as a servant, a flower girl, a crossing sweeper," who had "mingled with rag-pickers, . . . made artificial flowers, . . . worked in sweat shops" (Ross 18), she was simply adept at taking on others' roles and perspectives, here the perspectives of males. Male perspectives that she takes on not just by writing of the education of males but by writing in the mode favored by twentieth-century crossgendering males—writing a piece of social criticism rather than, as in the case of most other twentieth-century crossgendering women, a work that explores consciousness and connection.

Banks's narrator Nell has just returned to England from Canada, and she and her husband decide to send their two children to—of all things—a council school, which is to say, a state-supported school for, effectively, the working classes. Friends are shocked. How can poor John hope to get along in life without attending first a preparatory school and then The School, the great public school that his father and other forebears attended? How can Nell be so cruel as not to send Mary to a poor widow who cannot send her boys to public school unless she takes in scholars?

The teachers at the council school are excellent, even if the facilities are not all that could be desired—the outhouses especially are reprehensible. But fortunately the mother of Nell's daily assistant lives next to the school, and John and Mary will be able to lunch there and to use her lavatory. Thus the effluvia of the class system erupt even here—what would one do without one's servants. Finally, however, the Nortons prove unable to overcome other caste aspects of British schooling: like most of his bright classmates young John does not win a scholarship to secondary school, and even though his family could pay to send him, that somehow doesn't quite seem cricket, given that less fortunate classmates cannot follow suit.[3] So Nell and her family decide to return to Canada; her children will once again know the joys of a democratic education. Like Dickens' Micawbers, the Nortons have to escape to the colonies—or rather the dominions—to find equity and just desserts.

Interspersed with all this are disquisitions on caning and fagging, the regressive examination system, the shifts to which parents, especially widows, are reduced to send their boys to "really good" schools (including high-class prostitution). The boys at the nearby preparatory school, to which the Nortons decide not to send John, spend a large part of their time in turning good Latin into bad English and good English into bad Latin. Then they go forth "prepared" for what is to follow. At the public school they "do" still more Latin or, it may be, Greek, treating these languages in a similar fashion to what they have done at the preparatory school. They learn to worship at the shrine of the God of Games, and they take in, or on, all the caning or the birching they are unable to escape by lying or by the application of special ingenuity in the science of how not to get found out. (89)

We also get to observe progressive and illuminating classes taught by John and Mary's superb teachers, each of whom is able to foster the individual talents of some fifty or sixty children.

Yet for all her high moral purpose and antitraditional moralizing, Banks does not escape some traditional themes from canonical school stories—though sometimes she gives them a new twist. We learn of children sending other children to Coventry; only Banks updates it by calling it boycotting. We learn of a somewhat effeminate boy sent off to his father's school and running away, but refusing to tell tales—even though he has been all but sodomized, behavior generally considered heinous enough to justify violating the code (see Orwell, "Such" 39). And as in the typical school story, we eventually learn who the guilty party was—the narrator deduces it from the acute embarrassment of her M.P., who has a son at the school.

There is even a fight or two with a bully. The first, endorsed, is a fight with a bully from the unsavory prep school, someone who has been torturing a little boy from the council school. The second, not endorsed, in fact aborted by an admirable headmaster, would have been with the most upper-class boy at the council school, next to John of course, the son of a down-at-heels former army officer, now a drunk.

Occasionally, too, Banks gets some mileage out of playing out prevailing norms to their contradictory conclusions. A peppery uncle arrives to berate the Nortons for "sending my nephew's children to a school for raggamuffins [sic]" (69). The narrator comments on how Uncle James "regards the father as the only parent, an attitude in which he is, of course, upheld by the present barbaric law," yet he nevertheless expostulates to Nell, "It's your business, as his wife, to keep him from going to extremes" (69). As the narrator comments, "This was a novel 'point of view' certainly from Uncle James, who believes thoroughly in a wife's submission to her husband's decrees, and has so reared his own wife, the dear, kindly, placid Aunt Jane" (69–70).

Unfortunately Banks doesn't proceed in like manner with contradictions closer to the heart of her story. Her narrator admits that she met Jack because her brother was Jack's fag—"so I mustn't be too hard on The School!" (7). And there she drops this contradiction—that the public school she despises has nonetheless made her family possible. When the case is made that Jack didn't turn out too badly, for all that he attended The School, she simply responds, "Jack's what he is in spite of, not because of, the public school system" (12). And that's that—with no further evidence proffered.

Another evasion is that Banks denies the possibility of finding a feasible school in England. With the Nortons it's either public school or council school, nothing in between. Though a cousin has mentioned a third alternative: "a *crank* school, where the boys learn their lessons out of doors, and live on nuts, like squirrels, and wear sandals and all that crazy sort of thing" (57, Banks's italics). A radical school, in short, of which there were many, each with its own philosophy—surely some such school would suit the Nortons. But choosing such an alternative would fail to indict the British educational system. In playing out the tension between personal and societal, between plausible motivations and social criticism, even though she gives some prominence to the personal realm of family, Banks gives precedence to the societal, wants to make social criticism more than to make sense of the plot.

Yet another potential contradiction that Banks tries to sweep under the rug has to do with the class system that she keeps castigating. She uses her child characters to offer a child's-eye view, critical of society—John is apt to wonder "why, Mums, have we got a nice big house, with plenty of bedrooms, when Tom Bailey's father and mother and sisters and little brother live in two rooms?" (201). On the other hand, when the narrator is waxing enthusiastic about the many virtues of her house, she notes, "We had running water fitted in all the bedrooms, not forgetting those which our domestic workers would use . . ." (116–117). It's nice that the servants have running water, but why are there any in a family that feels so strongly about democratic values? As if in justification, the narrator goes on, a few pages later, to explain how everyone helps with the housework, even Mary (Nell doesn't mention John), and to clarify the role of her housekeeper—excuse me, "assistant working manager"—

> Mrs. Adams is not in any sense a "servant," though much of the
> housework is done by her. She is the daughter of a Canadian farmer
> and the widow of a Canadian soldier. She has her pension from the
> Canadian Government, besides her salary from us. She came to live

with us soon after our arrival in Canada, and as she had never been to England, but had a keen desire to see the Motherland, she gladly accompanied us when we returned home. (124)

For all that she made her breakthrough into British journalism by working as a maidservant and writing up the experience—she readily admits that her goal had not been to better the world but to find something to write about (*Autobiography* 92)—Banks shows little real sympathy for such workers; she cannot imagine not needing them, or their not needing their employers.

Much as she tries to evade the contradictory, Banks also tries to repress the irrational. As becomes particularly clear when Mary's teacher encourages children and parents to come up with deodorized Mother Goose rhymes because, as Mary notes, that redoubtable matron "told cruel poetry about children and animals" (233). So Mother Hubbard, upon finding her cupboard bare, bakes her dog a beautiful scone. The old woman who lived in a shoe gives her children bread and treacle, then kisses their sticky faces as she tucks them into bed. In short, let's shield our children, so they won't be prepared for the world; let's deny their aggressive impulses; let's project onto them the blinders that we wish we could wear ourselves. Only in the matter of fighting does Banks allow two versions to stand, though then too she tries to abort one and sanctify the other, to sanctify the one that challenges the class prejudices of a prep-school bully.

Overall, there are ruptures in Banks's text, but she doesn't pursue them. She may describe John meeting a kind lady on a school trip, someone who said she "earned a dishonest living writing up things that everybody believed were true, when they weren't" (48). And thereby Banks hints at some of the play of truth and fiction in her own work, neither biography (Banks was not named Norton, nor married, nor a mother), nor full-fledged fiction, nor full-fledged treatise. But she never follows up such hints, either in the plot (the lady vanishes) or thematically.

Another woman who crossgendered in the twentieth-century male mode, the mode of social criticism—though after the men seem to have given it up—is the British Doreen Wallace. She, too, like Banks, follows a conscious male model, though this time a nineteenth-century one. Frequently invoking Dickens, Wallace wrote *Sons of Gentlemen* (1953) to reveal the abuses permitted by the new Education Act, whereby anyone can claim to run a boarding school and attract, among others, lower-middle-class boys who didn't get into grammar school and whose parents don't want to send their boys to a mere secondary modern.

Wallace's satire is far more restrained than Dickens', though. Perhaps in part she wants her story to be more believable. But also she wants to allow for the possibility of compassion and reform—she admits familial values. She laments the loss of family attachments, in musings on the British eagerness to tear boys away from their families, connecting the process with imperialism, noting how, "if one were fated to spend one's time fighting wars in foreign parts, the hardening process had its usefulness—homesickness was got rid of in childhood, instead of sapping the strength of the young emigrant or soldier" (60). She goes on to ask, if such a process presumably makes a man of a boy, "did one have to jettison all tenderness and sensibility, in order to be a man?" (60). And the novel chronicles the introduction of tenderness—and family feeling—into the sorry excuse for a school at Baconsthorpe Hall. For once the alcoholic proprietor physically collapses, the school is taken over by the compassionate usher and the neighboring parson and his family (though, oddly, the erstwhile proprietor will stay on as a figurehead, receiving parents, still providing a false front). The proprietor's long-suffering wife, who will continue to be the cook, effectively adopts the Smike figure, a boy who has worked for his keep to stay at the school but has been kept so busy he hasn't been able to attend lessons. And the new arrangements will be conducive to yet another kind of family as well, we are assured at the end, since they will throw the usher and the parson's daughter very much together.

Wallace thus attempts, like other women, to meld school and family stories. And unlike in her other novels, where she expresses considerable ambivalence about educating women and portrays romance that "inevitably sours" (Leonardi 128), she here allows the desirability of both education (though for boys) and heterosexual romance. Yet satire does not meld well with compassionate domesticity; the happy ending is a cop out.

In the 1930s women settled down to write boys' school stories in earnest. And what stories. Like other school stories for adults—and there have been many in the twentieth century, by such writers as Hugh Walpole, Antonia White, Dorothy Bussy—these pay some attention to the perspectives of the teachers. The crossgendering women likewise pay some attention to females. Sometimes their focus seems to be on the interconnections of characters associated to varying degrees with a school; sometimes more on the consciousnesses of a few individuals.

In the former, the attention to the lives of the adults, their loves, their families, makes the school setting almost accidental. The public school is a marker less of genre than of milieu, a middle- to upper-middle-class milieu, rather like the manor house in nineteenth-century novels. Perhaps a marker that, for women, was especially attractive as a site once forbidden to them, still largely forbidden—both the fictional and real sites. So the women characters' penetration of the boys' school is a metaphor for the women authors' penetration of boys' school fiction—and of their penetration of the male mainstream of literature.

Such metaphoric penetration is clearest perhaps in the case of Angela Thirkell, who set a series of novels in Trollope's imaginary Barsetshire—directly encroaching, in other words, on male fictional terrain. Her novels have been described as "light fiction compounded of gentle irony, grave absurdity, and urbane under-statement" (Kunitz and Haycraft), of "gaiety, a fetching inconsequence, and a pretty and at times delicately malicious wit" (Roberts 781).[4] Several touch fleetingly on school. *The Headmistress* (1945), for instance, centers on the village of Harefield, during wartime. A girls' boarding school has temporarily taken over Harefield Park, and we see the headmistress being assimilated to village society, along with the various haps and mishaps of village life—who is thinking what about whom. Even more fleetingly touching upon school is *Love Among the Ruins* (1948): one of the half dozen or so main characters becomes a master at a preparatory school, and one of the several gatherings that brings characters together is Parents' Day at the school. In both novels the school has taken over a manorial house—a metaphor for how the marker of gentry milieu has shifted from manor to school.

More centrally concerned with school is Thirkell's witty *Summer Half* (1937), which happens partly at a boys' school but is largely a romantic comedy, as one assistant master falls out of love with the headmaster's daughter and another falls in love with yet another's sister. So family is important, even if the women characters tend to be rather flat, unlike most of the men. It's fitting, furthermore, that Colin Keith, a new assistant master, stays at Southbridge for only a term before going on to read law. Much as school is simply a convenience as a setting for Thirkell, it is a temporary convenience for Colin.

Thirkell succeeds in gaining complexity—and in creating humor—through ironic dialogue, interchanges seemingly at cross-purposes. Yet the complexity of the interchanges serves more to elicit wit than to hint at unplumbed depths or to question the premises of the school story. Or to put it more snidely, as a reviewer in the *New Yorker* has, the book is "written with such good humor and sly wit that it seems more important than it really is" (63).

Yet it's impossible to avoid the depths altogether: working largely from the perspective of the masters, Thirkell does succeed in ironizing some standard tropes. Most of her effects are achieved through reversal—starting with the deflating note with which she prefaces the book: "It seems to be extremely improbable that any such school, masters, or boys could ever have existed" (6). Unlike writers of canonical school stories, she is pretending not to seek verisimilitude.

Though she does in fact go on to claim greater verisimilitude than previous school stories. Before going to the school, Colin succeeds in frightening himself by imagining a sensationalized school story: "falling in love with the headmaster's wife, nourishing unwholesome passions for fair-haired youths, . . . being despised because he hated cricket, being equally despised because he didn't know the names of birds, possibly being involved in a murder which he could never prove he hadn't committed, certainly marrying the matron" (8). Yet as Colin's housemaster Everard Carter tells him upon arrival, "It is all very civilised. No pillow fights, barring-outs, or if you prefer it barrings-out, stealing of exam. papers, or Damon and Pythias. Not even a passion for the headmaster's wife. I really don't know what boys are coming to" (36).

In a similar vein, the key person to impress is the butler: the servants generally have the upper hand, both at home and at school. And of course it's not the masters but the boys who run the school. When Colin admits to Carter that he did not come to teaching out of a liking for boys, but is, rather, "terrified of them," Carter says, "You're all right, then . . . Once they've got you where they want you, they treat you very kindly. The wheel has come full circle, Keith. . . . [T]he boys are our masters. Benevolent tyrants, I admit, but despots. It is far more difficult to expel a troublesome boy than to dispense with the services of an unpopular master" (37). Certainly the boys assume poses of superiority. They even claim to be above watching the masters (though of course they're not): "To watch assistant masters quarrelling is a sport unbecoming to our age and station. Flies on a window-pane if you like; masters, no" (40).

And the boys' perspective is prominent. In one prank a boy ties up Hacker's chameleon "in red paper with its head sticking out, and put it in Winter's desk with a note to say that it had gone Red in sympathy with his political views" (89–90). The head's response to this prank on one of his assistant masters? "'Devils,' said Mr. Birkett, in a loving voice" (90)—continuing, of course, the redness motif. Or the boy Morland can be casually offhand about plagiarism in the course of praising the headmaster's book: "I thought Mr. Birkett's *Determination of Logical Causality* was very interesting . . . I read it in the school library, and I used a bit in an essay for Mr. Winter, but he spotted it, and told me to remember that there were some very useful little signs called notes of quotation" (144).

Teaching generally goes by reversal, as the master Winter indicates when he muses on the possibility of starting a small prep school but is unsure "whether it would be a crank school or an anti-crank school. I believe anti-crank would pay better now. Parents, even crank ones, are a bit sick of their children not washing behind the ears. I'll have a pure fascist, regimented school. After all, the boys are much more likely to react to the left if they are taught imperialism at school" (43).

On the other hand, if the masters find that the boys' athletic pursuits sometimes get in the way, some of the boys, certainly the ones with whom we are concerned, are substantially in agreement—whether a boy deliberately comes last in a race or, better yet, "by well-timed references to a poisoned insect bite, got matron to put a large bandage on his leg and so scratched from all events" (93). Certainly both boys and masters find their house dishonored by the winning of athletic prizes, at least certain ones, such as that for the consolation race. No matter that Hacker "never meant to" win—"It's the worst knock the House has ever had" (109). Still, when Hacker is praised by the headmaster's imbecilic daughter—"a punishment far beyond his desserts"—other boys change the subject, inquiring whether there was indeed "a boy in 1929 who got the Scripture Prize" (110). Everard admits that there was and, thanking the boy named Morland, adds, "That was a depth to which Hacker has not descended. Well, Hacker, you won't do it again here, and I daresay you'll never be tempted again" (110).[5]

It follows from all these reversals that the best way to be nice to a person is to contradict him. As one precocious schoolboy notes, "Sometimes if people are feeling a bit down, it is rather a help to be contradicted. It peps them up" (151). Or when Hacker, studying late at night, absentmindedly causes both a fire and a flood in Carter's house, there is a confrontation between the masters Lorimer and Carter, "a pitched battle between Senior Classics and Housemastering" (50), each blaming the other for what has happened, over excellent sherry. The two reach a friendly agreement, an agreement underscored by the way in which they speak the opposite of what they mean:

> "How I loathe boys and their ways," said Mr. Lorimer, who had been teaching for thirty-five years and took promising boys to his home in Scotland every holidays.
>
> "About mid-term I could kill every boy in my house with joy," said Mr. Carter, who liked being a housemaster more than anything in the world, and usually enlivened the tedium of the holidays by taking boys to Finland, or Mount Athos. (50)

Thirkell's writing can be delightful, and sometimes she delicately probes complex issues. But she is so intent on being witty that for the most part the book just skims surfaces.

Even more incidentally set at school is Iris Murdoch's *The Sandcastle* (1957), an early novel generally given little attention in the Murdoch canon, "criticized for its decided thematic similarity to the conventional literature of women's magazines" (Todd 36). Yet the echoes of names in Thirkell—Everard, Carter, Mor (a truncation of Morland?)—suggest that Murdoch is working as well in a new school-story tradition. As Donna Gerstenberger has noted, "Murdoch's novelistic structures are, by and large, traditional, her characters middle- or upper-middle class, their interactions largely polite, even when outrageous, their conversations often cerebral . . ."—yet she is nonetheless fundamentally concerned with the irrational, with the "terrors of existence" (15).

In *The Sandcastle* Murdoch uses some of the scaffolding of the school story, yet like Thirkell she focuses more on the adults than on the boys. She focuses particularly on the relationships of the master Mor: in his private life, to his wife and children and the young woman painting the portrait of the retired headmaster; in his more public life, to the school itself and to the possibility of shifting to a career in politics.

Displacement is at the heart of the book, as Murdoch displaces the canonical school story, displacing the focus on boys, displacing institutional allegiances with personal ones (even displacing, somewhat, logic with magic, a gypsy appearing at moments of transgression, Tarot cards seeming to govern destiny). William Mor's allegiance seems to be more to the retired head Demoyte than to the current one, the Reverend Everard (Revvy Evvy), or even to the school itself. Through Demoyte Mor meets the painter Rain Carter, his attention displaced from the school to the retired head to the painter of that head.

Much as Thirkell's Colin Keith is moving on from teaching school, so, it turns out, is Murdoch's Mor: instead of disrupting his family, instead of running off with Rain, he simply disrupts his relationship with the school, leaving it, it appears at the end, to run for Parliament. It's as if he needs to sever his connection with the school to maintain his connection with his family: thus does Murdoch dramatize the crosscutting overlay of allegiances common in school stories by women—opting here, unlike most twentieth-century women writers in quest of independence, for family. Yet it's a man who so opts. If Murdoch "sees little barrier between men's and women's minds" (Dipple 88), then perhaps for her crossgendering has become an effortless androgyny, embodied in her melding of traditionally gendered genres as well, the school story and the popular romance. Yet it's significant that it's a man who opts for family connections and that no matter how trapped he finally feels, he still has opportunities for wider public action.

The life of the school itself figures little in *The Sandcastle*. Its grounds, the terrain that must be covered in searching for someone, are more important than its boys. And we never enter the perspectives of any of the school-boys. We may enter that of Mor's daughter Felicity, as she sneaks onto the school grounds to see her brother. But we never enter that of her brother Donald. Not when Felicity meets him, having successfully made her clandestine way to his room. Not when he is so disturbed by the arrival of Rain Carter at the house cricket match that he is bowled. Not even when he makes the mad attempt to scale the school tower, nearly falls, is rescued by the exertions of Mor and others, and runs off into the night, staying away long enough to miss the chemistry exam that might have enabled him to attend Cambridge. So Don too is displaced, displaced further by being expelled from school because of a rule against attempts to scale school buildings. Males here are wrested from school.

As in her other novels Murdoch identifies, as she admits, "more with my male characters than my female characters" (Chevalier 82), more with Mor than with his wife or with Rain. Yet although Rain is primarily an object in the story, her subjectivity is hinted at: "She is implicitly re-instated as female *subject* by the terms of her own Oedipal family romance" (D. Johnson 17, Johnson's italics). Murdoch herself has stated that she is "very interested in problems about the liberation of women, particularly, for instance, in so far as these concern education" (Chevalier 82).

Hence the role of young women in the story seems to be to penetrate the bastions of male prerogatives. Rain penetrates the precincts of the school, penetrates the defenses of Demoyte in painting him, penetrates Mor's defenses too. And when Felicity sneaks into St. Bride's to see her brother, she acquires some of the traits attributed to boys in school stories: she "did not have any particularly reverential attitude towards authority, and her conscience functioned vigorously enough in complete detachment from the adult world of prohibition and exhortation which surrounded her, and which she often failed completely to make sense of" (126). At the end, Don's choice not to go on to university but to work in the business of a family friend makes it somehow feasible for Felicity not to leave school for a secretarial course and possibly to consider university. Felicity gains access to male prerogatives, much as Murdoch's working at the lode of the school story helped her to penetrate the literary mainstream—though, curiously, previous commentators have missed the school-story connection, focusing instead on Murdoch's use of popular romance conventions, and have been dismissive of the work within the Murdoch oeuvre.[6] Or perhaps they have not missed the school-story connection, but vaguely associating schools and school stories with juvenilia and puerility, they have been all the more inclined to be dismissive.

Six years earlier there appeared a crossgendered school story in a somewhat different vein, a story that is not just incidentally set at school but that focuses on school, a story focusing as much on consciousness as on connection: Margery Fisher's *Field Day* (1951). If Thirkell and Murdoch tend to use the boys' school setting more as a marker of milieu, as male territory to invade, Fisher—and, as we shall see, D. Wynne Willson—is more inclined to reconceptualize school and the school story. Fisher, having herself taught in a boys' public school during wartime (Carpenter and Prichard), sensitively captures a day in the life of a school.

Her book is unusual, first, in that she enters the perspectives of representatives from all parts of the school: not just those of boys, not just adding those of masters, but also the perspectives of women, including a housemaster's wife, her sister, and a young servant. The housemaster's wife is trying to cope with not having children, hoping she is pregnant, and with the servant's having taken a picture, torn from a book, from a boy's locker. The housemaster is trying to cope with an injured ankle that enforces his absence from the annual Field Day exercises. The boy who is his head of the house is trying to decide whether to stay on at school to try for a scholarship or to join the army.

The book is also unusual in being set during wartime—a time for unusual measures, such as hiring the housemaster's sister to teach French, a time when women can be empowered, temporarily at least, by the absence of men. A time when, in short, crossgendering may become more thinkable: just as Hale was empowered to write of Rachel's public activities in *Mrs. Merriam's Scholars* (1878) by the real experiences of women teaching freedmen during the Civil War, so is Fisher empowered to write of experiences to which she became privy, as a teacher at Oundle, during World War II. The salience of the wartime setting is only enhanced by the choice of day to focus on: Field Day, a day when the boys of various houses, now in platoons, enact a "mimic battle" (64). Thus does Fisher underscore the connection between the playing fields of school and the fields of war.

Though always with complex irony. The boy who was previously head of the house has already died in the trenches—but of appendicitis.

Characters do something almost stereotypical but then break out of the stereotype, often only to revert to type again. The housemaster's dreamy wife, Lucy, becomes assertive for a moment, then reverts to docility; she learns once again that she is not pregnant and is terribly disappointed, but also a little relieved. Her independent-minded sister Anne learns that she will get to teach and is eager to do so, but that eagerness derives partly from the extent to which she misses her husband, absent at the front, and Lucy recognizes how much Anne will miss looking after her children. And finally, as Lucy notes, her methodical husband Arthur for the first time decides something "on personal grounds and not on principle" (227)—letting her keep on the errant servant as nursemaid for Anne's children—thereby allowing a feminine principle a moment of triumph. Though Fisher also allows that keeping Joyce on, a fourteen year old not only guilty of theft but with little sense that what she did was wrong, is not conducive to the long-term well-being of the household: "There was no doubt that Lucy's plan for Joyce was in many ways a short-sighted one" (236). Or perhaps that is only what Arthur thinks. Yet still, the last we see of Joyce, talking with fellow servants of the new job, she is not contrite but rather is starting "to believe she had acquired the job on her own merits" (249).

Neither indicting war nor celebrating it, Fisher neither indicts nor celebrates school, though the possibilities she finds for connection, even if temporary, are more celebratory than condemnatory. Especially since she finds possibilities for women in the orbit of this boys' school. She may not be revolutionizing the educational system or the school story, but she is unearthing a potential here, in the British boys' public school, that no one else had.

The highlight of twentieth-century crossgendered school stories—and the key precedessor text for Fisher—is D. Wynne Willson's *Early Closing* (1931). In a survey of children's literature Fisher lists *Early Closing* as one of four adult novels (the other three are by men) that will give a boy a better idea of what public school is like than a canonical boys' story will (*Intent* 171).[7] As for Willson herself, little is recorded of her life, except that she died the year after *Early Closing* was published, at age twenty-four—the title of her novel having been too prophetic. Yet she writes the school story as Woolf might have written it. And like other women modernists—more even than other women modernists—she has been denied recognition.

Willson's story may not seem significantly different from contemporary stories by men—for by the 1930s men were writing, for adults, more sophisticated, more jaded and cynical, stories about schooling. Yet despite her sophistication, Willson is not particularly jaded or cynical. A character may reflect, "But there was nothing like facetiousness for privacy. In all that cackle, who was to see your thoughts?" (274). Yet unlike Thirkell's characters, with their bright chatter, Willson's nevertheless communicate moods and feelings and caring—just as Willson does, through gentle irony.

Early Closing offers a range of perspectives, representing those of both boys and masters and also that of a sister who doesn't attend the school yet is uncannily informed about it. Like Martineau in *The Crofton Boys* (1841), Willson finds a female proxy in a boy's sister. This sister in *Early Closing*, Lavender, asks about "'Teacher' and 'Frog,' and whether Penhurst was still as old for his years; and how Nigel and Gray had enjoyed being prefects, and whether Johnny liked fagging for Gray, and how Rat Day had gone off?" (148). When Nigel and Johnny remain unresponsive, a visiting master attributes their discomfort to

> the fact that it was unnatural in a sister to know so much of the everyday goings-on of school life. Of course it was quite in order that sisters should take an interest in these affairs; but it went down better, Fenn opined, if it was an old-fashioned, wide-eyed, simple feminine interest; with a fondly-foolish idea to be set right here, and a quaintly-foolish question to be answered there. (148–149)

Neither Willson nor Lavender is that old fashioned.

Willson succeeds in capturing shimmering impressions of school, of the seasons that mark its moods, vignettes of high points (such as Rat Day, when men from the village bring their ferrets and mongrels to kill rats) and low points (such as the day that the housemaster William—everyone calls him by his first name—ran over the dead pig). Not to mention more than the usual quota of classroom scenes—of Johnny struggling with mathematics, of the skill of Johnny and his friends in getting a master sidetracked, of the subtleties of ragging. The teacher nicknamed Teacher, accustomed to inattention and indiscipline, discovers "a growing tendency to listen to what he had to say; and this troubled him; for the attention paid him by these Philistines was, he considered, out of all proportion to the significance, not of what he had to say, but of what his remarks could mean to their unopened minds" (178). Over time he discovers the direction of their innuendoes— the sounds like popping corks, the allusions to Bacchus, the naming of the classroom the "Jug and Bottle"—yet there are no concrete misdemeanors that would justify punishment, and, without any sense of the source of the alcoholic allusions, he is immobilized. Overall, there are far more classroom scenes in *Early Closing* than scenes devoted to athletic contests (though athletics are rarely far from the boys' thoughts).

Willson also portrays moments of epiphany, often with nature—and often not at school. It's in connection with such an epiphany, as if enabling it to happen, that a kind of laming, of convalescing, occurs—a latter-day echo of the nineteenth-century women who lamed their schoolboys to tame them, temporarily or permanently. Nigel, the older of two brothers on whom we focus at Willson's school, is convalescing at home after a toboggan accident. For once, he is, like his sister Lavender, at loose ends, though only temporarily. In any case, Nigel doesn't know what to do with himself, at least not what he will do once he leaves Oxford, which he will be attending in the fall. As his sardonic housemaster William has remarked, with respect to Nigel's academic plans, "I gather that your final choice is now narrowed down to Greats, History, Forestry, Agriculture or Law" (79).

As for Lavender, she hasn't known what to do with herself for some time. She is restless. She longs for greatness yet wonders if she lacks intellect and pluck, if in fact she is "but an ordinary person, without enough to do" (155). Certainly the master John Fenn, visiting her family, has thought as much: when musing on her extraordinary interest in Nigel and Johnny's doings at school, he decided that her "peculiar interest came from pure affection and from insufficient home-interests. Of course, it must be that" (149). What home interests does she have? "A restless laziness possessed her. She knew she couldn't write; her painting, though more successful than her father's, had no character, and her 'cello was going from bad to worse" (156). Perhaps when she travels to Paris to study the cello she will find what she is lacking.[8]

The stasis that Nigel has attained thus resembles that of his sister, creating, in his case, a liminal time of transition before he goes to Oxford. His invalidism provides, then, not so much an instrument of moral regeneration, as it would have in the previous century, but a pause for reflection—though as in the previous century, it implicitly feminizes and infantilizes him. He is granted time to reconnect with his childhood, remembering how it tasted to eat early peas, how "the garden walls were as high as cliffs" (249). He recalls his school life, which now too is "a life retreating into memory and reminiscence" (250). And he drives to a bridge—a bridge he had visited the end of the previous summer with his brother and sister, a bridge that had then evoked a multitude of childhood memories, of going there in a pram or with his father to fish from it. So he visits again this trope of transition, this threshold image.

And he experiences an epiphany. Sitting in a beech wood, he sees a brilliant cloud, and he remembers a day at school the previous autumn, a day when he watched small boys playing rugby: "And it was one with the vigour that rose in him at the moment—surging up, a sense of confidence and power and great possessions" (270). It's a feeling of energy and certainty, of impersonality, of timelessness and loveliness, somehow echoing, bringing to fulfillment, moments of his childhood—"as when in childhood he had felt suddenly glad, with no accounting for it; capering in a shining excitement before a nurse who said he would be crying before bedtime. And so he was, invariably" (271). So too does Nigel descend from this moment of exaltation—"and by his analysis he lost it" (277)—but he descends to greater wisdom. He tries to recapture the moment, but this kind of transcendence can only come unforced: "It was gone as dew from the grass. The very early morning of his life was over. A bright promise in the skies was overcome by creeping greyness, the early closing of his vision" (278). Yet he reaches a sense of harmony, of peace, if no longer of exultation: "Now in this moment life unfolded before him with all its striving and tangle of human relationships— long, full, absorbing, prosperous maybe, or sorrowful" (278). He moves from an individual ecstasy of connection with nature to a more sober but peaceful sense of connectedness with others.

This moment of connection is connected, appropriately, with similar moments in the text. John Fenn's thoughts and conversation at a dinner party anticipate the imagery and feeling of Nigel's moment of epiphany and subsequent recollection in tranquility. Fenn recollects a moment the previous year in Switzerland, when he experienced a kind of communion with nature, "the snow scarce melted," "the sun hot upon the moss and primroses," "the woods below, transparent, thin, with red-brown glooms and purple shadows," "the wind approaching through the pine wood—and, coming and coming, it never reached him!" (209–210). Fenn then has another moment of communion—signaled by a smile across the room—with Teacher. For his host has been feeling unhappy, weighed down by his pupils' allusions to drink, and is quick to see mockery in trifles. Even, concretely, in the trifle served at the dinner party. The cook has left the sherry out by mistake, bringing to mind "Alcohol: Blue ribbon—what twinges they both gave him still!" (211). But then, like Clarissa Dalloway and Peter Walsh finally communing at the end of a party, he suddenly sees "John Fenn smiling at him; a companionable smile, guessing his thoughts. And suddenly the cloud lifted for good and all, and was blown beyond his horizon. He saw the affair in its true light, and oh, the delightful unimportance of it all, and of them all, and of himself!" (211). Teacher smiles back, knowing peace of mind again, knowing that he will "live through the noise they made in the Middle School," and "he beamed round his table. The sun was out again" (211, 212). Thus the cloud of alcoholic innuendo lifts, will no longer bother him. The references to sun and cloud further connect this moment to Fenn's on the mountainside the year before. And both connect to Nigel's moment of epiphany while convalescing.

Yet if Nigel's illumination occurs in connection with nature, the masters' are as likely to occur in a social setting—a subtle difference of Willson's work from those of her male predecessors and contemporaries. For she allows both for a solitary mode of connection, for the young male alone, and a sociable mode, for the more mature male—thus moving beyond adolescent Byronism to the tangle of humanity Nigel has dimly glimpsed ahead of him.[9]

Fenn also connects with Nigel—and with humanity—in another way, as we eventually learn—through Lavender. While visiting the Bentley family, Fenn finds himself falling in love with her. Not uncritically. He observes with distaste that when Nigel catechizes an old school friend about his shifting politics—"it was widely known that Compton-Mallett was passing through political distemper"—Lavender exchanges "glances of sympathy and commiseration" with the victim: "Now, thought Fenn, she shouldn't do that. She ought to stick to Nigel, even though he is showing off. Fenn was quite put out. He tried to get things straight in his mind" (158, 159). Though of course the lack of loyalty to Nigel is not the only reason why Fenn is put out. He goes on to rationalize that she must be one of those people who is "constitutionally disloyal," not vindictively, but as "the outcome of weakness, sympathy, and a faculty for seeing the other side to the question" (159). When Fenn and Lavender talk that evening, the narrator reveals Fenn's feelings in a throwaway phrase, sandwiched between the mundane: "John Fenn drew her out, listened and explained, and saw the facets of her character, for he loved her, and went on to talk of Certificate A" (160).

Fenn and Lavender eventually marry, we eventually realize—if we piece together innuendoes, attend to subordinate clauses and what is left unstated. For on the next page we get a glimpse of the future, learn that "she became engaged for a short time" to Compton-Mallett, and after that came her marriage. But marriage to whom? At the end of another chapter is another throwaway line: we learn that all of Nigel's family—Lavender as well as Johnny and their father—are early risers, including "in time her son, Nigel John Fenn" (251). And thereby are Nigel and Fenn connected, through Lavender, through the child and the child's name, as Lavender herself is connected to the boys' school, becoming engaged to someone met through the school connection, and marrying someone else also connected to the school.

Then there are the filiations of the title. Not only does the phrase "early closing" appear in connection with Nigel's sober reflections on his epiphany, on "the early closing of his vision" (278), but it also embodies the power of the unexpressed, Willson's metaphoric compression. We might expect "early closing," applied to a school story, to refer to an early closing of the school term. And in effect there is such an early closing for the injured Nigel, though the phrase is not used in this context. More importantly, Nigel's absence from school paradoxically brings together significant themes from school, much as, perhaps, Willson's own absence from the kind of school she describes enabled her to crystallize its essence. Though perhaps there is just a whiff, as well, of a sense of the limitations of school, that what is important happens outside it (while school yet remains a necessary catalyst). Overall this book keeps undermining longings for a kind of Romantic wholeness—while yet staying, like its title, within a tradition of Romantic melancholy, the impossible longing for wholeness.

We don't find here any explicit commentary on the themes that have characterized canonical school stories. There is no bully to overcome. No fighting. Little battle discourse.[10] Just a wry perspective on the dailiness of school life.

What attention gets paid to plagiarism, for instance—another node, like talebearing, in which the divergent interests of boys and masters can appear in bold relief—is wry, gentle, without recrimination, conveying neither outrage nor glee. There is a book owned by Johnny,

> an old book, tattered and frayed, handed down from generation to generation.
>
> On every page were scribblings, underlinings and remarks—his heritage. For there were answers written in, and hints and warnings; for of what use is it to know an answer, if unable to arrive at it convincingly?
>
> And these remarks were written in the same spirit that prompts tramps to mark the gate-posts of the penurious, and hotel servants their luggage. A good turn done those in the same trade; a fraternal kindliness found in those who have enemies in common. (200)

Though the disjunction of interests between master and pupil implied here—assuming that masters want boys to derive answers for themselves—is perhaps offset by a kind of connectedness, even of camaraderie, between the two camps. When the French master Clovis-Abel witnesses Johnny Bentley's distress with mathematics, specifically with plus and minus—"the signs went wrong, invariably, inevitably" (255)—the Frenchman offers a heuristic. If he calls "plus" his friend, and "minus" his enemy, then Johnny can apply tags such as "the enemy of mine enemy is my friend" (256) to work his way through algebraic multiplication. Though such help, humanizing the unhuman, is sufficiently unorthodox that "Clovis-Abel hoped that William would not mind his having helped Bentley with an explanation" (257)—and of course William doesn't.

Nor are other school matters always treated with reverence. Take, for instance, the topic of writing. When Nigel is working on an editorial for the Magazine, he asks his friend Gray, "About how many commas would you put to a page?" Gray suggests that for an editorial he'll "need a good few" and then goes on to suggest the structure of this species of writing: "a nice quotation to lead off with; and then you can work round via politics, economics, religion and moral science to the Public School Spirit, and fetch up with an indirect compliment to the Proprietor himself" (166). William too offers some parodic advice: "Just mind you give us our usual turgid bombast, my good boy. And then there'll be all those Minutes of the Societies, with one or two 'we's' to break the monotony of the third person" (167). This may not be writing for coursework, just for a magazine—yet the magazine still metonymically represented the School.

A few pages later we get Johnny's approach to writing:

> That evening his thoughts were in full spate. Away he went, untrammelled. For what is History but World-gossip?
>
> So he treated [the master] Warner to a wealth of irrelevancies, astounding and disconcerting. And his most flagrant opinions he just popped into inverted commas, and left Warner to puzzle them out. His unruled margins he bespattered with dates.
>
> He got it all done in twenty minutes and lay back panting.
>
> Now let the man correct the stuff! (170)

Not that writing itself is belittled. William has granted it status—this housemaster who deflects undermining by others by undermining himself, so that when he does state something we are apt to take it seriously, as seriously as we take anything—this William says of writing, "Nigel has it in him; and Johnny is bursting with something too" (231). He goes on to tell Lavender that "she must remember that although she might have her head in the clouds, in company with Shelley and others, the result of this communion, if she tried to reproduce it, would probably be inferior; but if sincere, quite printable" (233).

Willson herself has chosen the path of writing, excusing herself, it would seem, by way of William's comments. She further ironizes her dismissals of writing by herself using language with care and sensitivity. With respect to the matron, Willson says that "the approach of middle age had crystallised the ginger of her hair . . ." (13). Or with respect to the tennis-playing abilities of certain masters:

> Fenn's game was above the average; Warner's, too, was worth watching.
> So was Teacher's; he pranced forward between his first and second faults; a gambit which lent both style and incident to a game devoid of skill. (263–264)

Willson has had a few perceptive readers. Witness Fisher, cited earlier. Another is an anonymous reviewer in the *Times,* who put *Early Closing* in "the small class of books which hold the attention with what is on the page read without there being anything on that page to astound or to suggest that it is a preparation for some dramatic climax to come." The reviewer adds that in this plotless and seemingly patternless book, "the art of the writer may pass unrecognized until the reader remembers that he never stopped because puzzled at an incongruity or offended at a distortion, but that he did stop to chuckle over exhilarating dialogue or to reread a passage on spring or autumn for the pleasure given by the rhythm."

Yet few critics or historians even acknowledge the existence of Willson's book, and when they do they aren't quite sure how to treat it. Take Edward C. Mack. He briefly discusses Willson in his pathbreaking intellectual history of *Public Schools and British Opinion Since 1860.* He tries to classify works as to whether they are critical of public schools or fundamentally approving, a task that is feasible with most of the novels he discusses, quasi-realistic, quasi-moralistic, aimed at a popular audience. Uncomfortable with what he calls Willson's "disenchanted urbanity," he states, "The public school system in Miss Willson's pages hardly appears capable of arousing much enthusiasm or devotion, and without the ability to do this there can be no healthy survival" (414). But Willson's stance is too complex for his grid. Mack's response to her is further captured in a suggestively contorted sentence: he describes *Early Closing* as "a novel about public schools of so different a character from . . . any previous novels about schools, as almost—if the book were not so slight and the word so inappropriate to its tone—to constitute a revolution" (413).

Slight? Inappropriate? Mack senses a revolution that he doesn't quite grasp. For, unlike the authors of canonical school stories—and the fitting culmination of a study of crossgendered, noncanonical school stories—Willson subtly probes characters and conventions and dismantles canons. When women wrote about boys, when men wrote about girls, they reoriented the terms of the genre, at times even revolutionized them—creating sissies who are nonetheless sassy, tomboys who nonetheless tattle. Too often overshadowed by their canonical brothers, these authors—from Lamb with his seafaring tyke to Quebec with his happy-go-lucky lesbians, from May's tattling to Wood's secrets, from Johnson's exotics to Mathews' erotics—nonetheless bring to bear questions that elsewhere are begged. And sometimes, like Willson, like Alcott, they create a work that bears—that illuminates—the intensest critical scrutiny.

NOTES

1. Banks was acquainted with Wells (see *Remaking* 100). In fact, she admits that when she embarked on her investigations into British schooling, early in the 1920s, one of her first thoughts was to interview Wells, "who always had original ideas about education" (*Remaking* 237). He, however, was out of the country.

2. In the first volume of her autobiography, *The Autobiography of a "Newspaper Girl"* (1902), she seems particularly concerned to interrogate what it means to be a woman with a career; in the second, *The Remaking of an American* (1928), what it means to be American. She is quite self-conscious, in short, about both gender and nationality.

3. Though the Nortons do "make a provision for [two other boys'] higher education that will render them independent of the unjust scholarship system" (308–309). Banks notes in *Remaking* that only about 10 percent of eleven year olds in London County Council schools win scholarships or exhibitions (249)—and since only the scholarships, not the exhibitions, enable one to attend secondary school, significantly fewer than 10 percent win a free place in a secondary school. The number is so small that if a council school of a thousand or more students succeeds in having a winner—and many years it does not—it's likely to declare a one-day holiday for the whole school (244–245).

4. See Collins for an appreciation of Thirkell's work.

5. Not that all prizes are bad—Hacker does not seem to bring discredit on the house when, later, he wins prizes for Latin, Greek, Latin verse, Greek verse. On the other hand, Swan "disgraced the house by getting a reading prize given by the Chaplain" (121). He didn't mean to. And the boys decide that the only thing to be done is to play football with the prize book, *Sartor Resartus*—a reprise of the trope of the thrown book. When they succeed in breaking a glass ventilator with it, and the housemaster Everard comes in, he simply assesses the damage—four and six—and advises as he leaves that "now the ventilator is broken, you might as well go on using it. What with Hacker winning the Consolation Race and Swan the Reading Prize, this house has come pretty low" (121). And they do go on—until the book falls in pieces and they throw it away.

6. Dipple, for instance, counts it as one of two failures among Murdoch's first twenty novels (136).

7. For another brief account of Willson see my "Heading."

8. The narrator tells us that eventually, "By the time she was twenty-five, she had forgotten whatever it was the poets upset themselves for; and had forgotten how infinitesimal she was in the Universe; for she became important to those about her,

who counted on her for support and sympathy . . ." (160–161).

9. Though her climactic placement of Nigel's epiphany, near the end of the book, does give it priority—does reveal that Willson is not immune to the Romantic yearning for solitude and solipsism.

10. The closest approach securely frames and distances it, putting it in its place: a dining hall is graced with large, crude pictures of famous battles like Hastings and Agincourt—"the usual mediaeval brawl, warriors cheek by jowl amongst the lances" (103). William swears he will replace them once he can afford to, and send them "to adorn the walls of the Sick-house, and startle the malingerers there. . . . However these battle-scenes gave a homely, almost nursery atmosphere to the dining hall, not to be despised" (103). Thus is battle infantilized—though infantilization is not necessarily bad in this novel threaded with Romantic views of childhood.

WORKS CITED

SCHOOL STORIES

[Abbott, Jacob]. *Cousin Lucy at Study*. Boston: Mussey, 1842.

———. *Cousin Lucy's Stories: Stories Told to Rollo's Cousin Lucy, When She Was a Little Girl*. 1841. Reprint, Boston: Mussey, 1842.

———. *Rollo at School*. 1839. Reprint, Boston: Webb, n.d.

Adams, C[harlotte]. *Edgar Clifton; or, Right and Wrong: A Story of School Life*. 1852. Reprint, New York: Appleton, 1858.

Alcott, Louisa May. *Little Men: Life at Plumfield with Jo's Boys*. [1871]. Reprint, New York: Grosset, 1947.

Alcott, Louisa May. "Mamma's Plot." In *Cupid and Chow-Chow*. Vol. 3 of *Aunt Jo's Scrap-Bag*. Boston: Roberts, 1886. 115–127.

Anstey, F. *Vice Versa*. 1882. Reprint, Harmondsworth: Puffin-Penguin, 1985.

Baldwin, Mary R. *The New Boy at Southcott*. Reprinted in *Gurnet's Garden, and The New Boy at Southcott*. New York: Phillips, 1887. 135–282.

Banks, Elizabeth. *School for John and Mary*. London: Putnam, 1924.

Betham-Edwards, M[atilda]. *Charlie and Ernest or Play and Work: A Story of Hazlehurst School*. Edinburgh: Edmonton, 1859.

Blinders, Belinda [Desmond Coke]. *The Chaps of Harton: A Tale of Frolic, Sport and Mystery at Public School*. Edited by Desmond Coke. London: Chapman, 1913.

[Brewster, Margaret M.]. *Charlie Hubert; or, Consecrated Gifts*. 1857. Reprint, New York: Randolph, 1858.

Buckland, Annie. *Lily and Nannie at School: A Story for Little Girls*. London: Cassell, [1868].

Coke, Desmond. *The Bending of a Twig*. [1906]. Reprint, London: Milford, 1934.

Dane, Clemence [Winifred Ashton]. *Regiment of Women*. New York: Macmillan, 1917.

Densel, Mary. *Tel Tyler at School*. New York: Dutton, 1872.

Diaz, Abby Morton. *The William Henry Letters*. 1870. Reprint, Boston: Lothrop, 1899.

Edgeworth, Maria. *The Parent's Assistant; or, Stories for Children*. [1796]. Reprint, London: Routledge, n.d.

Eggleston, Edward. *The Hoosier School-Boy*. New York: Judd, 1883.

Eiloart, Mrs. [Elizabeth]. *[Ernie at School]*. [1867]. Reprinted in *Ernie Elton at Home and at School*. London: Routledge, n.d.

Farrar, Frederic W. *Eric; or, Little by Little: A Tale of Roslyn School*. 1858. Reprinted in *The Victorian Age (1837–1900)*. Edited by Robert Lee Wolff. Vol. 5, no. 2, of *Masterworks of Children's Literature*. New York: Stonehill, 1985. 1–203.

[Fenn, Ellenor]. *School Dialogues for Boys: Being an Attempt to Convey Instruction Insensibly to Their Tender Minds, and Instill the Love of Virtue*. 2 vols. London: Marshall, [1783?].

————. *School Occurrences: Supposed to Have Arisen among a Set of Young Ladies, under the Tuition of Mrs. Teachwell; and to be Recorded by One of Them.* London: Marshall, [1782].

Fenn, G. Manville. *Burr Junior: His Struggles and Studies at Old Browne's School.* London: Griffith, [1891].

Fielding, Sarah. *The Governess; or, Little Female Academy.* 1749. Reprint, with introduction by Mary Cadogan. New York: Pandora, 1987.

Fisher, Margery. *Field Day.* London: Collins, 1951.

Forsyth Grant, Mrs. G. [Annie]. *The Beresford Boys: A School Story.* Illus. by her son (a schoolboy). Edinburgh: Nimmo, 1906.

————. *The Boys at Penrohn: A Story of English School Life.* [1893]. Reprint, Edinburgh: Nimmo, n.d.

————. *Burke's Chum: A Story of Thistleton School.* Reprint, Edinburgh: Nimmo, 1896.

Gaylord, Glance [Warren Ives Bradley]. *Miss Howard's School.* New York: Carlton, 1866.

"The Glutton." In *Tales from the Mountains.* [1809]. Reprinted in Tuer 253–261.

Goddard, Julia. *The New Boy at Merriton: A Story of School Life.* London: Blackie, [1882].

————. *Philip Danford: A Story of School Life.* London: Blackie, [1890].

Hale, Edward E. "The Good-Natured Pendulum." In *The Ingham Papers: Some Memorials of Capt. Frederic Ingham, U.S.N., Sometime Pastor of the First Sandemanian Church Naguadavick, and Major-General by Brevet in the Patriot Service in Italy.* Boston: Fields, 1869. 1–19.

————. *Mrs. Merriam's Scholars: A Story of the "Original Ten."* Boston: Roberts, 1878.

Hall, Mrs. S. C. [Anna Maria]. *Daddy Dacre's School: A Story for the Young.* [1858]. Reprint, London: Routledge, 1859.

Hughes, Thomas. *Tom Brown at Oxford.* 1861. Reprint, London: Nelson, [1880].

————. *Tom Brown's Schooldays.* [1857]. Reprint, New York: Airmont, 1968.

[Johnson, Richard]. *The Little Female Orators; or, Nine Evenings Entertainment.* [1770]. 3rd ed. Reprint, London: Carnan, 1778.

Kenyon, E[dith] C. *Jack's Heroism: A Tale of Schoolboy Life.* London: Partridge, [1883].

Kilner, Dorothy [M.P., pseud.]. *Anecdotes of a Boarding-School; or, An Antidote to the Vices of those Useful Seminaries.* 2 vols. London: Marshall, [1790].

———— [M. Pelham, pseud.]. *First Going to School; or, The Story of Tom Brown, and His Sisters.* London: Tabart, 1804.

[Kilner, Dorothy]. *The Village School: A Collection of Entertaining Histories, for the Instruction and Amusement of All Good Children.* [c. 1783]. Reprint, London: Harris, 1831.

Kipling, Rudyard. *Stalky & Co.* 1899. Reprint, London: Oxford University Press, 1987.

[Knight, Helen C.]. *Annie Sherwood; or, Scenes at School.* Philadelphia: American Sunday-School Union, [1843?].

————. *Reuben Kent at School; or, Influence as It Should Be.* Philadelphia: American Sunday-School Union, 1844.

Lamb, Charles and Mary. *Mrs Leicester's School; or, The History of Several Young Ladies, Related by Themselves.* 1809. Reprinted in *Middle Period.* Edited by Robert Bator. Vol. 4, c. 1740–c. 1836, of *Masterworks of Children's Literature.* New York: Stonehill, 1984. 279–330.

Marshall, Arthur. "Look Out King Wenceslas!" *Lilliput* (1949). Reprinted in Cadogan, *Chin Up* 31–32.

Martineau, Harriet. *The Crofton Boys: A Tale.* [1841]. Reprint, New York: Appleton, 1842.

[Mathews, Julia A.]. "True to His Flag." In *Drayton Hall, and Other Tales, Illustrating the Beatitudes.* [1871]. New ed. Reprint, London: Warne, n.d. 483–567.

Mathews, Julia A. *Jack Granger's Cousin.* London: Nisbet, 1877.

May, E[mily] J. *Dashwood Priory; or, Mortimer's College Life.* [1855]. Reprinted as *Mortimer's College Life.* New York: Appleton, 1856.

———. *Louis' School Days: A Story for Boys.* [1850]. New York: Appleton, 1851.

Murdoch, Iris. *The Sandcastle.* 1957. Reprint, London: Penguin, 1987.

Old Humphrey [George Mogridge]. *Lessons Worth Learning for Girls.* London: Religious Tract Society, [1851].

Oliphant, Mrs. [Margaret]. *The Story of Valentine and his Brother.* 2 vols. Leipzig: Tauchnitz, 1875.

Optic, Oliver [William T. Adams]. *In School and Out; or, The Conquest of Richard Grant: A Story for Young People.* Boston: Lee, 1864.

———. *Poor and Proud; or, The Fortunes of Katy Redburn.* 1858. Reprint, Boston: Phillips, 1859.

Orwell, George. *A Clergyman's Daughter.* [1935]. Reprint, New York: Harcourt, n.d.

Quebec, Adela [Gerald Hugh Tyrwhitt-Wilson Berners]. *The Girls of Radcliff Hall.* N.p.: Privately printed, [1937].

Reed, Talbot Baines. *The Fifth Form at St. Dominic's.* [1881–1882]. Reprint, London: Oliphants, n.d.

Richards, Hilda [Charles Hamilton]. *Bessie Bunter of Cliff House School.* London: Skilton, 1949.

Sharp, Evelyn. *The Making of a Schoolgirl.* 1897. Reprint, with introduction by Beverly Lyon Clark. New York: Oxford University Press, 1989.

Sherwood, Mrs. [Mary Martha]. *Robert and Frederick: A Book for Boys.* 18[4]2. London: Bohn, 1859.

Sherwood, Mrs. [Mary Martha] and Mrs. [Sophia] Kelly. *Boys Will Be Boys; or, The Difficulties of a Schoolboy's Life: A Schoolboy's Mission.* London: Darton, 1854.

Strickland, Susannah. *Hugh Latimer; or, The School-Boys' Friendship.* London: Dean, 1828.

Tales of the Academy. Vol. 1. [c. 1820]. Reprint, London: Cowie, 1825.

Thirkell, Angela. *The Headmistress.* New York: Knopf, 1945.

———. *Love Among the Ruins.* New York: Knopf, 1948.

———. *Summer Half.* 1937. Reprint, London: Hamish Hamilton, 1949.

Trevor, William. "Nice Day at School." Reprinted in *The Collected Stories.* New York: Viking, 1992. 154–167.

Tuer, Andrew W., ed. *Stories from Old-Fashioned Children's Books.* 1899–1900. Reprint, Detroit: Singing Tree, 1968.

[Tuthill, Louisa C.]. *The Boy of Spirit: A Story for the Young.* 1845. Reprint, Boston: Crosby, 1846.

Wakefield, Priscilla. "The Cautious Mother." In *Juvenile Anecdotes, Founded on Facts, Collected for the Amusement of Children.* 1798. 7th ed., 1825. Reprinted in Tuer 400–402.

———. "The Grateful School-Fellow." In *Juvenile Anecdotes, Founded on Facts, Collected for the Amusement of Children.* 1798. 7th ed., 1825. Reprinted in Tuer 396–398.

Wallace, Doreen. *Sons of Gentlemen.* 1953. Reprint, Leicester, UK: Ulverscroot, n.d.

Walpole, Hugh. *Jeremy at Crale: His Friends, His Ambitions and His One Great Enemy.* London: Cassell, 1927.

[Warner, Anna Bartlett]. *The Prince in Disguise.* [1862]. Reprint, London: Wesleyan Conference Office, [c. 1880].

Wells, H. G. *Joan and Peter: The Story of an Education.* New York: Macmillan, 1918.

Willson, D. Wynne. *Early Closing.* London: Constable, 1931.

Wilson, Colin. *The Schoolgirl Murder Case.* New York: Crown, 1974.

Wood, Mrs. Henry [Ellen]. *Orville College: A Tale.* 1867. Reprint, London: Bentley, 1890.

SECONDARY AND OTHER SOURCES

Aaron, Jane. *A Double Singleness: Gender and the Writings of Charles and Mary Lamb.* Oxford: Clarendon, 1991.

[Abbott, Edward]. Sketch. In *Abbott's Young Christian: A Memorial Edition.* With a Sketch of the Author by One of His Sons. New York: Harper, 1882. 1–109.

Adams, John R. *Edward Everett Hale.* Boston: Twayne, 1977.

Adams, Oscar Fay, ed. *A Dictionary of American Authors.* 5th ed. 1904. Reprint, Detroit: Gale, 1969.

Ake, Mary, et al. *A Canon of Children's Literature.* Children's Literature Assn., [1985].

Alcoff, Linda. "Cultural Feminism versus Post-Structuralism: The Identity Crisis in Feminist Theory." *Signs* 13 (1988): 405–436.

Alcott, Louisa May. "The Brothers." *Atlantic Monthly,* Nov. 1863. Reprinted in *Hospital Sketches and Camp and Fireside Stories.* Boston: Roberts, 1869.

———. *Little Women.* 1868. Reprint, with introduction by Ann Douglas. New York: Signet-Penguin, 1983.

———. "Transcendental Wild Oats." 1874. Reprinted in *Alternative Alcott.* Edited by Elaine Showalter. New Brunswick, NJ: Rutgers University Press, 1988. 364–379.

———. *Work: A Story of Experience.* Boston: Roberts, 1873.

Allibone, S. Austin. *A Critical Dictionary of English Literature and British and American Authors Living and Deceased from the Earliest Accounts to the Latter Half of the Nineteenth Century.* Philadelphia: Lippincott, 1870.

Anthony, Katherine. *The Lambs: A Story of Pre-Victorian England.* New York: Knopf, 1945.

Armstrong, Nancy. "The Occidental Alice." *differences* 2.2 (1990): 3–40.

Atwood, Margaret. *The Journals of Susanna Moodie: Poems.* Toronto: Oxford University Press, 1970.

Auden, W. H. "Honour." In Greene 9–20.

Auerbach, Nina. *Communities of Women: An Idea in Fiction.* Cambridge: Harvard University Press, 1978.

Avery, Gillian. *Behold the Child: American Children and Their Books 1621–1922.* Baltimore: Johns Hopkins University Press, 1994.

———. *Childhood's Pattern: A Study of the Heroes and Heroines of Children's Fiction, 1770–1950.* London: Hodder, 1975.

———. With the assistance of Angela Bull. *Nineteenth Century Children: Heroes and Heroines in English Children's Stories 1780–1900.* London: Hodder, 1965.

Avery, Gillian, and Julia Briggs, eds. *Children and Their Books: A Celebration of the Work of Iona and Peter Opie.* Foreword by Iona Opie. Oxford: Clarendon, 1989.

Baker, Theodore. *Baker's Biographical Dictionary of Musicians.* 6th ed. Revised by Nicolas Slonimsky. New York: Schirmer, 1978.

Banks, Elizabeth. *The Remaking of an American.* Garden City: Doubleday, 1928.

Banks, Elizabeth L. *The Autobiography of a "Newspaper Girl."* 2nd ed. London: Methuen, 1902.

Barry, Florence V. *A Century of Children's Books.* 1922. Reprint, Detroit: Singing Tree, 1968.

Bator, Robert. Headnote for *Mrs Leicester's School.* In *Middle Period.* Edited by Robert Bator. Vol. 4, c. 1740–c. 1836, of *Masterworks of Children's Literature.* New York: Stonehill, 1984. 281.

Belenky, Mary Field, Blythe McVicker Clinchy, Nancy Rule Goldberger, and Jill Mattuck Tarule. *Women's Ways of Knowing: The Development of Self, Voice, and Mind.* New York: Basic, 1986.

Belsey, Catherine, and Jane Moore, eds. *The Feminist Reader: Essays in Gender and the Politics of Literary Criticism.* New York: Blackwell, 1989.

Benson, Theodora. "Hot-Water-Bottle Love." In Greene 35–44.

Benstock, Shari. *Women of the Left Bank: Paris, 1900–1940.* Austin: University of Texas Press, 1986.

Berners, [Gerald] Lord. *A Distant Prospect.* London: Constable, 1945.

———. *First Childhood.* New York: Farrar, 1934.

Betham-Edwards, M. *Reminiscences.* Rev. ed. London: Unit Library, 1903.

Betham-Edwards, Matilda. *Mid-Victorian Memories.* With a Personal Sketch by Sarah Grand. New York: Macmillan, 1919.

Bhabha, Homi. "Of Mimicry and Man: The Ambivalence of Colonial Discourse." *October* 28 (1984): 125–133.

Billman, Carol. "Edward Everett Hale." In Estes 197–203.

Black, Linda. "Louisa May Alcott's 'Huckleberry Finn.'" *Mark Twain Journal* 21.2 (Summer 1982): 15–17.

Blackburn, William. "'Moral Pap for the Young'? A New Look at Louisa May Alcott's *Little Men.*" *Proceedings of the Seventh Annual Conference of the Children's Literature Association.* Baylor University, March 1980. Edited by Priscilla A. Ord. [New Rochelle]: [Iona College], 1982. 98–106.

Boles, John B. "Jacob Abbott and the Rollo Books: New England Culture for Children." *Journal of Popular Culture* 3 (1973): 507–528.

Bond, Donald F., ed. *The Spectator.* Vol 1. Oxford: Clarendon, 1965.

"Books for Boys and Girls." *Literary World,* Nov. 1877, 94.

Botume, Elizabeth Hyde. *First Days Amongst the Contrabands.* 1893. Reprint, New York: Arno, 1968.

Boyarin, Daniel. "Paul and the Genealogy of Gender." *Representations* 41 (1993): 1–33.

Brantlinger, Patrick. *Rule of Darkness: British Literature and Imperialism, 1830–1914.* Ithaca: Cornell University Press, 1988.

———. "What Is 'Sensational' about the 'Sensation Novel'?" *Nineteenth-Century Fiction* 37 (1982): 1–28.

Briggs, Julia. "Reading Children's Books." *Essays in Criticism* 39 (1989): 1–17.

———. "Women Writers and Writing for Children: From Sarah Fielding to E. Nesbit." In Avery and Briggs 221–250.

Brinnin, John Malcolm. *The Third Rose: Gertrude Stein and Her World.* Boston: Little, 1959.

Bristow, Joseph. *Empire Boys: Adventures in a Man's World.* London: Harper, 1991.

Brodhead, Richard H. "Sparing the Rod: Discipline and Fiction in Antebellum America." *Representations* 21 (1988): 67–96.

Burdan, Judith. "Girls *Must* Be Seen *and* Heard: Domestic Surveillance in Sarah Fielding's *The Governess.*" *Children's Literature Association Quarterly* 19.1 (1994): 8–14.

Burstyn, Joan N. *Victorian Education and the Ideal of Womanhood.* London: Croom, 1980.

Bushman, Richard L. *The Refinement of America: Persons, Houses, Cities.* New York: Knopf, 1992.

Butler, Marilyn. *Maria Edgeworth: A Literary Biography.* Oxford: Clarendon, 1972.

Cadogan, Mary. "Absolute Mascots: Bessie Bunter and Co." In Cadogan, *Chin Up* 35–44.

———, ed. *Chin Up, Chest Out, Jemima!* Haslemere, UK: Bonnington, 1989.

———. "Eighty Years of the Spiffing Schoolgirl." In Cadogan, *Chin Up* 9–20.

Cadogan, Mary, and Patricia Craig. *You're a Brick, Angela! The Girls' Story 1839 to 1985.* Rev. ed. London: Gollancz, 1986.

Calvert, George H. *The Gentleman.* 1863. 3rd ed. Boston: Dutton, 1866.

Carnes, Mark C., and Clyde Griffen, eds. *Meanings for Manhood: Constructions of Masculinity in Victorian America.* Chicago: University of Chicago Press, 1990.

Carpenter, Humphrey, and Mari Prichard. *The Oxford Companion to Children's Literature.* Oxford: Oxford University Press, 1984.

Catano, James V. "The Rhetoric of Masculinity: Origins, Institutions, and the Myth of the Self-Made Man." *College English* 52 (1990): 421–436.

Cathcart, Rex. "Festive Capers? Barring-Out the Schoolmaster." *History Today,* Dec. 1988, 49–53.

Cawelti, John G. *Apostles of the Self-Made Man.* Chicago: University of Chicago Press, 1965.

Chevalier, Jean-Louis, ed. *Rencontres avec Iris Murdoch.* Caen: Université de Caen, 1978.

Chodorow, Nancy. *The Reproduction of Mothering: Psychoanalysis and the Sociology of Gender.* Berkeley: University of California Press, 1978.

Christian, Barbara. "The Race for Theory." *Cultural Critique* 6 (1987). Revised and reprinted in *Gender and Theory: Dialogues on Feminist Criticism.* Edited by Linda Kauffman. Oxford: Blackwell, 1989. 225–237.

———. "Shadows Uplifted." In *Black Women Novelists: The Development of a Tradition, 1892–1976.* 1980. Reprinted in *Feminist Criticism and Social Change: Sex, Class and Race in Literature and Culture.* Edited by Judith Newton and Deborah Rosenfelt. New York: Methuen, 1985. 181–215.

Cixous, Hélène. "Sorties: Out and Out: Attacks/Ways Out/Forays." In *La Jeune née.* 1975. *The Newly Born Woman.* Translated by Betsy Wing. 1986. Reprinted in Belsey and Moore 101–116, 229–230.

Clark, Beverly Lyon. "Fairy Godmothers or Wicked Stepmothers? The Uneasy Relationship of Feminist Theory and Children's Criticism." *Children's Literature Association Quarterly* 18.4 (1993): 171–176.

———. "Heading the Class of the School Story: Three Lost Works." *Junior Bookshelf* 56 (1992): 47–50.

———. Introduction. *The Making of a Schoolgirl.* By Evelyn Sharp. New York: Oxford University Press, 1989. 3–23.

———. "Not for Children Only." *Wheaton Quarterly,* Fall 1989. Revised and reprinted as "Books for Children Deserve to Be Part of Literary Studies." *Chronicle of Higher Education,* 17 Oct. 1990, B2–B3.

———. "A Portrait of the Artist as a Little Woman." *Children's Literature* 17 (1989): 81–97.

———. "Reconstructing Dorothy Kilner: Anecdotes as Antidotes." *Children's Literature Association Quarterly* 14.2 (1989): 58–63.

———. "Thirteen Ways of Thumbing Your Nose at Children's Literature." *The Lion and the Unicorn* 16 (1992): 240–244.

Collins, Laura Roberts. *English Country Life in the Barsetshire Novels of Angela Thirkell.* Westport, CT: Greenwood, 1994.

Coolidge, Susan. "Holiday Books for Children." *Literary World,* Jan. 1878, 143.

Costa, Richard Hauer. *H. G. Wells.* New York: Twayne, 1967.

Courtney, Winifred F. "*Mrs Leicester's School* as Children's Literature." *Charles Lamb Bulletin* n.s. 47–48 (1984): 164–169.

Crandall, George W. "Emperors and Little Empires: The Schoolmaster in Nineteenth-Century American Literature." *Studies in American Humor* 5 (1986): 51–61.

Crowley, John W. "*Little Women* and the Boy-Book." *New England Quarterly* 58 (1985): 384–399.

Cutt, M. Nancy. *Mrs. Sherwood and Her Books for Children.* With Facsimile Reproductions of *The Little Woodman and His Dog Caesar* and *Soffrona and Her Cat Muff.* London: Oxford University Press, 1974.

Darling, Richard L. "Children's Books Following the Civil War." In *Books in America's Past: Essays Honoring Rudolph H. Gjelsness.* Edited by David Kaser.

Charlottesville: University Press of Virginia, 1966. 64–84.

———. *The Rise of Children's Book Reviewing in America, 1865–1881.* New York: Bowker, 1968.

Darton, F. J. Harvey. *Children's Books in England: Five Centuries of Social Life.* 3rd ed. Revised by Brian Alderson. Cambridge: Cambridge University Press, 1982.

———, ed. *The Life and Times of Mrs. Sherwood (1775–1851): From the Diaries of Captain and Mrs. Sherwood.* London: Wells, 1910.

Davie, Donald. "Maria Edgeworth." In *The Heyday of Sir Walter Scott.* London: Routledge, 1961. 65–77.

Davis, Angela. "Reflections on the Black Woman's Role in the Community of Slaves." *Black Scholar,* Dec. 1971, 2–15.

Demers, Patricia. "Mrs. Sherwood and Hesba Stretton: The Letter and the Spirit of Evangelical Writing of and for Children." In McGavran 129–149.

D'Emilio, John. "Capitalism and Gay Identity." In *Powers of Desire: The Politics of Sexuality.* Edited by Ann Snitow, Christine Stansell, and Sharon Thompson. New York: Monthly Review, 1983. 100–113.

Demos, John. *Past, Present, and Personal: The Family and the Life Course in American History.* Oxford: Oxford University Press, 1986.

Denning, Michael. *Mechanic Accents: Dime Novels and Working-Class Culture in America.* London: Verso, 1987.

Derrida, Jacques. "The Law of Genre." Translated by Avital Ronell. *Glyph* 7 (1980): 202–232.

———. "Limited Inc abc . . ." Translated by Samuel Weber. *Glyph* 2 (1977): 162–254.

Dhingra, Lavina. "The Making of Schoolgirls: Girls' School Fiction of the Nineteenth and Twentieth Century." Senior thesis, Wheaton College, 1989.

Diffley, Kathleen. "Where My Heart Is Turning Ever: Civil War Stories and National Stability from Fort Sumter to the Centennial." *American Literary History* 2 (1990): 627–658.

Dipple, Elizabeth. *Iris Murdoch: Work for the Spirit.* Chicago: University of Chicago Press, 1982.

Douglas, Ann. *The Feminization of American Culture.* 1977. Reprint, New York: Discus-Avon, 1978.

———. Introduction. *Little Women.* By Louisa May Alcott. New York: Signet-Penguin, 1983. vii–xxvii.

Downs-Miers, Deborah. "For Betty and the Little Female Academy: A Book of Their Own." *Children's Literature Association Quarterly* 10.1 (1985): 30–33.

Drotner, Kirsten. *English Children and Their Magazines, 1751–1945.* New Haven: Yale University Press, 1988.

———. "Schoolgirls, Madcaps, and Air Aces: English Girls and Their Magazine Reading Between the Wars." *Feminist Studies* 9.1 (1983): 33–52.

Duberman, Martin Bauml. "'Writhing Bedfellows' in Antebellum South Carolina: Historical Interpretation and the Politics of Evidence." In Duberman et al. 153–163, 513–515.

Duberman, Martin Bauml, Martha Vicinus, and George Chauncey, Jr., eds. *Hidden from History: Reclaiming the Gay and Lesbian Past.* New York: New American Library, 1989.

Dunae, Patrick A., "Boys' Literature and the Idea of Race: 1870–1900." *Wascana Review* 12 (1977): 84–107.

"Editor's Literary Record." *Harper's New Monthly Magazine,* Jan. 1878, 308–311.

Eiloart, Mrs. [Elizabeth]. *[Ernie Elton, the Lazy Boy].* [1865]. Reprinted in *Ernie Elton at Home and at School.* London: Routledge, n.d.

Elbert, Sarah. *A Hunger for Home: Louisa May Alcott and* Little Women. Philadelphia: Temple University Press, 1984.

Eliot, George [Mary Ann Evans]. *The Mill on the Floss.* [1860]. Reprint, New York: Pocket, 1956.

Ellis, Havelock. *Sexual Inversion.* Vol. 2 of *Studies in the Psychology of Sex.* 3rd ed. 1915. Reprint, Philadelphia: Davis, 1922.

Emerson, Ralph Waldo. "Self-Reliance." 1841. Reprinted in Lauter et al. 1: 1511–1528.

Erisman, Fred. "The Strenuous Life in Practice: The School and Sports Stories of Ralph Henry Barbour." *Rocky Mountain Social Science Journal* 7 (1970): 29–37.

Estes, Glenn E., ed. *American Writers for Children Before 1900.* Vol. 42 of *Dictionary of Literary Biography.* Detroit: Gale, 1985.

Evans, Walter. "The All-American Boys: A Study of Boys' Sports Fiction." *Journal of Popular Culture* 6 (1972): 104–121.

Eyre, Frank. *British Children's Books in the Twentieth Century.* Rev. ed. London: Longman, 1971.

Faderman, Lillian. *Surpassing the Love of Men: Romantic Friendship and Love Between Women from the Renaissance to the Present.* New York: Morrow, 1981.

Ferguson, Kathy E. "Interpretation and Genealogy in Feminism." *Signs* 16 (1991): 322–339.

Fiedler, Leslie A. *Love and Death in the American Novel.* 1960. Rev. ed., 1966. Reprint, New York: Stein, 1975.

———. *No! In Thunder: Essays on Myth and Literature.* 2nd ed. 1971. Reprint, New York: Stein, 1972.

Fisher, Margery. *Intent upon Reading: A Critical Appraisal of Modern Fiction for Children.* 1961. Reprint, New York: Watts, 1962.

Fitzgerald, James Edmund. Letter. *The Times,* 20 Dec. 1865, 6.

Fletcher, Sheila. *Feminists and Bureaucrats: A Study in the Development of Girls' Education in the Nineteenth Century.* Cambridge: Cambridge University Press, 1980.

Foster, Edward Halsey. *Susan and Anna Warner.* Boston: Twayne, n.d.

Foucault, Michel. *Discipline and Punish: The Birth of the Prison.* 1975. Translated by Alan Sheridan. 1977. Reprint, New York: Vintage-Random, 1979.

Fox-Genovese, Elizabeth. *Within the Plantation Household: Black and White Women of the Old South.* Chapel Hill: University of North Carolina Press, 1988.

Freeman, Gillian. *The Schoolgirl Ethic: The Life and Work of Angela Brazil.* London: Lane, 1976.

Freud, Sigmund. "Three Contributions to the Theory of Sex." In *The Basic Writings of Sigmund Freud.* Translated by and edited by A. A. Brill. New York: Modern Library, 1938. 551–629.

Friedman, Susan Stanford. "Post/Poststructuralist Feminist Criticism: The Politics of Recuperation and Negotiation." *New Literary History* 22 (1991): 465–490.

Frith, Gill. "'The time of your life': The Meaning of the School Story." In *Language, Gender and Childhood.* Edited by Carolyn Steedman, Cathy Urwin, and Valerie Walkerdine. London: Routledge, 1985. 113–136.

Garber, Marjorie. *Vested Interests: Cross-Dressing and Cultural Anxiety.* New York: Routledge, 1992.

Gates, Henry Louis, Jr. *Figures in Black: Words, Signs, and the "Racial" Self.* New York: Oxford University Press, 1987.

Gay, Carol. "Jacob Abbott." In Estes 3–11.

Geller, Evelyn. "Tom Sawyer, Tom Bailey, and the Bad-Boy Genre." *Wilson Library Bulletin,* Nov. 1976, 245–250.

Gerstenberger, Donna. *Iris Murdoch.* Lewisburg: Bucknell University Press, 1975.

Gilbert, Sandra M. "Costumes of the Mind: Transvestism as Metaphor in Modern Literature." *Critical Inquiry* 7 (1980): 391–417.

Gilbert, Sandra M., and Susan Gubar. *The Madwoman in the Attic: The Woman Writer and the Nineteenth-Century Literary Imagination.* New Haven: Yale University Press, 1979.

———. "Sexchanges." *College English* 50 (1988): 768–785.

Gillespie, Joanna. "An Almost Irresistible Enginery: Five Decades of Nineteenth Century Methodist Sunday School Library Books." *Phaedrus*, Spring/Summer 1980, 5–12.

Gillespie, Joanna. "Schooling through Fiction." *Children's Literature* 14 (1986): 61–81.

Gilligan, Carol. *In a Different Voice: Psychological Theory and Women's Development*. Cambridge: Harvard University Press, 1982.

Girouard, Mary. "Lord Berners." In *The British Eccentric*. Edited by Harriet Bridgeman and Elizabeth Drury. London: Joseph, 1975. 9–22.

Godkin, Edwin Lawrence. "Chromo-Civilization." *The Nation*. Reprinted in *Reflections and Comments 1865–1895*. Westminster, UK: Constable, 1896. 192–205.

Green, Martin. *Dreams of Adventure, Deeds of Empire*. New York: Basic, 1979.

———. "The Robinson Crusoe Story." In *Imperialism and Juvenile Literature*. Edited by Jeffrey Richards. Manchester, UK: Manchester University Press, 1989. 34–52.

Greene, Grahame, ed. *The Old School: Essays by Divers Hands*. London: Cape, 1934.

Grey, Jill E. Introduction. *The Governess; or, Little Female Academy*. By Sarah Fielding. London: Oxford University Press, 1968. 1–82.

Griffen, Clyde. "Reconstructing Masculinity from the Evangelical Revival to the Waning of Progressivism: A Speculative Synthesis." In Carnes and Griffen 183–204, 265–271.

Grimké, Charlotte Forten. "A Teacher from the North." In *The Journal of Charlotte Forten*. 1961. Reprinted in *Black Women in White America: A Documentary History*. Edited by Gerda Lerner. New York: Vintage-Random, 1973. 94–99.

Gubar, Susan. "Blessings in Disguise: Cross-Dressing as Re-Dressing for Female Modernists." *Massachusetts Review* 22 (1981): 477–508.

Hale, Edward E., Jr. *The Life and Letters of Edward Everett Hale*. Vol. 2. Boston: Little, 1917.

[Hale, Edward Everett]. "Education of the Freedmen." *North American Review* 101 (1865): 528–549.

Hale, Edward Everett. *A New England Boyhood*. [1893]. Reprinted in *A New England Boyhood and Other Bits of Autobiography*. Vol. 6 of *The Works of Edward Everett Hale*. Boston: Little, 1910. 1–208.

———. *Ten Times One Is Ten*. 1870. Reprinted in *Ten Times One Is Ten and Other Stories*. Vol. 3 of *The Works of Edward Everett Hale*. Boston: Little, 1899.

———. "Where Shall Polly Go to School?" *Cosmopolitan*, May 1892, 111–115.

Halttunen, Karen. *Confidence Men and Painted Women: A Study of Middle-Class Culture in America, 1830–1870*. New Haven: Yale University Press, 1982.

Hamblen, Abigail Ann. "The Divided World of Louisa May Alcott." In *Webs and Wardrobes: Humanist and Religious World Views in Children's Literature*. Edited by Joseph O'Beirne Milner and Lucy Floyd Morcock Milner. Lanham: University Press of America, 1987. 57–64.

———. "Louisa May Alcott and the 'Revolution' in Education." *Journal of General Education* 22 (1970): 81–92.

[Hamilton, Charles]. *The Autobiography of Frank Richards*. London: Skilton, 1952.

Hansot, Elisabeth, and David Tyack. "Gender in American Public Schools: Thinking Institutionally." *Signs* 13 (1988): 741–760.

Haraway, Donna. "Situated Knowledges: The Science Question in Feminism and the Privilege of Partial Perspective." In *Simians, Cyborgs, and Women*. New York: Routledge, 1991. 183–201.

Harden, Elizabeth. *Maria Edgeworth*. Boston: Twayne, 1984.

Hendler, Glenn. "Tom Sawyer's Masculinity." *Arizona Quarterly* 49.4 (1993): 33–59.

Hildebrand, Ann Meinzen. "The Dreary Time: The Ethos of School in Award-Winning Fiction for Children, 1960–1980." *Children's Literature Association Quarterly* 11.2 (1986): 82–85.

Holloway, Jean. *Edward Everett Hale: A Biography*. Austin: University of Texas Press, 1956.

Honey, J. R. de S. *Tom Brown's Universe: The Development of the English Public School in the Nineteenth Century*. New York: Quadrangle, 1977.

Howarth, Patrick. *Play Up and Play the Game: The Heroes of Popular Fiction*. London: Eyre, 1973.

Hughes, Felicity A. "Children's Literature: Theory and Practice." *ELH* 45 (1978): 542–561.

Hughes, Winifred. *The Maniac in the Cellar: Sensation Novels of the 1860s*. Princeton: Princeton University Press, 1980.

Hulme, Peter. *Colonial Encounters: Europe and the Native Caribbean, 1492–1797*. 1986. Reprint, London: Routledge, 1992.

Hunter, Jim. "Mark Twain and the Boy-Book in Nineteenth-Century America." *College English* 24 (1963): 430–438.

Hurston, Zora Neale. *Their Eyes Were Watching God*. 1937. Reprinted with Foreword by Sherley Anne Williams. Urbana: University of Illinois Press, 1978.

Inglis, Fred. *The Promise of Happiness: Value and Meaning in Children's Fiction*. Cambridge: Cambridge University Press, 1981.

Irigaray, Luce. "Ce sexe qui n'en est pas un." 1977. Translated by Claudia Reeder. In *New French Feminisms: An Anthology*. Edited by Elaine Marks and Isabelle de Courtivron. Amherst: University of Massachusetts Press, 1980. 99–106.

Jackson, Mary V. *Engines of Instruction, Mischief, and Magic: Children's Literature in England from Its Beginnings to 1839*. Lincoln: University of Nebraska Press, 1989.

James, Louis. "Tom Brown's Imperialist Sons." *Victorian Studies* 17 (1973): 89–99.

Jameson, Fredric. *Marxism and Form: Twentieth-Century Dialectical Theories of Literature*. Princeton: Princeton University Press, 1971.

———. *The Political Unconscious: Narrative as a Socially Symbolic Act*. Ithaca: Cornell University Press, 1981.

———. "Towards a New Awareness of Genre." *Science-Fiction Studies* 9 (1982): 322–324.

Jan, Isabelle. *On Children's Literature*. 1969. Translated by Catherine Storr. Preface by Anne Pellowski. New York: Schocken, 1974.

Johnson, Barbara. *A World of Difference*. Baltimore: Johns Hopkins University Press, 1987.

Johnson, Deborah. *Iris Murdoch*. Bloomington: Indiana University Press, 1987.

Jones, Jacqueline. *Labor of Love, Labor of Sorrow: Black Women, Work, and the Family from Slavery to the Present*. 1985. Reprint, New York: Vintage-Random, 1986.

———. *Soldiers of Light and Love: Northern Teachers and Georgia Blacks, 1865–1873*. Chapel Hill: University of North Carolina Press, 1980.

———. "Women Who Were More Than Men: Sex and Status in Freedmen's Teaching." *History of Education Quarterly* 19 (1979): 47–59.

Jordan, Philip D. "A New Look at Some 'Bad Boys.'" *Books at Iowa*, April 1977, 19–34.

Jump, J.D. "Weekly Reviewing in the Eighteen-Sixties." *Review of English Studies* n.s. 3 (1952): 244–262.

Kahn, Madeleine. *Narrative Transvestism: Rhetoric and Gender in the Eighteenth-Century English Novel*. Ithaca: Cornell University Press, 1991.

Kaplan, Cora. "Pandora's Box: Subjectivity, Class and Sexuality in Socialist Feminist Criticism." In *Making a Difference*. Edited by Gayle Greene and Coppélia Kahn. 1985. Reprinted in *Sea Changes: Essays on Culture and Feminism*. London: Verso, 1986. 147–176.

Keith, Sara. "Gruesome Examples for Children: The Real Purpose of Mr. Fairchild." *Notes and Queries* 210 (1965): 184–185.

Kelly, R. Gordon. *Mother Was a Lady: Self and Society in Selected American Children's Periodicals 1865–1890*. Westport, CT: Greenwood, 1974.

Kelly, Sophia, ed. *The Life of Mrs. Sherwood (Chiefly Autobiographical), with Extracts from Mr. Sherwood's Journal during His Imprisonment in France and Residence in India*. London: Darton, 1857.

Kerber, Linda K. "Separate Spheres, Female Worlds, Woman's Place: The Rhetoric of Women's History." *Journal of American History* 75 (1988): 9–39.

Keyser, Elizabeth Lennox. *Whispers in the Dark: The Fiction of Louisa May Alcott*. Knoxville: University of Tennessee Press, 1993.

Kilgour, Raymond L. *Messrs. Roberts Brothers Publishers*. Ann Arbor: University of Michigan Press, 1952.

Kilner, Dorothy. *The Life and Perambulation of a Mouse*. 1783–1784. Reprinted in *Middle Period*. Edited by Robert Bator. Vol. 4, c. 1740–c. 1836, of *Masterworks of Children's Literature*. New York: Stonehill, 1984. 221–270.

Kirk, John Foster. *A Supplement to Allibone's Critical Dictionary of English Literature and British and American Authors*. Philadelphia: Lippincott, 1891.

Knoepflmacher, U. C. "The Balancing of Child and Adult: An Approach to Victorian Fantasies for Children." *Nineteenth-Century Fiction* 37 (1983): 497–530.

Kowaleski-Wallace, Beth. "Milton's Daughters: The Education of Eighteenth-Century Women Writers." *Feminist Studies* 12.2 (1986): 275–293.

Kristeva, Julia. "Women's Time." Translated by Alice Jardine and Harry Blake. *Signs* 7 (1981). Revised and reprinted in Belsey and Moore 197–217, 240–242.

Kunitz, Stanley J., and Howard Haycraft, eds. *Twentieth Century Authors: A Biographical Dictionary of Modern Literature*. New York: Wilson, 1942.

Laird, Susan. "The Ideal of the Educated Teacher—'Reclaiming a Conversation' with Louisa May Alcott." *Curriculum Inquiry* 21 (1991): 271–297.

Lauter, Paul, et al., eds. *The Heath Anthology of American Literature*. 2 vols. Lexington: Heath, 1990.

Lawrence, George. *Guy Livingstone*. 1857. Reprinted with an introduction by Sheila Kaye-Smith. New York: Stokes, [1928].

Leonardi, Susan J. *Dangerous by Degrees: Women at Oxford and the Somerville College Novelists*. New Brunswick, NJ: Rutgers University Press, 1989.

Lesnik-Oberstein, Karín. *Children's Literature: Criticism and the Fictional Child*. Oxford: Clarendon, 1994.

Levi-Strauss, Claude. *The Raw and the Cooked*. Translated by John and Doreen Weightman. 1969. Reprint, New York: Harper, 1975.

Loesberg, Jonathan. "The Ideology of Narrative Form in Sensation Fiction." *Representations* 13 (1986): 115–138.

Lofts, W. O. G., and D. J. Adley. *The Men Behind Boys' Fiction*. London: Baker, 1970.

———. *The World of Frank Richards*. London: Baker, 1975.

Lucas, E. V., ed. *The Works of Charles and Mary Lamb*. 7 vols. New York: Putnam, 1903.

Lurie, Alison. *Don't Tell the Grown-Ups: Subversive Children's Literature*. Boston: Little, Brown, 1990.

MacDonald, Ruth K. *Louisa May Alcott*. Boston: Twayne, 1983.

Mack, Edward C. *Public Schools and British Opinion 1780 to 1860: An Examination of the Relationship between Contemporary Ideas and the Evolution of an English Institution*. London: Methuen, 1938.

———. *Public Schools and British Opinion Since 1860: The Relationship between Contemporary Ideas and the Evolution of an English Institution*. New York: Columbia University Press, 1941.

MacLeod, Anne Scott. *American Childhood: Essays on Children's Literature of the Nineteenth and Twentieth Centuries*. Athens: University of Georgia Press, 1994.

———. *A Moral Tale: Children's Fiction and American Culture 1820–1860*. Hamden: Archon-Shoe String, 1975.

Maison, Margaret M. "Tom Brown and Company: Scholastic Novels of the 1850s." *English* 12 (1958): 100–103.

Mangan, J. A. *Athleticism in the Victorian and Edwardian Public School: The Emergence and Consolidation of an Educational Ideology.* Cambridge: Cambridge University Press, 1981.

"Maori Sketches." *Cornhill Magazine* 12 (1865): 498–512.

Marquis, Claudia. "Among the Cannibals: Early Adventurers in New Zealand." Unpublished ms.

Marrs, Edwin W., Jr., ed. *The Letters of Charles and Mary Anne Lamb.* 3 vols. Ithaca: Cornell University Press, 1975–1978.

Marsden, Jean I. "Letters on a Tombstone: Mothers and Literacy in Mary Lamb's *Mrs. Leicester's School.*" *Children's Literature* 23 (1995): 31–44.

———. "Shakespeare for Girls: Mary Lamb and *Tales from Shakespeare.*" *Children's Literature* 17 (1989): 47–63.

Marsh, Margaret. "Suburban Men and Masculine Domesticity, 1870–1915." *American Quarterly* (1988). Reprinted in Carnes and Griffen 111–128.

Martin, Jane Roland. *The Schoolhome: Rethinking Schools for Changing Families.* Cambridge: Harvard University Press, 1992.

Martin, Robert K. "Knights-Errant and Gothic Seducers: The Representation of Male Friendship in Mid-Nineteenth-Century America." In Duberman et al. 169–82, 515–17.

Mathews, Julia A. *Our Four Boys.* [1872]. Dare to Do Right Series, vol. 2. Reprint, New York: Carter, 1881.

McCurry, Niki Alpert. "Concepts of Childrearing and Schooling in the March Novels of Louisa May Alcott." Dissertation, Northwestern University, 1976.

McGavran, James Holt, Jr., ed. *Romanticism and Children's Literature in Nineteenth-Century England.* Athens: University of Georgia Press, 1991.

McKeon, Michael. *The Origins of the English Novel 1600–1740.* Baltimore: Johns Hopkins University Press, 1987.

Merchant, Peter. "'Fresh Instruction o'er the Mind': Exploit and Example in Victorian Fiction." *Children's Literature in Education* 20 (1989): 9–24.

Michie, Helena. *The Flesh Made Word: Female Figures and Women's Bodies.* New York: Oxford University Press, 1987.

Miller, Nancy K. "Emphasis Added: Plots and Plausibilities in Women's Fiction." *PMLA* 96 (1981): 36–48.

Mitchell, Sally. "Children's Reading and the Culture of Girlhood: The Case of L. T. Meade." *Browning Institute Studies* 17 (1989): 53–63.

———. *The Fallen Angel: Chastity, Class, and Women's Reading, 1835–1880.* Bowling Green: Bowling Green University Popular Press, 1981.

———. Introduction. *East Lynne.* By Mrs. Henry Wood. New Brunswick, NJ: Rutgers University Press, 1984. i–xviii.

Moi, Toril. *Sexual/Textual Politics: Feminist Literary Theory.* London: Methuen, 1985.

Moon, Michael. "'The Gentle Boy from the Dangerous Classes': Pederasty, Domesticity, and Capitalism in Horatio Alger." *Representations* 19 (1987): 87–110.

Moore, Jane. "Promises, Promises: The Fictional Philosophy in Mary Wollstonecraft's *Vindication of the Rights of Woman.*" In Belsey and Moore 155–173, 233–237.

Murphy, Ann B. "The Borders of Ethical, Erotic, and Artistic Possibilities in *Little Women.*" *Signs* 15 (1990): 562–585.

Murray, Patrick. "Maria Edgeworth and her Father: The Literary Partnership." *Eire-Ireland* 6.3 (1971): 39–50.

———. *Maria Edgeworth: A Study of the Novelist.* Cork, UK: Mercier, 1971.

Musgrave, P. W. *From Brown to Bunter: The Life and Death of the School Story.* London: Routledge, 1985.

Myers, Mitzi. "The Dilemmas of Gender as Double-Voiced Narrative; or, Maria Edgeworth Mothers the Bildungsroman." In *The Idea of the Novel in the Eigh-*

teenth Century. Edited by Robert W. Uphaus. East Lansing, MI: Colleagues, 1988. 67–96.

———. "The Erotics of Pedagogy: Historical Intervention, Literary Representation, the 'Gift of Education,' and the Agency of Children." *Children's Literature* 23 (1995): 1–30.

———. "Impeccable Governesses, Rational Dames, and Moral Mothers: Mary Wollstonecraft and the Female Tradition in Georgian Children's Books." *Children's Literature* 14 (1986): 31–59.

———. "Reading Rosamond Reading: Maria Edgeworth's 'Wee-Wee Stories' Interrogate the Canon." In *Infant Tongues: The Voice of the Child in Literature.* Edited by Elizabeth Goodenough, Mark A. Heberle, and Naomi Sokoloff. Detroit: Wayne State University Press, 1994. 57–79.

———. "Romancing the Moral Tale: Maria Edgeworth and the Problematics of Pedagogy." In McGavran 96–128.

———. "Socializing Rosamond: Educational Ideology and Fictional Form." *Children's Literature Association Quarterly* 14.2 (1989): 52–58.

———. "'A Taste for Truth and Realities': Early Advice to Mothers on Books for Girls." *Children's Literature Association Quarterly* 12.3 (1987): 118–124.

Nelson, Claudia. *Boys Will Be Girls: The Feminine Ethic and British Children's Fiction, 1857–1917.* New Brunswick, NJ: Rutgers University Press, 1991.

———. "Sex and the Single Boy: Ideals of Manliness and Sexuality in Victorian Literature for Boys." *Victorian Studies* 32 (1989): 525–550.

"New Zealand." *The Times*, 16 Sept. 1865, 9.

Newby, P.H. *Maria Edgeworth*. London: Barker, 1950.

Newsome, David. *Godliness and Good Learning: Four Studies on a Victorian Ideal.* London: Murray, 1961.

Newton, Judith. "Making—and Remaking—History: Another Look at 'Patriarchy.'" *Tulsa Studies in Women's Literature* 3 (1984–1985). Reprinted in *Feminist Issues in Literary Scholarship.* Edited by Shari Benstock. Bloomington: Indiana University Press, 1987. 124–140.

Nichols, Beverley. *The Sweet and Twenties.* London: Weidenfeld, 1958.

[Nodelman, Perry, ed.]. *Touchstones: Reflections on the Best in Children's Literature.* 3 vols. W. Lafayette, IN: Children's Literature Assn., 1985–1989.

Noel, Thomas. *Theories of the Fable in the Eighteenth Century.* New York: Columbia University Press, 1975.

Obituary of Joanna Ho[o]e Mathews. *New York Times*, 30 April 1901, 9.

O'Brien, Sharon. "Tomboyism and Adolescent Conflict: Three Nineteenth-Century Case Studies." In *Woman's Being, Woman's Place: Female Identity and Vocation in American History.* Edited by Mary Kelley. Boston: Hall, 1979. 351–372.

[Oliphant, Margaret]. "Sensation Novels." *Blackwood's*, May 1862, 564–584.

Omasreiter, Ria. "Maria Edgeworth's Tales: A Contribution to the Science of Happiness." In *Functions of Literature: Essays Presented to Erwin Wolff on his Sixtieth Birthday.* Edited by Ulrich Broich, Theo Stemmler, and Gerd Stratmann. Tübingen: Niemeyer, 1984. 195–208.

Orwell, George. "Boys' Weeklies." *Horizon* (1940). Revised and reprinted in *An Age Like This 1920–1940.* Vol. 1 of *The Collected Essays, Journalism and Letters of George Orwell.* Edited by Sonia Orwell and Ian Angus. New York: Harcourt, 1968. 460–484.

———. "'Such, Such Were the Joys . . .'" *Partisan Review* (1952). In *Such, Such Were the Joys.* New York: Harcourt, 1953. 12–63.

Osborne, Edgar. "In Defence of the School Story." *Junior Bookshelf*, July 1947, 62–69.

Pearson, Elizabeth Ware, ed. *Letters from Port Royal: Written at the Time of the Civil War.* Boston: Clarke, 1906.

Pedersen, Joyce Senders. *The Reform of Girls' Secondary and Higher Education in*

Victorian England: A Study of Elites and Educational Change. New York: Garland, 1987.

———. "The Reform of Women's Secondary and Higher Education: Institutional Change and Social Values in Mid and Late Victorian England." *History of Education Quarterly* 19 (1979): 61–91.

Petzold, Dieter. "Breaking in the Colt: Socialization in Nineteenth-Century School Stories." *Children's Literature Association Quarterly* 15.1 (1990): 17–21.

Pickering, Samuel, Jr. "Allegory and the First School Stories." *Opening Texts: Psychoanalysis and the Culture of the Child.* Edited by Joseph H. Smith and William Kerrigan. Baltimore: Johns Hopkins University Press, 1985. 42–68.

Pickering, Samuel F., Jr. *John Locke and Children's Books in Eighteenth-Century England.* Knoxville: University of Tennessee Press, 1981.

———. *Moral Instruction and Fiction for Children, 1749–1820.* Athens: University of Georgia Press, 1993.

Pleck, Elizabeth H., and Joseph H. Pleck, eds. *The American Man.* Englewood Cliffs, NJ: Prentice-Hall, 1980.

Pleck, Elizabeth and Joseph H. Pleck. Introduction. In Pleck and Pleck, American Man 1–49.

Pollard, M. "Maria Edgeworth's *The Parent's Assistant*: The First Edition." *The Book Collector* 20 (1971): 347–351.

Poovey, Mary. "Cultural Criticism: Past and Present." *College English* 52 (1990): 615–625.

———. *Uneven Developments: The Ideological Work of Gender in Mid-Victorian England.* Chicago: University of Chicago Press, 1988.

Population Schedules of the Eighth Census of the United States 1860. Washington, DC: National Archives, 1967.

Postlethwaite, Diana. "Mothering and Mesmerism in the Life of Harriet Martineau." *Signs* 14 (1989): 583–609.

Price, Lawrence Marsden, ed. *Inkle and Yarico Album.* Berkeley: University of California Press, 1937.

Protherough, Robert. "'True' and 'False' in School Fiction." *British Journal of Educational Studies* 27 (1979): 140–153.

Quigly, Isabel. *The Heirs of Tom Brown: The English School Story.* London: Chatto, 1982.

Quinlivan, Mary E. "Race Relations in the Antebellum Children's Literature of Jacob Abbott." *Journal of Popular Culture* 16.1 (1982): 27–36.

Raven, Simon. "Sneak House." In *John Bull's Schooldays.* Edited by Brian Inglis. London: Hutchinson, 1961. 121–127.

Reed, John R. *Old School Ties: The Public Schools in British Literature.* Syracuse, NY: Syracuse University Press, 1964.

———. "The Public Schools in Victorian Literature." *Nineteenth Century Fiction* 29 (1974): 58–76.

Reimer, Mavis. "The Family, the School, the World: Inside and Outside in Mary Molesworth's *The Carved Lions.*" Children's Literature Assn. Conference. Trinity University, Hartford, CT. June 1992.

"Renewal of War in New Zealand." *The Times,* 19 Aug. 1863, 10.

Review of *Early Closing,* by D. Wynne Willson. *Times Literary Supplement,* 24 Sept. 1931, 726.

Review of *Jack Granger's Cousin,* by Julia A. Mathews. *Publishers' Weekly,* 27 Oct. 1877, 492.

Review of *Summer Half,* by Angela Thirkell. *New Yorker,* 4 June 1938, 63.

Review of *The Life of Mrs Sherwood,* by Sophia Kelly. *Christian Remembrancer.* Reprinted in *Living Age* 43 (1854): 339–362.

Reynolds, David S. "From Doctrine to Narrative: The Rise of Pulpit Storytelling in America." *American Quarterly* 32 (1980): 479–498.

Reynolds, Kimberly. *Girls Only? Gender and Popular Children's Fiction in Britain, 1880–1910.* Philadelphia: Temple University Press, 1990.

Richards, Jeffrey. *Happiest Days: The Public Schools in English Fiction.* Manchester, UK: Manchester University Press, 1988.

———. "The School Story." In *Stories and Society: Children's Literature in its Social Context.* Edited by Dennis Butts. New York: St. Martin, 1992. 1–21.

Richardson, Alan. "Reluctant Lords and Lame Princes: Engendering the Male Child in Nineteenth-Century Juvenile Fiction." *Children's Literature* 21 (1993): 3–19.

———. "Wordsworth, Fairy Tales, and the Politics of Children's Reading." In McGavran 34–53.

Riehl, Joseph E. *Charles Lamb's Children's Literature.* Salzburg: Institut für Anglistik und Amerikanistik, Universität Salzburg, 1980.

———. "Charles Lamb's *Mrs Leicester's School* Stories and Elia: The Fearful Imagination." *Charles Lamb Bulletin* n.s. 39 (1982): 138–143.

Roberts, Frank C. *Obituaries from the Times 1961–1970.* Reading, UK: Newspaper Archive Developments, 1975.

Rose, Jacqueline. *The Case of Peter Pan or the Impossibility of Children's Fiction.* 1984. Reprint, Philadelphia: University of Pennsylvania Press, 1993.

Rosenberg, Charles E. "Sexuality, Class and Role in Nineteenth-Century America." *American Quarterly* 35 (1973). Reprinted in Pleck and Pleck, *American Man* 219–254.

Ross, Ishbel. *Ladies of the Press: The Story of Women in Journalism by an Insider.* 4th ed. New York: Harper, 1936.

Rotundo, E. Anthony. *American Manhood: Transformations in Masculinity from the Revolution to the Modern Era.* New York: Basic, 1993.

———. "Learning about Manhood: Gender Ideals and the Middle-Class Family in Nineteenth-Century America." In *Manliness and Morality: Middle-Class Masculinity in Britain and America 1800–1940.* Edited by J. A. Mangan and James Walvin. New York: St. Martin, 1987. 35–51.

Rowbotham, Judith. *Good Girls Make Good Wives: Guidance for Girls in Victorian Fiction.* Oxford: Blackwell, 1989.

Said, Edward W. *Orientalism.* 1978. Reprint, New York: Vintage-Random, 1979.

Saul, E. Wendy. "The School Story in America, 1900–1940: A Socio-Historical Analysis of the Genre." Dissertation, University of Wisconsin, Madison, 1981.

Saul, E. Wendy, and R. Gordon Kelly. "Christians, Brahmins, and Other Sporting Fellows: An Analysis of School Sports Stories." *Children's Literature in Education* 15 (1984): 234–245.

Schwager, Sally. "Educating Women in America." *Signs* 12 (1987): 333–372.

Scott, Joan W. "The Evidence of Experience." *Critical Inquiry* 17 (1991): 773–797.

Scott, P. G. "The School Novels of Dean Farrar." *British Journal of Educational Studies* 19 (1971): 163–182.

Scott, Patrick. "The School and the Novel: *Tom Brown's Schooldays.*" In *The Victorian Public School: Studies in the Development of an Educational Institution.* Edited by Brian Simon and Ian Bradley. Dublin: Gill, 1975. 34–57.

———. "School Novels as a Source Material." *History of Education Society Bulletin* 5 (1970): 46–56.

———. "The Schooling of John Bull: Form and Moral in Talbot Baines Reed's Boys' Stories and in Kipling's *Stalky & Co.*" *Victorian Newsletter* 60 (1981): 3–8.

Sedgwick, Eve Kosofsky. *Between Men: English Literature and Male Homosocial Desire.* New York: Columbia University Press, 1985.

———. *Epistemology of the Closet.* Berkeley: University of California Press, 1990.

"Settled Among the Maoris." *All the Year Round,* 21 Nov. 1863, 309–312.

Shavit, Zohar. *Poetics of Children's Literature.* Athens: University of Georgia Press, 1986.

Sherwood, Mrs. [Mary Martha]. *The History of the Fairchild Family; or, The Child's Manual.* [1818, 1842, 1847]. Reprint, London: Hatchards, 1880.

Showalter, Elaine. *A Literature of Their Own: British Women Novelists from Brontë to Lessing.* Princeton: Princeton University Press, 1977.

Sinclair, Keith. *A History of New Zealand.* 3rd ed. London: Allen, 1980.

Sitwell, Edith. *Taken Care of: The Autobiography of Edith Sitwell.* New York: Atheneum, 1965.

Small, Sandra E. "The Yankee Schoolmarm in Freedmen's Schools: An Analysis of Attitudes." *Journal of Southern History* 45 (1979): 381–402.

Smedman, M. Sarah. "Not Always Gladly Does She Teach, Nor Gladly Learn: Teachers in *Künstlerinroman* for Young Readers." *Children's Literature in Education* 20 (1989): 131–147.

Smith, Daniel Scott. "Family Limitation, Sexual Control, and Domestic Feminism in Victorian America." *Feminist Studies* 1 (1973): 40–57.

Smith, David C. *H. G. Wells: Desperately Mortal.* New Haven: Yale University Press, 1986.

Smith, Naomi Royde. *The State of Mind of Mrs. Sherwood.* London: Macmillan, 1946.

Smith-Rosenberg, Carroll. *Disorderly Conduct: Visions of Gender in Victorian America.* New York: Knopf, 1985.

Spivak, Gayatri Chakravorty. "Three Women's Texts and a Critique of Imperialism." *Critical Inquiry* 12 (1985). Reprinted in Belsey and Moore 175–195, 237–240.

St. John, Judith. *The Osborne Collection of Early Children's Books 1566–1910.* Toronto: Toronto Public Library, 1958.

Stein, Gertrude. *Everybody's Autobiography.* London: Heinemann, 1938.

Stowe, Harriet Beecher. *Uncle Tom's Cabin.* 1851–1852. Reprint with introduction by Alfred Kazin. Toronto: Bantam, 1981.

Strickland, Charles. *Victorian Domesticity: Families in the Life and Art of Louisa May Alcott.* Foreword by Robert Coles. University: University of Alabama Press, 1985.

Summerfield, Geoffrey. *Fantasy and Reason: Children's Literature in the Eighteenth Century.* Athens: University of Georgia Press, 1985.

Swint, Henry L., ed. *Dear Ones at Home: Letters from Contraband Camps.* [By Lucy and Sarah Chase.] Nashville, TN: Vanderbilt University Press, 1966.

Tate, Claudia. "Allegories of Black Female Desire; or, Rereading Nineteenth-Century Sentimental Narratives of Black Female Authority." In *Changing Our Own Words: Essays on Criticism, Theory, and Writing by Black Women.* Edited by Cheryl A. Wall. New Brunswick, NJ: Rutgers University Press, 1989. 98–126, 230–234.

Tebbel, John. *The Creation of an Industry 1630–1865.* Vol. 1 of *A History of Book Publishing in the United States.* New York: Bowker, 1972.

Thomas, Keith. "Children in Early Modern England." In Avery and Briggs 45–77.

Thorpe, Margaret Newbold. "Life in Virginia, by a 'Yankee Teacher.'" Edited by Richard L. Morton. *Virginia Magazine of History and Biography* 64 (1956): 180–207.

Todd, Richard. *Iris Murdoch.* London: Methuen, 1984.

Toklas, Alice B. *What is Remembered.* New York: Holt, 1963.

Tompkins, Jane. *Sensational Designs: The Cultural Work of American Fiction 1790–1860.* New York: Oxford University Press, 1985.

Townsend, John Rowe. *Written for Children: An Outline of English Children's Literature.* Rev. ed. Boston: Horn Book, 1974.

Tregear, Edward. *The Maori-Polynesian Comparative Dictionary.* Oosterhout, the Netherlands: Anthropological Publications, 1969.

Trelawny, Edward John. *Adventures of a Younger Son.* 1831. Reprint, edited with an introduction by William St. Clair. London: Oxford University Press, 1974.

Trensky, Anne. "The Bad Boy in Nineteenth-Century American Fiction." *Georgia Review* 27 (1973): 503–517.

———. "The Saintly Child in Nineteenth-Century American Fiction." *Prospects* 1 (1975): 389–413.

Trousdale, Ann M. "Why Is This Teacher Smiling? Portrayals of Teachers in Picture Books for Young Children." *Feminist Teacher* 6.3 (1992): 25–31.

Tucker, Nicholas. "*Vice Versa*: The First Subversive Novel for Children." *Children's Literature in Education* 18 (1987): 139–147.

Vicinus, Martha. "Distance and Desire: English Boarding-School Friendships." *Signs* 9 (1984): 600–622.

———. *Independent Women: Work and Community for Single Women 1850–1920.* Chicago: University of Chicago Press, 1985.

Wallace, James D. "Where the Absent Father Went: Alcott's *Work.*" In *Refiguring the Father: New Feminist Readings of Patriarchy.* Edited by Patricia Yaeger and Beth Kowaleski-Wallace. Afterword by Nancy K. Miller. Carbondale: Southern Illinois University Press, 1989. 259–274.

"The War in New Zealand." *The Times,* 15 Dec. 1863, 5.

Ward, Alan. *A Show of Justice: Racial "Amalgamation" in Nineteenth Century New Zealand.* Toronto: University of Toronto Press, 1973.

Ward Jouve, Nicole. *Colette.* Bloomington: Indiana University Press, 1987.

Washington, Booker T. Excerpts from *Up From Slavery.* 1901. Reprinted in Lauter et al. 2: 853–877.

Wechselblatt, Martin. "Gender and Race in Yarico's Epistles to Inkle: Voicing the Feminine/Slave." *Studies in Eighteenth-Century Culture* 19 (1989): 197–223.

Weedon, M. J. P. "Richard Johnson and the Successors to John Newbery." *The Library* 5th ser. 4.1 (1949): 25–63.

Weeks, Jeffrey. *Coming Out: Homosexual Politics in Britain, from the Nineteenth Century to the Present.* 1977. Reprint, London: Quartet, 1979.

———. *Sexuality and Its Discontents: Meanings, Myths and Modern Sexualities.* London: Routledge, 1985.

Wells, H. G. *Experiment in Autobiography: Discoveries and Conclusions of a Very Ordinary Brain (since 1866).* New York: Macmillan, 1934.

Wernham, John, and Mary Cadogan. *The Greyfriars Characters.* Vol. 2 of *The Charles Hamilton Companion.* Maidstone: Museum, [1976].

Williams, Charles. *George Mogridge: His Life, Character, and Writings.* London: Ward, 1856.

Wilson, Harriet E. *Our Nig; or, Sketches from the Life of a Free Black, in a Two-Story White House, North, Showing that Slavery's Shadows Fall Even There.* 1859. Reprint, edited by Henry Louis Gates, Jr. New York: Vintage, 1983.

Wilson, Mona. *Jane Austen and Some Contemporaries.* Introduction by G. M. Young. London: Cresset, 1938.

Wolfson, Susan J. "'Their She Condition': Cross-Dressing and the Politics of Gender in *Don Juan.*" *ELH* 54 (1987): 585–617.

Wood, Charles W. *Memorials of Mrs. Henry Wood.* 3rd ed. London: Bentley, 1895.

Wood, Gordon S. *The Radicalism of the American Revolution.* 1991. Reprint, New York: Vintage, 1993.

Wood, Mrs. Henry. *East Lynne.* 1861. Reprint with an introduction by Sally Mitchell. New Brunswick, NJ: Rutgers University Press, 1984.

Woolf, Virginia. "Mr. Bennett and Mrs. Brown." 1924. Reprinted in *Collected Essays.* Vol. 1. New York: Harcourt, 1967. 319–337.

———. Review of *Joan and Peter,* by H. G. Wells. *Times Literary Supplement,* 19 Sept. 1918. Reprinted in *H. G. Wells: The Critical Heritage.* Edited by Patrick Parrinder. London: Routledge, 1972. 244–247.

Wright, Terence. "Two Little Worlds of School: An Outline of a Dual Tradition in Schoolboy Fiction." *Durham University Journal* 75.1 (1982): 59–71.

Yacovone, Donald. "Abolitionists and the 'Language of Fraternal Love.'" In Carnes and Griffen 85–95.

Yellin, Jean Fagan. "From *Success* to *Experience:* Louisa May Alcott's *Work.*" *Massachusetts Review* 21 (1980): 527–539.

Yuill, Phyllis J. *Little Black Sambo: A Closer Look.* New York: Racism and Sexism Resource Center for Educators, 1976.

Zagarell, Sandra A. "Narrative of Community: The Identification of a Genre." *Signs* 13 (1988): 498–527.

Zwarg, Christina. "Fathering and Blackface in *Uncle Tom's Cabin.*" *Novel* 22 (1989): 274–287.

Zwinger, Lynda. *Daughters, Fathers, and the Novel: The Sentimental Romance of Heterosexuality.* Madison: University of Wisconsin Press, 1991.

Author and Title Index